Psychology of developing children

P. M. Pickard, M.A., A.B.Ps.S.

Formerly Principal Lecturer
Maria Grey College of Education

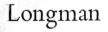

Longman

LONGMAN GROUP LIMITED
London

*Associated companies, branches and representatives
throughout the world*

© Longman Group Ltd 1970

First published 1970

ISBN 0 582 32491 2 cased edition
ISBN 0 582 32492 0 paper edition

Printed in Great Britain by
Spottiswoode, Ballantyne and Co Ltd,
London and Colchester

To my husband Christopher Bailey

Acknowledgements

I wish to express my thanks for very detailed criticism, to Professor Sir Cyril Burt, Professor Stephen Wiseman and Professor Philip Vernon.

Author and publisher are indebted to the following for permission to reproduce copyright material:

The editor of the *British Journal of Mathematical and Statistical Psychology* for an extract from 'The Multifactorial Theory of Inheritance and its application to Intelligence' by Burt and Howard, first published in the *British Journal of Statistical Psychology*, 1956.

We are grateful to the following for permission for the use of diagrams:

Cambridge University Press for Figure 24 from Coghill, *Anatomy and the Problem of Behaviour*; Ginn & Company Ltd, for Figure 21 from Obrist and Pickard, *Time for Reading: Teachers' Manual*; Heinemann Educational Books Ltd, for Figure 6 from Penrose, *Outline of Human Genetics*; Miss Rhoda Kellogg for Figures 15 and 20 from *What Children Scribble and Why*; Methuen Publishers for Figure 13 from Fisher, *Brit. J. Ed. Psychol.*, 35, Pt 1, 1965; The Editor of *Nature* and Miss Kellogg for Figure 17; University of Iowa for Figure 14 from Smith, *Univ. Iowa Studies in Child Welfare*, Vol. 3, No. 5; University of London Press Ltd, for Figure 27 from Tanner, *Education and Physical Growth*; Weidenfeld & Nicolson for Figure 3 from Gregory, *Eye and Brain*; John Wiley & Sons Inc., for Figure 23 from Boring, Langfeld and Weld, *Introduction to Psychology*, 1939; Yale University Press for Figure 1 from Robbins *et al.*, *Growth*. Figure 26 is reproduced by permission of the Controller H.M. Stationery Office from *Mathematics in Primary Schools*, *Curriculum Bulletin*, No. 1, 1969. Table 16.6 and Figures 2 and 25 are redrawn from *Introduction to Psychology*, 3rd Edition, by Ernest R. Hilgard, copyright, 1953, © 1957, 1962, by Harcourt, Brace & World, Inc. and reproduced with their permission, and Figure 5 from Victor C. McKusick, *Human Genetics*, © 1964, reprinted by permission of Prentice-Hall Inc., Englewood Cliffs, New Jersey, U.S.A.

Contents

Figures

Foreword

Education in the primary, and particularly in the infant, school has been revolutionised in the past fifty years or so, largely as a result of the teachings of psychologists which have given a new insight into children's needs and the nature of their mental processes and learning. Through the work of Froebel, Montessori, Freud, Binet, and more recently Piaget in Europe, of Dewey, Thorndike, Terman, and Moreno in the USA, Burt, Susan Isaacs and Dorothy Gardner in this country, and many others, schools have become far happier places, where most children actually learn more that is of value to them than in the days of 'payment by results'. Teaching and the bringing up of children are no longer treated as drilling them in correct habits; we realise that they are active, curious, social beings and that we can get their cooperation by taking account of their interests and their mental capabilities at different ages.

It is particularly important, then, that the teacher should have a good knowledge not only of the psychology of the age group she is dealing with, but also of how her pupils grew that way, from birth onwards. There is a vast amount of information, scattered in many books and articles, and it is difficult for the student to know where to turn for a general survey which will cover both the more abstract theories and the concrete applications of psychology. Miss Pickard has long experience both as a psychologist in child guidance work, and in the training of infant and junior school teachers. Her book ranges widely, but is always lively and interesting. Clearly she is talking about real children, yet at the same time she explains many technical aspects of the subject simply and clearly.

A noteworthy feature of the book is its insistence on the need to understand what kind of research goes into the development of our knowledge of children, i.e. how the psychologist arrives at his conclusions. She has, moreover, particularly stressed the contributions of British psychologists which are often unduly neglected in some of the available textbooks, for example from American sources. Thus much of the book consists of summaries of particular researches published in this country, which she integrates with her general picture of the development of babies, preschool and school-age children. This approach has its difficulties but, together with her advice on reading it should be especially valuable in stimulating the student to read original sources more widely.

I am glad, then, to recommend this as an introduction to the topic, not only to students and teachers, but also to many intelligent parents who want to know more about the minds and behaviour of their own children.

P. E. VERNON
Emeritus Professor of Psychology
University of London,
Institute of Education:

Professor of Educational Psychology
and Senior Research Consultant,
University of Calgary, Alberta

Introduction

The inborn nature of children, some people say, is obvious. One has only to see how they behave when no one is in charge of them to know that they are savage little creatures at heart, who have to be disciplined into sufficient social courtesy to take their place in a civilised community. If they are not taught the rules, they cannot be blamed for being unruly. Indeed, there is something in these accusations. An unattended nursery class, a junior gang off on some escapade, or a group of restless adolescents, all seem bent on destruction.

The aim of education today, still very far from being realised, is to develop each child fully. This aim applies to all children, no matter how gifted, normal or retarded they may be intellectually or artistically. As we attempt to carry out this objective, we find that there is far more potential in children, whatever their abilities, than was previously recognised. With the help of research, not only do we expect more, but our expectations become more realistic. For instance, we now find that, given plenty of interesting experience and plenty of opportunity to talk about the experiences, children's vocabularies can be far richer and far more precise than previously believed. But we also find that children can apparently use words correctly, when they have not understood their true meanings. Many words thus used become a façade concealing misunderstanding.

Left in this predicament, children grow into adults who fail to communicate properly. An example of how one can help children to use words more correctly will make this clear. A group of gifted children went to visit Wisley Airfield in the summer of 1967. They had themselves made arrangements to go, because they had noticed interesting planes flying over their school. They leapt out of their bus carrying slide rules and other paraphernalia used by modern children at work, and looked around. One boy waved at all the radio apparatus and asked if it was radioactive. A possible way to answer would have been, 'Well, it is radio apparatus and it *is* very active. But radioactive material is something different; it is a heap of chemicals which mostly comes from nuclear power stations.'

Children's use of words is only one example of how our expectation of children goes up but also has to be realistic. To promote it we have to see that our own use of words is very precise. For instance, biology is the study of life and psychology is the study of the behaviour of living things; therefore psychology is a branch of biology. We also have to distinguish between the way such words are used by the specialist and the way they are used by the general public. There is a difference in the meaning of the word *intelligence* according to whether it is being used by a specialist or by a lay person. The specialist now uses it as Plato originally explained it in the third century B.C. Plato came to the conclusion that there was a directing or governing force in the mind. In *Phaedrus* he uses an analogy with the most skilled machine control of his time. 'To tell what it really is', he wrote, 'would be a matter for utterly superhuman and long discourse, but it is within human power to describe it in a figure.' He then likens this governing force to a charioteer who has to direct the horses. When his word was translated into Latin it became *intelligentia*, from which we get our word intelligence.

But the non-specialist uses this word in quite a different way, and the way in which the word became debased is interesting. With the fall of the Greek and Roman civilisations, the books were scattered and many lost. A few were preserved in churches. But the break in cultural tradition resulted in deterioration of meaning for some terms. There has to be discussion, teaching, disagreement and thrashing out of fresh ideas, both between contemporaries and between generations for continuity and development of ideas. The word *intelligence* degenerated from a directing activity of the mind to no more than readily available information, much as the word 'gen' is used today (indeed, this colloquialism may well be an abbreviation for the word). Over several centuries this became the meaning in literature. Macbeth asks of the witches:

> Say from whence
> You owe this strange intelligence.
> *Macbeth*, I. iii.

Plato's meaning of the word *intelligence* was revived by Herbert Spencer (1820–1903), whose *Principles of Psychology* (1855) was one of the first two textbooks of psychology to appear in Britain. He borrowed from biology the idea of an analytical or discriminative activity of the mind coupled with a synthetic or integrative process; and for the controlling element he revived Plato's notion of governing activity in the mind.

Another area in which the specialist has to break away from what 'everybody' is supposed to know is that of personality. There are literally hundreds of words to describe personality. But the specialist has to do more than make a list of words. He has to conduct experiments and report the facts he is able to establish. For example, research has to be conducted on the child's notion of himself. This may seem unnecessary to the lay person, or even dangerous. But research shows that the greater danger lies in not doing so. In terms of our aim of developing each child's potentiality, children who think too little of themselves fail to do as well as they should. Far too many children are leaving our schools with too low an opinion of themselves, thus reducing the quality of their activities as adults.

In order to obtain and exchange psychological information one needs a dictionary which defines certain words of common speech in the narrow senses used by the educational and psychological specialist. The *Concise Oxford Dictionary*, which includes *information* and *news* in the definitions of intelligence, is not discriminative and therefore not helpful to this end. A useful dictionary for students is Drever's (1952) *A Dictionary of Psychology*. A more expensive but much more comprehensive one is the American *A Comprehensive Dictionary of Psychological and Psychoanalytical Terms* by English and English (1958). It is extremely helpful for clarifying the highly technical concepts of psychology.

An increasing amount of research on child development is now going on, particularly in Britain and the United States. But in 1946 Fleming reported in *Research and the Basic Curriculum* that practice in our schools is at least thirty years behind our research findings; and the drive to improve the situation has only begun in the last few years; so the situation is not yet much better. In order to get the latest information a student has to read original papers. There are grave dangers in relying upon lectures. A lecturer may be biased or may lack the particular interests of a student; or a legitimate comment in one context may be misleading when put in another context. Anyone interested in progressive education has to be ahead of textbooks.

But reading original papers can be very time-consuming for a student and the difficulties fall into two categories: obtaining the papers and understanding them when they have been obtained. Let us first look at the problem of reading original papers for information. Scientific papers are not written in order that students can follow their conclusions. They are written for the authors' expert colleagues, to give factual information; and much of this information concerns methods used in coming to conclusions, which are presented in a form intended to forestall criticism. In addition to this they are written in a style intended to convey supreme objectivity, which Dixon (1968) describes in *New Scientist* as unnecessary and comic contortion of syntax which can easily be avoided. The following is an example, given by him, of what it would be like if we communicated with children in this extraordinary style:

'Daddy, I want cornflakes this morning. Must I have porridge?'
'Yes. It has been suggested by Mummy that, in view of the external

coldness, the eating of porridge by you will cause an increase in bodily temperature. Furthermore, in regard to the already-mentioned temperature considerations, your grandma-knitted gloves and wool-lining hooded coat will have to be worn.'

'May I have some sugar on my porridge?'

'The absence of sugar in the relevant bowl has been noted by Daddy at an earlier moment. However, further supplies of this substance are now being brought by Mummy from the appropriate vessel that is present in the kitchen.'

Dixon concludes by saying, 'My guess is that the way scientists write and talk must be a potent discouragement for the bright youngster hovering between science and "the humanities".' He maintains that the difficulty in reading original papers is not the technical terms, which are taken with ease through television science programmes, but this obscure and unnecessary style.

Let us assume that a student interested in the information in one of these papers is able to make notes which have greater clarity and simplicity of style than the article. The titles are often long, in order to indicate the nature of the information. The first thing to look for is a heading, usually in smaller print, called *Abstract* or *Summary*. Most scientific papers, if they do not have such a heading, have a paragraph before the references or appendices, headed 'Summary and Conclusions'. Some articles have both, and the tailpiece is usually more informative. If more information is required on a particular aspect, the subjects mentioned in the abstract correspond to the order of the paper itself. By skim-reading in this way you can quickly trace the particular topic of interest. It is better for a student to read many scientific papers quickly for the pith of their contents, than to read fewer papers all through.

But reading in this way means that one often has to refer back to a particular paper later for further details, perhaps for an essay. It is often a time-wasting shock for students to come from the protective secondary school where homework is set and given in and marked, to a college where there is a library and it is up to the student to find what he wants. The first notes that a student makes on the first articles or books that he reads can be quite valuable a decade later, with a little practical guidance. An index file and a loose-leaf notebook are needed and that is all. The file can be a proper one bought at any stationery shop, or an old shoe box and postcards. Let us say that a student attends a child development course and the first book he gets from the recommended reading list is John Bowlby's *Child Care and the Growth of Love;* also that he has been struck by the information that the parents remain the greatest influence in a child's life, with the teacher only second. His eye is caught by an article on 'Parents and Education' in a friend's copy of *Educational Research*. Here we have a book and a journal. The file has to have two sections, one for books and one for articles. He takes a card from the book section and fills in the following information:

> Bowlby, J. (1953)
>
> Child Care and the Growth of Love
>
> Pelican: Great Britain
>
> Pp. 190. 2s. 0d.

That is all the information required to review the book, make a reference list to an essay, or refer to it in an M.Ed. thesis. Even if he has bought the book, someone may have borrowed it, just when he is tired after writing an essay but wants to put a proper reference list. In a very similar way, he completes a card for the article section:

> Banfield, J.   Ed. Res. 9/1/66
> Bowyer, C. and
> Wilkie, E. (1966)
>
> Parents and Education
>
> [*Below, he makes one or two notes to remind him what the article is about*]
> Survey in N.E. and London area—most parents concerned about children's ed. Parents should be told more of methods in schools their children attend.

The figures at the top right are volume, number, and the date repeated for fear of slips. It is also useful to mention any relevant articles put in the reference list.

The book of notes also has to be in two parts (until it grows to two volumes, perhaps years later), one for articles and the other for books. Each section has a page of index at the front, so that one can see quickly whether one actually made some notes, or just 'meant to do so'. Let us assume that our student has never in his life made notes on a book, though he has cribbed a few ideas from time to time in his homework. He does not know how to set about it. There are two ways of reading the book: (1) very slowly and pausing frequently to make notes; or (2) at normal speed, with notes made afterwards. If one wants to read many books, the first way takes too long. But riffling through a book and then reading fast may mean that one is not sure what notes to make afterwards. Yet alternating slow and fast reading does not prove satisfactory. Even if the student ends up with just one page of rather poorly written notes, they can be valuable notes because they are points that interest *him*.

He can take a piece of rough paper and, as he reads swiftly, he can jot down the number of a page on which there is something of special interest. If he is afraid he will not remember what it was, or where it was on the page, he can put a dash by the number to show roughly whether it is high, middle or low on the page. When the book is finished, he can very quickly make notes of exactly what he wants. If he does not remember what interested him when he looks back—this is a sign that he was not really interested and the point is not at present of importance to him. The title and author should be at the top, and use of a different colour helps to make titles stand out. He might have twenty or fifty pages to study and make notes from. It is wise to put the number of the page in the margin for each point, in case a more careful study of a particular point proves useful later. Many references are given so that each student, as he directs his attention along a particular line, can pursue the many sources on this particular aspect.

Obtaining required articles can present difficulties. The college may not take the particular journal; or the required issue may be borrowed or missing. Most libraries now have photocopy apparatus. It costs about a shilling a page to make a print, but many colleges only charge half price when the student makes the print. If the photocopy has to be obtained from elsewhere, for instance the British Museum, it is wise to write for an estimate. A long article may at the beginning and end only use part of a page; this can be quite expensive. Some students have such vivid visual imagery that they can recall the exact page on which they have read information, and they see no occasion to make notes. But in this age of technical means of storing information, by computer and so on, memory is not now considered as important as it used to be. What matters today is to be able to put information into new orders, so that fresh insights are obtained.

When the student has to write an essay he can take out the relevant cards from his index, both for books and articles, and arrange them in what seems a logical order. He may rearrange them several times before he is satisfied. But when he has an order which looks right, the cards give the numbers of his relevant notes. It is at this point, when working out a fresh approach to a theme, that he may find his notes deficient in some important way and wish to go quickly to the original article or book again. If, in the summary on his card he has listed items of the bibliography, he may now wish to skim-read several more articles before beginning the essay.

In the present book the majority of articles referred to are British, since these concern cultural settings with which our students are familiar; and they are predominantly from *Educational Research* and the *British Journal of Educational Psychology* because these can be found in most college libraries, or may even be taken by the students themselves. But there is another reason for stressing British research. So many American textbooks are used that we tend to underestimate the importance of our own little-publicised work. Take, for instance, the important subject of college and the training of teachers. *Educational Research* has published an article on this which has 60 per cent American research references. We shall see in our final chapter that there are many reports of important British researches on this subject which have simply been ignored. American work concerns primarily a different culture.

When books and journals are missing, as they all too often are, this is not a simple situation of theft for resale. Here we touch on the irrational. If colleges knew how to stop this 'forgetting to return books' they would do so for reasons of economy. In fact they should do so in the interests of accurate thinking. The 'forgetting' is Freudian in the sense that it is due to wishful thinking about reading a book. Because 'I really am going to read it' never turns into 'I have read it', unrealism bypasses the whole subject; the fact that the book has been taken but remains unread is repressed. Every librarian knows that students are not the only offenders in this matter. When a list of missing books is posted, it is excellent discipline for each person to go straight to his own bookshelf and see if any of them are there. This is rational behaviour.

Whereas scientific journals may have articles written in the unnecessarily obscure style already referred to, text books of psychology may have another defect. Where research information is lacking authors often obtain a smooth style by generalising without sufficient evidence. There are two main ways of checking whether a writer subordinates factual information to an elegant style; (a) to notice when the writing becomes too rounded, too self-sufficient; and (b) to become critical of helpful-sounding but unsupported generalisations. Take for instance the well-known film series using the alliterative style of 'terrible twos' and 'thrusting threes' for titles: two-year-olds are not terrible to those who understand them, and many threes become withdrawn. For generalising: Gesell and Ilg's *Infant and Child in the Culture of Today* (1943): 'The eyes of a newborn baby are apt to rove around both in the presence and absence of a stimulus' (p. 18). We are not told upon how many observations of newborn children this generalisation is based; and many psychologists think that not enough observation of individual infants has yet been made for such generalisations by Gesell or anyone else, to be very reliable.

We are lamentably short of research into infancy.* Even the Americans, who have done much more research into this stage than we, complain bitterly of deficiency here. We must therefore attune ourselves to recognising precise observations by experts such as Piaget (1926, 1951, etc.), Lewis (1936) and Valentine (1942). A couple of examples will make this clear:

(*a*) *4th day*

T was wide awake, looking straight in front of him, motionless and silent. Three times in succession the crying of L (four years old) started him crying also. . . . As soon as L stopped crying, he too stopped. It therefore seemed to be a clear case of contagion, and no longer a mere starting off of a reflex by an appropriate stimulus.

Piaget *Play, Dreams and Imitation*, (1951), p. 8.

(*b*) *10th and 15th day*

Look of great interest when I contorted my face, especially at a yawn, and three times he opened his mouth (only once a proper yawn) when I gaped mine open. Day 15. Suggestion of mouth opening in response to mine; but a baby's lips are so frequently moving that coincidence is always possible.

Valentine *The Psychology of Early Childhood* (1942), p. 186.

There are many excellent examples of precise information in L. B. Murphy *The Widening World of Childhood* (1962), one of which is given here (p. 28). One soon learns to identify genuine firsthand information.

When the results of research work are quoted, we should note the date of the work. Sometimes textbook after textbook quotes the same research decade after decade, as if this were fresh information in the context of new insights on child development. An example of this (p. 92) is M. E. Smith's 1926 research into children's vocabulary development. It was undoubtedly a most valuable piece of research; but the reason why it is quoted so much is that it is discouragingly difficult to bring it up to date. We should be suspicious of the applicability of research nearly half a century old in a changing field.

* By the end of the 'sixties there are signs of improvement. The *Centre for Advanced Study in the Developmental Sciences* reports a January 1969 conference at the University of Sussex with 89 abstracts of current British researches on early developmental behaviour.

Bearing all this in mind, we might hope that a book intended to bring research of the last decade to the notice of students might be easy to read and at the same time up to date in its quoted facts. In terms of developing children, over and over again at the stage where a particular aspect of development should be examined, there is almost no information. Take, for instance, personality development at the infant school stage. Many thousands of adolescents and adults have filled in personality questionnaires and the results have been treated statistically with interesting results. But almost no research into the personalities of children at the junior school stage, let alone on infants, has been done. Yet teachers are expected to send each child up with a form assessing a number of personality traits.

This book is arranged in the order of stages in the development of a child. Between this introductory chapter and the final chapter on the teacher's rôle there are five stages:

Up to 15 months	True infant
15 months to 2½ years	Toddler
2½–5 years	Nursery school age
5–8 years	Infant school age ⎱ Approximating to ages in
8–12 years	Junior school age ⎰ D.E.S July 1965 circular 10/65

Each section begins with general development followed by language development. This arrangement of topics, by the age group to which each topic starts to be important is, on the whole, logical. It raises one difficulty: that too often most of the established facts refer to an older age group. The present arrangement therefore sometimes serves to emphasise the areas of our ignorance and indicate the lines of research into older children or adults which might be adapted to younger children. There is a slight danger here that people might argue by analogy that because adult personalities are shown to be such-and-such, we can assume that children's personalities are the same. We are more sophisticated than the Renaissance painters who depicted the infant Jesus on his mother's knee as a little man, a miniature adult. However, in order to avoid this pitfall, the research of the greatest living expert on how one phase of development evolves to the next, Jean Piaget, is described as early as the toddler stage of 15 months to 2½ years. This research goes right up to the adult stage of thinking; but it is put so early as a means of demonstrating the fundamental qualitative and quantitative differences between one stage of thinking and the next.

In the same way, nursery school teachers should know something of the child's concept of himself. Here the facts are thin, though it is known that awareness of oneself as a person arrives in the nursery school age group. So the subject of the self concept is introduced at the nursery school stage, together with known facts of the self concept of older children and adults. The reader having just read in the previous section on Piaget about the fundamental differences between stages, will not make the blunder of arguing, for instance, from the self-picture of students (into which there has been some research) to the self-picture of nursery school children (about which almost nothing is known). Another area where facts are thin is personality at the infant stage; but this is when teachers are expected to rate children on a five-point scale for various traits, so personality is introduced at this stage, together with known facts about older children and adults. The same applies to learning, which is also explained at the infant stage. These facts will, it is hoped, at least raise questions about earlier origins of the self concept, personality and so on, and provide a background for the students' observation. But again, the facts should not be assumed to apply out of their age group.

Again, we know little about the growth of language at the primary school stage, apart from M. E. Smith's researches (1926). This subject has therefore been combined with that of reading, the secondary phase of language. Substantial research has been conducted into the causes of failure to read; consequently we are now beginning to accumulate some facts on that aspect of language development.

This book is meant to bring to students the pith of what is and what is not known about developing children. The word 'developing' is deliberately ambiguous. It should be taken as both active and passive, both 'how to develop a child' and 'how to let a child develop'. It is particularly directed to contrasting the small but all-important body of fact known about children with the mass of opinion. For this reason, a great part of it consists of critical abstracts of research work. The author hopes two things of this emphasis: (a) that students will read in the original many of the papers referred to, once they have decided their special areas of interest; and (b) that they will be encouraged to do their own research in a field where so many opportunities exist. To the latter end, not only the bare results but some of the methods of the cited research workers have been quoted. Anyone wishing to pursue psychology as a career should study the British Psychological Society 1969 Supplement to the Bulletin. It is a mine of information on the work of British psychologists, edited by Foss.

Part 1
True infant:
up to 15 months

1. General development
0 to 15 months

When the sperm from the father meets the ovum of the mother the child is conceived. So the child begins as a single cell which is half from the father and half from the mother. When the cell divides it divides in such a way that both cells—and all subsequent cells—contain this same balance of hereditary material, equal amounts from each parent. A fuller description of the mechanism whereby the two gametes (as the original male and female cells are called) join is given in the section on heredity in Chapter 4. At the moment of conception the ovum is usually coming down from the ovaries, a journey which takes about four days. Once in the uterus the embryo rises to the top and settles into the wall of the uterus.

Towards the end of the second month the embryo, now called a foetus, is about half an inch long. It floats in a liquid with plenty of room for free movement at this stage. By three months it is about three inches long. The tiny bones are beginning to form and the mother needs extra calcium, so drinks extra milk. Both physiologically and psychologically a 'need' is something which the person, adult or child, requires in order to maintain a state of equilibrium. A lack, at certain times in foetal development may cause irreparable harm. Sufficient calcium when the bones begin to form is such a need, for equilibrium in development.

By the end of the fourth month the foetus begins to look like a human child, though the head is rather large and the body rather skinny. The change in form and proportion of the human body from first foetal stage to adulthood is astonishing. Figure 1 shows this by representing all stages as the same height. The heart and blood vessels have developed and filled with blood. For the blood, the mother needs extra iron. She also takes extra fresh fruit and vegetables for vitamins. As a result of medical research a pregnant woman can now have a normal diet, with just a few extras for calcium, iron, vitamins and so on. It is most important that the mother herself should maintain a healthy body and not become debilitated, her own equilibrium upset, through the baby taking more than she can spare.

By four months the foetus weighs about half a pound, and its weight doubles in the next month. The speed of growth is greater than at any time after birth. The teeth are beginning to form, so that still more calcium is needed, for teeth as well as bones. Sensible parents follow the doctor's diet instructions very carefully. But not all parents are sensible, so that months before it is born the foetus may be environmentally handicapped. All being well, by the end of the seventh month the baby weighs about two and a half

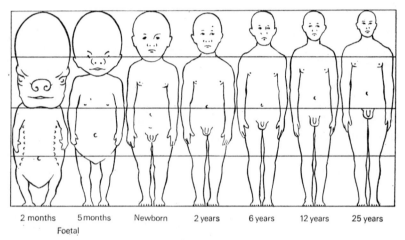

| 2 months | 5 months | Newborn | 2 years | 6 years | 12 years | 25 years |

Foetal

Figure 1. Body proportions during development.
Source: Robbins *et al.* (1928).

pounds. It has developed so much in complexity that, should it be born now, it would probably survive; and a month later it is almost as likely to live as a baby born at the full time, just over nine months from conception.

In the last two months of pregnancy the baby has grown so large that there is no longer room for it to kick and stretch in the fluid. Stone and Church (1957), in *Childhood and Adolescence* have reproduced five photographs of the foetus at different stages which show how much the foetus becomes confined. Of course, if there are twins the curtailment of movement will be even more severe; and this is one reason why twins tend to be born a little early. A singleton usually settles with head downwards as space becomes limited, ready to push out head first. Doctors may give a little gentle manipulation, if the foetus does not properly invert itself, to help it into the most favourable position. Midwives, who are today very highly qualified, look after the vast majority of births under the supervision of a doctor. They also advise the mothers during pregnancy, on clothes for themselves and equipment as well as clothes for the baby. They hold small classes for mothers at about the same stage of pregnancy, where they explain about diet and about the child's development. They run relaxation classes, where the pregnant women learn helpful exercises to practise and how to relax after effort. Experiences are exchanged at these classes. Some have older children; some have cooperative husbands; some have husbands who try to ignore the whole thing. The questions which others ask the midwife may be the very ones a shy mother has not cared to ask.

Nothing about our attitude towards the birth of a child today has done more good than these classes run by informed midwives. Some of the worries can easily be explained away; some need more careful handling. The regular attendance means that check-ups can be made, as to whether the diet is satisfying needs, whether there are twins or any other complications. Above all, the shared experience enables a woman to get into physical trim for the rhythmic labour of birth. The birth is a labour just as digging a vegetable patch is a labour. The mother-to-be who avails herself of this help from the community makes a joke of using the exercises to clean the house. If she is fortunate enough to have a husband who is deeply involved in her experiences, even eventually attending the birth, this really gives the child a fortunate prenatal environment.

Society thinks of birth as the time when successful labour is completed. But the first three days are so critical for the newborn child that, at least for the child, they should be included as part of the birth. As the foetus became more confined in the uterus, it became accustomed to remaining quiet. But movements of ribs and heart have begun. As soon as the doctor holds up the trickling infant, still attached to its mother by the cord, and taps it, the respiratory muscles begin to work. The expanded ribs automatically suck air into the lungs for the first time; and when the ribs relax again, the air is automatically forced out with a sound not unlike that of a collapsing balloon. The oxygen from the air in the lungs increases the heart beat; and the blood begins to circulate, carrying oxygen all over the body. Once the breathing starts, the now unnecessary cord can be cut—a minor matter no more painful than cutting the nails—and the placenta, also no longer required, can be cleared away.

The baby spends most of the time asleep, while the body becomes accustomed to breathing and circulating the blood. When he is hungry he wakes up, and then he has to make a third major physical adjustment, taking nourishment into the stomach through the mouth. Although it is true that the mother has given birth before the cord is cut, the child is not safely in the outside world until he can breathe, circulate the blood and suck. We owe the reduction in infant mortality to long and patient medical research. A newborn infant does not always start breathing as soon as he is tapped; he may need quite a little spanking. Consequently there is always tension until that first cry is heard. Nor does the baby always start sucking the nipple when he is hungry. The nipple may have to be given again and again before sucking starts. But once these critical first three days are survived, there is a high probability that the baby will live to draw his or her old age pension.

0–15 MONTHS

The period from nought to fifteen months is called infancy. The Plowden Report (1967) points out that schools for children of five to seven years are incorrectly named 'infant' schools. The misnomer reflects general ignorance about the development of children during their early years which was even greater at the time when the schools were started.

For the first few weeks of infancy the newborn child only needs warmth and nourishment and touch. Many will have seen on television how baby rats, monkeys and other animals become more alive if they are actually handled. For these first weeks mother and child still seem to be one person. The first unpractised movements of the mother in learning to bath and dress and feed him are experiences he needs. Strictly speaking, in the very first months a baby can thrive if a mother-substitute does these things—and a father makes an excellent mother-substitute. Even when a child can be attended to by his mother, it is a common mistake to think that a father's help is not useful in such matters as bathing, bottle-feeding or changing nappies. Quotations from Piaget and Valentine (p. 8) show that there is much behaviour for a father to take an interest in. As he becomes involved in the child's development he loses the sense of being displaced; or perhaps it would be more correct to say the parents can share a sense of displacement by the child.

An excellent example of our ignorance of fact and dependence on opinion about infants has recently been highlighted by J. and E. Newson (1965). In an enquiry of 709 Nottingham mothers of one-year-olds, they found amongst other things when these mothers stopped breast-feeding their children. Doctors and midwives encourage a mother to breast-feed as soon as possible after birth, partly because the sucking helps the uterus to return to its normal size, and partly for the baby. Four days after birth 83 per cent of these mothers were either breast-feeding or attempting to do so. But a large number of them had no intention of carrying on once out of hospital, or once home was normal again. Thus after two weeks only 60 per cent were still breast-feeding; and at the end of the first month only half were still doing so. A typical remark was: 'Of course, while the nurse was here I had to.' In this investigation there were two groups who interviewed the mothers: (a) Health Visitors, who are experienced in contacting mothers of young children; and (b) Mrs Newson herself, helped by sixteen other university people. Table 1 shows the percentage of breast-feeding during the first six months.

TABLE 1: *Mothers still breast-feeding babies at various ages (percentages)*

Samples	1 month	3 months	6 months
Health visitor (corrected)	53·5	28·5	13·0
University sample (corrected)	39·5	21·1	8·9

Source. J. and E. Newson (1965).

Notice how the mothers, associating the Health Visitors with the medical world, tended to give them answers somewhat prejudiced in favour of what they knew was medical expectation. The university group was used specifically to counteract this effect, and the replies they received were not prejudiced in this way. Manner of interviewing is an important point in research; it can influence the trustworthiness of replies.

In order to find out whether this early cessation of breast-feeding was peculiar to Nottingham, the Newsons examined the figures for four other investigations. Luton (1945), National Survey (1946), Newcastle (1947–8) and Bristol (1947–8). The average for all five surveys was: at 1 month, 65 per cent; 3 months, 44 per cent; and at 6 months, 29 per cent were still breast-feeding. The inference from all these surveys, is that breast-feeding is on the decline. When they investigated exactly who stopped breast-feeding early they found a class distinction (for class grouping see p. 229). The decline in breast-feeding is, they say, 'predominantly a working-class phenomenon'. The old opinion that working-class mothers stop breast-feeding in order to return to work proved not to be true. Only 3 per cent had returned to work. The reversal of expected trend seemed to be due to the attitude of the mothers rather than economic considerations. The wives of professional and other white-collar workers appeared to be strongly influenced by the demands of 'duty' and books of advice on child rearing often refer to breast-feeding as 'baby's birthright.' On the other hand, the working-class mothers were more prudish and objected to exposing the breast, even within the family circle.

The great value of the Newsons' report is that it is not advice based on opinions. It does not aim to advise at all, but merely to report what mothers actually do, no matter what advice they may have been given. A look at the contents in the Penguin Edition *Patterns of Infant Care in an Urban Community* (1965) will show that this book should be owned by any student interested in childbearing. It is delightfully written by authors who are themselves parents.

Since parents are subjected to such a barrage of advice on bringing up their babies, we might note the trends of the advice. In the middle of the nineteenth century families were so large and so many children died in the infant stage, that the children were scarcely credited with personalities. Indeed, the parents would choose a name and give it to one child after another, as the previous sibling died. Since so little was known, advice (based on protective feeling) was mainly to breast-feed and wrap the child up warm. When Mrs Beeton in *The Book of Household Management* (1861), advised giving infants fresh air and fewer clothes, she was making a highly original suggestion; and her advice was increasingly taken by mothers. By the turn of the century more and more books on babies were appearing. The attention given to food, clothing and schedules culminated in the widely practised Truby King method of strict schedules for feeding, bathing, etc. Innumerable children were fed by the clock and virtually woken up because it was time to go to sleep, not to be asleep. Thus the child-rearing pattern changed from all feeling to all thinking, from entirely subjective embrace to over-detached planning. Each system on its own had no place for the individual child's own likes and dislikes. But today an effort is made, in the advice given, to blend feeling with thinking in the handling of infants. The baby is allowed to be a person. However, even today, we must remember that advice is largely based on opinion. As the Newsons (1965) say: 'The truth is, of course, that in the present state of knowledge there is not a sufficient body of well-substantiated evidence about the facts and consequences of child rearing on which to base sound practical advice to parents.'

During the first weeks the baby asserts himself only by searching for the nipple—of mother or bottle—when he is hungry. Parents who can quickly find the rhythm of hunger in their own child are able to save themselves much distress. Hilgard (1953) describes an experiment with adults which shows on a graph the record of stomach contractions which correspond closely to reported hunger pangs. Figure 2 shows how this is done. One cannot argue the child's experience from the experience reported by an adult and one hesitates to subject a child to such an experiment for fear of doing lasting damage. Parents quickly learn to identify types of cry and it seems that the baby's hunger pangs can cause first discomfort and then real pain. Right from the start, it is bad for a baby to associate food with pain and prolonged crying. Amongst the many individual differences of children, such as height, weight and colouring, there are marked differences in how long a baby can go without food. This gives us the first of many lessons in finding what suits individual children.

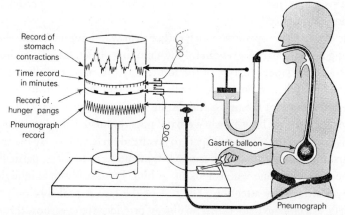

Figure 2. Hunger pangs and stomach contractions. Reported hunger pangs correspond closely to the periods when stomach contractions are at their maximum.
Source: Cannon (1934).

One of the big changes for a child once outside the mother, is that he is no longer close to the beating of his mother's heart. Salk (1962), working in the New York City Hospital with newborn babies, found there was less crying before sleep if the infants were put in a room where there was a simulated sound of a heart beat seventy-two times a minute for the first four days. This environment was more effective than silence or a lullaby. There is a fuller account of this investigation in Pickard (1965). Observers have found that the majority of mothers, both monkey and human, carry their newborn babies on the left arm. Medical advice has rationalised this by saying it leaves the right hand free for jobs. But with 287 mothers Salk found that a very high percentage of left-handed as well as right-handed mothers automatically held the child on the left side, close to the heart. One cannot yet say whether this is an inborn tendency. More probably the mothers quickly become conditioned to holding the baby the way which contents him most.

The mechanism for smiling can be seen within hours of birth. The baby makes a kind of grimace, with mouth stretched sideways and upwards at both corners. As his cheek pads are plump, he seems to smile with his whole face, including the eyes. Within a week or two he smiles in two ways: either spontaneously or in response to touch or sound. Here we have the roots of what will soon be social behaviour. In *Determinants of Infant Behaviour II* (ed. Foss, 1963) Wolff (pp. 113–60) gives an interesting account of research on infants smiling and follows this with an account of a family, with plates showing stages of smiling as the infant grows older. The old idea that the infant's smile is 'just wind' belongs to the time when infants' personalities had not been noticed.

The eyes are also operative much earlier than was thought. Within hours of being born the baby's eyes can follow a moving object, such as a swinging bell. Valentine (1942) reports of the fourth day, 'Appears to follow bright object a little when moved very slowly and not far (3 inches) from his eyes'. Indeed, this diary of the first fortnight, in *The Psychology of Early Childhood* (pp. 68–71), shows how much we have underestimated the first stages of life, as does also the work of Piaget (1951) already referred to. By the end of the first month the eyes have become bright and seem to focus, particularly on the eyes of anyone who is looking at him. Presumably the highlight of the eyes attracts his attention. The rest of the face is probably only seen vaguely, as a hideous mask causes no distress provided the eyes show through.

During the first three months the initial jerky movements become much smoother and more continuous. After the first weeks immense vitality is shown in movement. By the third month the spine becomes stronger. The head can be held up for several seconds while sitting. A child turns his head at a human voice and enjoys 'Boo!' He recognises his mother and greets her warmly. Everything goes to his mouth, still the most sensitive area for finding what things are like. He will even try mushy solids and make his approval or disapproval very clear. He begins to pick things up with forearm and hands, so needs a variety of objects with which to experiment. But he cannot deliberately let go. By the fourth or fifth month he may go four or five hours between meals. He may sleep through the night or just need one feed. If feeding has gone well, without anxiety and excessive crying, he may entertain himself for a while on waking, before crying. But if the feeding rhythm has not been found, then anxiety immediately accompanies hunger.

He likes the sound of the human voice. Fortunately mothers appear to have a built-in mechanism for 'nattering' to children. He will wait expectantly for her to return to the room, if he has learned that there will be the fun of her smile and greeting when she returns. This social training in patience and pleasure is very important. A child has no sense of time at all. As soon as he can recognise his own mother he becomes anxious with her departure from the room. So learning that she will return is an intellectual as well as an emotional step. When this event is combined with a game, he is greatly helped in the mastery of disappointment. 'Peep-bo!' is a very serious game.

By six or seven months the child begins to notice strangers. He does not like to play games with them, because they look different and do not do the usual things in the usual way. This is when the temperamental disposition of the child begins to show. One child will go quite soon to strangers, while another literally withdraws. A child who is unusually shy needs longer to get through the phase of watchfulness about strangers. With this behaviour the child observes more of the face than just the eyes. By now a mask on the face frightens him. He may mistake his mother for a stranger, if she appears in a strange party dress or new hat. She can quickly allay his fears by speaking. The picture of how his world is normally arranged is forming, otherwise he would not be taken by surprise over the new clothes. It is interesting to note that the familiar voice calms him. We tend to forget that the baby is receiving auditory as well as visual and touch impressions all the time he is awake. The important element of speech is intonation. If we say with an edge in our voice, 'I'll pick your toys up in a minute' he understands the edge but not the words.

At this stage, left to himself, he plays many absorbing games with his toys. The cortex, the outer covering of the brain, is sufficiently mature for him to open his hands now at will and let things go. Previously things he had grasped stayed in his hand until he forgot them and his fingers relaxed, or he rubbed them out of his hand against his body. Now he plays dropping them and naturally enjoys dropping them where they disappear, over the side of the pram. This exciting new stage of skill is still frequently mistaken for 'naughtiness'. He needs plenty to drop as well as some attached toys that he can still play with until someone kindly brings back the toys which have disappeared, so that he can drop them again.

He also examines everything minutely, testing the taste and whether it stretches or is soft to the face. The teeth are pushing through, so biting is important. There are wide differences in how much pain is felt with the teeth coming through. The temples may flush and he may put his hand there. A gentle adult hand on the temple can have a very calming effect. He finds his feet and pulls them up for inspection by eyes and mouth. The world of the family is becoming more stable. He notices his parents' moods and whether they are pleased or not with what he does. He knows the meaning of *No*, even though it is not a word to him. Already, one can aid his understanding by letting him have plenty to investigate and nothing within reach which is dangerous. However, crises arise from time to time because no one has noticed he can, for example, reach the teapot. This is where the emergency *NO* is vital. It should not be abused by using *NO* for things that do not really matter.

By the eighth and ninth month he can pull himself up to sitting, raise himself on hands and knees, may even start to crawl. Once he becomes mobile through crawling, the circle of harmful things out of reach has to widen considerably. Coal-scuttle and fire must be *firmly* barricaded, sideboards locked with key out of reach. Measures such as these can save much anxiety to adults and frustration to the child. He may go off in any direction. But even on a beach, he will not go very far. He wants to keep in touch. It is excellent self-discipline for parents to find out how far he will go and much better for the child to be allowed the independence he can himself tolerate. But, of course, open space is needed for this.

He loves to play with adults, especially passing things back and forth which practises the let-go reflexes. If you cover a toy with a box he will find it; but if you cover the toy with one of two boxes he cannot tell which covered the toy. He wants to feed himself and again parents need self-discipline as they see the food miss his mouth, going on his bib, even into his ear. He looks up at a dog barking in the street or a knock at the door, because he can now distinguish near from far sounds. With so much learning going on, mothers hope that he will soon be toilet trained. But control of the sphincter muscle depends on cortical development. Bowel control comes before bladder control, because an effort has to be made to push out the faeces. Bowel control usually comes *after* walking, if the mother is sensitive to the child's natural rhythm; bladder control does not come till much later.

By the last month of his first year the baby can usually stand, swaying. He pulls himself up and sits with a flop. Then he cruises sideways holding on to furniture. Though he cannot talk more than the odd word, he understands many words and short sentences. He can wave goodbye, usually with closed fists. Analysts tell us that at no time in our lives do we have such an upsurge of power as when we begin to walk; except perhaps when we first drive a car. Liberated from just sitting, he investigates everything and goes out of the door to see where people disappear to. No wonder that, in this intense excitement, he forgets to talk.

By the time he is a year old, there are many signs of thinking as he tries to manoeuvre his toys, and also his family. The next three months are largely occupied in consolidating the learning of the first year. As his walking be-becomes steadier he begins to control his bowels. There are many accidents but he has seen that the faeces go in his pot and is interested to get them to the right place, provided nobody fusses him. He knows where his clothes go, and puzzles over his mirror reflection, looking behind for someone. After the lull in use of words, he begins to use short sentences. He makes mistakes about what adults mean, but adults also make mistakes about what he means. Sensitive as he is to facial expression now, he will mistake a frown for intense anger, such as he sometimes feels himself when frustrated. His superego, his idea of what adults expect him to be like, is forming. This is the process by which we incorporate the moral standards of our society and is therefore very important. Some children seem far more sensitive to adult approval and disapproval than others. The question of 'obedience', except to the danger-cry of No, does not yet arise. It is best to keep danger away until he is a little older.

He still has absolutely no sense of time. Everything is NOW. So conversation should be about shared experience. An expedition yesterday comes to his mind when mentioned and is again NOW. Talking about something he will do tomorrow cannot have meaning, unless he has done it before. His social contacts are developing rapidly, now that he can interpret facial expressions and intonations. But he will still play on his own, given plenty of toys, and he will repeat the same experiment so often that he appears to have an inborn compulsion to repetition. Infancy is the time when his play is nearest to the play of animals. He learns to judge distance, space, what will fit into what. He also wants to imitate and makes his toys do some of what adults do. There is also an element of making toys represent situations, so that he can repeat the situations until he understands them; for instance when he enjoys Peep-bo with his toys he is finding out that things which disappear can come back again. But this symbolic play is much more developed in the next stage.

Let us look at an example of neuromuscular adjustment which the child has to make and interpret, of a kind which we have long since forgotten. This will explain a little of his absorption in what he is doing. He has to sort out single and double images and learn to ignore the double ones, as he learns to focus his eyes. A simple experiment will bring back to the reader the forgotten double images. Hold a finger at arm's length in front of the light switch; then focus alternatively on the finger and the light switch. When one is in focus, the other has a double image. This works at about a dozen feet from the switch. But some people have a little difficulty in reverting to seeing the double images. A good popular book indicating the great complexity of vision is the paperback *Eye and Brain* by Gregory (1966). It has attractive coloured pictures, and deceptive diagrams, as in Figure 3, which appears sometimes to have the spot at the front and sometimes at the back of the cube. We have learned to discipline this oscillation of attention through learning to identify the nature of such objects from past experience. Because we usually only glance at posters when passing them on the road, poster artists have to be very careful to avoid reversible pictures, for instance by exaggerating the perspective of the cube in Figure 3, so that the spot keeps stationary, either at the front or at the back. But the very young child has to make many experiments before he can stabilise his visual perception of the world around him.

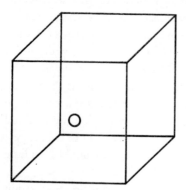

Figure 3. Oscillating figure.
Source: Gregory (1966).

During the fifteen months of infancy the development of a child is extremely rapid. The helpless and almost motionless newborn, preoccupied with starting mechanisms for breathing by lungs, feeding by mouth and circulating blood, is transformed to a child who can stand and walk, communicate, and judge adult reactions. Given a secure routine, he makes widening social contacts and enjoys the company of those who enjoy him. Far more of this development is innate than was previously realised. Smiling, awareness of eyes and expression, sympathetic response to the behaviour of others, are largely emotional reactions which are born in us. But language is not born in us, and we shall treat it separately.

2. Speech development
0 to 15 months

In less than twice the time of pregnancy the helpless organism battling for air is able to use air for speech. The reason why speech is now generally accepted as man's greatest asset is quite simple. The wild animals bring up their young carefully by showing them how to do things and preventing them from harm. But they always have to demonstrate on the spot. By use of a word as a symbol for an object (e.g. a horse) or event (e.g. thunderstorm) man can refer to things and people and events when they are not present. This lifts communication out of the present alone, so that it embraces the past and the future. Through this single asset man has created and handed on the whole complex fabric of culture. Thus we can speak of Homer though we are born many centuries later and may never go to Greece. Many philosophers have in the past speculated on the origins of speech, but the simple fact seems to be that after the cortex has reached a certain degree of complexity, using a sound as a symbol for an object, event or person appears to be a natural step. All known groups of men, no matter how isolated, have invented language, but unlike the dance symbols of bees, languages are not the same in every colony of the species because not innate.

The cortex normally reaches the required degree of complexity during infancy. Children usually know a few words when about one year old. Sampson, to whose work we shall refer later, points out that the delicate mechanism of speech involves a subtle coordination of ear, larynx and brain. The larynx is the upper part of the windpipe and the vocal cords are formed by folds in the membrane at the top of the larynx. The first cry a baby gives is not due to manipulation of vocal cords but to air rushing up the windpipe. But Piaget's (1951, see p. 8) observation at four days shows the start of coordination of ear and larynx. And by the end of infancy, after many months of practice, the child can not only exercise the neuromuscular control to make the sound he wants, but can use the sound as a symbol, as speech.

We can learn much by studying the practice stages. Very soon the mother can detect differentiation of cries. Lewis, in *Language, Thought and Personality* (1963), describes the sequence of the earliest sounds. The discomfort and comfort cries are quite distinctive. But as he points out, what is not so obvious is that for the child himself his early utterance has its rudimentary 'meaning' and the nature of his early utterance is a potent influence on the growth of his language. The sequence of sound-making is broadly the same in all children everywhere. Lewis traces three stages of vowels and consonants with both discomfort and comfort cries. Table 2 gives his sequence of emerging vowels and consonants. In view of our paucity of research on very young children

TABLE 2: *The stages of early spontaneous utterance*

Stage	Discomfort cries	Comfort sounds
I. Vowel-like	(i) Onset: immediately after birth	(i) Onset: when the discomfort-cries have already begun to appear
	(ii) Narrow vowels: e, ɛ, æ, a	(ii) Open vowels: not clearly defined, a, o, u
	(iii) Often nasalised	(iii) Rarely nasalised
II. Earlier consonantal	Sounds made by partial closure: w, l, ŋ, h	Mostly back consonants: g, ɡ, x, k, r
III. Later consonantal	Front consonants, usually nasal: labial, m dental, n	Front consonants, usually oral, sometimes nasal: labial, p, b, m dental, t, d, n

Source: Lewis (1963).

and the now recognised importance of language, this is a book which students would be well advised to own for reference.

Such careful notice of the routes by which infants reach speech is a fairly recent feature of child development. It was assumed that the sounds were 'purely emotional'. But adult conversation also conveys emotion, through intonation and inflection. 'I'm not sure about that,' can be said in very different ways, and the roots of conveying pleasure or pain by how it is said lie deep in the first comfort and discomfort cries. An adult who is pleased that a student has raised an interesting problem says so with relaxed throat, as if glad that both will have to go a stage further in thinking. But one who is insecure, or whose antagonism has been roused by the aggressive way the question was put, may retaliate with the sharp speech of distress.

By the second month a child makes several different sounds, when crying; and he listens to human voices. Listening is part of conversation; we take turns to speak, otherwise the speech becomes a monologue. As the child listens, he begins to perceive the sounds adults make. By the third or fourth month, perhaps earlier, he coos and makes noises back, to people or music. By the sixth and seventh month he coos or crows for pleasure. Now he begins to babble. The impulse to babble is innate; even deaf children babble at this stage, though they cannot hear the speech of those around them. Babbling covers more or less every known sound made by man. By the eighth or ninth month the child not only babbles, but babbles back when people talk to him. He may even say *Dada* or *Mummum*. These are fairly easy sounds to make and, as we can see from Table I, they belong to Lewis's third stage, of comfort sounds. So parents give themselves names which are easy for the infant to say and are associated with comfort.

These words, with perhaps one or two names of objects, have definite meaning for the child by the time he is a year old. But it is still extremely difficult for us to gain a picture of this meaning. There is a development towards the idea of 'man' when the child calls the postman or the policeman 'Dada'. But all these words are usually forgotten, or more exactly go into disuse for a while, in the excitement of learning to talk. When he begins to talk again the words are used again, but often in very simple sentences. It is most important to remember that words learned may be retained, at least for a while, even when not exercised in speech. If, when he speaks again, the child uses simple sentences, then he has been listening to the speech around him, and forming schemata of how one manipulates words.

Hayakawa (1966), Professor of English in San Francisco State College, points out that children, as newcomers to the language, do not just learn words; they learn the rules of the language at the same time. He says even linguists are only just beginning to understand this. A child who says, 'I runned' has never heard the word 'runned'. He makes it up by analogy with other past tenses he has heard. When a child proves more logical than the English language, we should listen with great attentiveness. So often we laugh at the 'mistakes' children make, when it is the language we speak which is illogical. Hayakawa gives an excellent description of a child's relief when the adult understands. When his daughter was three she asked to see the 'popentole'. After a moment of puzzlement he asked if she meant the Lincoln Park totempole. She said 'Yes' and having got her point across, she played contentedly for another twenty minutes, singing to herself. Younger children often have a temper tantrum when adults fail to understand them; so do children of three when surrounded by adults who cannot receive their communications.

27

The month by month stages which have been given are only very approximate. Children differ in verbal ability, in perception of sounds made by themselves and others, in environment of adults who have time or ability to give them attention and verbal stimulus. Children sometimes make their meaning very clear before they have the words, as the following extract from L. B. Murphy, *The Widening World of Childhood* (1962) shows.

> Greta, at fourteen months, had many wishes, needs and interests; she did not talk much and had few words. But she communicated a great deal, with considerable expressiveness and motor agility. Waking up in the morning she pointed at the window shade, looked toward her mother and motioning upward, indicated that she wanted the shade to be pulled up, then she stood up in her crib, leaned far over the edge, and pointed down to indicate that she wanted to get down. If she was picked up without being offered anything to eat she became restless and when asked, 'Do you want a cracker?' nodded her head vigorously, with wide approving smiles.

This child also demonstrated that she understood what was said to her, before she talked much herself.

Somewhere between eleven and seventeen months a child obeys simple commands: 'Give that to Mummy' or 'Take this spoon'. Somewhere between twelve and twenty months he begins to obey a simple *No*, provided you give him time to understand. To us it is a word meaning 'You must not do that', but to the child it is not speech but an emotional cry inducing fear or inhibition. The young of wild animals are also naturally obedient when warned of danger. Leverets wait in the form while the hare seeks food; young foxes wait in the holes while the vixen goes food-seeking; and kittens will cease to investigate at a spit-command from the cat. Parents should remember that children also have a built in mechanism for obedience when definitely forbidden to do something dangerous. A child only learns to ignore *No* when it is constantly used unnecessarily.

Somewhere between thirteen and fifteen months a child first greatly enjoys hearing nursery rhymes and jingles, then tries to join in. Now the babbling changes. The nonsense is babbled with great emphasis, the high voice going still higher and dropping down low. This is how we say rhymes and stories to them and they imitate our exaggerations. Thus we can see that, over the fifteen months of infancy, a child rehearses the various aspects of speech; control of ribs for intake of air, control of larynx and tongue, and of vocal cords for inflection; he also rehearses attending to speech around him, to alternating speakers, and so on. Probably one of the most important points is for adults to get into the habit of attending very carefully to what the child is trying to say. Only by attending to a child can we encourage a child to attend. This does not mean that one has to attend to a child the whole time. Fortunately children need a good deal of time in which to play and investigate on their own. But every child needs full attention for part of the time; and caring for children becomes much more interesting when we begin to notice the way in which their minds work. This is nowhere more true than in the early stages of speech.

3. Heredity and environment

Most thoughtful parents wonder, as they look at their newborn baby, how much of what he will become is determined by heredity (over which they have no control) and how much is determined by environment (much of which they can control). In order to understand how best to manipulate the environment we have to gain some idea of the nature of heredity. Over many centuries people have been interested in pedigrees of physical and mental traits. The first unsystematic studies led to many anecdotes, superstitions and myths; but it was a long while before anyone thought of keeping systematic records of successive generations. The first record of this kind seems to have been in the eighteenth century, when it was noticed that certain peculiarities tended to run in families. In 1752 the mathematician and naturalist Maupertuis recorded a Berlin family of four generations in which every generation had some people with extra fingers and toes. Being a mathematician, he worked out the frequency of the occurrence of extra fingers and toes to be expected in a population the size of eighteenth-century Berlin. This calculation is made according to the *theory of probability*. One of the concerns of this theory is to work out the likelihood of two different properties—in this case supernumerary digits and a common heredity—being both possessed by an individual if there were no connection between them; then to compare this with the ascertained fact, and to draw conclusions about the presence or absence of a causal relation between the properties.

Maupertuis found that the chance of a person having extra fingers and toes in Berlin at that time was one in twenty thousand. With such a very small chance of having extra fingers and toes, it was striking to find so many people in one family with this unlikely characteristic. If today we heard of four generations of one family, each with several members who had won vast sums of money on premium bonds (Ernie), we should suspect that something had gone wrong with the machinery for selecting wins by chance. Maupertuis suggested that so many people in one family with deformed hands and feet could not be explained on the basis of chance alone. His work influenced the subsequent study of heredity in two ways which are basic to modern genetics: (a) he linked the chance element and theory of probability to concepts of inheritance; and (b) he started scientific recording of traits noticeably clustered within single families

From the eighteenth century onwards, increasingly accurate records have been kept of families with some observable peculiarity which is rare in the population as a whole and frequent within a particular family. Some of these peculiarities are harmless, such as colour blindness which is no worse for an individual than being tone deaf; some are lethal, causing early death, such as haemophilia, a deficiency of the blood which prevents clotting to staunch a wound or scratch, thus causing the sufferer to bleed to death before old age; and some, like the extra fingers and toes, are little more than embarrassing in a world where the vast majority of people have five. From study of peculiarities in relation to probability theory, geneticists have been able to trace the inheritance of normal traits, such as eye and skin colour.

But the link between mathematical theory and observable characteristics was not easy to understand. Maupertuis's suggestion was not followed up for about a century. Then Mendel (1822–84), an Austrian biologist of peasant stock, who became an Augustinian monk and taught in the monastery school, made an intensive study of succeeding generations of garden peas, which have the advantage over human families for study of heredity that generations occur much more frequently. He developed pure strains of peas, for colour and size of flowers, height of plants, and so on. To do this he had to segregate plants, so that white flowers were only pollinated by white plants, tall flowers by tall plants, and so on. Mendel introduced into genetics the idea of *segregation*, which is the division of plants or animals into two classes by a single hereditary trait. He then crossbred plants of pure white flower with plants of pure red flower and recorded the results. He found that the flowers in the first generation of offspring were not pink but mixed red and white. From this kind of observation of various segregated traits with some ten thousand plants, he was able to show in 1865 that the results of crossbreeding segregated traits could be predicted according to certain mathematical formulae. Such ways of predicting the results of crossbreeding are now called *Mendelian Ratios*.

Mendel's work was ignored for more than thirty years. This may have been because his work was published in the Proceedings of a little local society which hardly anyone read. At that time scientists thought that when two plants or animals united the offspring would have a *blending* of the different traits. According to their ideas, when Mendel crossed the white and red flowers he 'ought to have obtained' pink offspring. They thought that the result of marriage of a dark African with a blond Scandinavian would be coffee-coloured offspring, and of course some of them are. If this blending always happened, all variety would long since have been lost. Darwin noticed that, despite the theory of blending, evolution of species had maintained great variety, and he put this down to spontaneous 'sports' or changes. We now know that spontaneous changes called *mutations* do take place, for example as a result of radiation, and they are the main source of the great diversity of species and races. Mendel's idea of segregation of inheritable traits and forecasting results of mixed breeding was a major contribution.

Mendel called whatever it was that caused a plant to have a particular colour or size of flower, or a particular height, a 'factor'. Today the various elements of inheritance which pass on instructions for development are called factors or *genes*. Until the invention of the electron-microscope no one had ever seen a gene. Now the double-helix structure, which in theory consists of genes, has been seen; but by the end of the 'sixties research workers were not certain whether what they had seen was actually a gene. The behaviour of genes can be worked out statistically and what happens in development can be guessed or observed. There is nothing strange to modern science in

Male cell
or gamete (Gk. *gametes*, husband)
or sperm (L. *sperma*, seed)

Female cell
or gamete (Gk. *gamete*, wife)
or ovum (L. *ovum*, pl. *ova*, egg)

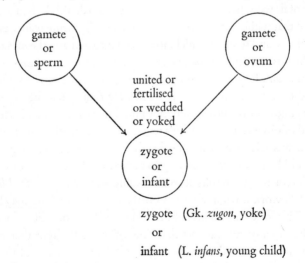

gamete
or
sperm

gamete
or
ovum

united or
fertilised
or wedded
or yoked

zygote
or
infant

zygote (Gk. *zugon*, yoke)
or
infant (L. *infans*, young child)

Figure 4. Sex cells or gametes.

nobody having seen a gene. The physicist has not seen an electron and the civil engineer has not seen the stresses and strains revealed by his calculations. At first geneticists imagined the genes to be like beads strung on threads. But calculations show that each gene can be analysed further, so that prediction becomes increasingly elaborate and increasingly accurate.

Had the scientists of Mendel's day given his work the attention it deserved, they would have found that, in addition to establishing incontrovertibly the existence of segregation, he was faced with a problem which looked remarkably like blending. He got the results he expected with peas, but when he carried out the same experiments with beans, no matter how carefully he purebred white flowers and purple flowers, if he crossed them the offspring gave a whole series of colours from purple to pale violet and white. Mendel correctly surmised that here a number of genes were involved. Today we have two terms for these two situations: (a) when the trait is traceable to the effect of a single gene, this is referred to as *unifactorial inheritance*; (b) when the trait is traceable to the effects of a series of genes, this is referred to as *multifactorial inheritance*. The former is monogenetic inheritance and the latter is polygenetic inheritance.

The attention of twentieth-century geneticists has now turned to the mechanisms whereby inheritance operates. These mechanisms are extremely complex; many questions are far from settled. But it is possible to follow a much simplified outline. First we should clear up some confusion arising through use of interchangeable terms: 'factor' has meaning other than just 'gene' whereas 'gene' has not. Both of them refer to characteristics which are segregated, such as height, colour, etc.

Then there are a few words which appear in various forms and if we get the source of these words clear, many apparently strange words also become clear. The word 'zygote' comes from the Greek word to 'yoke' or join together—an essential first step in producing the next generation. A *zygote* is the initial stage, the moment of conception when the heredity from the male is linked to the heredity from the female in any plant or animal. In humans, the zygote is the infant. The word zygote is linked to two Greek words, 'homo' meaning the same and 'hetero' meaning different. When we meet the word 'homozygous' we know that the same has been yoked, for instance red-flower gene to red-flower gene; and in the same way we know that 'heterozygous' means that different elements are yoked, for instance white-flower gene to red-flower gene.

In Figure 4 some of the double, and even triple terminology is shown in graphic form, together with some of the derivations. These derivations show that, though the words of Greek and Latin origin may sound so different, the concepts which these words symbolise are closely related. Zygote is the better word for the newly conceived offspring, as it covers all plants and animals, whereas infant does not.

Both the sex cells, the sperm and the ovum, have a fixed number of *chromosomes*, or coiled threads each consisting of a large number of strands. These chromosomes are the elements of heredity. Penrose has likened these 'instructions for development' to recipes. The recipes consist of heredity material from previous generations. The hereditary recipes produced in each sperm by an individual male are somewhat different. So are the recipes produced in each ovum by an individual female. Which sperm reaches which ovum is a matter of chance. Once the zygote is formed, the heredity is fixed. There are twenty-three chromosomes from the ovum. These pair up in the zygote, so that there are twenty-three pairs of genes of similar effect opposite each other. It is difficult to imagine how microscopic the instructions or recipes are. It has been estimated that if all the recipes for all people in the world today, at the moment of their conception, were added together, the

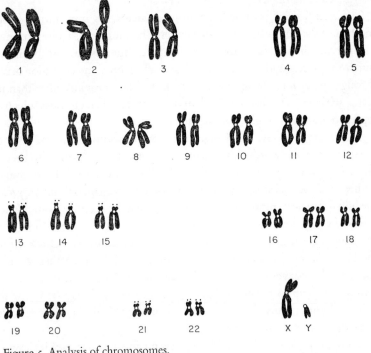

Figure 5. Analysis of chromosomes.
Source: McKusick (1964)

chemicals (known as D.N.A.) in their initial chromosomes would weigh about three-quarters as much as a postage stamp.

The newly formed zygote grows by cell division. Every time the cell divides, the twenty-three pairs of chromosomes divide exactly. When there are two cells, each cell has an exact replica of the original twenty-three pairs of chromosomes. When the child is born, or the student goes to college, or the old person dies, every cell in the body has an exact replica of the original twenty-three chromosomes. A drop of blood from any person, put under a powerful microscope, reveals the nature of the original chromosomes in the first zygote cell. The word chromosome is made from two Greek words meaning colour and body, because, at a certain moment in chromosome division, the chromosomes can be coloured and seen under the microscope. During this moment of division the chromosomes develop constrictions like waists, and it is possible to arrange them in order of size and constriction. Figure 5 shows a set of human chromosomes, analysed and set out in order. All the numbered ones are called *autosomes*; they are not the ones concerned with sex. But the two lettered ones at the end are the *sex chromosomes*. As these two sex chromosomes are not the same size, we can see that these are the chromosomes of a male; the female has two sex chromosomes of the same size. The autosomes are the same for a man or a woman, but the sex chromosomes are XX for a woman and XY for a man. It was a surprise for the geneticists, when they found that masculinity was inherited through an extra *small* chromosome. But if, with Penrose, we think of the Y chromosome as an extra small book of recipies, the size of the book does not affect the quality of the recipes.

It is not yet known by what process the chromosomes divide, but the stages of division have been photographed under the microscope. Figure 6 shows diagrammatically the process of division in six stages, from interphase to interphase. The third phase is the one where the chromosomes are best coloured and seen. When division is over, the chromosomes return to coils.

Along the chromosomes there are the factors or entities or concentrations of recipes which are called genes. Though they have not been seen, there is incontrovertible evidence for their existence. Figure 7 shows diagrammatically a pair of chromosomes, one from the father and one from the mother, with marks to show the position of pairs of genes, each one of a pair concerned with the same aspect of development.* When the chromosomes from each

* The physical equivalent of this process is now in process of being revealed, and it appears that each gene is strung out on a long helical (corkscrew) molecule like a message inked in morse code along a tape, except that there are three pairs of organic groups instead of the two symbols, dot and dash, of morse.

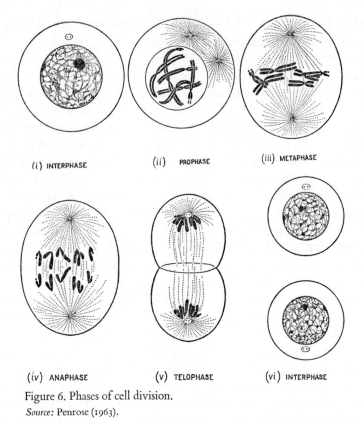

(i) INTERPHASE   (ii) PROPHASE   (iii) METAPHASE

(iv) ANAPHASE   (v) TELOPHASE   (vi) INTERPHASE

Figure 6. Phases of cell division.
Source: Penrose (1963).

parent pair up, genes concerned with similar aspects of development form an allelomorphic pair or for short, alleles (pronounced al-eels). Within very small limits, there is a range of places where a particular gene may be placed, and this is called a *locus* (pl. *loci*). The word locus does not just mean place; it is a term from mathematics, meaning a total of all possible positions of a moving or generative element. Thus the locus is the exact position within

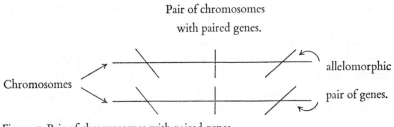

Pair of chromosomes
with paired genes.

Chromosomes

allelomorphic
pair of genes.

Figure 7. Pair of chromosomes with paired genes.

36

which alleles can be situated. One individual can only have alleles on one position in the locus; the exact position is not the same for everyone. So, in a whole population of individuals, there may be five or six positions within one locus, for the alleles. However, the alleles of one locus, though slightly differently placed in different individuals, are all concerned with variations of the same trait.

Different species have different numbers of chromosomes. This puts a limit on the amount of interbreeding between species, since all of both sets of chromosomes in the zygote have to pair very exactly. A mouse has 20 pairs, a dog 39 pairs, and man has, as we have seen, 23 pairs. When the alleles form, they may have the same instructions, for instance for development of red flowers. If we use A to represent this recipe for red flowers, then the alleles are AA. Or the instructions may be for white flowers, and if we use a for white flowers, the alleles are aa. When the instructions are the same for an element of development such as flower colour, the plant or animal is called *homozygous*, because the same instructions have been yoked and whichever is followed, the result will be the same. The plant or animal only follows one set of instructions, not both. Figure 8 shows this graphically.

Homozygous   Homozygous

AA
pure
red
flowers

aa
pure
white
flowers

AA Purebred genes coded for red flowers
aa Purebred genes coded for white flowers
Figure 8. Homozygous colour coding.

If you crossbreed these two pure strains, one for red flowers and the other for white flowers, then each can only contribute from its own pure genes. The parent on the left can only offer the A recipe and the parent on the right can only offer the a recipe. Figure 9 shows this graphically. The first generation offspring only have recipes for red *or* white flowers. If these offspring are inbred, with no further crossbreeding from outside, interesting possibilities happen. Those who know the theory of probability can see at once what arrangements might happen. Figure 10 shows this graphically. Since red and white is the same as white and red, there are three kinds of flowers which could appear in the second generation: pure white, pure red, and mixed red

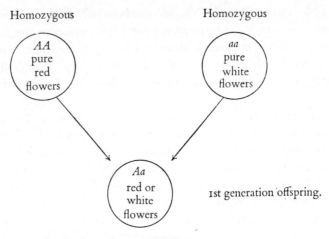

Homozygous   Homozygous

AA
pure
red
flowers

aa
pure
white
flowers

Aa
red or
white
flowers   1st generation offspring.

Heterozygous

Figure 9. Heterozygous colour coding.

and white. By the time these plants have been inbred for several generations, the offspring settle down to a proportion of about one white to one red to two red-and-white flowers. This approximate estimate of what colours to

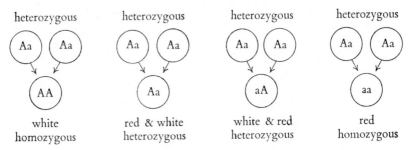

heterozygous   heterozygous   heterozygous   heterozygous

Aa   Aa   Aa   Aa   Aa   Aa   Aa   Aa

AA   Aa   aA   aa

white   red & white   white & red   red
homozygous   heterozygous   heterozygous   homozygous

Figure 10. Offspring of heterozygous union.

expect forms one of the Mendelian Ratios; and ratios can be predicted, provided that the pedigree is known.

Even before the theory of blending had been superseded by that of segregation, scientists had realised that something could be learned of heredity from identical twins, whose eye and skin colour, stature and so on, appear so close. Let us see what happens when humans give birth to twins. Figure 11 shows the two kinds of twins: identical and fraternal. It is not yet known by what mechanism some zygotes divide into two children at an early stage, with identical sets of chromosomes. But the incidence of monozygotic or identical twins is about the same throughout the world. If the zygote divides into more children, then the resulting triplets, quads, etc., are identical. The Dionne quins are five identical children, with identical sets of chromosomes.

Fraternal twinning has a very slight tendency to run in families. The fact that fraternal twins may be very alike or very unalike reminds us that, although all genetic development is inherited, we do not inherit all that could be inherited from our parents. Chance decides which genes come from the father and which from the mother at the moment of conception. Fraternal

Fertilisation of one ovum by one sperm, and early division to two identical children.

Fertilisation of two ova by two sperms and normal development of two children.

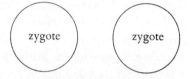

Monozygotes (one yoking) or identical twins or uniovular twins.

Dizygotes (two yokings) or fraternal twins or diovular twins.

Figure 11. Twins.

twins are conceived within a matter of hours of each other, but they may be very different. We sometimes forget that we inherit our genetic differences as well as our genetic likenesses. Frequently fraternal twins seem more alike than other brothers and sisters, simply because children born in normal sequence are not seen together at the same age.

Another cause of variety, in both plants and animals, is that only one of the two sets of instructions at each of the alleles can be carried out. Thus, though there are instructions for eye colour from both parents, one will dominate and the other recede. The gene which guides development is called the *dominant gene*, and the gene which is, so to speak, in abeyance is called the *recessive gene*. Strictly speaking, it is the trait and not the gene which is dominant or recessive. Very occasionally, both traits develop to some degree. For instance, when a ginger cat mates with a black cat, the kittens are ginger or black; but tortoiseshell cats show both ginger and black fur, inherited from the ginger and black parents. Recessive genes are not useless; they are a rich investment of possible future adaptation, for offspring in different conditions. Nature's 'experiment' in developing two sexes has been a very fertile way of developing variety of heredity.

The genes of some traits are located on the sex chromosome. Colour blindness and haemophilia are both traits resulting from genes on the male chromosome. They cannot be developed fully through the female chromosome, so both these defects pass from the father, through the daughter, to her sons. There are far more colour blind men than women, and yet, when a woman has a markedly colour blind son, careful tests now show that the mother usually has some slight colour disability. The proportion of colour blind men to colour blind women is about 30 to 1. Traits originating from genes on the sex chromosome are called *sex linked*. Haemophilia is fortunately much rarer than colour blindness, but is well known because Queen Victoria had a son with this disability and it spread through him to other European royal families. The incidence of colour blindness in schools and the reasons why teachers should be aware of any children who either cannot see colour (very rare) or can only see a limited amount of colour, are clearly set out by Waddington (1965) in an article on young children and colour blindness.

Sometimes the same trait appears in both men and women but takes a somewhat different form because of the peculiarities of constitution which distinguish the sexes. Stature is an example of this. Boys and girls normally grow to a height somewhere between the height of the two parents. But the male constitution is such that it produces greater height than the female constitution. When a trait appears in somewhat different form in the two sexes it is called *sex influenced*. Premature baldness is sex influenced. Women tend to have more hair on their heads than men, and less hair elsewhere. A bald father has a fifty-fifty chance of passing this characteristic of less than usual hair on the head to a son. However, here too, the mothers of bald sons tend to have less luxuriant heads of hair than other women. The mothers are usually more or less unaffected carriers of the sex influenced trait.

In order to make some of the processes clear, isolated traits have been discussed; but the developing individual has immense complexity, with not yet known numbers of genetic causes for development. Very rarely chromosomes break and join up in the wrong order, or extra chromosomes appear, and so on. The whole complex structure is so well adapted to survival that minor changes can be tolerated. But major changes are usually destructive, since the new form is not so well adapted for survival; and there are either no offspring or only a very few generations before the change dies out. Obviously some changes must be suited to better adaptation, or there would be no evolution. It may be that the higher intelligence in man results from what Darwin called some 'sport' and we now call a mutation.

Penrose gives a diagram of various chromosome disorders and one of these, mongolism, is of considerable educational importance. In Figure 12 one can see the normal chromosomes for a man and a woman. Those who have not studied biology may not know the symbols for male and female. The circle with an arrow represents the male. It therefore appears over the XY chromosomes in Figure 12. The circle with a cross under it appears over the XX chromosomes. In the past any form of mental retardation or deficiency was regarded as a shame and disgrace to parents, implying that they must themselves have very inferior intelligence or have done something to displease the gods. Today, geneticists are able to show that mongol children have three instead of two of the twenty-first chromosome. This in some way prevents all-round development of brain and body. This discovery, that mongolism is due to faulty chromosome development, has reorientated the minds of well-informed people towards mongol children.

Man has always considered the possibility of breeding away any defects. The Greeks exposed what they thought were defective children. *Eugenics* is the attempt to improve the inborn qualities of a race. But we are still far from knowing exactly what are the essential qualities; and an even more serious problem is that exceptionally fine qualities often appear together with certain defects. Take, for example, the exceedingly unpleasant complaint of migraine. Amongst those who have suffered acutely from it are G. B. Shaw, Thomas Mann and Freud, Diaghilev was diabetic and Dostoievsky epileptic. We do not want to throw out the baby with the bath water. Because hereditary defects tend to be unproductive, there are relatively few of them; and because so many of the more complex traits are dependent on many genes with many steps between the various alleles and the ultimate trait, the whole individual is a closely interlocking system of development.

One of the major discussions of the last decade or so has been about how much intelligence is a matter of heredity. In 1956 Burt and Howard published a paper on the multifactorial theory of inheritance and its application to intelligence. They put forward a hypothesis mentioned in several previous papers by Burt that, among normal persons, differences in intelligence are determined by a large number of genes partly multi- and partly uni-factorial, segregating in accordance with Mendelian principles. From these assumptions, with due allowance for dominance and assortive (not just random) mating, they derive formulae for the correlations to be expected between siblings, parents and offspring, and remoter relatives. Their data from school

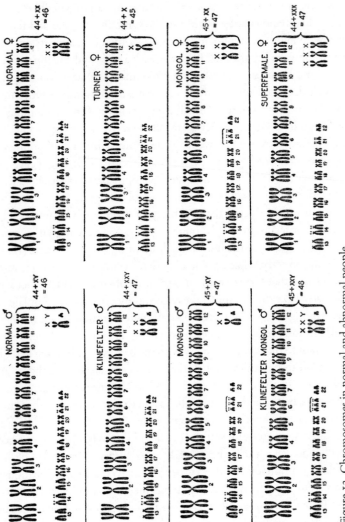

Figure 12. Chromosomes in normal and abnormal people.

Source: Penrose (1963).

surveys are in almost complete agreement with the predictions according to Mendelian principles.

Burt and Howard first define 'intelligence' as innate, general cognitive ability, with cognitive meaning directive thinking as distinct from feeling. We shall examine later how this definition was developed. The central assumption of their hypothesis is that, so far as genetic influences are concerned, an individual's measurement for intelligence is determined by a large number of independent factors, each of whose effects is small, similar and cumulative. Since intelligence is, by their definition, innate, it must be passed on to succeeding generations through the mechanisms of heredity which are now well established. Using 'factor' interchangeably with 'gene', they give these mechanisms in six postulates:

1. Each factor, though itself invisible and indeed hypothetical, may be thought of as a *definite location on one of the chromosomes*.
2. Each factor has *two alternative forms* (allelomorphs), of which one or the other will be carried at corresponding loci on corresponding chromosomes.
3. Every factor *preserves its nature and form* unaltered from one generation to another; it never changes, vanishes or blends, however often its observable effects may seem to do so.
4. Every *gamete* (whether egg or sperm) contains one and only one *specimen* of each factor, never both; every *zygote* or union of two gametes contains *two specimens* of each factor, one derived from the male parent and one from the female parent.
5. As a result of the separation of the chromosomes during the nuclear divisions which precede the formation of gametes (egg and sperm), the two factors thus brought together in the zygote will again be *segregated* in the gametes, the distribution of the factors from each pair being determined purely by chance; and when yet another zygote is formed by fertilisation they will be *recombined* in pairs, the type of re-combination being once again determined purely by chance.
6. The segregation and recombination of each pair occur *in complete independence* of the segregation and recombination of other pairs, so that the final reassortment is also determined by chance.

They point out that these postulates do not deny the occurrence of other events, such as mutation, sex linkage, chromosome irregularities, etc: but for the purpose of the present argument, these complicating possibilities may be temporarily disregarded as negligible or irrelevant. The essential feature of the Mendelian hypothesis lies in the fact that both the segregation of genes and their recombination are wholly determined by chance; therefore, as Mendel said, the expected results may be predicted according to the rules of probability. Even in the most elementary form, the problems of heredity are primarily statistical problems. They then explain the kinds of calculation involved in prediction for unifactorial and multifactorial inheritance:

(a) *Unifactorial inheritance.* Simpler instances of alternative forms of the same gene responsible for alternative structures: e.g. *A* producing tall peas, *a* producing dwarfs; *B* producing coloured blossoms, *b* producing white. The gene *A-a* results in four possible combinations: *AA Aa aA* and *aa* or three distinct types of height, since the middle two are the same. Similarly the coloured or white flowers *B-b* result in four possibilities: *BB Bb bB* and *bb* or three distinct types of colour, since the middle two are again the same. In thus estimating the outcome in the long run, account has to be taken of the hypothetical genotype and the observable phenotype, that is to say between the genetic characteristics of the individual resulting from the properties of the genetic material transmitted by the parents, and the characteristics ultimately observed or measured, since the latter will be affected by the interaction of his various genes with each other, with the rest of his body, and with his own particular environment. Thus, so far as observable characteristics are concerned, it frequently happens that the heterozygous individual, *Aa* or *aA*, appears superficially to be identical with one of the homozygous, such as *AA*. In such a case, *A* is said to be dominant and *a* recessive. But what appears identical to the naked eye may be distinguishable under biochemical tests: 'dominance' is therefore a developmental feature rather than a genetic feature.

(b) *Multifactorial inheritance.* Here the various genes all affect the *same* character or trait, and are responsible not for quantitative but for qualitative differences. When Mendel crossed white and purple beans and got a whole range of colours, he concluded that the colours were due, not to a single factor or gene, but to a series of factors, $A_1 + A_2 + \ldots$ and their alternatives, none of which dominates the other and which together produce the grading of colours. The authors then discuss the factor analysis necessary to prediction in this more complex situation. Mendel failed to secure sufficient bean offspring to confirm his multiple gene conclusion, but it has since been amply confirmed in experiments on wheat, maize, tobacco plant, etc.

In the final sections of their paper, Burt and Howard analyse school surveys of observable or measurable intelligence and show that there is almost complete agreement between coefficients of the schools data and the theoretical figures. They also make an analysis of the variance of the assessment obtained, and an assessment of the contributions of genetic factors and non-genetic factors respectively.

The fact that problems of heredity are primarily statistical is not yet widely understood. And the fact that intelligence is primarily a matter of heredity is also not widely understood—or rather, is not widely accepted, because reactions frequently tend to be emotional. Intelligence is therefore an interesting subject by means of which to examine heredity and environment. So let us examine what has happened to the concept since Spencer took up Galton's idea of a *general intellectual ability together with special abilities* and called this 'intelligence'. The idea was quite revolutionary. By the end of the nineteenth century most so-called psychologists adhered to the traditional doctrine of specialised 'faculties' ('powers of the mind' such as memory, will and attention), or explained the working of the mind in terms of 'association' (experience of one event becomes connected with experience of another because they happened close together in time, place, etc.)

But Spencer was well supported by experimentalists. The psychologist Sherrington (1906) used the phrase 'a hierarchy of neural functions'. Biologists make extensive brain study with animals. A recent example is Young (1964), who for many years studied how the octopus discriminates and controls the information it collects. During the evolution of animals, and the growth of young children, cognitive (thinking) processes differentiate into a hierarchy of more specialised abilities: sensory, perceptual, associative and relational. Experimental study of the brain leads to this conclusion: in matters involving thought, the brain acts as a whole (though certain areas have certain specialised functions) and *no part of the brain works in isolation*. This idea of intelligence was condemned by the faculty psychologists and associationists as too speculative. Those who wish to study in detail the fallacies of the logicians' and philosophers' approach will find them discussed by Burt in *The Backward Child* (1937) pp. 462–3.

McDougall collected a team (W. Brown, Burt, Flugel, and later Spearman) to find out the facts about general and special abilities. They constructed tests for a survey and the following were their conclusions (Burt, personal communication):

1. The team decided to seek not *a* general factor but the 'highest common factor'. To do this Burt suggested Pearson's method of principal components (factor analysis). The results demonstrated the evidence both of a general and of special abilities.

2. To demonstrate that the general factor was cognitive (thinking not), conative (willing) or motivational (emotional), a large correlation table was subsequently obtained including both types of assessment. General ability then appeared as a large but distinct group factor uncorrelated with motivation.

3. To demonstrate that differences in this general ability were largely innate, correlations were obtained for members of the same family, but different degrees of affinity, parent and child, uncle and nephew, first and second cousins, etc. The most conclusive data are: (i) the correlations between orphans brought up in residential institutions almost from birth, with the intelligence of their parents; (ii) the correlations for identical twins brought up from birth in separate and very different homes; (iii) the comparison of correlations obtained for different degrees of affinity with the values deduced from neo-Mendelian genetics, with a known value for preferential (not chance) mating, yields so complete an agreement in every case that it is clear that the determining factor must be the genes transmitted from parents to offspring at each stage.

Thus they reached the conception of a mental tendency which is:

1. *cognitive* (or directive) rather than motivational (or dynamic);
2. *general* (i.e. applicable in all directions) rather than specialised (like speech or memory);
3. *innate*, in the sense of 'dependent on the individual's initial genetic endowment'.

For this innate, general, cognitive ability they borrowed Spencer's specialised term 'intelligence', which was not generally used. But through intelligence testing in the First World War, the term became known to journalists and consequently debased, just as other scientific terms such as 'salt', 'gas' or 'energy' have become loose in meaning. Much discussion of heredity versus environment with regard to intelligence founders because the specialist and journalistic meanings are confused.

In order to disentangle the various aspects of intelligence, Burt suggested three forms of the letter 'g', symbolising the general cognitive factor:

1. 'g' or the estimate of intelligence (P. E. Vernon's Intelligence A).
2. 'γ' or gamma as the hypothetical quantity (P. E. Vernon's Intelligence C).
3. 'G' or the journalistic 'intelligence', no more than 'general mental efficiency at the time of speaking' (Hebb's Intelligence B).

No psychological dictionary so far published attempts to define either (2) hypothetical gamma or (3) journalistic Gee. But there are many attempts to define the scientific estimate of (1) little gee, often several attempts within one dictionary, for example two in H. C. Warren (1934); two in Drever (1952); and six in English and English (1958). It is imperative not to confuse little gee, the legitimate scientific estimate of intelligence *either* with hypothetical inheritance which can never be measured *or* with journalistic, diffused meanings. We shall be returning to more detailed study of intelligence in Chapter 19, with special reference to the methods and meaning of scientific estimates.

Vernon (1968), as others before him, points out that ability depends not only on genes but also on cultural environment, physiological conditions before birth, adequate proteins and vitamins, possible brain damage at birth and so on. These are all aspects of the environment which can undoubtedly affect the building up of healthy brain tissue and therefore the capacity of the brain for further development. The newborn baby has only the minimal sensory-motor reflexes. But he is a living organism with a strong drive to preserve himself and master his environment. Sherrington (1955) in his Gifford Lecture on *The Brain and its Work*, says 'Life has an itch to live'. Growth depends on his interaction with a stimulating and educating environment. Give a child what he requires in the way of environment—physical, mental, social and so on—and his unmeasurable hypothetical inheritance of intelligence can function well; deprive him of these environmental essentials and that same hypothetical inheritance will fail to function well.

Make a scientific estimate of a child's 'g' or estimated intelligence when he has been environmentally deprived for three or four years; then put him for three or four years in a rich environment and again test his 'g'—the results will show a substantial rise in 'g'. This is because the rich environment has enabled his inherited intelligence to function better, resulting in a higher estimated 'g'. Unfortunately Burt's suggested use of letters (as in chemistry) to distinguish the three main aspects of intelligence, never caught on. This was probably because one could not go into court and tell the magistrate about a defective child's amount of 'g': so 'intelligence' became of general use, to the detriment of clear thinking in some educational psychology.

The whole of cultural development is dependent on the fact that what is born in us can be affected by learning. Modern research shows that the two most potent factors in learning are language and first hand experience. Curiously enough, these two factors of language and first-hand experience have, in past educational systems, worked in opposition; moreover, we cannot even yet say with confidence that this does not happen in any of our schools. Century after century teachers of all kinds have fallen into the same trap: thinking they have to teach children by telling them what other people have experienced. This is back to front. First the children have to experience things and people that matter to them, and then they develop language which has meaning to them because they *know what the words stand for*. From this sequence interest widens to what others have done and thought and found out. At any stage in primary or secondary school work, where learning seems to have slackened, a return to this basic environmental arrangement—first experience which involves the child, then conversation about it—will improve the situation. When children are constantly in a rich and varied environment, then vivid experience results in constant learning and language development.

Heredity and environment should not be discussed as if they are opposition theories, but rather as if they are two sides of a coin which together make up the amount. The essential points about heredity are: that innate potential cannot be measured quantitatively but we can make relatively crude measurement of the extent to which the potential has been developed by the environment. The essential points about environment are: that research has shown how environments can successfully be adapted to foster innate potential, and the two most effective ways of doing this are: (a) opportunities for the children to have their own rich variety of experiences, and (b) opportunities for speech development through these experiences.

At first glance it might seem that this chapter goes into the mechanisms of heredity in far too great detail. This is not so. Until the twentieth century there have only been opinions about the importance of heredity and environment to man. Now, at last, we are receiving facts about the importance of environment from many experiments. But facts about heredity have been known for more than half a century. Intelligence conforms to Mendelian principles and this fact cannot be discredited by the opinions of people unable to see how observable facts conform to mathematical theory. Therefore modern students should be given the opportunity to see how the facts on heredity are obtained. Only then can the students make their own evaluation of the importance of the two sides of the coin. There would be no value without both.

Part 2
Toddler:
15 months to 2½ years

4. General development
15 months to 2½ years

The stage of about 15 months to 2½ years is sometimes known affectionately as the toddler stage. Children enter this stage having reached about as high a level of behaviour as they can without language. Though some are able to say a few simple sentences, many cannot. But, like the child signing for the blinds to be drawn (p. 28), they can now show by their behaviour that they have foreseen the results of actions before they occur. They are emerging from the completely egocentric stage and becoming more objective, as they move around and learn to detect what is near and what is far away, what they can push and lift and what is too heavy for them to move. Whereas in infancy the mouth was the main source of information about what objects are like, now hands and face are important for textural perception. A good many things still go into the mouth, particularly at bedtime when behaviour tends to regress. But hands and eyes and ears all increasingly give clues to the nature of the environment; and particularly the hands explore the topology of objects. In an experiment by Fisher (p. 74) we shall see how sensitive children are to the relief or surface moulding of objects as they touch them; and this topological perception is of paramount importance during the toddler years. One frequently sees a child of this age apparently 'idly' fingering some object, while staring into space. This may be a moment of vivid topological perception.

Each stage of thinking and perceiving has to be fully experienced before the next stage of thinking and perceiving can be entered satisfactorily. Therefore toddlers need plenty of things which they are able to perceive topologically. The more we aid their thinking, the more reliably they will pass on to the next stage, after about 2½ years of age. This means that they need toys of all textures, from shiny wooden doll to soft teddy-bear; also toys and books of many different colours. They will learn to discriminate colours better as they learn the names for colours. Then toys should be of different sizes, shapes and weights. The bit of old bent metal tube, and a feather fallen from a blackbird, may be treasured, even taken to bed. The differences in weight, texture, moulding and smell are all part of the child's learning. A toddler heaving a box almost too large to shift down the garden, is taking a first step in the study of physics. We shall see in Lovell and Ogilvie's conservation of weight experiments (p. 76) that children in the junior school are handicapped in forming concepts of weight, if they lack experience of this kind. As Peel says (p. 72) children need plenty of experience demanding no more than topological awareness and capacities.

In *Infant and Nursery Schools* (1933), Burt and S. Isaacs have given us an imperishable and brilliant account of how to handle the emotional life of preschool children. They point out that, since the child's emotional life centres on the nutritive impulses of his body, it is a serious educational mistake to treat feeding and excretory habits as purely physiological and local mechanisms. Regularity in times for feeding and opportunities for voiding are essential; equally important are the gentle modes of handling him, with calm and confident manner. Quiet, positive encouragement, showing the child what to do and how to do it, is far more effective than scolding or punishment or emphasis on what he should not do. Successes should be emphasised; failures should be minimised; and above all, any feeling of shame or hostility should be avoided.

As was explained in the section on infants, by the toddler stage bowel control can have begun. If one finds the time of day when voiding is likely to happen, training is relatively simple. But the sphincter muscle which controls urine works in a way which is much more difficult to train. Until about two years it works automatically, at the reflex level. As soon as sufficient urine has collected, the sphincter muscle relaxes to let the urine pour away. This muscle cannot be trained until the cortex of the brain reaches a certain level of complexity, usually at about two to three years, sometimes later. A clever mother may learn to catch the drips on most occasions, but that is her own training, not the child's. As far as the child's training is concerned, there are three stages. First the child comes to say he has wet his pants, an initial step which should receive mild appreciation. Then he comes and says he is wetting his pants, a further step which should receive mild appreciation. Finally he comes and says he wants to do so, which should receive the same mild appreciation. At this stage there may be many lapses, when the lavatory is not reached in time. But if the trip to the lavatory and for clean pants is made a cheerful expedition at each of the three stages, then the child can learn much more quickly that the lavatory has to be reached in time if pants are to be kept dry.

Anger rises to a peak during the second year. Emotions cannot be controlled until they have been experienced. At no other time is there such a gap between, on the one hand, the great strength of feeling and impulses, and on the other hand, the weakness of understanding and power of control. Because of the strength of impulses the child has to be preserved from danger; because of the weakness of understanding and power of control, frustrating him on account of dangers he has not seen may precipitate bursts of uncontrollable anger. These temper tantrums give a shot of adrenalin to his blood-stream which literally make him 'hopping' angry. The energy biologically designed for attack or flight may make a child leap into the air with rage, no matter where he is, in garden or house, inside or outside the shops of the high street. Keeping calm helps him to learn much quicker that these storms pass and can eventually be controlled.

Each toddler seems to be two people, one devastatingly charming and the other impossibly objectionable, and this is how each child sees the adults to whom he is most closely tied. Later, they enjoy tales of wicked stepmothers and cruel fathers, going through in stories their earlier tempestuous reactions to adults. But at two the child really believes the loving adults have suddenly changed to terrible monsters; he projects his own storms of hatred upon them. This cherub-and-gargoyle swing between love and hate is to be seen in sculpture on many churches and cathedrals. Stone and Church (1957) have a beautiful picture of a naked toddler, and they point out that this is the model for the cherubim and cupids of Renaissance painting. Adults who understand the strain and stress which a child of two goes through, from within and from without, can by deliberate and determined effort be calm and gentle, thus giving a child the chance to move towards integration.

One of the most noticeable effects of language upon children of this age is the discovery that answers to many puzzling things can be gained by asking questions. So many *why?* questions are asked that adults find it impossible to answer them all. It is as well to recognise that there are three kinds of *why?* questions, each requiring a different kind of reply. First there is the *why?* of intellectual curiosity. This can be extremely taxing to answer, as the subject of the question may seem too complex to explain to so young a child; or the subject may never have been noticed, or was once noticed and then forgotten. The child asks why the water splashes, why biscuits make crumbs, why it is foggy. These questions are difficult, first because we have to see whether we know the answer, and then because we have to see how much of the answer could have meaning for the child. Wherever possible the answer, or preparation for the answer, should have practical experience. For instance, one could suggest that the child finds out more about splashes. Does water always splash? What happens if you put a feather or a piece of cotton on it? He has clearly been wondering about splashes and this gives him a directive for further experimentation. If you can get him to a stage where *he* suggests that bigger or heavier things push the water harder than smaller or lighter things, then he has answered part of his question himself. Then a reply, such as that runny things are more easily pushed apart than solid things, will have meaning to him. But the important thing that has been done here is beginning to build an attitude of finding out for himself. Incidentally, giving him something to do about his question gives you time to select something brief and suitable for the answer. It is astonishing how, with a little training, one can learn to give this kind of short and simple reply almost automatically. From such replies the child receives important intellectual and social 'nourishment', as well as a knowledge of words with real meaning.

A great deal of frustration, to both adult and child, can be avoided if the other two kinds of *why?* questions, which have nothing to do with intellectual curiosity, are identified and given quite different kinds of answers. The second kind of *why?* is as unexpected as if the child had hit you. You ask him to put his hat on, something he loves doing, and he says very crossly, *why?* without making any attempt to put it on. If adults mistake this situation for intellectual curiosity, they can be victimised. The child is upset about something and retaliates with what he imagines is reciprocal aggression. It is very difficult to indicate in general terms what might have caused the upset. Children of two have many cares which we have in the past failed to appreciate. Pitcher and Prelinger (1963) collected stories from many children and these examples from the children of two show, from their spontaneously chosen themes, some of their troubles:

Boys of two
'Boy fell out of car. He went in car again. He fell in water.'
'He broke it. He's OK. He didn't broke it. It's all right. The little boy fixed it.'
'Pussy scratched. He cried. He's a bad boy. He banged. He stopped crying. He's a good boy. He cried again.'
'Tractor fall down boom. Fall right down and hurt his head off. And he run, run, run.'

Girls of two
'The kitty meowed. The boys hit the kitty with a stick. The kitty scratched him.'

'The mommy just spanks me. When it is time to go to Eleanor's she goes to Eleanor's. Then she goes back home.'
'Once upon a time there was a dog. He cried. He needs his mommy. The mommy comes. Then she had a bottle.'

Of thirty two-year-old boys' stories, only two have no disaster, such as animals or children hurt or run over. Of thirty two-year-old girls' stories only ten have no disasters. We become so preoccupied with keeping a child 'safe' that we overlook his many awarenesses of dangers around him. It is very fruitful to look for the cause of upset with the aggressive *why?*, since it may show us what to do next. In the instance of the hat, we decide quickly whether the hat matters. If it does not, then we give in gracefully. But if possible we also trace back what can have upset him. Were we unnecessarily sharp with him, in our alarm, when he got hold of the bread knife? The above stories show that two-year-olds are intensely accident-conscious. Perhaps the hat does matter, because it is raining. So one gives the child a huge hug and says, 'It is raining so we can't go out without hats. I wasn't cross about the knife, only frightened you'd cut yourself.' It is the hug that answers that question, by showing that you do still love him.

The third kind of *why?* is simply a bid for attention. The child is below subsistence level in social contact, perhaps when the parents are entertaining other adults. The child leans against you, climbs on your knee, puts his hand over your mouth to stop you talking, asks questions he has asked before, asks silly questions; and if you still won't show him he belongs to you, he begins to behave 'badly'. When his parent gets cross, well, he is cross, too. That is better than no attention. Sometimes the parents choose public occasions to answer these questions as if they were motivated by intellectual curiosity. The child knows they are showing off and he does the same, resulting in social disaster. When mothers treat such situations well, they allow their child on to the knee, give close contact, and every now and then give a few seconds of undivided attention to the child. The attention may be to a toy he is clutching, a button on his coat, something unexpected that comes out of one's own pocket. What the attention is about does not matter. Having had his social contact brought back to equilibrium, the child can return to his toys.

Though we are still so short of facts about very young children, a conference held in 1969 at the University of Sussex suggests that the subject is now beginning to interest research workers. The conference was on current research in Great Britain into the early development of behaviour. The report contains some eighty abstracts of research in progress.

5. *Speech development*
15 months to 2½ years

During the period 15 months to 2½ years speech develops to language proper. By the end of this time a child may have a vocabulary running into hundreds of words which he uses in sentences three, and even four words in length. Most of us could get along quite well in a foreign country if we had this much language equipment. As the importance of language for communication has become recognised over the last century, various writers have expressed theories. Darwin in *The Descent of Man* (1871) wrote that language owes its origin to the imitation and modification of natural sounds. Infants imitate the sounds around them and enjoy playing rhythmically with repetitions. Toddlers continue to do this with great delight, now often taking a word they understand, such as the name of their house or street, and converting it to a nonsense song. Indeed, poets use this music of words as part of their medium. It is surprising that there has been no serious research into what one might call the music of words. According to Hearnshaw (1964), the first psychologist to draw attention to the social factor in language was Lewes (1817–78), a neglected writer. Lewes did no more than point out that human language was a social, not an individual product. As the toddler's world widens from the totally egocentric to increasing objectivity, the socialising effect of language becomes increasingly important. The toddler develops from 'No! Mine!' or a wordless tug-of-war to 'Can I have a turn?' and ability to wait a little.

Then Romanes (1848–94), a gifted man of Scottish descent, wrote that the power of translating ideas into symbols was the essential distinction between man and animals; and that language was the needful condition for the attainment of conceptual thought. A concept is a general meaning. It is an idea or property that can be understood of two or more individual items. We have already met an example of this generalising, in the infant who used the comfort-sounding word *Dada* of the postman (p. 27). The ability to generalise, to form concepts, depends upon the development of the cortex or outer covering of the brain. Wherever men have developed, the brain is sufficiently complex for concept formation, and language is invented; that is to say sounds begin to be used as symbols. With the aid of adults and an already established language, many children begin to learn a few words at the infant stage. The importance of this grasp of how language works must not be underestimated; but the real use of language usually develops during the toddler stage. A number of converging lines of development indicate that considerable intellectual effort is involved in this early speech: the child attends to what is said before he can say anything, he uses correct intonation before he knows how to form the words, the increase of vocabulary is extremely slow at the start, and a sudden upsurge of emotion causes speech to regress or fade into emotional cries.

As so often happens in psychology, attention was drawn to the development of speech, not by the toddler stage when speech really starts to operate effectively, but by failure of this development which resulted in older children having speech defects. Centres for speech therapy are a twentieth-century phenomenon. In 1906 Manchester and Glasgow opened classes for stammerers; then speech clinics were opened at St Bartholomew's Hospital, London, in 1911 and St Thomas's Hospital, London, in 1913. Burt (1937) found, in his survey of London children, that about 5 per cent had speech defects.

Through clinical work on speech, considerable interest in normal speech development was aroused. Seth and Guthrie published *Speech in Childhood* (1935), Lewis published *Infant Speech* (1936); and other writers devoted sections of books to the subject, for example, Valentine's *The Psychology of Early Childhood* (1942), Chapter 20. The books by Lewis and by Valentine were detailed studies of the authors' own children. Since both these fathers became professors, there is quite a high probability (no more) that the children were above average in verbal ability. In studying their works, one can see that both had gifted wives, which raises the probability that the children recorded in these books had more than average ability. An example of the insight of Lewis's boy K's mother is given on p. 61, and Valentine acknowledges his wife's contribution in the preface. It is important to notice that records of the behaviour of their own children by professors are liable to show that these children are more advanced than most children.

Surveys of language development are extremely difficult to conduct. The simplest form of investigations is a count of vocabulary, but as we saw (p. 27) children do more than just learn words; they learn grammar and word order at the same time. Two surveys of the 1920s are extensively quoted, because there does not appear to have been anything comparable since. Descoeudres reported on 300 children of Geneva in *La mesure du langage de l'enfant* (1924). She asked questions and gave simple tasks to large and small groups, listened to children playing in the park, and so on. A couple of years later Smith published *An Investigation of the Sentence and Extent of Vocabulary in Young Children* (1926), a study of the language development of 273 children aged 8 months to 6 years. There was a marked similarity in the account of language

TABLE 3: *Average size of children's vocabularies: 8 months to 6 years*

Age (years, months)	N	I.Q.	Vocabulary		
			Number of words	Gain	Yearly gain
0–8	13		0		
0–10	17		1	1	
1–0	52		3	2	3
1–3	19		19	16	
1–6	14		22	3	
1–9	14		118	96	
2–0	25		272	154	269
2–6	14		446	174	
3–0	20	109	896	450	624
3–6	26	106	1,222	326	
4–0	26	109	1,540	318	644
4–6	32	109	1,870	330	
5–0	20	108	2,072	202	532
5–6	27	110	2,289	217	
6–0	9	108	2,562	273	490

Source: M. E. Smith (1926).

development by Descoeudres in Geneva and Smith in Iowa. The total vocabularies, age for age, show almost exactly the same average number of words in the two localities, and the relative importance of the various parts of speech are amazingly similar, despite the differences between French and English. Smith had a somewhat improved though similar question-and-answer method, and as her work confirmed that of Descoeudres, it is worth having a look at her list. Table 3 gives the whole range, up to 6 years. Accounts of this preschool investigation (only Britain starts compulsory schooling at 5 years) are extensively quoted in American textbooks of child development. It is as well to note that these references are to the one survey (often to different parts of it) in America, conducted a long while ago.

However, until we have research on similar lines in Britain, we may fairly safely assume that the toddler's vocabulary may develop from about 20 to over 400 words.

Gates *et al.* (1942), also in America, combined the data of McCarthy (1933) and Davis (1937) to give average number of words per remark. Table 4 gives the results of this combination of researches for American children aged $1\frac{1}{2}$ to $9\frac{1}{2}$ years.

From this we may again fairly safely assume that, at the beginning of the toddler stage, the children are only just beginning to pass the one word sentence, e.g. 'Dolly!' meaning 'Give me my dolly!'; and by the end of this period the children are able to produce a complete sentence, 'Give me

TABLE 4: *Average number of words per remark at different age levels*

Age in years	Average no. of words	Age in years	Average no. of words
$1\frac{1}{2}$	1·2	4	4·4
2	1·8	$4\frac{1}{2}$	4·6
$2\frac{1}{2}$	3·1	$5\frac{1}{2}$	4·6
3	3·4	$6\frac{1}{2}$	5·3
$3\frac{1}{2}$	4·3	$9\frac{1}{2}$	6·5

Source: Gates *et al.* (1942).

dolly'. From the final stage of Table 4, the $9\frac{1}{2}$ year average of $6\frac{1}{2}$ words, we can see that the length of sentence at the end of the toddler stage is nearly half way to the length of sentence used just about a year before secondary school. When we come to discuss reading we shall find from the work of Burroughs (1957) of Birmingham that there is a very wide range of individual differences. With Burroughs's five-year-olds he found a range in size of vocabulary from 56 to 578 words. This range of individual difference is confirmed as early as $1\frac{1}{2}$ to $2\frac{1}{2}$ years by Sampson, whose investigation we now examine.

Sampson (1956, 1959), at Leicester, started a most valuable longitudinal research under the title *A Study of Speech Development in Children*. The 1956 report is on children of 18 to 30 months. She describes in detail the method of selecting a representative sample of fifty children, who were given three individual interviews of half-an-hour, at six-month intervals at the beginning and end of a year, and once mid-way. There were twenty-five boys and twenty-five girls. She used a set of toys similar to that of McCarthy (1930). Using similar experimental design means that results can better be compared.

Only two of Sampson's 150 interviews were not in the child's own home. Almost all these children had said as their first word 'dada' or 'mama'. She classified preverbal speech in the first interview as 'incomprehensible'. Table 5 gives the decline of incomprehensible speech during the year of this investigation. She suggests that this is more than a practice period. There is purposeful practice and even the preverbal phase has the purposeful character of speech. Stern and Stern (1928), Lewis (1936), and others have pointed out that babbling cannot be understood unless the social and emotional stimulus behind it are taken into account. Sampson thinks the same is true of the jargon at 18 months, which is often highly charged emotionally.

TABLE 5: *Percentage of incomprehensible responses by age and sex*

	18 months	24 months	30 months
Boys	60	24	7
Girls	62·7	28	8
Both	61·35	26	7·5

Source: Sampson (1956).

Tracing the order in which speech sounds emerge, Sampson found first vowel sounds, then vowel-and-consonants together, then single words, followed by combinations and sentences. By $2\frac{1}{2}$ years the balance of elements in vocal expression had changed completely from that of her first interview at $1\frac{1}{2}$ years. She found that those with the worst language development had by the end, scarcely reached the average of the whole group at the start. That is to say that by age $2\frac{1}{2}$, some were only at the average $1\frac{1}{2}$ year level. These verbally slower children could only, at $2\frac{1}{2}$ years, say such poorly enunciated sentences as 'I don' wan',' while the verbally advanced could, for instance, say clearly, 'It sticks when you turn it over.' Using, as criteria of progress, absolute grammatical correctness plus number of responses and word combinations, she made an assessment of quality responses, which can be seen in Table 6. Then Sampson added length of sentences and, combining quality with length of sentences, she found a steady progress from sounds to sentences, with again a wide range of individual differences. There was a high correlation between quality and length of sentences.

She concludes that, although maturational processes explained much of the speech development recorded, there were other factors of two kinds: (*a*) goal-direction, for instance in circumstances where a child was motivated to say, 'I want my sweetie'; and (*b*) variety in environmental stimulus, which included such factors as the emotional atmosphere, equipment such as toys and books, example and encouragement. She rated the homes for environments fostering speech and found a moderate correlation between speech quality and home environment. She therefore ends this valuable report with: 'No unequivocal evidence as to the effect of environmental simulus, in contrast to the force of maturation, in developing speech, was obtained, but there were some indications of its contributory importance.' The next stage of Sampson's study (1959), is to be seen in Chapter 9, when these same children are about five years of age.

TABLE 6: *Quality responses (word combinations and sentences) by age and sex*

	Boys			Girls		
	18 months	24 months	30 months	18 months	24 months	30 months
Number of quality responses	46	377	1008	62	437	977
Mean no.	1·84	15·08	40·32	2·48	17·48	39·88
σ	4·69	13·89	25·58	4·79	19·92	25·55

Source: Sampson (1956).

σ (sigma) standard deviation or measure of the dispersion round the mean of a whole distribution.

The influence of motivation on language learning as early as the toddler stage is very important. The child wants, for instance, a sweet. He learns to say 'Sweetie', and later 'I want my sweetie.' In learning to say what he wants, he has the learning reinforced by the reward, whatever it may be. We shall later discuss this kind of reinforcement of learning. A rich language environment can result in earlier transition from material rewards to command of situations by language becoming the reward. Lewis (1963 p. 73) reports how K, when just over 2 years 4 months, had his toy dog in the pram and held it up when he saw a dog, saying, 'K got own doggie!' Six months later, when given a grand new toy dog and asked which should go to bed with him, replied, 'My own old doggie what always do sleep with me.' Incidentally, this child who is not yet three shows remarkable ability with the rules of language (see p. 27).

With a little imagination and ingenuity, experiments might be devised which revealed word meaning. Razran (1936) conducted an adult experiment of interest here. He knew six languages. The experiment was to put the word 'saliva' in all these languages on cards, and intersperse the cards with nonsense words on other cards. Each time the word 'saliva' appeared in one of the six languages, a dental roll of cottonwool was put in his mouth and he thought only in the language of the presentation. Subsequent saliva tests on the cotton wool showed that the amount of saliva corresponded with how well he knew each language. His native Russian occasioned most salivation.

Mateer (1918) tested fifty children ranging in age from 1 to 7 years; she put a pneumatic tambour on the throat to record swallowing, blindfolded each child and put a drop of chocolate into the mouth. She checked how soon a child began to salivate and swallow on being bandaged, and found much individual difference in learning this conditioned reflex. A conditioned reflex (see p.181) is a reflex which begins to work, not at the primary stimulus, but at a secondary stimulus associated with the primary one; here, having a bandage put over the eyes is the secondary stimulus, which is associated with a chocolate drop coming. These two experiments by Razran and by Mateer show the kind of ingenuity which could be used in investigating young children's language development. In Chapter 9 we shall look at an ingenious language experiment with somewhat older children, devised by the Russian psychologist, Vygotsky.

As a matter of fact it is not just about infant language development that we need more information. Somehow we have managed to treat speech as our blood-stream, into which no experimenter may 'stick pins'. The result of this attitude is that we are still grossly uninformed about language. We impute to infants degrees of immaturity which we have not ourselves outgrown. For instance, Henle and Hubble (1938) of America report on egocentric adult conversation. They made surreptitious recordings of snatches of conversation overheard in two groups, one of college women and the other of an unselected group of men and women. More than 40 per cent of the remarks made were ego-related. More recently, Kirkman (1967) of Cardiff reported an investigation of command of vocabulary among university entrants. More than 2,000 first-year undergraduates from seven universities and colleges were given a test of general vocabulary. The purpose of the investigation was to see whether differences of vocabulary appeared in different faculties. Differences were striking. Out of a possible score of 72, the following averages emerged: Arts: 55·50; Social Science: 52·90; Pure Science: 48·70; Applied Science: 44·67; Agriculture: 44·66. There was evidence that wide reading improved the use of the English language; in fact, a student's customary diet of reading-matter, including newspapers, was reflected in his command of English. They give an entertaining collection of howlers demonstrating that students have not understood words they use. Perhaps the most dramatic demonstration of misuse of English is the number of students who did not know the meaning of *lucid*. If the reader does not know, he should look it up in the dictionary before reading how some of the students who had won university places defined it. A very large number of students did not know what it meant and here are some of their definitions: 'not clear, hard to find, mysterious, lewd, life-like, sweet, dishonest, slow, thick, without any real meaning, flexible, dubious, dark and dreary, watered down, limp, complete, full, free from inhibitions, cool, smooth, elaborate, rash, uncertain, crafty, watery, dry, docile, loose, delicate, gentle, undesirable, immoral, dull, half-hearted, lightly coloured, warm, thin, luke-warm, and slippery [character].*

Nothing could more forcefully underline our need to connect words with things, people and experiences they symbolise. Piaget, whose work we shall examine in the next chapter, said that children picked up words they heard and used them sometimes quite correctly, without any idea of their true meaning. He called such word-usage a 'façade', covering failure to understand what the word really symbolised. Thus we have to see that the words used by children are in the context of known experience. What can be the real talking point, subjects for the genuine use of words for communication, with children of 15 months to $2\frac{1}{2}$ years? There are material objects known to them, such as their clothes and body, their house and toys; there are places, such as visits to parks and other people; there are the things they can do, developing skills in feeding, dressing and washing; and there are their developing ideas of themselves, as well as of other people. If, during the preschool years, we root communication securely in words that children understand then the primary and secondary schools *and* the universities can develop language from secure foundations.

* The word *lucid* is used on p. 65. Any of the above definitions of lucid would cause grave failure of communication, would in fact fail to give a clear idea.

6. Piaget

Our understanding of preschool children will be much helped if we pause now to examine the work of Piaget, the Swiss psychologist who has been experimenting for more than forty years to find out how children of all ages think. There are certain problems in learning about his work, and the first problem to be faced is that his books are not easy to understand. The Swiss-born French-speaking Nathan Isaacs (who ran the Malting House School with his wife, Susan Isaacs) found even the original French of Piaget's records almost as obscure at times as the English translations. Nearly all the reports of British investigations to check Piaget's findings use such phrases as, 'By this Piaget seems to mean ...', 'We take it that Piaget concludes ...', and 'He seems to have used ...'.

The next problem in understanding Piaget's work concerns the experimental conditions of his investigations, which frequently fail to conform to British standards. For instance, Piaget lumps together his colleague Inhelder's carefully controlled investigation of the whole Geneva school population and his personal observation of his own children. These two forms of investigation, each important in its own way, cannot legitimately be combined to give one set of results. Then, until quite recently, Piaget has not taken into account mental age (see p. 224), though this concept was invented by Binet more than twenty years before Piaget began his researches, and was published in Piaget's native tongue, French. In the 1920s Susan Isaacs took Piaget to task for considering the development of thought by chronological age only. She was, at that time, running the Malting House School, and convinced that motivation had—or could have—a powerful effect upon development. In a lively correspondence, each affected the other's point of view.

There was another outstanding psychologist of that time who had also read Piaget's first reports with very critical attention. This was Vygotsky, a Professor at Moscow University. He unfortunately died young, before his work was translated from the Russian. When Piaget read Vygotsky's *Thought and Language* (English translation 1962), he expressed great regret that he had had no opportunity to read it at the time of its original Russian publication, in 1922. The influence of Vygotsky's attitude to young children's development is to be seen in Russian experimental work of very fine quality now being conducted by his one-time students, such as Luria. We shall refer to their work again in Chapter 9.

Referring to work similar to Piaget's but independent of him, Burt (1962d) includes researches by Sir Percy Nunn, Professor H. R. Hamley, and Dr Susan Isaacs, who became director of the Department of Child Development at the London Institute of Education; also statistical work in other European countries, for instance Binet in France and Meumann in Germany. The Americans were late in becoming interested in Piaget, so the greater part of their work has also been independent of Piaget. But despite the criticisms of Piaget and the fact that many others were working on similar lines, historians will look back on Piaget as a great twentieth-century psychologist.

What, then, is Piaget's great contribution? During his long life he has had one preoccupation: *the way in which thought develops*. On this subject his theories are rigorous; and he has produced information so astonishing that the very strangeness of the stages of thought development he propounds makes him difficult to understand. His concepts of mental development are not even common currency among educationists yet. So perhaps we might say that, in devoting his great gifts to this one aspect of psychology, he has been able to give a remarkably clear picture of the way thinking develops from infancy to adolescence; that is to say from a much earlier stage than has been of interest to most research workers, to virtually the mature adult way of thinking. He has reported on a greater span of cognitive development than anyone else, which is a valuable contribution to twentieth century understanding. Others can reproduce his experiments. Indeed, others have been doing so, as nearly as his sketchy descriptions permit, using more rigorous methodology.

Nathan Isaacs (1961), who read the greater part of Piaget in French as well as English, wrote a brief introduction to Piaget's work, *The Growth of Understanding in the Young Child*, which is quite first-class. It is easy to read and—remarkable with Piaget—completely lucid. Because of the strangeness of the stages which Piaget describes, no one can regard himself as a serious student of Piaget who has not either conducted some of Piaget's experiments or witnessed a demonstration. It is quite easy to arrange for a group of students, between them, to work with all ages and all types of experiment, then come together and give each other a joint demonstration. Another excellent book for planning such practical work is *A Teacher's Guide to Reading Piaget* by Brearley and Hitchfield (1966). After carrying out such experiments, students would be interested to read the original; and the original would be much clearer because the subject-matter had been experienced. Another valuable source of information is Chapter 10 of Lewis's *Language, Thought and Personality in Infancy and Childhood* (1963), on language and concrete thinking.

Berlyne (1957), at Aberdeen, wrote a good survey, 'Recent developments in Piaget's work', of development in psychological functioning from birth to adolescence as seen by Piaget. Berlyne first defines the *0 to 2 years sensorimotor stage*, when the child reaches the highest level without language, can represent the results of actions before they occur, gradually becomes less egocentric and more objective as he learns about size and shape, near and far, and so on. He then defines the *2 to 4 years pre-concept stage*, in which the child has a hazy notion of similar things, but is not yet able to generalise firmly enough to form proper concepts. Between two and three a child begins symbolic games; starts rôle playing and 'make-believe'. Then comes the *4 to 7 years stage of intuitive thought* when the visual impact of apparatus in an experiment, the visual perception, no matter how deceptive, decides his answer; he is still perception-orientated but sometimes has gleams of further understanding. Then comes the *7 to 11 stage of concrete operations*. A basic stock of reliable precepts becomes organised into coherent systems, so that the child can reason, provided he has the coalesced situation before him 'for a little preliminary examination' (Piaget 1960, p. 221). Piaget calls this 'operational thought', since the child can reason through having operated the material in his mind. During this stage the child can use classes through grouping, relations through ordering, and numbers through classification plus ordering. Last comes the *11 to 15 years stage of formal operations*. At about 11 years the child can apply operational thought to practical problems and by 15 years he reaches the final stage, going through solutions in his mind, backwards as well as forwards, in reversibility. The childhood journey from perception to thought about abstractions of size, weight, motion, and so on, takes some fifteen years. Piaget writes of a child 'decentring' himself and becoming aware of the 'conservation' of size, weight, etc. Thus these properties can be understood, apart from himself, in abstract thought.

A detailed study of the phases of development described by Piaget is easier if attention is directed along the line of Piaget's own interest. What interests

Piaget is the inward working model which each child builds. By means of this model the child sees how to regulate information and behaviour. Piaget traces the development of this working model, from the tiny infant receiving impressions with sensations to the adult able to find solutions to abstract problems within his mind. Piaget is not interested in *when* the various phases of the model are reached; but he is greatly interested in *how* each phase is transformed to the next phase. He is not interested in the age at which a child starts building a fresh phase of the model, but in what happens to the model for the child to move into the next phase of thinking. He has tested so many hundreds of children that, had he been interested in statistical techniques, he could have given means with standard deviations for the *durations* of phases. But he did not do so for the main part of his work. We should therefore make the following kind of adjustment when we read the ages he gives: e.g. for '4 *to* 7 years' read 'from about 3 to 5 years *to* about 6 to 8 years'. Irritating though this may be to those who are troubled by the lack of statistical methodology, we must not allow ourselves to be distracted from what Piaget is really talking about; namely how the changes in the working model take place.

Another problem is the vocabulary which Piaget selects. He worked so long before other countries became familiar with his research, that he developed a private, almost unique vocabulary. But here we have to be careful. The words are no stranger than the mental processes he describes. We have to see that we do not blame the unfamiliar use of words when what is really totally strange to us is the way the children's minds work.

Piaget sees the child as the agent of his own learning. This is a concept becoming increasingly familiar to us, as more and more children are guided to learn by their own doing. But he explains in detail just how the child is able to learn through his own agency. In *Play, Dreams and Imitation in Childhood* (1951) he describes two active processes by which the child learns: imitation and play. Imitation is copying the action of another more or less exactly; and in doing this, the child accommodates himself to the other person. Piaget calls the process of learning by imitation *accommodation*. Play is an activity released from this more or less exact copying, which leaves the child free to contribute creatively, and to find out what meaning the game has for him. In play the child works inventively, using symbols for what he means, and so digests the situation thoroughly. Piaget calls the process of learning by play *assimilation*.

There is no sharp line of demarcation between accommodation and assimilation. Much play is imitative; and much imitation is play. However, both forms of learning are essential and equally important; therefore there has to be an *equilibrium* of learning by imitation (accommodation) and learning by play (assimilation). Moreover, this equilibrium undergoes a development, which will become clearer once we examine the development of the working model. At the very beginning, when the child receives sensations and has no notion that anything persists if he does not experience it, Piaget calls the child *egocentric*. But later, when the child begins to realise that things may persist without him, Piaget calls the child increasingly *objective* while decreasingly egocentric.

As the child becomes more objective, in the sense of recognising space, time, volume, etc., outside himself, he begins to approach abstract thinking. When this happens, the equilibrium changes from egocentric equilibrium dependent upon learning through the senses, to an objective equilibrium now becoming quite independent of sense perception and free to work by ideas. Thus the two ways in which the child can be his own agent in learning— imitation and play—change from egocentric dependence upon senses to objective manipulation of concepts, which can be freely arranged and rearranged. Piaget calls this mobile operation, whereby concepts or general ideas can at any time be arranged one way or another in the mind, *reversibility*. This phase of being able to preserve and organise reliable concepts is called *conservation* by Piaget; and the actual process of building up complexes of concepts he calls *concrete operations*. According to the *Concise Oxford Dictionary* the verb 'concrete' can mean 'to form into a mass'; thus concrete operations evidently means coalescing operations; and what are coalesced at this stage are the now properly generalised concepts. If this is so, then 'concreting operations' might have been a more meaningful translation. Armed with at least some of the terms Piaget uses, let us look at the evolution of the working model which the child forms, remembering that the name of the phase usually describes the final stage of that phase.

THE MAIN BUILDING PHASES OF THE INWARD WORKING MODEL

The first 18 months: the sensori-motor phase
The child explores the world with his mouth, he pushes and pulls, he co-ordinates hand and eye while investigating, and so on, until patterns of experience begin to form in his mind. At the start of this phase his senses bring no impression of even the most rudimentary persistence of anything; what is experienced only exists while he is experiencing it. Gradually he begins to recognise his mother, certain objects, and events such as bathing;

then he learns to expect some of them, which implies their persistence. Towards the end of this phase the variety of his purposive behaviour shows that he already has a simple inward working model of the world. Piaget writes of this transition from nothing but sensation to the first awareness of outer objects as a transition from complete egocentricity to increasing objectivity. This transition enables the child to build into his model information which will later lead on to perception of space, time, and other abstractions.

18 months to 4 years: the pre-concept phase

The child incessantly expands and enriches his world. He repeats experiments such as pushing a pencil through a cane chair or climbing through a hoop, over and over again, as if to verify that he knows now what happens. During this phase the advent of language adds a new dimension to his ability to build the working model; now experiments can be conducted in speech; and when they fail, they can be corrected in further speech. He questions, listens, answers, talks and imagines; speech opens new worlds of thinking which he might never reach or might never be able to manipulate if he did reach them. Most of the ideas and images in his mind remain vague and unstable; and his thinking cannot move far away from the present situation without getting lost. So much that he thinks he has discovered proves later to be quite wrong that his working model itself is in a state of flux. But towards the end of this phase some notions of space, time, order and so on, are beginning to persist. Piaget calls this the stage of *pre-concepts* because the way to form and test concepts is being discovered, but too much is proving on further investigation to be wrong, for the concepts to be properly generalised and preserved yet.

4 to 7 years: the phase of intuitive thought

Now the child has carried out so many experiments in such a variety of ways that certain of the pre-concepts remain fairly stable and so can be generalised as genuine concepts, resulting from manipulation of sensory impressions. He builds into his working model the first hazy notions of space, of time, of movement and speed, of number and measurement, and of elementary logical relations such as whole and part, classes and subclasses, or serial order. He is still largely perception-orientated; he still goes mostly by how things strike him from where he stands. But by the end of this phase he begins to have gleams of understanding, as certain notions are remembered from previous experience and can influence his immediate idea of how things look. The inward model begins to include these fleeting notions that facts might be other than they seem. A piece of plasticine looks more when it is rolled out, but perhaps it might still be the same amount; a quantity of water looks more when poured into a tall thin jar, but perhaps it does not increase. The barely crystallised concepts of number, perspective, measurement, floating and sinking, moral judgments and so on, can be used in making judgments, although the child is scarcely aware of them. Piaget calls this phase *intuitive thought* because the child frequently jumps to the correct solution, just as adults do at times, without knowing how the answer arrived.

7 to 11 years: the phase of concrete operations
During this phase the child increasingly advances to reasoning much as normal adults can reason, provided he has before him the practical problem 'for a little preliminary examination'. He constantly builds into his model fresh concepts which will stand the test of further examination. Now he can begin the operation of concreting or massing together concepts. As the model requires less and less dismantling (on account of erroneous pre-concepts), he can group together more and more clusters of concepts and rely on them to work as a whole. Although the concepts originated from sensory experience, they now become one-removed from sensory experience, as increasingly intellectual activity. This influences the nature of both assimilation through play and accommodation through imitation, both of which also progress towards intellectual activity. And as a result, this essential equilibrium begins to change from a predominantly sensory to a predominantly intellectual balance. Concepts such as speed, mass, length and volume can stand for other circumstances than those in which the concepts first began to form, and so can reliably be conserved as clusters in the working model. Whole sets of concepts taken together can go into the working model to form distinctive schemes of operational thought. Relational reasoning becomes possible, either mathematical or logical.

11 to 15 years: the phase of formal operations
As the child becomes accustomed to working distinctive schemes of operational thought, his powers of abstract thought develop. What in the previous stage were concepts of mass, speed, volume, and so on, now advance to the abstractions of geometry, mechanics, and formal aspects of all the sciences. Remembering the vagueness of ages given for the various phases, we can now see that some children may not reach the final phase of formal operations until 17 years or more, and a few are unable ever to reach it. This implies

that there should be much experimentation in practical situations until children are well into secondary school. But of course the cleavage between abstract and practical reasoning is not as clearcut as this suggests. For all their abstract calculations, scientists very frequently resort to practical work to check calculations. The electronics engineer makes a prototype, to find out whether the invention he thought out really works; and Euclid doubtless drew many triangles before stating his theorems. The twentieth-century lesson we are learning is that forcing a child to abstract reasoning too soon actually obstructs the final phase. The nature of the development of the inward working model is such that each phase has to be gone through fully if genuine formal thinking is to be achieved.

Psychologists began their own rigorously scientific experiments reproducing apparatus as exactly as they could from Piaget's accounts of the actual experiments upon which he had based his conclusions. Peel (1959), at Birmingham, wrote an account of an experimental examination of some of Piaget's schemata concerning children's perception and thinking, and discussed their educational significance. His students had been testing some of Piaget's schemata experimentally and Peel's article reports on four of the investigations. Two of the experiments, with children of 2:9 to 7:9, tested their haptic (cutaneous or touch) perception and spatial relations in drawing; the other two experiments with children 7:8 to 14:11, tested their logical and moral judgments. Large numbers of children, groups ranging from thirty-two to sixty, were put in Piaget-type situations. The account of the experiments makes interesting reading, including the appendices which give some of the stories used. In conclusion Peel makes two general points: (a) the work done gave no evidence of the parts played by maturation and by experience; from certain unpublished experimental work at Birmingham, probably both maturation and experience are important; (b) it appeared that each phase of development is necessary for the emergence of later more mature phases. From these two generalisations Peel concludes: 'It would seem that the more experiences we can provide of materials, and reading and questioning at the appropriate level the better.' The first two experiments, with children of 2–6 years, showed that children of this age are only capable of seeing, depicting and executing topological features and patterns. Slow developers would take longer to reach Euclidean or geometric awareness.

Since this affects infant school work we must get the distinction clear. If you draw a man on a sheet of rubber and then stretch it, the man changes shape, whether you keep the sheet flat or strain it over, for instance, a football. But the head is still next to the body, and the legs remain connected to body and feet. Topology is the systematic statement of the properties of spaces that do not change under one-to-one continuous transformation and are independent of magnitudes. Thus we see why young children's drawings appear to us 'out of proportion'. The children are only concerned to link in correct relations the various parts; they ignore magnitude. But the geometry of Euclid which most of us learned at school is the statement of properties of spaces, defined according to certain axioms and postulates about magnitude and direction. In Euclidean geometry a drawing which is the wrong shape would be incorrect. Haptic or cutaneous or touch perception is important for topological perception. The right items in a drawing are in the right relationship to other items, but shape is still not properly perceived.

Since the first two experiments support Piaget, Peel says this should affect the teaching of manipulative, drawing, writing and reading skills to young children. We must give plenty of experience that demands no more than topological awareness and capacities. Peel's last two experiments, with children of 7 to 15 years, also confirm Piaget's work. The three phases of logical judgment could be seen. Peel therefore says much greater care is needed, in grading passages for children in primary and secondary schools to study so that questions evoke the full range of response, from intuitive to logical stages. Since the main concern of educationists is, or should be, to train the children's thinking (not just reading and writing), there should be more opportunity for active answering as opposed to passive reading, to give the experience at each level necessary for progression to the next. The critical period appears to be the first three years of primary school. The findings on moral judgment were not quite so conclusive, but were at least suggestive of a sequence which might help teachers of religious knowledge, history and English. If the purpose is to discover the maturity of judgment, then material and questions need to be chosen which reveal the full range of phases. If the most mature phase of autonomous (independent) moral judgment is to be naturally and permanently achieved, the children need plenty of experience of active reading and questions.

In 1965 two other people published investigations relevant to these two groups of experiments reported by Peel: Goldman on moral judgments and Fisher on haptics. Goldman (1965) of Reading, in 'The application of Piaget's schema of operational thinking to religious story data by means of Guttman scalogram', describes an experiment with a random sample of 200 children, age range 6:1 to 7:11. To assess Piaget's schema of operational thinking (the 7 to 11 year organisation of reliable percepts into coherent systems through concrete operations), Goldman got some forty responses from each child and arranged the scores by chronological age, by mental age, by total scores and also by Guttman's Scalogram, which is a cumulative scale. In all five systems of scoring he found that Piaget's operational thinking was valid for the stories they had used. This result has profound relevance for the theory of children's religious cognition. Religious thinking depends on the normal mental development of children. They cannot draw undistorted inferences from religious stories until the original experiences in the Bible can be understood. This supports previous work by Goldman (1964a). In a book on *Religious Thinking from Childhood to Adolescence* he shows that children pass through three phases: pre-religious, sub-religious and religious. Whether the final stage is reached or endures through adolescence depends on whether adolescents are able or willing to apply the higher levels of formal operations to religion. This book is an illuminating empirical study of concern to all interested in religious education.

The other investigation relevant to Piaget's work reports experiments on haptic and space experience with younger children. G. H. Fisher (1965), of Newcastle-upon-Tyne, opens a series of articles on 'Developmental features of behaviour and perception' with an article on visual and tactile-kinaes-thetic shape perception. In the introduction he refers to research on haptics and topology by Piaget and Inhelder. (All the articles on Piaget have most valuable references for further reading.) Incidentally Fisher is one of the many writers who impute imprecision in descriptions of the Geneva experi-ments: 'Since it is not possible to obtain a complete list of the objects used in the studies conducted by Piaget and Inhelder,' he writes, 'a sample of thirty common household and play objects was selected, each of which was prob-ably to be found, seen and perhaps handled by children in the majority of English homes.' Fisher conducted two experiments. The first experiment was on the Non-manipulation Paradox. The following objects were assembled:

TABLE 7: *Objects for non-manipulation paradox experiment*

1. a cardboard box	11. a fountain pen	21. a child's shoe
2. a book	12. a teaspoon	22. a woolly toy
3. a pencil	13. a milk bottle	23. a tea-cup
4. a penny	14. a comb	24. a pair of scissors
5. a table-knife	15. a banana	25. an egg-cup
6. a doll's table	16. a fork	26. a tooth-brush
7. a plastic beaker	17. a saucer	27. a pipe
8. a metal thimble	18. a top	28. a hammer
9. a rubber ball	19. a saw	29. a whistle
10. a glass marble	20. a torch	30. a pair of spectacles.

Source: Fisher (1965).

In the pilot experiment seventeen children of 2 to 6 years handled the objects without seeing them. The most easy were the banana and the penny; and the most difficult were the thimble and the torch.

For the main experiments the thirty objects were reproduced in wood for size, shape and weight, so that only touch cues would be given. Each original object was photographed and full-size black and white matt prints were mounted where the child could see them. He could indicate which object was being identified by his hands while out of his sight through the holes. This is the sort of informal instruction given: 'Let's play a game like blind-man's buff.—Now put your hands through these holes and I will give you

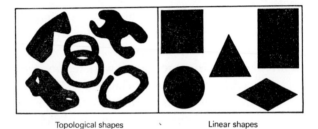

Topological shapes   Linear shapes

Figure 13. Examples of topological and linear shapes.
Source: Fisher (1965).

a toy (frequently one of the child's own toys was used for a few trials). Can you tell me what it is? Now let's try another. . . .' The results of this first experiment suggest that important cues for recognition of objects at this age are textural rather than spatial.

Fisher's (1965) second experiment was on the topological-primacy hypo-thesis. Piaget and Inhelder (1956) argue that the achievement of a spatial coordinate system which is essentially linear is not complete until the age of about 8 or 9 years. They interpret their haptic shape perception experiments as indicating a gradual development from using 'primitive' topological re-lationships to using linear or Euclidean relationships based on a vertical–horizontal system of coordinates. Fisher prepared sets of ten linear and ten topological shapes, as near as possible to the 'rough sketches of some of the shapes' reported by Piaget and Inhelder, and photographed them. Figure 13 gives examples of Fisher's shapes. Elsewhere, G. H. Fisher (1963) gives exact details of object measurements, etc., so that others can duplicate his investiga-tion. The subjects of his experiment were twenty-six children of 1:7 to 5:0 years, and the controls were twenty-six children of 1:8 to 5:1 years. Both groups were given plenty of experience of the objects before the experiment began. The controls did the experiment exactly as it had been done for Piaget and Inhelder. But the subjects were given nonsense names for the shapes to be investigated and could say the name as well as point to the shape. Fisher found that subjects and controls could all recognise most shapes by four years. The subjects, who had been given names, could identify linear shapes more readily than topological ones; and the controls, who had not been given names, could identify topological shapes more readily than linear shapes. Fisher concludes that Piaget's topological-primacy hypothesis should be replaced by a linear-primacy hypothesis. He suggests that children, who stand erect by about one year, complete their vertical–horizontal perception of space by about four years. From his detailed account of experimental procedure we may safely assume that he hopes others will affirm or refute his adverse criticism of Piaget resulting from the second experiment.

For some time Lovell of Leeds, with his students, has conducted a comprehensive programme of experiments along the lines of Piaget's schemata on conservation and logic. Lovell has also written a book, *The Growth of Basic Mathematical and Scientific Concepts in Children* (1961), which Burt (1962) recommends to teachers and students, despite certain criticisms. Lovell (1959) made a study of 'Some aspects of the work of Piaget and Inhelder on the child's concept of space' with about 140 boys and girls aged 2:11 to 5:8. There had to be some changes of children due to illness but the mean age was 4:5. The results indicated that the straight Euclidean shapes were the hardest to identify. Lovell does not mention giving nonsense names to the shapes, so this may account for his results differing from Fisher's second experiment. However, Lovell speculates whether the child's world is quite as different from the adult world as Piaget suggests. Then Lovell and Ogilvie (1960) made a study of 'Conservation of substance in the junior school child', using as subjects almost the whole of one junior school, boys and girls. (In French 'conserve' can mean 'preserve' and Piaget uses it in the sense of 'retention in memory'.) They made one major experiment, and two subsidiary ones arising from the results of the main experiment. The results were strongly in favour of Piaget's three stages, but these stages were not as clearcut as Piaget suggested; there was considerable overlapping of stages. They draw attention to the following points for junior work: (1) some children may be at an earlier stage during the first two years of junior school; (2) Piaget-type experiments are in themselves learning situations; (3) there is a grave danger in accepting a child's apparent understanding at face value; (4) inability to understand the conservation of substance may affect the lives of children and adults more than is generally realised, e.g. some children would pay more

TABLE 8: *Conservation of substance (giving the proportions of children in the three classes)*

	Average age		Conservation	Transition	Non-conservation	Total
	Year	Month				
1st year	7	8	30	27	26	83
2nd year	8	10	44	8	13	65
3rd year	9	9	73	15	11	99
4th year	10	8	64	7	4	75
			211	57	54	322

Source: Lovell and Ogilvie (1960).

money for a piece of toffee in one shape than another; and (5) certain verbal confusions, such as *bigger* and *fatter*, exist in the first two years of junior school.

The following year Lovell and Ogilvie (1961) reported a similar study of conservation of weight in the junior school child. According to Piaget only conservers can execute logical compositions (In French 'composition' can mean 'examination' or 'investigation'.) Table 9 gives the proportion of children in the three classes used by Lovell and Ogilvie. Comparison of Tables 8 and 9 shows that conservation of weight comes later than conservation of substance. This means that children can retain in their minds notions of quantity of material they are studying before they can retain in their minds notions of the weight of such material. The authors present their results in six interesting tables. They conclude that invariance of weight develops in part through prolonged and varied experience of the physical world. The concept of quantity of substance arises earlier since visual perception assists, whereas visual perception can actually mislead in judgment of weight. As said of the previous experiment, the tests used are in themselves learning situations. But Piaget's experiments are only one kind of test that could be used in the development of concepts.

TABLE 9: *Conservation of weight*

	Conservation	Transition	Non-conservation	Total
1st year	2 (4%)	3 (5%)	52 (91%)	57
2nd year	26 (36%)	26 (36%)	21 (29%)	73
3rd year	32 (48%)	13 (20%)	21 (32%)	66
4th year	124 (74%)	22 (13%)	22 (13%)	168
Total	184	64	116	364

Source: Lovell and Ogilvie (1961).

Then Lovell, Mitchell and Everett (1962) reported an experimental study of the growth of some logical structures. They carried out a series of experiments on ten primary school children of 5 to 10 years, and ten ESN (educationally subnormal) school children of 9 to 15 years. The work with the normal children confirmed the findings of Piaget and Inhelder fairly well. The extension to ESN children showed the limited ability of these children to develop logical structures. All these articles by Lovell and his co-workers give very detailed accounts of the nature of each experiment and much fuller results than would be appropriate here.

Case and Collinson (1962) of Birmingham report on the development of formal thinking in verbal comprehension. They wished to find out whether children's inferences in history, geography and literature followed Piaget's stages of thought, and used as subjects ninety children from primary and secondary schools. Generally, their results confirmed Piaget. But, as Lovell and Ogilvie found conservation of weight affected by practical experience as well as maturation, so Case and Collinson found formal thought in language affected by cultural background, width of experience and verbal repertoire as well as maturation.

S. Jackson (1965), in an MEd thesis at Manchester, reported an investigation on the growth of logical thinking in normal and subnormal children. He had two groups of forty-eight children, one with IQ 90–110 and the other with IQ 60–80. The six tests he used came from Piaget and Inhelder, *The Growth of Logical Thinking from Childhood to Adolescence* (1958), and he scored as they had done. Then he used a Guttman-type cumulative scalogram. He then ranked correlations between logical thinking and (1) chronological age and (2) intelligence. On the whole the results agreed with Piaget and Inhelder. But many of the older subjects did not reach the level of logical thinking Piaget's work predicted. Also there were very wide individual differences. These two reservations are important and underline Piaget's single-minded concern with *how* one stage develops into another, not with *when* it happens. Only extensive statistical work can give data on when one might expect the fresh stages, and on just how wide the deviations above and below these norms (due to individual differences) are likely to be.

In summarising these British experiments designed to prove or disprove the theories on stages of development in thought put forward by Piaget, we can say that on the whole they confirm Piaget's work. More rigorous scientific design has produced information which has not been of interest to Piaget. The most important further information, resulting from careful statistical work with large groups of children has been of three kinds: (1)

there is a good deal of overlap in stages, e.g. a level of thought reached in one type of test may be above or below the level of thought a child can achieve in another type of test; (2) there are very wide individual differences, so that chronological age for achievement of a new level of thinking is a poor guide without indications of the deviations to be expected in a normal group; (3) maturation is not the only factor; for example, the level of thinking attained may be influenced by previous practical experience, cultural environment, verbal ability, motivation, and so on. Many psychologists in various countries have been studying these three further aspects, arising from psychological statistics, for the last four or five decades. However, Piaget's prolific results, assembled in a long career, have brought new light specifically to the way in which one stage moves to the next, from infancy to adolescence, transmuting precepts-according-to-where-a-child-stands to *abstract* concepts which can be manipulated in thought alone.

Amongst the reasons why more research along the lines of Piaget is urgently needed are the three following: (*a*) so that teachers can themselves see the ways in which children of differing ages and differing abilities work out the problems; (*b*) so that teachers become more accustomed to the real nature of learning situations; and (*c*) to obtain the large numbers of scores under different circumstances of age, mental ability, social and cultural environment, etc., enabling psychological statistics to give further information on averages, deviations from the average, individual differences, improved tests, and so on.

7. Play
15 months to 2½ years

The experimental play, so like the play of young animals, continues still with marked tendency towards repetition. But now the child becomes increasingly aware of successful conclusion to some pattern of behaviour he has been repeating; he then moves on to some fresh activity. The repetitions give necessary practice. They are part of the drive towards mastery, both of the environment (including people) and of his own body. The new feature, awareness of success and moving on to the next activity, means that previous patterns of behaviour are now integrated into the whole system.

There is also a development on the social side. He begins to be interested in other children. At first there is no question of playing with them. He examines another baby in a pram with intense attention. If he is in the same room as another child of nearly two, each will play with his own toys, fully aware of the other child, but the two children play in parallel. Then he will approach the other child, as if he were an object, another toy. When he tries to touch the other's eye or hold his hair, there is trouble. He has never before played with anyone not able to defend himself and he cannot make out what the trouble is. This is the moment of misunderstanding by adults in the past. Toddlers seem to be savage with each other, to the destruction of play. Superficially, it looks as if they have to have social behaviour 'put into' them. But this is not so. They want to play together. To begin with, they need only short spells together, with long periods of parallel play, so that the necessary self-discipline demanded by social living has time to develop.

But the most interesting new feature is phantasy. A toy is used not for what it is, but as a symbol for something else. As we have seen (p. 66), Piaget puts this symbolic play, rôle-playing and make-believe at about 2½ years. Thus the symbolism essential to language development is used in many kinds of play, both with and without words. In understanding symbolic play, it is essential to realise that the ability to symbolise is a complex mental process. As Romanes said in the nineteenth century (p. 56), it is the ability to symbolise which sets man apart from animals, rather than language itself. Symbolism is used in many areas such as mathematics, music, and mime, as well as in language; and the brain becomes sufficiently complex for symbolism towards the end of the toddler stage, when actual vocabulary size is no more than some four hundred words and may be very considerably less.

Symbolic play is carried on for very long periods and with what seems like inexhaustible energy. For a long time psychologists could not find out the source of this immense energy. The two-year-old is too tired to walk the last 200 yards home and you wonder whether you should carry him. Instead, you suggest that you and he are teddybears stumping home for dinner. Suddenly the child is transformed to dynamic energy, all tiredness forgotten. The source of this great energy seems to be as follows. During the infant stage a child has to find how he can get what he wants from adults. If he smiles he gets a drink; if he screams he does not get it. In countless ways he finds what behaviour is effective and what behaviour is ineffective. He makes many mistakes. He projects his own feelings on to the adults. When he is angry and says, 'No!' he is very angry; so when adults gently and firmly say 'No!' to him, he thinks they are as angry with him as he was with them. He also does the opposite of projecting himself upon them; he introjects their apparent behaviour into himself.

In this way, at the infant stage, he learns that many forms of behaviour do not work. We can see from the egocentric nature of projection and introjection, that his ideas about what works and what does not work, that is, what he may and may not do, are not very objective. He is only just beginning to move to objective ideas about the world by two years of age. What he must not do, he rejects. It is gone, vanished, does not exist. Of course, today we know that his impulse to scream and do other things that do not work, does not vanish. He has, one by one, repressed these unacceptable impulses into the unconscious part of his mind; and he knows no more how he does this than he knows how he circulates his blood or takes oxygen from the air when he breaths.

This system of repressing unacceptable impulses works quite well at the infant stage. But by the toddler stage a child's unconscious mind is getting as full of unacceptable impulses as Pandora's box; and the multitude of repressed wishes are fighting to get out, just as all the little creatures in Pandora's box fought to get out. Indeed, the story of Pandora and her box is a myth symbolising this very situation. The child's dilemma is that he feels both anxiety at doing what his parents do not like and anxiety at trying to hold down any more unacceptable impulses in his unconscious mind. The solution to the child's dilemma is found by the child himself. He projects one of his 'wicked' or unacceptable impulses upon, say, his teddybear. He announces that Teddy has wet his pants, teddy has made a pool on the floor. The pool may have been made by the child himself, but this is behaviour which does not exist. So he beats the bad, bad teddy for unforgivable behaviour. The repressed energy comes out with jet-force.

The name of Freud (1856–1939) is, of course, associated with all this. When he first talked of repressed impulses the medical profession was in just such an uproar as when Harvey (1578–1657) announced that blood circulated. Revolutionary ideas always cause this kind of disturbance, because people become set in their ways of thinking as they grow older. But nowadays Freud's books can be got from any public library. A good starting point for reading Freud might be *Totem and Taboo* (1919) or *The Psychopathology of Everyday Life* (1904). Sometimes one can get these books as paperbacks, but Freud is so interesting to read that the paperbacks keep running out of print. Incidentally, Freud was not the first to discover that part of the mind was unconscious. This has been known by artists for a very long time. What he discovered was the mechanism by which repression worked. Of course it upset people to have the lid of Pandora's box lifted and find that some of the impulses they had repressed when two and three years old still existed.

So children project their unrecognised wishes on to their toys. The unacceptable impulses have a little time in the open and appear to be very disintegrative with a lot of beatings and smackings. But much more than this happens. Many of the impulses do not need to be totally shut away. The child may not be allowed to scream for a sweet, but he may scream as he runs round a field. The child has another chance to think about his forbidden wishes and when the game is over, not all of it need be shut away again. Repetition is very noticeable. Day after day, a child may spank his teddy for wetting his pants. Then perhaps the mother stands up for the teddy mildly, saying, 'Teddy is very little. It is not *so* bad when you are little to wet your pants. Give him a hug and tell him he is your very own teddy still.' Maybe he will do so now, or perhaps a little later. He has noted that his mother thinks wetting pants is not the terrible event he thought it was. The conflict is beginning to be resolved. The initial stage of disintegration thus swings towards an improved integration, and the child becomes more objective through clearer thinking.

Part 3
Nursery school age: 2½ to 5 years

8. General development
2½ to 5 years

Since this is the period when all who wish to (and most do) should be able to send their children of 2 to 5 years to nursery schools, it is here referred to as the nursery school years. A discussion of the nursery school problem is to be seen in Chapter 10. As can be seen from Figure 1, during the years 2 to 5 the proportions of the body change from what we might call the cherubic to much nearer those of the adult. Tanner (1961) gives a graph which indicates that by 5 years the head and brain are about 90 per cent of adult size. Ways of assessing developmental age are becoming increasingly sophisticated, particularly with reference to skeletal and dental development. But Tanner says little can be learned by merely, for example, counting the number of teeth which erupt during this period.

The most striking feature of this stage is phantasy. The cause and nature of these phantasies has already been mentioned (p. 80–1). It may well be that adults have failed to give due attention to the nursery school years precisely because the symbols the children spontaneously select veil too thinly what is being symbolised, such as scatology and mutilation. Nonsense chants and stories prove to have most unconventional meanings, when one attends to them. Even the garments chosen for play are mainly symbolic: a ring of string for a crown, a long veil for a wedding, and so on. Dramatic play in groups of three or four children may go on for half an hour or more. There are frequent changes, as one child in policeman's helmet goes off to dig sand or another in trailing gown wants a swing or slide. Weddings are daily occurrences, though the ceremony may be frequently delayed, as bride or groom goes off to do something else.

Friendships and hatreds are equally unstable. Feelings are intense and quarrels break out. One will be moody, another quick-tempered. But the reasons for quarrels change. At 2½ or 3 years, quarrels are usually about possession. There may be wordless struggles over toys or cries of 'Mine!'. But the indifference to being bumped into or walked over changes and there is quick retaliation, at 4 years, for what is taken to be physical attack. Playing together begins with, perhaps, one child holding a bucket and another filling it with sand, or one child pouring water into another child's jar. It is interrupted by one of them noticing something else of interest and cheerfully wandering off. But by 4 to 5 years, two children can carry on a long-term project, such as building a garage with bricks, for perhaps half an hour.

There is little exact information about the imaginary playmates that many children of 4 or 5 years make up. They give them 'nonsense' names, which have an origin, though difficult to trace. These companions are so real that a child will burst out crying if some thoughtless adult sits on one, not realising that he or she is in that particular chair. Ames and Learned (1946) estimate that roughly 20 per cent invent them; but from asking students, Stone and Church (1957) think 50 per cent is nearer the truth. These companions usually vanish as suddenly as they come, perhaps with a casual wave of goodbye; and adults who do not know they have departed can again be in trouble for talking about a non-existent person.

Bladder control may be established early in this period, or may not be established till towards the end. Children of 3 and 4 very much enjoy going to the lavatory. They will take with them whatever they are playing with, even travelling there by scooter. Much of their conversation is scatological. At a later stage the references are veiled, as in the Opie example quoted by Lewis in *Language, Thought and Personality* (1963, p. 209). The Opies (1959) give many examples under Parody and Impropriety, which will doubtless recall others from the reader's childhood. But there is no veiling at the nursery school stage. A child will tell another child, or the teacher, or no one in particular how 'a pussy pissed in another pussy's eye'. This is a perfectly normal verbal expression of aggression at round about 3 years.

The toddlers' preoccupation with mutilation now begins to undergo a change. The stories collected from children of 2 to 5 years by Pitcher and Prelinger (1963), which were mentioned in Chapter 4, show an evolution, year by year. The two-year-olds just state the disaster, e.g. Boy. 2:8. 'Tractor fall down boom. Fall right down and hurt his head off'. But during the 3:3 to 3:11 stage some attempt is made to bring the trouble to a satisfactory ending, which we can recognise as a first attempt at resolution of conflict. Success is patchy at first, but the move towards integration is unmistakable. Of the sixty stories by boys aged 3 years, twelve were still simple disaster statements, but more than twenty made some attempt to master the situation. For instance, 'He was just teasing the man', 'he got home, he ate his supper', and 'he didn't go any more.' Of the sixty stories by girls aged 3 years, fourteen were still disaster statements, but about fifteen (one cannot always be quite sure) had attempted satisfactory conclusions. For instance, 'The rattlesnake came and kissed him and they were friends' (after blinding the boy), and 'Then she runned to nursery school, just like I am.'

By 4 years of age the children told much longer stories, still with much violence, but frequently with well-expressed happy endings: 'The garbage man took them into the truck and throwed them away, and then that was the end of the witches', or 'we're all friends; tiger can you be our friends? Yes, we'd be friends. And they were all friends.' By 5 years the stories were longer still and more rambling. Though there were still accidents, cars slipping off the road, falling in the lake, and so on, the accidents are not the stark bulk of the story, and events follow in sequence usually to a final resolution, many with 'happy ever after'.

Thus we see that the deeply rooted preoccupation with mutilation, arising both from inner aggressive impulses which are disowned and from the outer environment which appears dangerously antagonistic at times, moves towards resolution. Intense interest in playing hospitals, with bandages, syringes, operations and corpses, is a partial sublimation.

Humour has an important part to play in the battle for integration. To be able to laugh at fears, or at least to half-laugh at them, is a step in the right direction. L. J. Stone and Church (1957) report the following lunchtime conversation at Vassar College Nursery School:

JOHN: We'll cut off his arms.
ELLIE: We'll saw off his legs.
DON: Let's hang him up in a tree and tickle him.
JOHN: Let's poke him full of black and blue marks.
ELLIE: Let's cut off his hair and put it in the sandbox.
DON: Let's cut out his grunties.
JOHN: Let's smear him all over with grunties ...
ELLIE: Let's make him eat lots of grunties.
JOHN: We'll wrap it up in some paper—not cellophane—some yellow paper, and then tie some string around it.

Note the move towards veiling the 'grunties' theme by final wrapping in non-transparent paper. Quite apart from having psychological insight about the normal scatological level in this conversation and the important part played by humour in mastering the aggression-mutilation anxieties, it is by no means easy to catch what the children are saying without interrupting the spontaneity.

Through their play, conversation and stories, the children pass from the first powerlessness in face of disaster to attempts at commanding dangerous situations. When we bring stories to a genuine resolution of conflict at the end, we set them an example in thinking, which shows them how to go deeper in thinking than just tacking a happy ending onto an unresolved struggle. Certainly by 5 years, though fact and fancy are still interchangeable there is a growing insistence on realism in situations of stories and drama.

Along with discovery of causality, that a pushed boat floats along water, a dropped brick falls, or a shout causes an echo, nursery school children are interested in the causes of birth and death. At 3 to 4 years a child asks where he came from. Unprepared adults frequently 'fail to hear' the questions and say the children never ask. A lively child always asks this, as soon as he is aware of himself as a separate person. Sensible parents just state the facts very simply. There are now many books on the subject, though few of them are better than K. de Schweinitz's *How a Baby is Born* (1931). Points which should be borne in mind include the following: A conscious effort should be made to answer unemotionally, and particularly to accept anything the child says as perfectly normal. When saying the child develops inside the mother, say there is a special place or bag; otherwise the child's birth is confused with faeces or 'grunties', which society expects a child to lose interest in eventually. The father's part must be quite explicit, otherwise the intellectually satisfying point of the child being half from his father and half from his mother at birth is lost.

As we can see, there are many moments in the telling where the mask of our own repressions can crack and reveal our own only partially resolved conflicts. Instantly the child absorbs this emotional disturbance associated with birth. If we make a determined effort towards integrity and explain in almost casual tones, the child accepts this attitude and will have no problem later in explaining to his own children. However, if we do not 'hear' or answer, a child of 3 to 4 years finds rest by making up a phantasy answer. All the phantasies of birth can be seen in religious paintings of the Virgin Birth from the early Renaissance time: birth through the ear, the eye, the navel, and so on. Children intuitively know they are the same flesh as their parents and have to make up how they become separated if we do not state the facts clearly. One last point of importance is that the child will ask and ask again many times and each time the answer unfolds a little more. This repetition of the facts is the only way to counter the force of the child's own phantasy explanations.

The questions about death can be much more disturbing. With birth we aim at security in love and understanding, but in the high vitality of having a young family, few young parents have given much thought to their attitude to death. Yet children visit the butcher, find dead animals and even hear of the death of grandparents, right in the period of coping with mutilation problems. We know from books like M. E. Mitchell's *The Child's Attitude to Death* (1966) that children of 3 and 4, in their ambivalent swings of love and hate, can for instance kill the ladybirds they really love; and have to face the fact that they cannot bring them alive again in reality as in the omnipotence of phantasy thought. Even those who are orthodox in religion and can tell of a happy future life cannot give much help if they are confused themselves. Both the religious and the humanist adults have to make a great effort to be calm and steady in helping these very young children to accept death as part of reality.

The psychoanalysts think that fear of death is closely linked to fear of life. A person who develops sufficient self-discipline to live fully is not greatly worried by the thought that he will not live for every. Conversely, a person full of unresolved conflicts is irrational about everything, including death. We can handle children's questions about death much better if we have ourselves pondered calmly on matters of life and death. A book which widens the horizons of thought here, is N. O. Brown's *Life against Death: the psychoanalytic meaning of history* (1959). The opening chapters require considerable intellectual effort, but the final chapters, though easier, do not have full meaning without the earlier ones. Brown argues that neurosis, an ill-defined mental disorder, is an essential consequence of civilisation or culture. If we do not learn to differentiate between sufficient and surplus, then luxury results in impoverishment. The neurotic alleviation of anxiety by gaining more and more possessions obscures the fact that we have an impulse to die as well as an impulse to live. We cannot reach equilibrium while we are irrational about this normal life-and-death dialectic, this testing of truth by discussion.

It is not just about direct questions on death that we need to be prepared. The phantasies of nursery aged children show that they not infrequently wish to inflict death. We handle this better, as we ourselves reach equilibrium on life and death. Children of this age frequently have an unmistakable urge to strike dead a new baby whose arrival disrupts the home routine. 'Feed me with a bottle, too.' 'Dress me,' 'Hug me,' a child will beseech, with face riven by jealousy. The child's newly forming repressions, which he is sorting out in play, are stripped from him and his behaviour inevitably regresses. This can be exasperating to the mother, temporarily enveloped in the biological urge to devote her entire self to the new baby. In the Pitcher and Prelinger collection of children's stories there is one such story by a girl aged 3:6.

> Once there was a baby and he got killed. The big hunter got the baby. He put him on the stove and cooked and ate him up. It was happened. The little girl ran a hundred miles. She fell down. Then she called her mommy. And her mommy put a Band-aid on it. They got another baby and he got shot too. And another baby, and he got shot.

One scarcely needs to be a psychoanalyst to interpret the symbolism of this story. To react oneself with horror is naïve. Such reaction to the new baby is normal and the child needs understanding. Very soon the three-year-old becomes attached to the new baby. Then the conflict between love and hate can be resolved in play; but the play more quickly leads to resolution if the parents know what the child has to go through. To react with understanding is psychologically sophisticated.

There is a fairly recent American study by Lois Barclay Murphy (1962), a research psychologist at the Menninger Foundation which shows very clearly how adults may have to cope with their own problems while helping the children to master theirs. It is a longitudinal study, reported in *The Widening World of Childhood*, of thirty-two children from the age of a month onwards and details are so well recorded that the case histories read like personal letters. Anyone intending to do research on young children should read it for its careful methodology. Two children had serious misfortunes, one losing a tip of a finger and the other contracting polio. The accounts of how the parents mastered their own reactions to these misfortunes is quite as remarkable as the accounts of how the children did the same.

A book which covers the whole of the primary school stage, with special reference to the nursery school years, is Lee's *The Growth and Development of Children* (1969). It would make good introductory reading. The generalisations made are well-supported by astute observations which those who know children can recognise as genuine and perceptive. For instance (p. 68) an account of twenty minutes' observation of how two three-year-olds who speak different languages get into communication through play. That one can recognise genuine observations (and they can be seen in the teaching practice notebooks of many students) is in itself an interesting point. The important quality of the many observations in this book, as well as the work of Susan Isaacs (1929, 1930, 1932, 1933, etc.), L. J. Stone and Church (1957), L. B. Murphy (1962), and many others quoted here, is that the observers are free of cliché-thinking, and so the children are interesting because their reported behaviour is original.

Understanding children of nursery school years gives great stimulus to their language development. But the young child's limited vocabulary is definitely not the barrier to understanding them. The real barrier for many adults is that they themselves tend to use symbols without remembering what exactly is being symbolised. This is a root cause of cliché-thinking. Children of 3 or 4 can greatly embarrass such adults by not realising that this has happened—or could happen—and so mentioning the basic fact that the adult has forgotten or repressed. A good nursery school teacher can take all that children of two to five are liable to talk about, be it scatological or aesthetic.

9. Speech development
2½ to 5 years

All authorities agree that children greatly increase their vocabularies during the years 2½ to 5. But to give norms and averages is extremely difficult. As Lewis says in *Language, Thought and Personality* (1963), the measurement of vocabulary is 'peculiarly fraught with difficulties'. Earlier work, particularly in the United States, tends to be more precise about norms and averages than most authorities would care to be today. M. E. Smith (1926), whose extensive studies were highly thought of, said that a child of 2½ years knows more than 400 words and one of 5 years knows about 2,000 words. Fowler Brooks shows how steep such a rise would be (see below). But in 1957 Templin, also in the

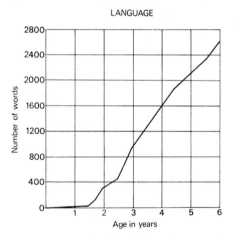

LANGUAGE

Figure 14. Growth of Vocabulary from Smith (1926).
Source: Brooks (1926).

United States, in *Certain Language Skills in Children*, uses samples of speech, as representative as possible, and commits herself to no more than that there is a steady growth of vocabulary.

Burroughs (1957), in a Birmingham University monograph, reports a study of the vocabulary of 330 children of 5 and 6 who were about to start reading. The average vocabulary was 273 words. This is considerably lower than the figures usually given in American studies, such as M. E. Smith (1926), Boring et al. (1939). Indeed Boring and his colleagues write that at 2 years a child knows about 300 words, at 4 years about 1,500 words, at 6 years about 2,500 words, at 12 years about 7,000 words, and that students know about 15,000 non-technical terms, plus 52,000 derivatives of root words, plus words learned in the study of science and foreign languages. Whether six-year-olds in America really have vocabularies nine times that of English ones only further research will show.* It is interesting to note that in Burroughs's survey of some thirty studies during this century before his work, only three originated in Britain. More important than the average number of words used by children at the end of the nursery school years is the fact that there are wide differences in the number of words used by individual children. Burroughs found that individual lists varied between 56 and 578 words. This is of educational importance, as a teacher needs to know which children should have extra help in verbalising experience.

Growth in understanding of words is basic to proper communication. Vygotsky (1896–1924), the Russian psychologist, describes in *Thought and Language* how thought and speech are related. He maintained that thought and speech are neither the same nor completely separable. They come together in a third element: *word meaning*. He argued that the essence of word meaning is a generalised reflection of reality, and this generalised reflection is also the absolute distinction between sensation and thought. We have already seen how the infant first calls his or her father *Dadda* and then calls the postman and policeman *Dadda*, moving towards a generalised idea of 'man'. But the child does not call the bath or cup 'man'.

Vygotsky said that the primary function of speech is communication in social intercourse. Lewes had drawn attention to this earlier (p. 56). The difference between animal signs and human language, between a frightened goose flying off and a human calling out 'Danger!', is this generalised element. Thus what enables us to communicate thought through word meaning is this generalising. The goose has a sensation which makes it react by flight; the human already knows a number of situations which can be potentially dangerous, so can understand from the word, that there is danger before seeing what this particular danger may be.

* Research now indicates that British children on the whole reach a somewhat higher level on the Stanford-Binet vocabulary test than American children.

As the nursery school years approach, the child becomes more and more aware of the meaning of words, provided they are attached to experiences he has had. But the years from $2\frac{1}{2}$ to 5 are much more than just a period when the quantity of words known increases; they are a period when over-generalising has to be curtailed. The child no longer calls a cow and a horse a bow-wow. He can identify a cow when he sees it, whether he has seen one this colour before or not. He learns that 'chair' is not just his high chair, but also the armchair that his father sits in to read the paper; and there are other chairs. But the stool his mother sits on to peel the vegetables is not a chair. 'Why not?' he asks. In order to refine his generalisations, he needs to have his question answered. Words are a tool for categorising the variety of objects, people and events.

Students often speculate whether they are thinking of the same word when, for instance, someone says 'blue'. Experiments have been done with colour naming and matching and shown that those who are not colour blind do choose the same colours for the various colour names. R. W. Brown and Lenneberg (1954) went further. They did an experiment which showed that subjects who knew the names for colours with a wide range of shades, selected better than those who did not. This reminds us of Fisher's experiment (p. 75) where nonsense names helped the children to remember shapes. A common fund of language gives us a common fund of experience, discrimination and thinking. In regions where objects or animals are very familiar, many more names for them are invented. Eskimos have many names for snow, as Arabs have for camels. There are many more names for trees in English than in Norwegian, as Norway does not have 'the oak and the ash and the bonny-ivy tree'. Whorf (1950, 1954), a student of Red Indian languages, found one of these languages made no distinction between brown and red, another between nouns and verbs, and yet another between past, present and future. Thus, where discrimination is careful, language becomes enriched; and where language is rich, discrimination can be more accurate. Language and thought, through word meaning, promote discrimination and integration.

The years $2\frac{1}{2}$ to 5 are particularly important, now the children are learning to live together; it is a time when children can hammer out a common language. Because they share many experiences, they can share word meanings. The child entering the group takes over words and concepts from the group. He also contributes in this way to the group. Thus equilibrium within the group is approached, through increasing communication. Old meanings are subtly blended with new ones. 'Mummy', which previously meant one particular person, now begins also to represent a relationship between a woman who has a child and that child. These puzzling developments are played out with dolls. More abstract concepts, such as being 'kind' or 'cross' are greatly helped by stories. A group listening to the same situations in tales begins also to hammer out a common code of behaviour. The child listening to the story is both involved and detached. If the story becomes too exciting, then the detachment goes, and opportunity to think clearly is disrupted. Just as the child of fourteen months could make her wishes clear before she could talk (p. 28), so these children—given opportunity for calm attention—can grasp social situations in stories beyond their ability to discuss them.

At the toddler stage, when naming things and getting them to the right place in the right order is still an intellectual effort, children like stories about things they know, items for laying the table, getting dressed, and so on. They still enjoy these tales, during the $2\frac{1}{2}$ to 5 years, but they also want stories about behaviour. Their phantasy life, basically a matter of human relationships, is very active. By the middle and end of this period they should have worked through many of the worse conflicts between their blind self-centred wishes and what can work in society. No matter how antisocial their behaviour may at times appear, children are basically social; they wish to live with others and are prepared to compromise, to discipline their blind wishes, in order to attain the reward of social living. However, these blind impulses come up in their play for hours on end. Therefore, it helps them very much to have stories with simple conflicts in them. The old woman in the vinegar bottle finally saw that she had made a mistake to grumble so much. Stories which have a satisfactory resolution help the children to bring their phantasy play to satisfactory resolution. A major difference between nineteenth century and modern stories is that today one does not point out the moral. The child is shown a situation, one which appears to be almost out of hand, and then shown how it can work out well. To point out the moral defrauds the child of seeing for himself how it worked, as explaining a joke before telling it defrauds the listener of seeing the joke for himself. Further details about the importance of stories can be seen in the final chapters of Pickard's *I Could a Tale Unfold* (1961).

Nursery school children leave us in no doubt of the importance of stories to them. The experiences shared in stories give them shared experiences and common language beyond the confines of home or school. Since an important aim is to increase the common fund of word meaning, the stories in their construction and illustration should be worthy of the children's attention. For their language to be enriched, in addition to stories the children need increasing experience with things and events. They also need to hear adults using words correctly; and the adults have to introduce correct terms at moments of interest. Faulty speech also has to be corrected. But this calls for great sensitivity, since the long-term objective is to foster confident enjoyment of communication through talking.

Stages can be traced in conversation amongst the children themselves. First one child makes a statement to another child. The second child may be surprised or interested but does not reply. Then two children make statements to each other, neither set of statements having any connection. This second stage runs something like this:

'My car has red wheels.'
'Dolly is crying.'
'I can push it.'
'She is hungry.'
'I can push it hard—like this!'

The third stage is when one child notices, with surprise and indignation, that the other child is talking about something else.

'I'm talking about my *car*!'
'My dolly's got blue knickers.'
'Silly!'

When each notices what the other is talking about, real conversation starts. Very naturally, as with adults, the children now tend to associate with friends who are interested in the same things. But it is worth noticing that, even at earlier stages, the children enjoy sitting together and chatting, neither really listening to the other, but both enjoying the sociability of the occasion.

Although we have not yet statistical data sufficient for producing reliable norms, the pattern of development can be seen throughout this stage. At the beginning talk is of their own possessions and very possessive; but then the children can exchange information, perhaps with many irrelevant details or some essentials left out. By 4 to 5 years children can use language to co-ordinate group activity for some agreed goal; there is eventually less blind self-assertion and egocentric speech. Sympathy and understanding in conversation emerges in stages: first a child stops playing to stare at a crying child, and may even start crying; but by 5 sympathy can be astonishingly mature, 'Take mine!' or 'I'll blow your nose, then you won't cry', and so on. The first *dog* or *cat* develops into *dog bark* or *cat meow* by nearly 3 years; and by 4½ to 5 years conversations are about the attributes of, for instance, dogs

and cats, showing that concepts are starting to form. Mainly differences between things or events and people are noticed. Similarities come later. But
there is the dawn of similarities in analogies. A child sees a cow being milked
and says, 'Water can'.

Another area of speech development is the way in which a child speaks to
himself. The Russian Professor Luria, one-time student of Vygotsky's,
speaking at the London Institute of Education in 1957, described one of
Vygotsky's experiments which has profoundly affected Russian experimental
work with young children. Vygotsky (see Luria 1961) would ask a preschool
child (up to age 6 or 7 in Russia) to do a simple practical task (such as drawing
or tracing a picture), and would then make the task more complicated, e.g.
there would be no pencil or drawing-pins to fix the paper. Children of
3 to 4 years proved helpless in the face of such difficulty and appealed to
adults for help, doing nothing till help came. Children of 5 to 7, if given no
help, tried to find a way round the difficulty; and they had an outburst of
active speech addressed in part to the adult but chiefly to anyone. Vygotsky
used Piaget's term 'egocentric speech'. Attention to what the child was saying
showed that this was very different from 'egocentric babbling'. At first the
child talked about the situation in which he found himself, as verbal orienta-
tion to surroundings; then his talk spread further, to include his previous
experience. Vygotsky concluded that these two phases of the outburst of
speech, talking about the present situation and then relating it to past experience played a decisive part; the child's speech was involved in social relationships, the child was able to discuss with himself and begin to form new
functional systems of which speech was a part. At a still later stage this inner
discussion can precede activity and eliminate unsuitable activity, without
performing it to see if it works. We in Britain have been slow to follow this
lead. But Joynt and Cambourne (1968) of Australia, following Luria, have
constructed a valuable experiment on psycholinguistic development and
the control of behaviour. They describe in detail the procedure, show
common elements in the development of Australian and Russian children,
and conclude that early speech must be encouraged.

Mistakes in speech deserve very careful attention, as well as correction
because they reveal the emerging schemata of the mother tongue. L. J. Stone
and Church (1957) give some interesting examples: permission key of a car,
nokay as the opposite of OK, I am so being have, a car busying along, etc.
The remarks are original and might have been correct: the key does 'permit'
the car to go. Emotional tone may be correct, as with the child who furiously
said to her mother 'You wrong number!' Words may also be used incorrectly

through misunderstanding of relationships, particularly over marriage, which figures so largely in phantasy play. 'When Mummy is dead, I shall marry Daddy', or a couple of boys are bride and bridegroom. Where our strictest taboos are touched upon, we have to be particularly calm in explanations.

At times the questions become extremely difficult to answer because they are wrongly asked. There is no right answer to a wrong question. If a child asks of the fallen leaves, 'Who put them there?' we can only say, 'No one', which is no answer to the child. We may embark on explanations about the wind, but the child may have no idea what we are talking about. A girl of 4, known to the author, was asked to hurry up in the bath. She started to hurry with the flannel, then stopped and asked, 'How do my hands know what to do?' The mother did her best to explain that something equivalent to instructions came from inside her head. The child replied, 'But I did not speak to them.' The physiological explanation, the only 'right' answer, went over the child's head. But the mother was most interested by the sudden insight to the child's way of thinking. There are two guiding principles in answering. First, all that we say must be true to the best of our knowledge; then we can defend the simplicity of our earlier answers when we expound further at a later stage. Secondly, we can build up a fund of goodwill over answering, by giving short and simple answers to questions motivated by intellectual curiosity which present no difficulty; then when we have to say, 'I don't think I can answer that properly till you know a little more', this will be accepted readily.

Language development during the nursery school years proves far more complex than was previously realised. This complexity is such that there are serious difficulties in trying to make scientific study of the development of vocabulary size, length of sentences, word meaning, and so on. The child with a poor vocabulary is usually reluctant to start speaking and when he begins, he speaks slowly and often softly. The teacher who wishes to encourage such a child to develop better powers of communication, is presented with a whole series of time-consuming barriers to success, and is sorely tempted to overlook this child, letting the fluent chatterers fill the air with talk. But the fluent chatterers also need guidance in better use of words. A good case for nursery schools could be made on grounds of language development alone. Children of 2 to 5 years should have expert help available for developing man's greatest single asset—speech.

10. Nursery schools
2½ to 5 years

The stage of development 2½ to 5 years is here called the nursery school years because this is the stage when parents should be able to send the children to experts in child development for part of the day if they wish to do so. An arbitrary age of 2½ has been chosen because it fits in the scheme of this book; nursery school could be available at two or three years.

Less than a century ago many children of 2½ to 5 had to work. In many countries they still do. Kidd, in *Savage Childhood: a study of Kafir children* (1906), describes children of three years building effective traps for birds, fish and small game. Writers on other cultures, such as Mead (1956), describe children of 5 years managing canoes alone and so on. In the British cottage sweat shops children of 3 and 4 years worked, for instance, with the bobbins for lace making, and by 5 they often had regular working hours. All students learn, in history of education, of children pushing trucks in the mines. There seems to be no record of children younger than 2½ being trained, so presumably this was the age when children first proved trainable. Schooling in Britain became compulsory at 5 in 1870, specifically to save children from such sweated labour in the industrial revolution. This is why in Britain school starts at least a year before other countries. We cannot console ourselves that in a manner of speaking, we started nursery schools at 5 with compulsory schooling, because lessons were extremely formal and many children could not understand the alphabet, which they were set to learn. Such children might have been very much happier left at home to do practical work with bobbins.

Of course, with school starting in a couple of years, it was not worth beginning to train the younger ones. So then a most extraordinary sociological phemonenon emerged. Overnight, with compulsory schooling, children of 2½ to 5 years literally became unemployed. They must have plagued their busy parents beyond endurance. By hindsight, we can see now that some provision should have been made for these children who had already proved

99

themselves teachable. Children of $2\frac{1}{2}$ to 5 need occupation, and schooling of a different kind should also have been a compulsory provision, though without compulsory attendance. The work of Froebel with young children and with teacher training was known from the early nineteenth century. But he does not figure in histories of education because nobody took seriously the idea of educating young children. Lilley in *Friedrich Froebel* (1967), gives a scholarly and most interesting account of his ideas and how they spread abroad, to illuminate work with young children. The author quotes Froebel as saying: 'The ability of a human being to grow in felicity to his full power and to achieve his destiny depends solely on a proper understanding of him in childhood. He must be understood not only in his nature but also in his relationships, and treated in ways which are appropriate.'

By the end of the nineteenth century the plight of British children aged $2\frac{1}{2}$ to 5 was highlighted by the decaying slums left in the wake of the industrial revolution. In 1910 Margaret McMillan, a woman of great ability and vision, started the first open-air nursery school, in Deptford, London. Cresswell's *Margaret McMillan* (1953) describes her life and works. After her death Burt wrote that she somehow managed to integrate in a kind of synoptic vision a practical synthesis of child psychology, child medicine, and child training in an inspired educational plan. The nursery school movement had an inspiring start and teachers became well qualified, although academics in colleges persisted in drafting the least gifted students to 'looking after nursery school children'.

What exactly is the position now? According to the Nursery School Association of Great Britain and Northern Ireland, in 1965 there were the following schools:

TABLE 10: *Nursery schools in England and Wales* (1965)

	Schools	Children	
		Full-time	Part-time
Local education authority nursery schools	461	23,914	7,975
Direct grant nursery schools	16	672	255
Independent nursery schools, recognised as efficient	9	286	102
Other independent nursery schools	196	5,141	1,685
	682		

According to the Plowden Report there were 2,100,000 children aged 2 to 4 years in 1965. If we take away the independent nursery schools, which are neither supported nor recognised, we have 486 nursery schools with 33,204 children either full time or part time in them. This leaves over two million of these educable children still 'unemployed'. Of course, there are a handful of other arrangements, such as unrecognised nursery schools, child minders, factory child minding and so on. Staff in these establishments lack the necessary expertise.

With the British tradition of starting nursery schools in very bad areas and giving priority to the worst cases, any nursery school research needs careful scrutiny to find whether the children selected are severely handicapped environmentally. Douglas and Ross (1964) published an investigation on the later educational progress and emotional adjustment of children who went to nursery schools or classes. Unfortunately the 130 children followed-up and compared with national averages were not only from very poor circumstances; the percentage from poor housing, poor maternal care, large families, and so on, was considerably worse than national percentages, as Table 11 shows:

TABLE II: *Nursery schools: socio-economic background (percentages)*

Background	Investigation	National averages
Mothers working more than ten hours a week	38·9	18·4
Living in poor houses	60·3	49·4
Given poor maternal care	19·0	12·5
With five or more in family	19·3	15·0
Lower manual working class	45·1	41·6

Source: Douglas and Ross (1964).

Evidence from research for the Plowden Report (II, p. 365) shows a connection between school attainment and poor home circumstances, particularly poverty and maternal care. Since the early years bear the heaviest impact of adverse environmental forces, the writers strongly recommend that nursery schools for the under-fives are essential for encouraging a healthy attitude to school and teacher and education. They also recommend that some 5 per cent of teachers should be specifically trained in social work. In the section of this book on training nursery school teachers (p. 102) suggestions are made which apply equally to children from rich and poor environments. While fully conceding the special contribution that nursery education can make to children who are handicapped by environment, we must not let this important issue distract us from the fact that most children of 3 and 4 are ready for expert help in their learning. The development of the National Association of Pre-School Playgroups is witness to the fact that thoughtful mothers, of other than the lowest social class, are aware that their children require some proper provision for active growing. One of the ways in which we can tailor our educational system to suit the new demands of modern knowledge for economy of learning is to provide enough genuine nursery schools for all who need them.

Government expenditure on sufficient nursery schools will only be justified if enough able students can be persuaded to prepare themselves for work in nursery schools. This can only be done as a reorientation of attitude towards the importance of the nursery school years develops in those holding high office in the educational world; the same proportion of 'BEd students' has to be expected from nursery school specialisation as from primary and secondary specialisation. The 'subject' in which such nursery specialists have to attain higher qualification is the behaviour of children. Nursery school teachers are the first educational specialists with whom children come in contact. The manner in which these children are first inducted into society outside the home is crucial for all subsequent development. For instance, the way in which these children's often difficult questions are answered affects their attitude to asking questions; without skilled encouragement, many children lapse into phantasy answers made up by themselves, or even appear to stop enquiring.

There are major world problems, such as that of mankind's aggression, which nursery students have to face, in order to get into perspective the long-term objectives of their work. No other section of the educational service so constantly handles children's naked aggression. We have to think in terms of nursery students being as capable as others of contributing to thought here. This has only been done in the past by a few very enlightened educationists. There is a new climate of thought about the aggressive behaviour of all animals, including man, which indicates that mankind alone has become trapped in a war ritual which could exterminate him.

The position is not that the poor nursery school teacher should be overburdened with these terrible problems; but that only the able nursery teacher can find out what we need to know about how to help nursery children to conform to social living with a minimum of harmful ritualisation. Books which students in training should discuss include Lorenz's *On Aggression* (1966), Ardrey *The Territorial Imperative* (1967), and Morris's *The Naked Ape* (1967). There is no greater authority on aggressive group action than Lorenz; with great patience he builds up his argument that war, being a ritual and not innate, can be changed. Ardrey also argues that a common cause for war lies in our ignorance of man's animal nature. Morris gives us a wide survey of our close relationship to the haired apes. These books have added so much to our understanding of what used to be regarded as 'prehistory' that they are bound to give new perspectives to our thinking about cause and effect in our society. We are told, for instance by N. O. Brown (p. 89), that Western development is motivated by neurosis in us all. It may be that accelerating technological development is not the prime cause of our present confusion. It could perhaps stem from that major step in human development when men gave up the immediate food rewards of hunting for the delayed rewards of agriculture. This gives a new slant to the need to accumulate stores or wealth. Some temperaments find it very difficult to wait long for rewards. The neurotic behaviour of some delinquents appears to be related to inability to tolerate long delay in receiving rewards. At any rate, the idea is worth consideration, and stands up before examination of some early agricultural communities. The Pharaohs, leaders of such communities, even stock-piled for the next world in their pyramids.

A symposium was held at the British Museum on the subject of aggression, where specialists in zoology, physiology, psychology, psychiatry and sociology pooled views. These are reported in a useful book by Carthy and Ebling, *The Natural History of Aggression* (1965). J. A. C. Brown in *Techniques of Persuasion from Propaganda to Brainwashing* (1963) shows the skilled organisation of aggression, industrial or national, with intent to cause people to think one way or another.

Many students feel that the cultural heritage which has been handed to them is so confused by undisciplined aggression that they hesitate to accept it. In the past, students who were being prepared to look after little children were not expected to bother about such major issues; people believed that all they needed was 'mother-love'. Now the tables are turned and we must have the information that major issues can contribute; Gorer says in *Exploring English Character* (1955) that, for the English, aggression is so confused with guilt that parents will not even tolerate it in their children. Whether this need be so is a matter on which the nursery expert should be able to give us information. Nathan Isaacs in an unusually wise pamphlet on *What is Required of the Nursery-Infant Teacher Today?* (1967) said that it is particularly the well-trained nursery and infant teachers for whom depth of understanding is a necessity.

11. Self concept

Some psychologists, for example Jersild (1952), believe that enabling a child to build a trustworthy picture of himself is the main task of education. Cattell (1946) calls the self the keystone of personality, which integrates all levels of personality to one dynamic structure or unified sentiment. We would therefore expect to study reports of the start of this picture of the self in the crucial first five years of life. But a hunt through the literature reveals almost nothing, in Britain or America, concerning the preschool age.

The reason for this paucity of information is not hard to find. In order to see what an individual thinks he is, the obvious thing to do is to ask him. That means that he must introspect, must contemplate his own behaviour and report what he finds. This has been done in America, with many groups of school children, and the replies organised into psychological categories. A certain amount has been done in Britain. But it is not a technique which could usefully be used on very young children. Moreover, British psychologists and philosophers have mainly been interested in introspection about the self only at a high philosophic level.

In 1885 the Cambridge philosopher Ward published an article in the *Encyclopaedia Britannica* which many consider to be a masterpiece on the philosophy of the mind. Hearnshaw (1964) includes the following points in his summary of this article: 'There is always a self or subject of experience, which can never be explained in terms of experience, but is itself the explanation of the unity and continuity of experience. The self can never be left out of any psychological analysis.' Hearnshaw maintains that between the wars, British psychology, like the government of that time, remained largely conservative. Thus British psychologists were uninfluenced by foreign psychological thought and were stimulated to little if any research. The outcome of this was that the only source of information in the self was the introspection of learned men.

One might think that this could have little connection with the training of teachers. But a few training colleges were becoming interested in current thought about the mind. In 1879 Maria Grey College, in London, invited Sully to lecture to students; and the following year the newly formed women teachers' college at Cambridge invited Ward to do the same. Ward gave a series of lectures entitled 'Mental science and its special relation to teaching'. Many students who attended these lectures themselves eventually became lecturers in colleges throughout the land where teachers were being trained.

One of the ways of training students of psychology to introspect is to ask them to notice what goes on in their minds as the meaning of a complex proposition 'dawns'. Sometimes several seconds pass before the meaning of such a proposition becomes clear; and it is by no means easy, at first, to catch the thought processes that lead to understanding. The complex propositions may be complicated statements or questions or aphorisms. There is little difficulty in coming to a decision as to whether one agrees or not. But then coming to a decision is very much easier than sustained thinking. A decision can be arrived at by tossing a coin.

In a moment the reader will come across one such aphorism, embedded in the text, so that it will not have caught the eye in riffling through the book, which would ruin the experiment. The reader should pause after reading the next sentence and see whether he can catch anything going on in his mind before answering the question: 'The smaller a woman's foot, the larger the shoemaker's bill—is this true?' It is by no means easy to catch yourself coming to a conclusion. Here is another one which looks easier, but remember before you read it that the purpose of the experiment is not to answer the question but to note what came into your mind before you decided your answer. 'What are you going to do during the next holidays?' The answer may be sad or gay or undecided, but perhaps several thoughts came into your mind this time before you reached the answer: travel brochures, one or two people, a place or occupation. It might be anything to do with holidays, or perhaps something quite different, to do with you personally.

When students are learning to introspect in this way, they usually work in pairs, so that they can take turns to do three things: ask the question, record the number of seconds before the answer is given, and take down the exact account of what went on in the mind *before* giving the answer. Here are three more complex statements, so that the interested reader can pause after reading each one, write down his introspection, and then estimate very roughly how many seconds he took to reach the answer. (1) 'Irrationality and superstition are specifically human characteristics. Is this true?' (2) "To give every-one his own would be to aim at justice and to achieve chaos. Is this true?' (3) 'One must be both sympathetic and cruel in order to be either. Is this true?'

A comparison of one's own first attempts to introspect and the introspec-tion of a highly qualified person will show how skilfully this source of infor-mation can be exploited by a trained person. During the Second World War, when University College, London was evacuated to Aberystwyth, the author began the study of introspection. After an extremely unsuccessful attempt with: 'The smaller a woman's foot, the larger the shoemaker's bill', J. C. Flugel, the professor in charge of the laboratory at that moment, offered to demonstrate. He was given : 'To fructify the past and to create the future: let that be my present. Can this be right?' After eleven seconds the subject of the experiment said:

Yes. Meaning slow in rising. I was vaguely disturbed by the fact that I remembered it slightly. Then my attention concentrated on the word 'fructify' rather, with vivid auditory and motor imagery. Changed to vague visual dim picture of a fruit tree with white blossom *and* fruit together. Then almost in a flash the conceptual meaning of the whole burst upon me together with a rather satisfying feeling of familiarity. Some relief at the thought that I could answer it satisfactorily (though the answer was not yet there). Then very clearly the thought arose that to fructify the past meant to develop to the full the possibilities of what our predecessors had done. Dim visual image of a man in white classical costume; this had dim meaning of Greek philosopher; also very fleeting image of someone dressed in a chocolate coloured costume. He dimly meant more modern philosophy. This image persisted after the answer was given and acquired the meaning of Jeremy Bentham (though now I realise he was dressed in U.C.L. beadles' costume). 'To create the future'; I understood it perfectly but quite conceptually. Satisfying feeling that this was a noble kind of work, though no words corresponding to this came. Then this linked on to the idea of fructifying the past. There was a conceptual notion of continuity (without the word). At this point the whole thought became thoroughly clear and I answered 'Yes', with a satisfactory feeling of uplift. As I did so there was a momentary but fairly clear visual image of a woman with both arms extended. She seemed to be joining the past with the future. She wore uniform and there were men behind. (I now recognise this as derived from the poster in Aberystwyth Post Office, *It all depends on you!*

Training can greatly influence one's ability to watch what goes on in the mind. But there is also an inborn ability which varies with different individuals. Poets and dramatists, for example, have the ability to a high degree. This source of information is peculiar to man. One does not ask inanimate objects or animals how they feel or what they think; but one should ask man. However, what an individual says he is experiencing is subjective. There is no way of proving that what an individual says is going on in his mind is either true or untrue. Many people have thought that no valuable information could be obtained from introspection, because it is so subjective; they have also found some introspections so frank that they concluded it was an unwise activity.

After the Second Word War the Americans used a new approach to information from introspection. They asked many school children and students to write what they thought about themselves, and then traced trends in views on the self which varied according to age. The British followed some years later. Although the subjects of these experiments had to be able to write and so they give no information on nursery school children, we may gain insight on the kinds of information which can be elicited from younger children, if we examine the results of these experiments with older children and students.

Chown (1959) at Liverpool University, investigated what made 96 boys and 96 girls, in third to seventh forms of eight grammar schools, choose the occupations they intended to follow. She used questionnaires to find out their interests, behaviour traits and reasons for choice and their intelligence scores were available. Because she had asked them to introspect she was able to find that there was a definite connection between their spare time interests and occupations they intended to follow. This is information which we cannot afford to overlook. She found that level of intelligence had a limiting effect: those of highest intelligence made a free choice, but those of lowest intelligence tended to choose office work.

When the completed personality questionnaires were factor analysed, some interesting information emerged. Traits of confidence and sociability were independent. We tend to think of sociable people as having plenty of confidence and unsociable people as lacking confidence. But the fact that confidence is independent of sociability means that the sociable may or may not be confident; and also the retiring person may or may not be confident. Another important discovery was that the personalities and spare time interests of these children fluctuated less than is generally thought of adolescents. Chown concludes that children of this age would profit by training in assessment of self, but that some educationists think introspection is 'bad' for children.

There are signs in the 1960s that more psychologists in Britain are prepared to link introspection with empirical work. Rowlands (1961), an Australian working in London, wished to find what sort of boys are most likely to have high-level educational hopes and scientific interests. He gave a questionnaire, an attitude test, an interest test, a vocational aspiration test, and a projection test (see Chapter 14) to the entire fourth-form population of six boys' grammar schools within twenty-five miles of London, in all 654 boys of fifteen. He also gave personal interviews to 127 of the boys, but the interviews were qualitative and he sought objective quantitative data, so he did not report the interviews. The schools covered the whole social range, from independent schools at the top of the prestige scale down to maintained schools in a very industrial area. He then made a statistical analysis of the boys' replies.

He found a big gap between the number of boys who planned to go to the university from the schools most and least socially favoured. Twice as many from the socially favoured schools planned to go to university as of the socially less favoured ones. But economic status was not such an important determinant of educational aspiration as is sometimes thought. The replies indicated that cultural rather than economic factors were important. The potential scientist emerged as one who enjoys work as much as play, plans to do great things, and wants to get as much education as possible, even at the cost of effort and sacrifice. He concludes by saying that one brief careers interview is insufficient. Someone in the school should be responsible for accumulating all psychological and scholastic tests and other relevant information, to assist the growth of self-knowledge in each individual boy over a period of years.

There are some Masters Degrees summarised in the *British Journal of Educational Psychology* which report the use of introspection for obtaining data. A Masters Degree is normally expected merely to show that the postgraduate student knows how to conduct experimental work. It is not expected to produce valuable increase of knowledge. That is reserved for PhD research. From time to time summaries of MA or MSc or MEd theses are published because the results have made valuable contribution to knowledge. These are worth scrutiny, but there is another reason why it is useful to examine them. The theme of the investigation has to be accepted by the university. What concerns us now is that introspection has been accepted as a means of collecting data in experimental work by universities such as London, Manchester and Aberdeen.

Barrington (1966), for an MEd thesis at Manchester, investigated the effects of teaching elementary science by television and other methods. The point at the moment is that, in addition to a hundred-item test given three times (at the beginning and end of the five-week experiment, and four months later) he used a twenty-four item attitude test which he had constructed from work in three secondary schools using the same television science series. The attitude test finally constructed was a Likert procedure. That means that, instead of giving a two-step *Yes* or *No* answer, there was a five-step scale which allowed the boys to answer each of the twenty-four items by indicating whether they agreed with the statement very much or not at all or somewhere in between. This is a much subtler technique than just agreeing or disagreeing. By asking some 150 boys and girls to introspect about their attitudes, and linking their replies to other data from the experiment, he was able to draw some interesting conclusions about the children's attitudes. The less able children were enthusiastic about television science; but the more able the children the less they favoured television. The attitude of the children to television did not seem to affect their actual performance in the science achievement tests. These facts could not have been obtained without asking the children to introspect.

Kelley (1961), for an MA thesis at London, made an investigation of 117 boys of thirteen in an East London Grammar School. He constructed the questionnaires, which he used together with two testing programmes at the beginning and end of the experimental five months, to find out what factors influenced those who chose scientific subjects. Forty-five boys chose science, forty-three chose other subjects, and the remaining twenty-nine (who had no choice) were the control group. Those who chose science had a long-standing and stable interest in the subject, and felt it was definitely their own choice. Kelley found a considerable overlap of the choice between arts and sciences and suggests further research into social class influences, school influence and the children's ideal self.

Murdoch (1966), for an MEd thesis at Aberdeen, investigated the effect of transfer from primary to secondary school on the adjustment of 289 boys and 263 girls in Aberdeen. Three terms after the change of schools, the 552 children were asked to write half-hour essays to 'tell the story of your first few weeks in this secondary school, comparing it with your primary school. Think back and write about your feelings when you first started at this school and about your feelings now you have been here longer.' Some further directives were given to their introspection; and at the end four specific questions on adjustment were asked. Other data, including verbal reasoning ability, social class, etc., were available. Sixty per cent of the children reported some problem of adjustment; and 7 per cent, who declared that they preferred their primary school to the secondary school, were judged to have failed to regain the level of adjustment to school which they had attained before transfer. Apparently the majority made a rapid adjustment to the new school. There was a tendency for more intelligent girls to report less success in adjustment. Children in social classes I and II (see p. 229 for social classes) showed more success in adjustment to senior secondary schools than those from classes IV and V, but there was no difference between these groups in the children's adjustment to junior secondary schools.* Difficulties of adjustment were related to disapproval of changing classrooms; failure to make new friends; unpleasant treatment by older children; dislike of having several teachers instead of one; and failure to find the work more interesting than in primary school. All this information from the children themselves could be of much help to teachers who are anxious to welcome the new children into an atmosphere where learning is a pleasure.

Once children have been allowed to express their views, a number of minor adaptations of secondary routine by the class-teacher could make all the difference in helping children to adjust to secondary school. One or two children could be shown the routes to other classrooms and could take small groups along. The value of widening circles of friends could be the subject of discussions. The cooperation of older children could be won at the end of the previous year; this would counteract a great deal of school unhappiness due to older children's jealousy of the new intake. The class teacher could explain the value of specialist classrooms. And of course the disappointment of not finding secondary work more interesting then primary work is largely due to the curriculum being too abstract. Most children are not ready for much abstract work until at least the fourth form, and even then new subjects, which require new thinking, need much practical work so that strange ideas can be worked out in concrete situations (see. p. 66).

The importance of introspection in experimentation can be summarised in this way. One does not ask a lump of sugar how it feels as it melts in a hot cup of tea; but one must, where possible, ask people who are the subjects of a psychological experiment for their introspections. Introspection is peculiar to humans, and we cannot afford to lose this unique source of information. One individual introspection is subjective and qualitative; but a large enough number of introspections given under experimental conditions can be treated

---

* In the Scottish Educational System junior secondary seems to be equated with secondary modern.

statistically, and so become quantitative. It is, for instance, important to know that as many as 7 per cent (some 38 children) of the 552 children in Murdoch's experiment even after a whole year of secondary school, still regretted leaving their junior schools; also that 40 per cent (some 332 children) had had difficulty in making the adjustment. Teachers need to know the personality characteristics which may lead to such unhappiness, so as to help them to detect children likely to be in need of extra care in developing to the secondary level of education. Such information can be gained through statistical treatment of introspections. What the general public imagines 'introspection' to be is not what the educational or psychological expert means by the term.

We have already come across three references to the self. Chown (1958) thought adolescents needed help in assessing themselves objectively; Rowlands (1961) thought someone should accumulate relevant information over years to help children in self-knowledge; and Kelley (1961) thought there should be more research on the ideal self. All were concerned with adolescents and future work. Now let us see what else we can find about children's awareness of self in the literature. The information falls into three groups: first, speculation about self (largely adult and philosophical); then, indirect observation (when something else is being observed); and finally, direct scientific study of the self.

Towards the end of the nineteenth century those with a biological approach to young children, such as Darwin, Preyer, Claparède and Binet, began to take increasing interest in children's spontaneous activity. They discussed, from a philosophical and theoretical standpoint, the child's growing awareness of his *self* and its difference from what is *not self*. Early in the twentieth century McDougall (1908) published *An Introduction to Social Psychology*, in which he set out his view that there was a whole series of more than a dozen instincts born into man and other animals; and that environment encouraged these inborn impulses to focus on objects (including people) in what he called sentiments. He took the term 'sentiment' from an article in *Mind* by the psychologist Shand (1896) on character and emotions, in which he suggested that emotional dispositions centred round the idea of an object. According to McDougall by far the most important sentiment is the self-regarding sentiment. In Chapter 7 of his *Social Psychology*, he explains self-consciousness and the self-regarding sentiment. Hearnshaw (1964) describes McDougall as 'essentially theoretical'. He devotes a whole chapter to him in *A Short History of British Psychology*, which implies that his work has been important. In fact McDougall's *Social Psychology*, to his surprise, proved to be a bestseller. Up to 1928 there was at least one edition a year, sometimes three, and it was even reprinted three times during the Second World War, despite severe paper shortage. By this time some 62,000 copies had been sold. There are usually several copies in college libraries and the book is both easy and interesting to read.

But the term 'instinct' is not now used much and is mostly replaced by 'drive'. Incidentally 'drive' comes from America, where many German words are used, and is actually from 'Treib' (pronounced tribe) which is German for 'instinct'. The American *Psychological Dictionary* by English and English (1958) states that 'drive' is used in innumerable ways, often quite loosely, and gives as the most commonly used meaning: a tendency, initiated by shifts in physiological balance, to be sensitive to stimuli of a certain class and to respond in any of a variety of ways that are related to the attainment of a certain goal. This is very close to McDougall's definition of 'instinct' on p. 25 of *Social Psychology*. Certainly, some most rigorously conducted statistical investigations on factors of personality later in the twentieth century have indicated innate impulses which bear marked resemblance to McDougall's intuitive speculations about instincts and the part they play in the development of the self-regarding sentiment. As with introspection, so with instincts or drives, empirical evidence can be obtained through statistical treatment of large numbers.

The early theories about the self were followed by indirect empirical evidence. That is to say, information about the self emerged when something else, such as spontaneous activity or language development, was being studied. In the first chapter of *The Language and Thought of the Child* (1926), Piaget noted how a child often imitates without being aware of it, merely through confusion of his activity or his point of view with those of others. He refers to this in later work, for instance Piaget's *Play, Dreams and Imitation in Childhood* (1951), where he shows how carefully children can be observed. On p. 7 he gives the exact observations of a baby on the first night of birth which enabled him to conclude that the baby was crying at the sound of crying and not at any other sound. He concludes from his detailed observations that a child first floats in a 'undifferentiated absolute', in which there are no boundaries between himself and other objects or between outer and inner reality, but gradually a child makes distinctions between what is himself and what is not, thus separating himself from the external world.

Gesell and Ilg (1943), writing on the guidance of development in the home and nursery school, says 'We shall find that personality development is essentially a progressive finding of the self through reactions to, and progressive detachment from, other selves.' G. Murphy, in *Personality* (1947), writes that the process of differentiation is aided by the perceptions of the child. He perceives himself in many aspects. Through his eyes and touch he perceives the various parts of his body; through his ears he perceives the sounds he makes, and so on. Winnicott, from his extensive clinical work with very young children, says in *The Child and the Outside World* (1957), that from their earliest years children have to undertake the psychological task of building a conception of themselves as a 'self' with a relationship to reality as they begin to conceive it.

The process of separating himself from the rest of the environment is hastened by language, and a little information about the development of self has come indirectly from study of the beginnings of language. Gesell and Ilg (1943), estimate that by about 2 years a child begins to use *mine, me,* and *I*; and by 5 or 6 years he may make such statements as 'Johnny—that's me', 'I am I', 'I am a boy', 'I was a baby' and 'I grew'. Sherif and Cantril in *The Psychology of Ego Involvements* (1947), suggest that pronouns serve as conceptualisation of the self and others.

Lewis in *Language, Thought and Personality* (1963) gives a very precise account of a two-year-old which suggests that the concept of self can begin to form before the third year. Lewis's boy, K, used 'I' for the first time when he was 2 years 3 months and 2 days. His mother said, 'Smile for Mummy!' and he said 'I don't want to!' Eighteen days later he said 'I do this self'. His mother asked 'Who?' and he answered 'K'. Within the month (thanks to the mother's question), we can see that the concept of self was properly established. Six months later he could show in a complex sentence that he knew what he was doing and why. At 2 years 9 months and 2 days he was arranging his bed and said: 'I'm going to bed in a minute, 'cause I'm tired.' It is because of the precision of information on which this book bases generalisations about a phase of development on which we are still lamentably ignorant, that it is one which students would be well advised to own for reference. Lewis points out that the child moves towards the time when language may serve him as symbolising his attitude to other people, of formulating principles of conduct towards them, of symbolising and so enhancing his awareness of himself as an individual. Thus he becomes aware of the pattern of his personality as it is and as it might become—his ego and his ego ideal.

Before we move on to direct experimental investigation of the self with older children, let us clear up the term 'ego'. Ego is the Latin for 'I', myself, the person; it can be used of the inner, subjective self or of the outer self which others see. A student may feel so shy on joining a party that he is quite miserable; but to others he may appear cool and completely at ease. Symonds in *The Ego and the Self* (1951), defines the *ego* as the person which is an object and the *self* as the subject who perceives, thinks and acts. Not everyone abides by these definitions. We all appreciate the great difference between the inner and the outer person, but it is as well to notice which terms a particular writer uses for the two, in order to understand what the writer is saying. Similarly we all appreciate the difference between what we should ideally like to do or be, and how sadly we fall short of this at times; but here we are a little more fortunate as one of the terms is more precise. The ego is the person (not specifying whether inner or outer or both) and the ego ideal is what a person aspires to be. What we are at the moment searching is the development of the inner self, here called the 'self', and direct study is much simpler if the children are old enough for us to ask a class to write about themselves.

Havighurst *et al.* (1946), in America, were amongst the first to make such empirical enquiry. They tried to find out how the ideal ego evolved by asking children and adolescents to write brief essays on 'The person I would like to be'. They found, despite the difficulty of classifying some individual responses, a clear evolution from identification with a parent, through romantic and glamorous ideas, to a composite picture in late adolescence of desirable characteristics, often symbolised by a known or fictional young adult. Thus one can see that older adolescents are dependent on adults in their environment for development by identification of their ideas of self. A good example of a partial transition from the first, parental phase of identification was given by a seven-year-old girl (a relative of the author). She expressed annoyance that adults kept asking her what she was going to be. When it was suggested to her that she might think what she wanted to be, so as to have a ready answer, she paused for several minutes and then said 'I think I should like to be Mummy's *au pair* girl.' This was a partial detachment from the first phase, of identification with the parents.

Jersild's *In Search of Self* (1952), profoundly influenced American thinking about the self. Jersild pleads forcefully for help to be given to the child in understanding himself and in learning to accept himself. He quotes many authors as seeing the social origins of the self, such as Mead, Horney and Sullivan. Sullivan even claims that the self is made up of the 'reflected appraisals of other people'.

In seeking evidence, Jersild also used essays. What he sought was not the ego ideal but the ego, and he asked children to say what they thought was acceptable as well as what was unacceptable about themselves. He asked nearly 3,000 American children and students in schools and colleges to write on both 'What I like about myself' and 'What I dislike about myself'. He thought of fourteen categories under which he might classify replies and arranged them in order of psychological maturity. This did not prove very fruitful, as children of different ages were liable to refer to items in any stage of the maturity classification. However, a picture of development in thinking about the self did emerge. The younger subjects of the experiment tended to describe themselves in terms of external criteria, such as physical character- istics and clothing; but the older ones tended to describe themselves in terms of inner resources. One should perhaps remember that though the younger ones only talked about external details, they might already be conscious of inner resources though not yet ready to talk about them. Moreover, the transition of identification in the self-picture from parent to other young adult as object of admiration mentioned by Havighurst *et al.* may well be less complete than appears. Musgrove (1967) questions the current assumption that, even at student age, children have moved very far from parent identifi- cation. He asked a group of 572 Bradford students who would be most disappointed if their careers as teachers went wrong and the answers were overwhelmingly in favour of the parents. In *The Psychology of Adolescence* (1957), a subject on which many have written books, Jersild puts a new angle on personality and self-fulfilment; he points out that, when we wish to understand children, we do best if we seek to understand ourselves.

In the same year Strang published *The Adolescent Views Himself* (1957), in which she gives an account of essays set for an adolescent group. But she widened the enquiry to how they saw themselves, how others saw them, and what kind of person they would like to be. With the essay information she used information from other sources, such as autobiographies. She, too, found older adolescents much concerned with inner resources, with moral and spiritual values, which are basic to self-esteem; and the older children proved more introspective than the younger ones.

Another American publication at this time was an article by Taylor and Combs (1952) on self acceptance and adjustment. They investigated the hypothesis that better adjusted children would tolerate more criticism of themselves. They gave a personality inventory (see p. 165) to sixth grade children to measure their degree of adjustment. Then they gave a list of derogatory statements to the children and asked them to tick those true of themselves. The results supported their hypothesis: better adjusted children ticked significantly more derogatory statements as true of themselves than less well adjusted children. That better adjusted children should be better able to tolerate adverse criticism is a most interesting point to which we shall return. Phillips (1964) reports other experiments in an article on self concepts in children. It is worth noting that, of the fourteen references he gives at the end, none are from Britain and only one, by Staines, is from the British Commonwealth. Phillips himself writes from the University of the West Indies.

Staines (1958) of Australia opens up a quite new avenue of research on the self in 'The self-picture as a factor in the classroom'. He planned two experiments based on two hypotheses: (1) that teachers could be classified by the type of self-reference comment they made to individual children, for example 'Jack, you're tall. Help me with this', which values tallness, or 'You won't do for the queen—you're not tall enough', which devalues smallness; and (2) that the effect of value or devalue comments on children's self-picture could be measured. He confirmed both hypotheses in a most ingenious way.

First he found two infant and two junior teachers prepared to cooperate without knowing the purpose of the investigation. The head teachers rated the teachers as comparable for proficiency, and the classes were matched for numbers of boys and girls, age, intelligence and social class judged by their fathers' occupations. The four teachers allowed him to attend classes and to interview children at any time. All the teachers overwhelmingly made comments which stressed performance and status; and through personal interviews with individual children, he found that quite ordinary comments on success and failure by the teacher, or selection for unimportant jobs and rôles, were liable to be fraught with status implications and intense emotional content. After analysis of data, he found it possible to classify the teachers according to whether their self-reference comments aided the children in building a valuable self picture or not.

Then Staines conducted a twelve-week experiment with the two junior teachers with whom he had already worked, to see whether it was possible to detect any differences in the children's self picture when a teacher was consciously trying to help the children build a valuable idea of self. For the experimental group he chose the more popular man, 'Teacher A'; and for the control group he chose the less popular man, 'Teacher B'. Both groups of children were given a self-rating card test (see p. 166). Teacher A also rated each individual in his class for the categories on the cards; and by the time he had done this he was very familiar with many psychological terms used about the self. Then Teacher A compared how he had rated each child for each trait with how each child had rated himself for each trait. He made a note of where he and a child had given different assessments (differences of the ego and the self according to Symonds's definition); and he diagnosed which children appeared to need help in formation of a trustworthy idea of the self. Meanwhile Teacher B received no such help in diagnosing children's self problems or how to handle individual children; and as Teacher B was less popular, we may surmise that he was not helping the children towards self-respect. At the end of the twelve weeks both classes were again given the self-rating card test. When the results of the two self-rating tests were compared, all the differences were in favour of the experimental class, with Teacher A who had studied how to help individual children. The improvement in score of the experimental class over the control score was highly significant. In his conclusion Staines points out that new light had been thrown on the variables operating in the learning situation; these are now seen to be closely related to adjustment; they occur in every classroom but can be controlled by appropriate teaching methods; and they are the product of group situations as well as of individual attention.

Two investigators have followed up Staines's interesting work on fostering the development of self concepts. Zahran (1967) has written an article on 'The self-concept in the psychological guidance of adolescents'. His aim was to relate the self concept to the whole personality structure, and he used many tests some of which are discussed in Chapter 14. He suggests that self-rating alone is insufficient; to this should be added other factors, such as the kind of home and social environment. He found that information on interests was not so relevant to psychological guidance of adolescents as others had found with vocational guidance. He also found that self-acceptance had a positive correlation with acceptance both of and by others. It is an interesting thought that those who appear most intolerant with others may, underneath, be too intolerant of themselves.

The other investigation following up Staines is reported in a Manchester MEd thesis by Chadwick, 'Some effects of increasing the teachers' knowledge of their pupils' self picture' (1967). The subjects were three teachers and their three classes of children, aged 12 to 13 years, in a streamed secondary modern girls' school. The teachers were given written notes which they could discuss with the investigator. The children were given Staines's self-rating scales with an additional space for indicating that the answer was not known; also Cattell's High School Personality Questionnaire (see p. 165) and three NFER tests for English, Mathematics and Intelligence. Teachers rated the children; and three independent judges rated the teachers on self-referent remarks. The results suggested that the experimental teachers had incorporated their rôles, fostering the children's healthy self-conceptual development.

The data on the children's views of themselves does not seem so clear, but this might be because the A stream acted as controls, and A streams are encouraged to think better of themselves than B or C streams.

Phillips (1963) gave unstructured compositions to Jamaican and English students and scored them for 'The self concepts of trainee teachers in two sub-cultures'. All 326 students wrote on 'I myself: the person I am; the person others think I am, and the person I would like to be.' These three sections represented the self, the ego and the ego ideal, which Phillips calls the cognised self, the other self, and the ideal self. (This is an example of having to note what terms an investigator uses.) Analysis of what was written in the 120 English and 206 Jamaican essays showed three tendencies: (a) All the Jamaicans rated themselves significantly higher for ego and ego ideal than the English; (b) English ratings by men and women were about equal; but the Jamaican women rated themselves higher than the Jamaican men and were less self-accepting; and (c) self-ratings by mature Jamaican students were lower than the regular (younger) students.

In an article by Phillips (1964) already referred to (p. 116) many researches on the self concept are mentioned. From his wide readings Phillips suggests various possible reasons for the difference between the two subgroups in self-rating, such as awakening racial awareness and the Negroes' new pride in themselves. He quotes Hilgard on the operation of the mechanism in the self concept whereby the fundamental need to maintain or restore self-esteem can necessitate self-deception. Thus Phillips implies over-compensation for past undue subordination. He also refers to the matriarchal tendencies of the West Indies, whereby the Jamaican men and women both rate the dominant women more highly. Then he suggests that Jamaican students, having more educational opportunity than most of their fellows, will feel elated, whereas English students will compare themselves unfavourably with their fellows who attain places at a university.

This analysis of influences upon the formation of the self-concept in two subcultures is interesting. The British could add a factor which might not occur to a West Indian. This is the curious effect upon self-esteem for the British of belonging to a nation which once had an empire. The British are responsible for the matriarchy in the West Indies. Our so-called Christian forebears found slave labour more lucrative if there were no marriages, as this meant male slaves were more mobile. This is only one example of matters upon British consciences, seen in the perspective of history. Moreover, the wealth gained through slave labour was not even fairly distributed in our own country. Too few had a surplus of wealth and luxury. Then, as N. O.

Brown (1959, p. 89) suggests, instead of giving up wealth as an effective objective, the neurotic spiral of seeking more wealth to compensate for the dissatisfaction still accompanying present wealth, came into force. The welfare state was initiated to counteract this movement. But, as we shall see when we look at child guidance work with maladjusted children, just giving money to maladjusted people is not effective. Giving sufficient for material needs alone does not ease the emotional disturbance. With the vital material sufficiency must go an educational system which shares wisdom. We hope that this is now developing. It could be that the lower self-rating by the 120 English students in this small investigation was a sign of realistic acceptance of ourselves. The thought is worth consideration, since study of the self concept in others is bound to make us reappraise our own self concepts.

Before we leave the older children's views of themselves, some remarks on leisure and the adolescent, by D. Miller of the Tavistock Clinic, which appeared in *New Society* (1966), might help. He points out that all cultures have equivalent experiences with adolescents, of negativism, emotional withdrawal from adults, day dreams and so on. At no time in history have adolescents been able to manage too much leisure. As society devalues their efforts, so they retaliate with aggression that leads to subtle self-destruction. Mid-adolescence, from 14 to 17 years, says this psychiatrist, is an important period of identification, when the children can gain a firm feeling of self. To a surfeit of leisure, we might add that a surfeit of money given without understanding, cannot help anyone towards maturity.

What knowledge of the development of self have we gained so far and how can it help us to state what we require of research on the self concept of preschool children? There is Ward's authoritative 1885 statement that the self can never be left out of psychological analysis; thus any psychological analysis of preschool children must include consideration of the self. Then there is McDougall's analysis of instinctual drives and their integration through sentiments, the most powerful of which is the self-regarding sentiment. Any work with preschool children which includes reference to the self must recognise that the child's interest in himself as a person is motivated by the most potent of all concentrations of innate drives. Many authoritative psychologists in America (e.g. Havighurst, G. Murphy, Jersild, Taylor and Combs) and a few in Britain (e.g. Lewis and Winnicott) recognise the co-ordinating and integrative potentiality of the self concept.

Observation has shown that indications of the concept of self can emerge before three years. If this is true of children likely to be of high mental calibre, might it not also be true of the preschool population as a whole?

If not, when should we expect it? Careful analysis of vocabulary and sentence development is a way of finding out, since language is a way of symbolising attitudes, principles of conduct and awareness of the self, the ego and the ego ideal, as well as awareness of others. We need more data on such matters as too big a rift between the self and the ego ideal, which can compel a child to restore self-esteem by deception of himself as well as others.

Research on the self concept, first in America and now in Britain, shows that self-acceptance is a prerequisite of realistic self-criticism and development towards maturity. So far most of the work has been done with older children, by means of written introspections. It appears that adolescents need help in learning to assess themselves realistically; that teachers should learn how to keep more careful cumulative records of development; and that much more research is needed in all these areas. Information has been gained from older children which is of value to teachers and could not have been gained without asking the children to introspect. For instance, how much children like or dislike television as a medium for school learning seems to have little bearing upon how effective it is as an educational technique.

Again, children's answers show stages of development in the self concept. Preadolescents describe themselves in terms of externals and adolescents in terms of inner resources; identification goes through phases, first with parents, then with glamourised daydream people, and then with attractive young adults. But some observations suggest that untrained introspection revealed through written work may miss subtle awareness about which the child is not yet able to communicate. For instance, L. B. Murphy's child of 14 months (p. 28) could demonstrate what she wanted done, to an understanding mother before she had attained speech; and Jersild's category of traits in hierarchical order of maturity demonstrated that all ages of children indicate awarenesses, at times, of all levels of maturity. We have not yet sufficient data, or suitable techniques for finding such data, to know how aware preadolescents may be of their inner resources.

Information about the youngest children's self concept has to be obtained more indirectly, for instance, through the adult's skilled perception of the significance of stages of language development, understanding of the 'language' or symbolism of play, knowledge of the nature of early identification with parents, and ability to speak to a child in ways that foster a trustworthy self concept. The ways in which very young children can be observed can be studied in the works of such highly trained observers as Lewis (1963), Valentine (1942) and Piaget (1951), who kept records of their own children. Sampson's (1956) work with children of 18 to 30 months gives a design for genuinely scientific study of very young children. L. B. Murphy's (1962) record of children 'coping' shows how a theme for such an investigation can work like a hypothesis, with evidence to weigh up at the end. And the self concept is affected by the educationist. In our present urgent need for further data, what themes need investigation? The following suggestions include direct and indirect approaches to the self concept of very young children:

1. The self concept, from 2 to 5 years
2. Information given directly by children of 2 to 5 years.
3. Stages of behaviour indicating self awareness.
4. Adjustment and self-acceptance in play.
5. How sentiments for objects and people foster integration.
6. Stages of speech relevant to the self and others.
7. The most valuable kind of cumulative records for very young children.
8. Indications of understanding which precedes ability to communicate.
9. The background to babbling.
10. Identification with parents.
11. What stimulates aggression and self-assertion.
12. Stages of awareness of other children's rights.
13. Talking to oneself aged 3 to 5 years.
14. The teacher's self concept.

Part 4
Infant school age: 5 to 8 years

12. General development
5 to 8 years

There is a curious gap in our psychological knowledge of children from 5 to 8 years. The nursery school stage is enchanting to watch, and still spontaneous when questioned; the children of 7+ are accustomed to school and to school techniques of being questioned. So an odd position has evolved, in which some of our best empirical educational experiments have been going on in an area where we actually know least about the children. Educational writers are good on how to teach the children, as we shall see when we come to study reading; but references swing between the nursery stage and the gang stage, as if nobody was quite sure how the transition of development happened. Gabriel, in *Children Growing Up: the development of children's personalities* (1964), assembles what he can on the 5 to 7 year children and is forced to such generalities from Gesell and others as that at 5 children are more conforming, at 6 more petulant and at 7 more preoccupied (p. 189).

According to the Plowden Report (1967) the age of children at entry to 'infant' schools is more often 4 than 5 years. In the Plowden survey 66 per cent entered at 4 and 34 per cent at 5 years of age; and more than a quarter of them went into classes of over forty children. It is little wonder that appreciation of differences between individuals has tended to become submerged. From medical sources we have information on physical growth. Whereas in the first two years a child grows about 14 or 15 inches in height, in the third to sixth year he only grows 9 or 10 inches, that is, grows less in twice the time. Consequently, a loss of appetite need not cause anxiety to parents, as less food is required. The legs now grow rapidly and are 44 per cent of the adult length. The head is almost adult size, and as the legs grow, the topheavy appearance is lost. We have been mistaken in assuming that the great majority of children are toilet trained by five, and the Plowden Report recommends further research here. Teachers in infant schools should be well aware of the advice on attitudes to toilet training recommended by Burt and Isaacs (see p. 52). Towards the end of the infant school the children lose their baby teeth, a matter of great concern to them, which incidentally affects their speech for a while.

Muscular coordination improves rapidly, and the children can begin to run lightly on their toes, skip, dance to music, climb and walk with ease. However, under emotional stress all these movements regress. If you go round the district just before nine o'clock on the first day of term, the newcomers to school can be picked out by the way they cling to their mothers, take tiny steps, often with toes turned in, and watch the experienced children of 5 and 6 skipping, dancing, shouting happily. If you are near enough you can see the pupils of the eyes of the newcomers enlarged with anxiety, to which every reception class teacher should be most sensitive. Undoubtedly, part of the freer movement of those who have been to school is due to physical and musical education; but the dilated pupils of the newcomers indicate a glandular disturbance which inhibits movements.

Another physical change by school age is in the voice. The high piping of an earlier stage has gone, and the voice becomes resonant and precise. Because language development is now recognised as very important, detailed information is becoming available. Many children of 5 still have difficulty in perceiving the differences between, and therefore in mastering, s, f, and th. The approximation to a vocabulary nearing a thousand words is very crude, and there are extremely wide individual differences, due both to inheritance and to differences in degree of environmental stimulus. It is not easy for the busy teacher to foster confident speech in a somewhat non-verbal child who is quite overwhelmed by the gay chatter everywhere. Such children tend to withdraw and be overlooked. Another physical change is that the babyish cheek pads go, and faces begin to become more individual, forecasting adult facial expression. The way to see the range of facial expression now possible is to make a ciné-film, the camera man lying on the floor and filming upwards as children are busy with some problem. Our somewhat overlooked group of 5 to 8 years is now too big to pick up, but not tall enough for adults to study their faces easily as they bend over tasks.

Emotionally, the children are usually past the temper tantrum outbursts—at least at school. Regression to earlier phases is more likely to be seen in play, when a child will lie down with a teddy and explain that 'Teddy wants to be cuddled'. But during these transition years a curious change takes place in play. Gradually, as play sorts out more and more conflicts, the children become more aware of symbolism. They can no longer project their feeling in total unawareness of the projections actually being a part of themselves. Thus there is a move towards greater reality and play comes nearer to true drama. Performances are put on by groups and audiences are required. Gardner and Cass (1965) give some good examples of how the teacher herself spares time to be the audience or gets other children to be the audience, or is even audience to one child. This need for someone to witness the projection, as an audience, is part of the children's move to sharing, in drama, both conflicts and their resolution. In fact, identifications are shared. Much that could not be observed through asking questions, as the children begin to conform to the behaviour of other children, can be seen in play and dramatic activities, provided the teacher has some insight. Baird (1968), for an MEd thesis at Manchester, studied the rôle of the teacher with top infants in ten schools, and found the teachers gave priority to intellectual, then emotional, then social and lastly disciplinary development. Teachers will have to receive more intensive training in social attitudes, if society is to maintain control of its own development—now urgently necessary.

New ways of behaving are also being learned. Maturation is now not so important in social development. A child loves stories and wants to read. He knows how you hold a book and goes to the book corner. He practises holding the book, looking at the pictures and turning pages. Two points are important here: (a) he has to learn to turn the page by the outer edge instead of the inner, 'hinge' edge; and (b) the perception of pictures requires practice (we shall refer to this again). Many skills are now learned, independent of maturation; for instance, the practical achievements of mastering pencil and paint in pictures and writing patterns. Materials, such as wood, nails and string are now put to some purpose. Children learn many techniques from watching each other, and the teacher learns much about their capabilities by watching them.

We have learned something of their intellectual abilities from Piaget (see chapter 6). They are going through the change from pre-concept (2 to 4 years) to concrete operations and reasoning (7 to 11 years); the changeover takes about four years (4 to 7 years). Thus the infant school child is still perception-dominated, still dominated by what things look like from where he stands. But increasingly he has intuitive gleams of a later thought stage, when he will be able to reason, provided he has had the concrete problem before him. In *The Backward Child* (1937), Burt reports research which shows that a normal child of 7 years can carry out all forms of reasoning, provided the problem is sufficiently simple and clear. Reasoning depends essentially on the power to perceive logical relations, and to relate these relations in their turn, so that they form a coherent whole—a single consecutive argument, valid, consistent and conclusive. The kind of studies which will later be selected for these 'infant' children will depend very largely on their powers of reasoning. At least 10 per cent of children in infant schools are able to reason well before they reach the junior school, in practical situations; and as many will be unable to do so, after a year or more in the junior school. Therefore many infant school heads make an objective assessment of reasoning powers at the end of each final year, in order to forewarn junior departments of what to expect of individual children.

In *The Moral Judgment of the Child* (1932), Piaget reports two experiments, which set an example of how to find out children's level of thinking. He played many games of marbles and broke the rules himself. He found that below the age of 7 years children regard rules as absolute, sacrosanct; to the children rules are moral dictates, infringement of which will result in dire punishment. So the infant school children have not yet fully worked through the much earlier stage of placating adults, trying to do exactly what adults say, in order to win as much as possible of their own demands. Piaget also told many children a story in which a boy told a lie to his mother. He found that the younger children were much harsher in punishment, much more intolerant. Thus, most children are unable to see that rules are no more than arranged conventions and that errors such as lying could be forgiven, until the very end of the infant school.

One tends to think of children of 6 to 7 years as toughening up for the rigours of junior school life. Lee (1957) carried out in Devon an investigation of the effect of journeys to school in a rural area, which reminds us that the process of getting to school may be quite a tax on the emotional and physical development of such young children in an area where the population is sparse. Teachers in fifty-seven rural primary schools of Devon assessed 883 children on ten personality traits. Comparisons were then made between children who came to school by (*a*) a short walk, (*b*) a long walk, (*c*) short transport, and (*d*) long transport journeys. The results showed that for approximately equal times, transport journeys were associated with poorer adjustment than walking journeys. The boys showed poorer adjustment than the girls, and greater differences according to the length of journey. This apparent effect lessens with age in respect of walking, but not of transport journeys. Lee discusses this evidence in relation to fatigue and maternal separation and family circumstances such as isolated farms, child rearing patterns, etc. He comes to the conclusion that the most important factor is the prolonged separation from the mother. He recommends that this separation which is longer both in time and in distance, is crucial with such young children, from the child's perception of the accessibility of the mother. Further investigation might well show that the damage to ability to adjust may have been done in the previous year, when schooling started; but it might also show ways in which this handicap could be overcome.

Susan Isaacs has some interesting comments to make on aggression and social development, at the infant school stage, in *The Children We Teach* (1932) p. 92–7. From her own school she notes that, many times, a band of children under 8 formed, with someone shut out. 'Shall we bury Tommy in our castle?', 'Shall we kill Bobbie?' 'Shut John out ...' etc. The technique frequently used by the shut-out child was to project his social ostracism onto another child outside the group. A girl in the group said, 'Dan doesn't know what he is talking about.' Dan stamped his foot and said, 'Yes, I *do*. But I'll tell you who does not know what he's talking about. *Mark* does not.' This kind of social development lags behind individual development. As we guide children of 5 to 8 years towards the social living which they so urgently desire, we have to recognise that the strains of social living constantly cause a re-gression from the attained behaviour of an individual on his own or with adults. Those within a group get on so well for a time because they have temporarily rid themselves of hate and aggression by accusing 'outsiders' of these unacceptable traits. The ostracised child seeks to work his way back to acceptance by the group through displacing the group's projection onto someone else. This is the technique of the individual toddler who says 'I did not make that puddle, Teddy did it.' Individual and social development should be seen as a fugue, with group development following after individual development, through the same sequences. First the individuals and then the group have to experience self-acceptance before acceptance of others can lead to genuine tolerance.

Children in infant schools have seen through the projections of the toddler stage as individuals and are most anxious to conform. If we, so to speak, trade on this growing desire to conform we run the serious risk of allowing them to repress all individuality instead of helping them to resolve their problems. The area most in need of understanding guidance is that of social develop-ment, but we cannot even pretend to do this well until far more is known of the developing personalities of infant school children.

13. Speech and reading development 5 to 8 years

There is as yet very little precise information on how language develops throughout the infant school years. One aspect of intelligence tests, to which we shall come later, assesses verbal ability objectively, relating a child's knowledge of words to the level of words known by most children of the same age throughout the country. But here the child is asked to define certain words and no attempt is made to find out how many other words a child happens to know. Attainment tests, which assess how well a child learns what he has been taught, are concerned with reading ability rather than knowledge of language. The problem of finding out how many words a child at this stage knows is formidable since some vocabularies run into many hundreds, even thousands. The solution lies in the direction of Tamplin's samples. One can take samples of children covering all socio-economic levels; or samples of circumstances, such as free play and unscripted drama; or particular kinds of directive questioning, and so on.

D. E. M. Gardner, in *Experiment and Tradition in Primary Schools* (1966, pp. 125–35), describes in detail certain standard procedures for assessing language development. Six oral language tests were constructed and given individually. Although these were used, not for language development as a whole but to compare the effect upon vocabulary of formal and informal education, similar tests could be designed for more general application. It just happened that none of the children in her group came from less favoured home backgrounds. Incidentally the two types of educational system, formal and progressive, produced no significant difference in effect upon vocabulary. This is not surprising for a number of reasons. Not only was the period 5 to 7 years very brief; but the tests were given to six-year-olds (thus subtracting a school year) and owing to date of birth (see p. 279) the first two terms may be missed (thus subtracting almost another year). Thus insufficient time was allowed for effects, if any, to be noticed.

Evidence submitted to the Plowden Committee led them to conclude that poverty of language is a major cause of poor school achievement, and that attempts to offset poverty of language are best made as early as possible (vol. 1, p. 302). The reader is referred to data from Appendix 10 (vol. 2), which is a first report of the National Child Development Study. This is a report on all children (singletons) born in England between 3 and 9 March 1958, as far as August 1965 when they were just under $7\frac{1}{2}$ years of age. It is disappointing that there is no original approach to language development here, as the follow-up studies of this group could have been most revealing. There is a table of teachers' rating of oral ability and there is a longish section on reading; but of course oral facility, speaking with ease, does not cover the wider aspects of verbal ability, which embrace the capacity for understanding and dealing with verbal material; and children with quite outstanding verbal ability sometimes have very great difficulty in learning to read and therefore lose their confidence over reading and spelling to such an extent that their verbal ability is overlooked.

Since the present classroom situation concerning language is that attention has been mainly directed to reading, let us get learning to read in some historical perspective. Written language is a secondary symbolisation of the symbolisation of words; and this double symbolisation has over many centuries caused children great suffering. But man built fortifications, palaces, temples, even the first pyramids, before the alphabet was invented; he record-ed harvests and crops by scoring rocks, told such epics as the pre-Babylonion *Gilgamesh*, and painted exquisite pictures. It would be wrong to think there is no cultural achievement without literacy.

When we come to examine the pictures made by man, we find evidence of various stages of development, culminating in the first alphabet, with the first letter a bull's head. But the concept of alphabet development belongs to archaeologists. If you threw a girdle anywhere round the world today, you would probably find along that line—even today—every stage in the de-velopment of writing from no pictures to the alphabet. If we follow the stages which archaeologists have traced, this may help us in our work with children. First we have to notice that it is a history of writing rather than reading. According to Diringer (1962), who is one of the world's greatest authorities on writing, there was a very long period before about 20,000 years ago, when men certainly had language; that is to say a long period of verbal symbolism in thinking before writing. Then come the following stages:

1. *Embryo writing.* The now familiar paintings and drawings on the caves of southern France, Spain and Africa are examples of embryo writing. They are

schematic figures of animals, geometric patterns and crude objects. Some go back 20,000 years B.C. They are believed to be sympathetic magic, such as ritual gestures to ensure good hunting.

2. *Pictography.* These are a sequence of pictures, called pictograms, which tell a simple narrative. They have been found all round the Mediterranean, and also in America, central Africa, south-east Asia, China and Siberia. These sequences of pictures seem to have been as spontaneous to man as speech, and to have occurred to him wherever he was labouring to stabilise tradition. The stages are not clearcut but follow in graduated succession, for example Wober (1968) reports a stage between embryo writing and pictography: an illiterate African saw three sizes of bird in one picture as the same bird in three different positions.

3. *Ideographic writing.* To the inexperienced these seem like highly developed pictography. But scholars have found them to be very much more. The pictures are used in such a way that they convey abstractions, multiple associations and other subtleties. A simple circle may be the sun, but it can also be an ideograph for heat, light, the sun-god or day. A part of an animal may mean the part, or the whole animal, or animals of that kind. Ideographic writing, with remarkably similar symbols, has been found in all sorts of places, some of them with no apparent cultural link. It appears to be a natural next step in the struggle to make tradition more permanent.

4. *Analytical transitional script.* This is an ugly name for a most interesting stage. At first sight it seems like the previous step, ideographic writing. But again scholars find an entirely new element is added. The ideogram is combined with a phonetic element. The basic units are *words*. This transitional stage is found all over the ancient Near East and appears to have lasted some 3,000 years.

5. *Phonetic script.* This is the graphic counterpart of speech. Each element corresponds to a sound in a language. Phonetic script represents a direct and inseparable relationship between written and spoken language. In order to read phonetic script the reader has to know the language in which it is written. The single signs in phonetic writing may be of any shape and there may be no connection between the external form of the symbol chosen and the sound represented. There are two branches of phonetic script:

(a) *Syllabic script.* In syllabic phonetic script the smallest unit of subdivision is one syllable. This also seems to have arisen at various times in many parts of the world. Much of it retained the ideograms, the abstractions and multiple associations, etc. of the earlier stage. As a form of writing it was far more flexible and exact, and far less cumbersome than ideograms. The trouble came when a syllable had more than one or two consonants. For instance, from our own language, *family* is easy: fa-mi-ly; but *strength* is very difficult: se-te-re-ne-ge-the. The situation became worse with foreign names containing new sounds to be spelt. Although syllabaries, as they are called, are a step forward because of the phonetic element, the total number of syllables involved is very large.

(b) *Alphabetic writing.* This is the most extensive, intricate and interesting system of writing ever invented. It is now nearly universal with civilized people, passing from language to language with minimum difficulty. Scholars are almost certain that alphabetic writing had its origin at a single point in history, probably in Palestine or Syria, and probably towards the middle of the second millennium B.C. Diringer (1962) says that the invention of the alphabet required 'great intelligence (indeed genius)' and that the man or men who invented it was or were acquainted with most of the scripts current in the eastern Mediterranean at that time.

Thus we have pursued a course in the symbol of language which we would not now dream of doing with the more recently developed symbols of science. For over 2,000 years we have endeavoured to introduce children to reading by means of the highest abstraction of a genius. We would not, for instance, introduce young children to science by means of the completely logical system of signs used for electrical engineering. The only explanation is that we have been caught up in an archaic web of tradition from which we are now struggling to free ourselves by means of research findings about how people do actually learn to read. Now that archaeologists and historians have been able to piece together the sequence of ways in which mankind has recorded events, culminating in alphabetic writing, let us examine the spontaneous ways in which children record events of importance to them. We will look at progressive education, although many still formal schools are gradually introducing ideas evolved in progressive education:

6. *Patterns.* Alongside the history of writing as evolved by mankind there has been a development of rhythmic pattern-making, sometimes so intricate as to be severely obsessional. It is to be found on pots and weapons and on ritual clothing still to be seen in surviving pictures. Figure 15 shows the patterns extended even to the dressing of beards.

1. Today children have many experiences of great interest and importance to them. We are fortunate in that the official policy, laid down in the Plowden Report (1967), is that primary education as a whole should work through such child-generated interests.

Figure 15. Pre-camera drawings of archaeological finds by Botta, 1850. Ceremonial dress. Seventh century B.C.

Source: Botta, *Discoveries at Nineveh*, 1850.

2. From nursery school onwards, children working in creative activity want to paint pictures of what has aroused their interest. We cannot always interpret them and the children frequently cannot explain them (see Figure 16).

3. (a) *Embryo-writing.* Round about 3 and 4 years children frequently produce hitherto inexplicable geometric patterns and crude objects and figures of animals. Desmond Morris in *The Naked Ape* (1968) gives a good account of the evolution of these signs in children's spontaneous 'writings' and says that apes which can draw are unable to reach children's level of sign-writing.

(b) *Pictography.* Children have difficulty in seeing that a character on one page of a story book is the same character as that appearing on the next page. In *Books Before Five* (1954) White, a librarian, has published a diary of her daughter. She describes how it took many months for the child to see that the different pages of a tale contained *different* pictures of the *same* character. Children's early absorption with comic strips for many years may be due to

Figure 16. What children scribble
Source: Kellogg (1955).

mental processes associated with juxtaposition of events, and with the ease of dream-sequences.

(*c*) *Ideographic writing.* We have long used a form of ideographic writing, much enjoyed by children, in the keeping of weather charts: umbrella for rain, snowman for snow, etc. Many schools let the children keep individual records, with any sign they like for today's weather, and class records, with standard signs for all to interpret. This would bridge the gap between pictography and ideography, children adopting the standard signs in individual records as they saw their value. This idea could be developed in other ways, feeding birds (what foods they prefer to take from the bird tray), weighing objects ($<$ and $>$ with two objects), and stories: e.g. 'Tim (outline of boy) went out for a walk. He had no coat because (sign for sun). Soon clouds came (sign for cloud) so he ran home (outline of boy running) to get an (sign of umbrella).' A four-frame comic strip.

4. *Analytical transitional script.* Here we get our first hint of phonics. But note: the first hint of phonics was a stage that lasted 3,000 years. This is where we begin to put these look-and-say words which happen to be phonic in juxtaposition. In a moment we will show how this can be done in writing patterns.

5. (*a*) *Phonic syllabic script.* We have reacted so violently from the endless lists of syllables in ancient readers that we have tended to overlook this phase. Children's love of making their own rhymes and jingles and nonsense syllables comes in here. Chukovsky, a distinguished Russian poet, has collected children's spontaneous rhymes over many years. In *From Two to Five* (Eng. tr. 1963), he describes the unerring accuracy with which children rhyme, often surpassing the less good adult poets. We should try to produce poetry for this stage which is of better rhyming quality than that of pantomimes and annuals. Probably more play with words would also help. Here again, writing patterns can aid this stage.

(*b*) *Alphabetic writing.* This is, as Diringer says, the 'most intricate and interesting system'. We should let it dawn on children who are ready for it and then guide them individually or in small groups.

The love of pattern-making is a force which can help us in the progress to writing. Cizek, in Vienna, a most unconventional teacher, used it. Somehow his pattern-making reached the adult art classes of the East End of London, and at the turn of the century it began to be used in schools. Marion Richardson (1935) H.M.I., published a series of books showing how these could be used for learning to write. Next, C. Stone and Fairbank (1957) used it for italic writing. Then Obrist and Pickard (1967) showed how it could be used, amongst other things, for introduction of phonics. At a certain stage, alternate rows can be repetition of words such as *did, did, did*. Soon one or two children begin to notice. The rhythmic patterns are so much enjoyed by the children, that they can be used to aid the teacher in discovering which children are becoming alphabet conscious. You decide, for instance, to make one word-row *tap, tap, tap* ... and the next word-row *top, top, top* ... That day you 'happen' to have printed labels displayed by a tap and a top. Some child may notice even before the writing pattern time. Like all good insights, the discovery feels like a joke, a genuine *Aha!* experience (see pp. 183–4).

The evolution of children's writing bears some interesting resemblances to mankind's development towards writing. The geometric patterns of embryo writing are frequently spontaneously produced by children of about 3 and 4 years. Some work on phosphenes, the bright lights and patterns which enter the field of vision when pressure is put on the eyeball, suggests a possible connection between embryowriting and children's similar patterns. Scientists have investigated phosphenes for over a century. They can be produced by certain drugs, surgical stimulation of the visual cortex of the brain, and by application of electrodes to the temple. Little is known of their cause, but the present assumption is that they are due to preformed neurone networks in the visual system. When subjects sketch the patterns they see, they appear to be abstract patterns, mostly geometric in form. Knoll and Kugler (1959) published in *Nature* patterns, drawn by twenty-four adults, of arcs, stars, lines, dots, etc., which they said they saw with electrical stimulus of the cortex. The following year they published in the same journal an account of 520 drawings of phosphenes by 313 adults. They were able to group them into fifteen types, which can be seen in Figure 17. They linked this work with that of Kellogg whose book *What Children Scribble and Why* (1955) is based on 300,000 spontaneous drawings by preschool children of many races and nationalities in a Californian nursery school. She found twenty basic scribbles (see Figure 20), and 90 per cent of them were similar to the fifteen basic phosphene patterns in Figure 17. In an article by Kellogg, Knoll and Kugler (1965), the authors suggest a link between such 'outlines in geometric style' to be seen in drawings by young children and by neolithic man. They point out that there is a limited number of patterns, both in the children's drawings and in the neolithic rock drawings. We should bear in mind the possibility that, when children later learn to identify alphabetic letters, we may not be teaching the patterns; these may be built in to the visual cortex. We may be doing no more than teaching them the somewhat arbitrary selection of which known shapes shall be linked with which known sounds. In Parrot's *Sumer* (1960) there is a series of diagrammatic, schematised

In the February 1970 *Scientific American* there is a report of current research on phosphenes in New York which gives support to the hypothesis put forward here that we do not teach children the patterns of the alphabet (which are largely built in) but only the generally accepted conventions for which pattern shall represent which sound. Gerald Oster is now working with people who have gone blind, artificially stimulating their phosphenes with intent to teach them a phosphene alphabet through which they might read. Since these people have at some time had sight and probably seen print, the phosphene alphabet of which he writes ought perhaps to resemble our present alphabet as nearly as possible. The article is well worth reading.

Figure 17. Some interesting work on phosphenes.
Source: Kellogg, Knoll & Kugler (1965).

pictographs. Figure 18 shows some of them. They have marked resemblance to phosphenes, either basic or combined. Such pictographs evolved to a stage when they were set out in a sequence of frames. In Diringer's *Writing* (1962)

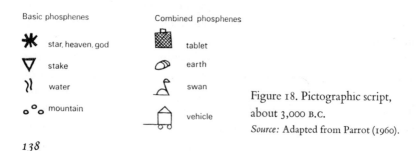

Figure 18. Pictographic script, about 3,000 B.C.
Source: Adapted from Parrot (1960).

there are various examples which have to be 'read' like a comic strip; one can be seen in Figure 19, on which the drawings have become too schematic to be classed as pictures.

Figure 19. Sumerian tablet.
Pictographic script, late fourth
millennium B.C.
Source: Diringer (1962).

In *What Children Scribble and Why* Kellogg gives a chart of the evolution of children's drawings, compiled from 300,000 nursery school drawings. Figure 20 shows this. Such evidence of the spontaneous developments of the young human mind needs much systematic research in connection with children's approach to alphabetic reading. We also need to study attitudes to reading which enable children to absorb the principle of alphabetic reading with such ease that they soon leave it behind and return to reading by word recognition, as all book-loving adults read. In compiling reading material, whether for publication or the equally important personal, home-made class-books and wall stories, we need more factual information on the lines of Burroughs's (1957) investigation of words used by children about to learn to read. The children in his research used words such as *backwards*, *blanc-mange*, *caterpillar* and *eiderdown*, all lengthy and far from phonetic. Children will learn a percentage of such words, because they are about experiences which matter to them; also because recognition of the pattern of a whole word, like ideographic writing, is a step in the natural development of mankind towards alphabetic reading. Once a child begins to notice that some letters make the same sound wherever they are in a word, a laborious process of decoding and encoding begins. This requires much practice. When we turn to the special problems of children with reading difficulty in Chapter 18 we shall find that word length is of importance. But there is almost no research on this.

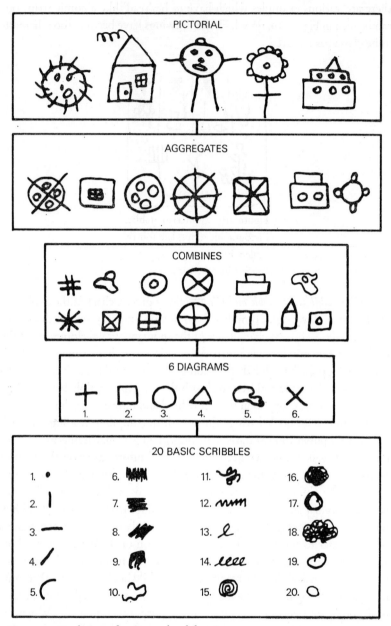

Figure 20. Evolution of nursery school drawing.
Source: Kellogg (1955).

When developing a scheme in *Time for Reading* (1967), Obrist and Pickard made a novel approach to information on length of words. The scheme was evolved in the normal way, based on the interests of present day children, for instance *aeroplanes, concrete mixers,* and the *underground;* and the vocabulary was controlled. The assumption was that it would be used in conjunction with a teacher's personal scheme evolved from the special interests of a particular class. The class teacher's scheme also requires control of vocabulary. This is the only way to ensure that there is sufficient repetition of new words; and also to ensure that not too high a percentage of interesting but very lengthy words is used. *Time for Reading* was based on such researches as are available; but there is little information yet about the best percentages for either repetition or word length in starting reading. There was a total of 17,000 words, 90 per cent repetition, in this scheme; but no record was kept of percentages of the various word lengths.

When the scheme was in proof stage the thirty sections of books, workbooks, cards and games were analysed by the Atlas Computer at the Cambridge University Literary and Linguistic Computer Centre. From the results a series of graphs was drawn, showing speed of introduction of new words and so on. One graph showed length of words throughout the scheme and the highest percentages were for words of four to six letters. In order to compare this with a normal adult reading vocabulary a graph was compiled from West's *A General Service List of English Words* (1964). Figure 21 shows both the word lengths of the 17,000 word scheme and the word lengths in an average adult reading vocabulary. Here we can see that the highest percentage of word length for the adults is also for words of four to six letters. But there are even higher percentages of these lengths of words in this reading scheme than the average reader meets. This is because beginners need much practice with medium-sized words.

Another difference to be seen in Figure 21 is that the adult graph extends considerably to the right showing that there are far more long words, from seven-letter words onwards, in adult reading matter. Only further research will show whether the assumption in this scheme is correct: that children learning to encode and decode the alphabet need much practice but should not be burdened with too many long words. In any case, it seems probable that the interesting long words are merely 'jumped at' look-and-say.

We also need experimental data on how many or how few repetitions are necessary with words which can be learned quickly, such as *ice-cream.* Incidentally, ice-cream vendors use Pavlov's technique (see p. 181) causing salivation by means of a bell, thus inducing classical conditioning in those who

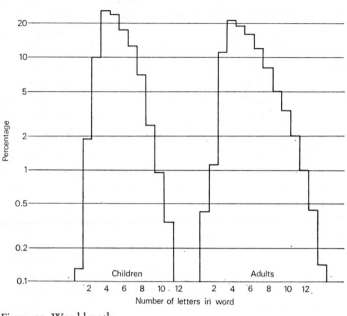

Figure 21. Word length.
Source: Obrist and Pickard (1967).

like and buy ice-cream after hearing a bell. One of our crudest errors seems to have been to think that rewards in the classroom have to be stars, prizes, position of seat, and so on. The child's need for acceptance by the group (including the teacher) is so subtle and pressing that a glance of appreciation and understanding far surpasses any of the tangible prizes. At least this is how it appears to sensitive teachers. Precise factual information here would be a great asset in the process of helping a child to think of himself as an interested reader. The first step for further research is clear definition of terms and this has now been done in an article by Southgate (1968) on 'Formulae for beginning reading tuition'. She suggests a formula for assessing reading success in any particular school which should add considerably to objectivity. This formula covers reading drive and teacher's competence as well as factors such as materials and procedure.

When children become 'alphabet-ready', they do not learn the alphabet *a* to *z*. Their attention may, for example, be caught by a letter such as *s* at the beginning of two different words they know. With help, they can see that *sit* and *sing* begin with the same sound as well. It is an individual discovery. Attention can be drawn to similar words which are phonic through words first learned look-and-say. It may be that children's love of rhyme should be classed as a form of 'syllabic interest'. There may be a syllabic enjoyment in the first very simple phonic dictation exercises. There are rarely more than four or five children ready for this at the same time. When experiments are done in such simple dictation the following points deserve consideration.

(1) *Aids to concentration*, e.g. time not exceeding five minutes, nothing to distract on tables, children with back to class (which leaves the teacher facing the others, who are self-employed). (2) *Aids to synthesis of letter and sound*, e.g. all watch as word said once, all repeat word, all watch as word is said again, all write without speaking. (3) *Understanding* (*a*) children tick words correctly spelt as teacher writes and spells each word out *and ignore failures*; (*b*) teacher keeps register of sounds or letters known by each child and gives a little further practice where sounds or letters have not been grasped, so that both children and teacher know what is known. Because children enjoy exercising any new skill, such activity can give great pleasure.

Quite a lot of research has been done into normal reading in the last decade. Let us see how relevant it is to the classroom. Since visual perception is involved, a study of this is essential. We are fortunate in having an almost popular Pelican book, *The Psychology of Perception* (1962) by M. D. Vernon of Reading, an outstanding authority on visual perception. It deals with how children learn to perceive, how adults perceive, and perception of special types of material, including reading. It is a background book which will make coherence of other kinds of books on reading. M. D. Vernon (1960) has also written an article on the development of perception in children which leads up to the problems of reading and number work. She begins by saying how hard it is for adults to understand the different way in which children perceive; then she traces, step by step, through the years, many kinds of perception. On visual perception, she shows the ages at which children can copy certain shapes, and concludes that until 6 or 7 years a child cannot perceive the relevant parts of a complex figure, as this requires understanding as well as visual perception. Learning involves more than visual perception. The child has to be involved and seek to understand. She says there is evidence that just giving children practice with visual shapes does not help them to read. When they are ready to understand reading they can adequately recognise the required shapes. Tracing language development she shows the importance of how a child is brought up. On the whole middle-class families encourage better articulation and language structure. Bernstein (1958) has shown how working class families make short, crude and obvious statements about immediate situations and feelings. Pringle and Sutcliffe (1960) have shown how handicapped in language institutional children are, through lack of individual contact with adults. When a class is approaching reading, individual differences of both intellectual gifts and social class have to be borne in mind, as a common fund of reading and number experience gives meaning to what is learned. M. D. Vernon (1960) opens her article by saying that despite much research the problems of learning to read are very imperfectly understood.

We suspect that the language development of children starting to read is a significant factor in reading success; but there is very little scientific evidence of this so far. The longitudinal study of speech and language development begun in 1956 (see p. 59) was reported again by Sampson (1959) when the same twenty-five boys and twenty-five girls had reached the age of 5 years. They were given tests of intelligence, vocabulary and language, mostly at school. Every child had made progress and the amount of this progress appeared to be related to both his family's occupational status and his own general intelligence. Correlations between the earlier and later rating, in 1956 and 1959, were positive but somewhat low. That is to say, one could not have made a very reliable prediction about future development from the tests at 18 to 30 months. There was some indication at 5 years that the boys were superior in precision and the girls in fluency of expression, but the sex differences were small. Descoeudres (see p. 58) had also noticed a connection between the developmental picture and the occupational status of the fathers and had attributed this to the material conditions of the home. But Sampson found a significant correlation between intelligence, and speech and language development; so she suggests that the environmental factor in the home is the intellectual rather than the material level. This is supported by the work of others, for example, Bernstein (1958), Lovell *et al.* (1964).

An interesting attempt has been made by Bruce (1964) of Cambridge to find out what is involved in understanding the principles upon which the alphabet is based. He took the first 500 words in the vocabulary which Burroughs (1957) of Birmingham had compiled, consisting of words known by the group of children about to begin learning to read at $6\frac{1}{2}$ years (see p. 59); and Bruce worked with a group of sixty-seven children in three Cambridgeshire infant schools with mental age 5+ to 9+. He found four barriers to be surmounted before alphabetic reading was properly established: (1) *words* and *sounds* had to be separated, as exclusive categories; (2) the children had to grasp what analysis was, in order to analyse the words to letters, (3) they had to be able to perceive the position of letters, and (4) to perceive the word sound as a whole. From an ingenious experiment, he found that a mental age of 7+ was necessary for the children to cover these four steps, and even at mental age 9+ they were not entirely sure of the last three steps. Further research will show whether, for most children, the process normally takes as long as this or not.

An investigation by Potts (1960) for an MEd thesis at Manchester will show the kind of problem met when scientific tests are applied to such a complex matter as reading. He made a factorial study of the relationship between the child's vocabulary and his reading progress at the infants' stage. He used 107 boys and 90 girls from eight infants' schools and did the statistical analysis with results from the following:

Chronological Age.
The Burt–Vernon Word Reading Test.
A Pictorial Test of Visual Discrimination.
The Moray House Picture Intelligence Test (Mental Age).
Net School Attendance.
The Schonell Silent Reading Test A.
A Test of Phonic Ability.
Social and Cultural Environment Rating.

But there was variation between schools as to when phonics were introduced and the Burt–Vernon test appears to favour children with considerable phonic skill. The fact that a child can read phonically does not necessarily mean that he can understand what he reads. All that Potts could conclude, on the basis of his statistical analysis, was that reading attainment and vocabulary extent are two different manifestations of general mental ability, which may or may not influence each other.

Sometimes cultural conditions provide interesting situations which one would not ethically be justified in imposing on children for scientific purposes. Tensuan and Davis reported such a case in 'The psychology of beginning reading: an experiment with two methods' (1965) from the Philippines. Philipino has logical spelling, and English, taught as a foreign language when school starts at 7 years, does not. In the area chosen for the experiment, the children in Grade I are taught to read the logically spelt Philipino by phonic, and the illogically spelt English by a variety of approaches. It has long been assumed that phonics was the best approach to Philipino and the aim of the experiment was to test this by using mixed approach for some Philipino classes. Ten elementary schools in different sections of Pasay City participated, each with at least one class using phonics and one using mixed approach. The study was longitudinal, covering the progress of children through the first three grades, and reading was judged by comprehension at the final stage. All began reading at 7 years. There were 1,050 children being taught phonics and 800 being taught by mixed approach; and they kept to the same groups for the three years. The results showed that: (*a*) teaching Philipino by mixed approach yields better results than direct phonic drill; (*b*) teaching by mixed approach is more helpful to English reading. Thus even the logically spelt Philipino is best learned by mixed approach; and even when Philipino is taught by phonic drill this makes no phonic-practice contribution to the foreign English. This would certainly seem to support Bruce's (1964) findings, published while the Philipino experiment was in progress, that children need a mental age of 7+ to make the necessary analysis involved in phonic reading, and particularly that phonic work is not entirely secure by mental age 9+ years. It certainly looks as if the Philipinos are making a wise move in delaying phonics until after 7 years.

The Philippine authorities went very carefully into the question of adopting the initial teaching alphabet (i.t.a.), the logical English alphabetical system initiated by Pitman. But, as we can see now, this is not a method of teaching reading. It is a way of making the alphabet more logical and is not directly concerned with research on when a child can cope with the processes involved in alphabetic analysis. There are some interesting articles on i.t.a., notably Downing (1962 and 1963), Downing and Gardner (1962), Southgate (1965), Downing and Jones (1966) and Swales (1967); and a comparative study of the influence upon spelling of look-and-say and i.t.a. is made by Peters (1967). Downing has long been associated with the big drive to get i.t.a. launched; and Southgate whose scheme of reading assessment was adopted for the Plowden Report, has advocated caution over i.t.a. since research must be long-term. The system of 'tidying up' the alphabet, so that each letter represents one sound, was first thought of by Dr Thornton, for many years President of the Washington Patent Office, and he published his suggestions in 1790. After three-quarters of a century the idea was taken up by Edwin Leigh. From that time onwards, there have been a succession of supporters for a logical alphabet. One day mankind will have to overcome inertia and make a new alphabet covering the whole world. For instance, the Russians have one letter щ for *sh-ch* as in *Ashchurch*. In English four letters are required for these two sounds; in Polish also four letters: *szcz*; in Czech two letters: *šč*; in German seven letters: *schtsch*. Once the alphabet is made universal and logical, its dissemination will probably be as follows:

(*a*) it is first developed for electronic apparatus; (*b*) it then has to be learned by typists; (*c*) and finally teachers insist that it is used in primary schools.

According to such authorities at the turn of the century as Reeder (1900) and Huey (1908) teaching reading phonetically has been the only method since the invention of the alphabet, until the eighteenth century. That is not to say phonetically was the only way to learn to read. Jesus would have been taught to read by the normal eastern method, which was to put books into the boys' hands and then recite each page in chorus. He may well have learned exclusively by this look-and-say method.

From time to time historical references show that only the logic of the letters was considered and it either worked or—more often—it did not. Today, from the work of Piaget and others we can see that children with mental age below 7 have not yet developed sufficient powers of abstraction to grasp the logic. The Greeks taught first the letters, then the syllables, and then after very long practice the words. The Romans did not teach reading until boys were 7 years of age. One wonders whether they had tried to teach it earlier and found it a waste of time. The Greek orator Quintilian brought to Rome the idea of teaching isolated letters. He said children could learn letters at an earlier age and must write letters before reading. As soon as a child could identify a letter he was given a block with the letter engraved and traced the letter with an ivory pen. Then he learned *all* syllables in both Greek and Latin; then words and finally sentences. Atticus Herodes had a son who suffered difficulty in learning the alphabet; so his father bought him twenty-four slaves each named after a letter, to play with.

During the dark ages, all school books were lost and when Charlemagne wished to extend literacy in A.D. 813 only one reading book for children could be found. This *Abecedarium* consisted of the alphabet, Credo, Paternoster, and to it was added Ave Maria. No secular material was added for children until 1524, when some sayings by wise men of Greece were included. The Puritans never accepted illustrations, which they regarded as sinfully interesting. The only practical work we know of in learning the alphabet is the girls' samplers treasured by many families and still to be found in antique shops. Then in 1791 Gedike thought that a word for something must strike a child exactly as the object struck him, and he produced a *Children's Book for First Practice in Reading Without the ABC or Spelling*. The bitterness evoked by the alphabetic method is perhaps best expressed by Comenius who said that schools were slaughterhouses of the mind.

We seem now to be thoroughly aware that a child has to be 'ready' to read but we are still very confused about how to tell when a child is ready.

When *Educational Research* commenced publication in 1958 it very properly started with a series of articles on reading. The first two were on the relative effectiveness of different methods and the value of whole-word methods, by J. M. Morris (1958, 1959) who has conducted a large survey of reading in Kent. Then there was a series on reading readiness by Standish (1959), Sanderson (1963) and Lynn (1963). The general impression is that reliable tests of reading readiness cannot yet be devised because we still do not know what mental processes cause children to learn to read. All that we can do is to try to become sensitive to the moment when what is still a 'miracle' is likely to happen; and for this purpose all articles on reading readiness should be studied carefully.

Thackray (1965) examined 'The relationship between reading readiness and reading progress' for a London MA thesis. He had as subjects 182 children from eleven schools, with average age 5 years 4 months. He tested them a second time, when the average age was 6 years, and a third time at 6 years 4 months. His principal conclusions from this sample were: (*a*) that there was a wide range of individual differences; (*b*) the Harrison–Stroud Reading Readiness Profiles as a whole proved a valid measure of readiness; auditory and visual discrimination correlated most significantly with reading achievement; general ability and home environment were also important; but emotional and personal attitudes were not significant; (*c*) girls showed superiority over boys on reading readiness, with regard to auditory discrimination and also ability and vocabulary; and (*d*) a mental age of $5\frac{1}{2}$ years was found adequate in this sample for beginning to read and then making steady progress.

With two recent researches (Bruce 1964 and Thackray 1965) giving apparently conflicting results, we can see that the matter of when children should start reading is by no means settled. Bruce maintains that the children in his group were unable to make full use of the alphabet until a mental age of 7+ years; and Thackray, with his group, found that a mental age of about $5\frac{1}{2}$ years was sufficient to start reading and then maintain progress. It might be that the start at 5+ years depends more on look-and-say than is obvious. The fact that one is 'teaching' the alphabet does not necessitate that the child 'learns' alphabetically. However, it begins to be clear that with the aid of various simplifying devices, such as coloured words or i.t.a. or J. K. Jones's (1967) Doman colour reading apparatus, children's visual and auditory discrimination is such that most can start learning to read between 5 and 6 years. But research indicates that the early lead is lost by about 8 years.

This brings us right back to basic philosophy of education. Do we have to teach something as soon as a child can learn it? Is this the best time? Are there advantages in deliberately delaying the start? Is the purpose of reading a mechanical achievement or are we seeking to avail ourselves of the new dimension, language development, in written form? If children need varied and interesting experience to talk about, they also need such experience at a higher level of intellectual effort to inspire them to read and write about it. When we have more information on the nature of learning to read, we can make a wise decision on when it should begin. If the decision is to be that reading should start at a later age, our troubles are not over. This will necessitate a much more profound understanding of how to direct children's creative play than is at present at all common in our schools. Learning to read is a new step in the child's mastery of his environment and genuine interest in the purpose of learning to read has to outweigh by far the self-discipline that it involves. So the purpose is the child's and concerns what he has done or wants to do. This is why no published reading scheme is complete; it must be complemented with the teacher's own personal scheme for her particular group of individual children.

Before leaving research on children's introduction to reading by various methods, some of the recent books on interesting children in reading should be mentioned. Children will want to make the intellectual effort to read and write if events are sufficiently interesting to them to be worth reading and recording. Burroughs's *A Study of the Vocabulary of Young Children* (1957) is important because it records the actual vocabulary of 330 Midland children aged 5 to 6½ who are about to start reading and the range of individual differences is from 56 to 578 words. Whatever the cause of this wide range—intelligence, verbal ability or socio-economic conditions—this great difference in experience of words presents a serious problem both for those who construct readers and for the teachers who introduce children to reading. Goddard's *Reading in the Modern Infants' School* (1958) is a handbook for practising teachers. The suggestions for children's activities will help the teacher about to start reading to encourage the vocabularies of all the class, and in so doing, to discover the ones most in need of vocabulary enlargement. Welding a common fund of language for a common fund of experience can help the start of reading, particularly if books and wall stories, as here suggested, are used. Diack's *Reading and the Psychology of Perception* (1960) has been criticised on the grounds that experimental conditions were not rigorous enough for today, so that the conclusions were not justified (Hopkins 1960). R. Morris's *Success and Failure in Learning to Read* (1963) is of great importance because it is a genuine attempt to introduce reading in ways that will guide the children's thinking, which presupposes the teacher's understanding of the nature of children's thinking.

By the end of the sixties attention really began to focus on how reading should be taught. The Morris (1966) and Goodacre (1967) reports on infant reading in Kent and London were out. Writing, reading and spelling began to be securely linked. M. L. Peters' (1967) *Spelling: Caught or Taught*, builds a good case for teaching it without ignoring the true purpose of creative writing. Clay (1961) studied the psychological processes whereby children apprehend the systems involved in reading and so can correct their own errors. Southgate (1968) published formulae for beginning to read and Goodacre (1969) reviewed published reading schemes. Downing argued the case for i.t.a. cogently, both on his own (1969) and with Latham (1969); and Jones (1968) did the same for colour story reading. Indeed, by 1970 how we were teaching reading was so much in the public eye that a letter from a teacher in the *Guardian* became headline news, because she said she had been warned by a publisher not to be disparaging of long-established schemes. In fact, educationists have both been presented with many modern schemes of reading and had their attention drawn to the fact that a few people receiving rich financial gains from long-established schemes is no proof that the old schemes are best. We must be prepared to suit the way in which we teach reading to the findings of modern research on the subject.

The Plowden Report (1967) devotes considerable space to reading from the varying standpoints of learning, in general individual ability, home background, and so on. There is a short but important paragraph (534) on reading 'readiness', which is seen as an active state for both teacher and child; the natural endowment of the child is stimulated—enough but not too much —for reading as for other skills. Appendix 7 in Volume 2 examines standards of reading at the end of the primary school years. One of the witnesses for this report was D. E. M. Gardner, successor to Susan Isaacs at the London Institute of Education. Anyone in doubt as to the difference between traditional and progressive education should read Gardner's descriptions of the two types of schools in the opening of Chapter 2 of *Experiment and Tradition in Primary Schools* (1966). Since we now know that a child has to become involved in reading before he can make the necessary intellectual effort, any books on progressive education are relevant to reading. These include Gardner's *Testing Results in the Infant School* (1942), *Long Term Results of Infant School Methods* (1950) and *The Education of Young Children* (1956).

Progressive education makes a twofold contribution to helping the whole nation towards literacy, each of prime importance. Children are actively motivated to making the intellectual effort to record their interesting experiences; and teachers, working from principles of child development, can adjust the nature of their stimulation to the stage of development of individual children. As mankind has enjoyed recording and come to see the value of records, so children are enthusiastic about recording and come to see its value. The children's first records may be so individual that each child has to explain the meaning of his record. Teachers are beginning to see that children more easily grasp the purpose of communal symbols if they are first given the opportunity to invent their own symbols or codes. This breaks down the learning of communal symbols to two steps: seeing that a code must be invented and then learning the communal code.

These steps in coding belong equally to many other spheres, such as mathematics and music. Two examples seen in schools by the author will make this clearer. In a Farnham primary school Mr French is well known for his modern approach to mathematics, through use of such apparatus as desk calculators and so on. Some boys of seven, wishing to record a discovery, invented their own histogram by sticking ping-pong balls on a sheet of paper. This was put up on the wall and explained to others. When later the headmaster explained the customary way of making a histogram, the boys did not find this difficult because they understood the purpose and only had to learn the conventional method. Also in the Froebel demonstration school at Roehampton, Miss Glynn-Jones has allowed children of the same age to invent their own ways of writing down tunes they have composed. After they have explained to each other how and why they have done this, they are ready to see the value of standard musical notation.

The stages of embryo writing, pictography, ideographic writing and so on through which mankind finally arrived at the great abstraction of alphabetic writing took many thousands of years. We should doubtless save ourselves much time in the long run, if we gave infant school children more time to see the purpose of symbols for reading and writing, before imposing the communal alphabet upon them. Teachers have, for over 2,000 years, had a fixation on the alphabet as the logical start to reading. How disastrous this is for many children becomes patently clear in the section on reading for children of 8 to 12 years in Chapter 18. The casualties by the way, the tears and suffering, are not just a remote matter of history of education. Any teacher who still imposes suffering on a child over reading is obstructing the child from later disciplining himself to read.

The modern approach to learning to read is not to leave a child to find his own way, but to see what help he requires. Though mankind did so much before the alphabet was invented, the world today is a literate place. Anyone who grows up unable to read notices, income tax forms, voting papers, and so on, is severely handicapped and exposed to exploitation. But in addition to these utilitarian matters, once a child can read, the development of his language takes a leap forward. Fresh sources of information and pleasure are opened; words and sentences are disentangled; the schemata of grammar and sentence construction which will have been discovered in spoken language are revealed in a new form which gives greater understanding; and the world of literature opens. It is imperative that we find the most efficient way to hand on this enrichment through man's greatest asset, language.

14. Personality

So far, in our study of preschool and young school children, many words, such as cheerful, moody or quick-tempered have been used to describe their behaviour. The act of observing and naming their behaviour is an analytical process. There are literally hundreds of words in our language for describing and discriminating the response of different personalities to circumstances. At first it seems impossible to generalise about personality, because it can be so varied. Indeed, personality has proved one of the most difficult areas of study for psychology. But half a century of scientific study has now begun to yield valuable results from systematic analysis. Before a child goes into the junior school the teacher is expected to give some description of his personality, often in the form of ratings; and the teacher will rate each child better if he is aware of some of the relevant work on personality.

But in reporting personality research we shall meet again some of the problems we met over the self. Almost no scientific study has been made of the personality of children under 8; which means that in order to understand the personalities of the youngest school children we have to examine what has been discovered about older children and adults to see if it helps us. As the various techniques for assessing personality turn up we shall have to pause and examine them. We shall meet some technical terms, but most of these will be valuable later for the study of such matters as intelligence. We shall, unfortunately, meet again confusion over terms, but by now we should begin to take these in our stride, as inevitable in a fairly new science.

The best approach would be to look briefly at the traditional classification of personality over many centuries, and then see how twentieth-century study of personality emerged. Most of us know, from our study of literature, the four traditional types of personality: phlegmatic (sluggish), sanguine (warm, optimistic), melancholic (depressed) and choleric (quick-tempered). Galen (A.D. 130–201), physician to Marcus Aurelius, was familiar with the writings of the earlier Hippocratic school of medicine in Greece, and extended their doctrine of four physiological groups based on 'humours' to a theory of four types of temperament. In Latin *temperamentum* means 'compounding' and Galen was concerned with lower-level emotional reactions, such as cheerfulness, bad temper, apathy, and so on. Some eighty of his treatises still exist, and show him to have been a practical as well as a theoretical scientist. Present knowledge of the autonomic and glandular systems shows that the theory of humours, as developed by Galen, was not so far removed from our modern theory of glandular secretions.

The first systematic attempt to classify personality seems to have been made by Wundt (1832–1920) in his Leipzig Laboratory. He wrote in 1910 that the entire system of feelings should be regarded as a 'three-dimensional manifold', which he compared with the latitude, longitude and altitude of a globe. Burt followed up Wundt's suggestions with experimentation. By combining statistical analysis with individual psychology he was able to find factors and components in a table or *matrix of correlations*. An analogy for the matrix is the way in which an apparently shapeless crystal splits, on a tap with a hammer, into its natural planes. The work which Burt undertook, with the help of a headmaster, within a year or two of Wundt's suggestion, proved germinal and has profoundly influenced later work. It will therefore be dealt with in some detail.

In a recent article Burt (1965) points out that today the term 'personality' is used in a somewhat narrower and more specialised sense, to denote the distinctive way in which any given individual's non-cognitive (non-intellectual) or dynamic tendencies are organised; these are the various affective (feeling), conative (willing) and emotional tendencies which chiefly determine an individual's interests, motives, preferences and whole social and personal behaviour. Since reports of his early studies of personality are scattered through various journals, some very difficult to obtain now, he summarises his main findings in this article.

Within five years of Wundt's suggested block system for classifying personality, Burt and Moore (1915) published the results of an investigation on 172 children of 9 to 11 years. Their aim was threefold:

1. to find out whether differences of temperament and motivation were partly due to heredity;
2. to see whether work at an early age could produce information from which development of an individual could be predicted as liable to neurosis or delinquency. *Neurosis* is an ill-defined mental disorder and *delinquency* is a relatively minor violation of legal or moral codes, especially by children;

3. to solve the teacher's puzzle as to why so many children of average or above average ability fail to reach standards to be expected of their ability.

Burt also had a subsidiary aim: to see if he could divert the uproar amongst psychologists over Spearman's announcement of a general factor of intelligence by discovering a general factor of emotionality.

The three main aims of Burt and Moore in 1915 are still amongst the most important objectives in personality research. Burt had been one of McDougall's (1871–1938) first students at Oxford and was interested in testing McDougall's classification of inborn properties. The emotion of fear accompanying the instinct of escape is a good example. The fear accompanying a toddler's screams over a nightmare is the same fear that a soldier can experience in battle. We have already seen how these feelings may cluster round some object forming what McDougall called a sentiment, the most important being the self-regarding sentiment.

Burt and Moore investigated McDougall's 'primary emotional tendencies', first because they were precisely defined and illustrated (an inestimable help to research workers), and then because they dealt with individual differences in traits which, on biological assumptions, were presumed to be innate or inherited. H. J. Eysenck (1953) a student of Burt's, finds instincts or drives in accordance with current biological and psychological views, and uses them for classification. Eysenck in Britain, and another of Burt's students, Cattell in America, are considered by many to be the two foremost workers on personality today. In *Occupational Psychology* each wrote on the other: 'Eysenck on Cattell' (1961) and 'Cattell on Eysenck' (1964). One must note that their opinions on primary emotional tendencies differ. However, Adcock (1965) has written an article on their differences (for which the reader needs at least some knowledge of statistics), in which he concludes that their disagreement is largely due to using different terms for much the same thing. Indeed, he ends with a glossary for readers of both authors 'For Cattell's *Anxiety* and Eysenck's *Neuroticism* read *Emotional reactivity*', and so on. So here again we are faced with the problem of interpreting terminology, as with the self and ego. Adcock thinks that the work of Eysenck and Cattell complement each other, as Eysenck works on one level of analysis and Cattell goes deeper, seeking source traits which he defines as factors.

In order to find out about the various emotional tendencies of each of their 172 children in 1915, Burt and Moore got the class teachers to give estimates of each child in the class, based on first-hand observation under standardised conditions. Such ratings of personality traits by teachers and others are still widely used. The traits have to be very precisely defined. Guilford (1936) gives the following example:

Is he slow or quick thinking?

Extremely slow	Sluggish, plodding	Thinks with ordinary speed	Agile minded	Extremely rapid

This is a five-point scale but the line is continuous to show that, as slow to rapid thinking is a continuous scale, one could mark anywhere on the line. However, for calculations an exact position above the definitions has to be given. Figure 22 is from Hilgard (1953) and gives definitions of five tendencies, with lines up to guide placing of mark. A constant error, to which Guilford says every judge falls victim is *the halo effect*. We judge our fellows in terms of a general mental attitude towards them; and there is a like mental attitude towards particular qualities. One result of this is to force the rating of any trait in the general direction of the general impression of the individuals rated, making the rating that much less valid. Having one trait only on a page would do something to pull the judge back from the general attitude error, or halo effect. Incidentally, in the Guilford rating example, and the second Hilgard example (see Figure 22), whether a child needs much prodding or not, is reminiscent of the traditional phlegmatic and sanguine classifications.

Here are a few recent researches which have used rating for part of their measurement. Thorpe (1959) got teachers to assess groups of adjusted and maladjusted children. Astington (1960) got teachers to assess children at various age levels. Hallworth (1964) got ten housemasters in a comprehensive school to rate all fourteen-year-olds, 138 boys and 140 girls, on fourteen traits. J. Rushton (1966) got teachers to rate 458 children of 11 years. Some colleges train students in rating by letting them rate themselves. R. S. Adams (1962), in New Zealand, got students training as teachers to fill in a self-rating scale, and results were so interesting that research on self-rating was extended to children. Morrison *et al.* (1966) got four girls from each of eight classes to rate their peers on twenty personality traits, in a coeducational secondary school, at two age levels: second and fourth year. Interesting information was obtained from this last experiment, both about development of judgment from second to fourth secondary school year and about differences in judging

A scale such as this one helps the judge to be specific about the basis for each of his judgments (American Council on Education; after Fryer and Henry, 1950).

Figure 22. A graphic rating scale.

Source: Hilgard (1953).

A. How are you and others affected by his appearance and manner?

Avoided by others	Tolerated by others	Liked by others	Well liked by others	Sought by others	No opportunity to observe

Please record here instances that support your judgment.

B. Does he need constant prodding or does he go ahead with his work without being told?

Needs much prodding in doing ordinary assignments	Needs occasional prodding	Does ordinary assignments of his own accord	Completes suggested supplementary work	Seeks and sets for himself additional tasks

Please record here instances that support your judgment.

C. Does he get others to do what he wishes?

Probably unable to lead his fellows	Lets others take lead	Sometimes leads in minor affairs	Sometimes leads in important affairs	Displays marked ability to lead his fellows; makes things go

Please record here instances that support your judgment.

D. How does he control his emotions?

Too easily moved to anger or fits of depression, etc.	Tends to be overemotional	Usually well balanced	Well balanced	Unusual balance of responsiveness and control
Unresponsive, apathetic	Tends to be unresponsive			

Please record here instances that support your judgment.

E. Has he a program with definite purposes in terms of which he distributes his time and energy?

Aimless trifler	Aims just to "get by"	Has vaguely formed objectives	Directs energies effectively with fairly definite program	Engrossed in realizing well-formulated objectives

Please record here instances that support your judgment.

157

the same or the opposite sex. P. H. Taylor (1962) turned the tables completely; he got more than 800 primary and secondary school children to rate their teachers for teaching ability. Thus we see that the 1915 rating of personality traits is still a technique much used.

H. J. Eysenck summarises research on personality rating in *The Structure of Human Personality* (1953); but, as we have seen, much rating research has been done since then. Today ratings are very frequently combined with personality questionnaires which consist of a series of questions to answer or inventories to check. In order to understand the findings, we have to study how these are constructed. Both Eysenck and Cattell have more faith in objectively constructed personality questionnaires or inventories than in rating. But Burt (1965) still thinks that no objective personality tests are as good as ratings by experienced teachers who have observed children year after year; and best of all are head teachers who have kept in touch with old pupils through taking an interest in their clubs and other activities. However, since so many teachers fail to train themselves thoroughly or to study the children later, he thinks it is better in practice to let a well-qualified educational psychologist conduct interviews.

In the 1915 research, besides ratings by teachers, Burt and Moore used a battery of 'would-be' objective tests, not unlike what are now called 'projection tests'. (Incidentally, the term 'battery' is used of a group of tests by analogy with the military emplacement of a group of guns; and without too much disrespect we might say they were 'gunning for' personality classification.) The term 'projection test' also derives from analogy, this time with the projection of a picture by a magic lantern, and this analogy has lead to a misunderstanding which should be cleared up. Let us take the Rorschach inkblot test as an example. This consists of a series of black or black-and-coloured blobs of ink which are made into symmetrical patterns by folding and pressing while still wet. Most students have done this in childhood, if not in the college art department. The Swiss psychiatrist Rorschach (1884–1922) used his own series and claimed to have invented this form of test in 1911. But this way of making a semi-formless pattern for testees to comment on has been used since the middle of the nineteenth century. When the testee says what the pattern looks like, nothing is projected literally from his mind on to the blot, in the way that the magic lantern projects the picture onto the screen. But something happens in his mind, as it does with the child who blames his teddy for misbehaviour.

Many British psychologists have, from the time of Stout (1860–1944), preferred to name the mental processes involved *apperception*. William James

(1842–1910) thought this term savoured too much of philosophical connections and persuaded the Americans to reject it—which they still do. Apperception is a mental activity familiar to us all. At first we see something of which we cannot make sense; then, by fusing what we already know with what the object looks like, we begin to see meaning. This can happen when we are off guard, as when we see something strange in the dusk and incorrectly apperceive a fallen log as a strange animal; or when we are under strain and think on first glance at an examination paper that none of it makes sense. Most of the time we identify objects around us by apperception and so orientate ourselves to our various environments. In order to avoid extremely naïve, crude and unjustifiable deductions about projection tests, we should think of them in terms of apperception. In these tests the contents of a particular sensory presentation, at first relatively indeterminate and meaningless, become clearer and more determinate; and so they acquire for the perceiver some kind of meaning, through the mental process of fusion with contents already more or less systematically organised in his mind. Although Rorschach himself made little or no mention of the mental processes involved, we know quite a lot about them from the experimental work of Bartlett (1916) and others.

What insight into personality might such inkblots give us? Let us take an extreme example. Soon after the Second World War the author was doing research with Rorschach inkblots and two men saw the same inkblot in strikingly different ways: one saw it as a lamp burning peacefully in a cottage window and the other saw it as savages boiling a cauldron of human bones. The one who saw it as something horrific saw three of the ten blots as horrific, while the other testee saw nothing horrific in any of them. The one who gave such troubled replies was an artist who had been in the RAF during the war and he was still suffering horrific war nightmares. Clearly something of emotional disposition was revealed, both by the one who gave 100 per cent reasonable responses and by the one who gave 33 per cent horrific replies.

The inkblot test is very difficult to score as an objective test. In the 1930s many German psychologists were extremely enthusiastic about the Rorschach test and called it 'rein empirisch'. But Vernon (1933) said that they called it 'pure empiricism' because they had no understanding of objective testing. Cattell (1946) criticises the vague premises on which Rorschach's own scoring is based and calls it a mixture of ill-defined intentions. Goodenough (1949) says the formulae for interpretation seem to have developed on a basis of chance relationships. H. J. Eysenck (1947) rightly refers to those who criticise it as the 'more cautious psychologists'. In spite of all this criticism of Rorschach scoring, inkblots as semi-formless stimulus to apperception can give valuable insight to mental processes and is widely used today.

There has been one factual study of scoring the Rorschach test by Sen (1950). A hundred Indian students were given a battery of tests including the Rorschach Test, which was scored in two ways: by orthodox Rorschach technique, and according to Burt's method of rating the content of responses. Also various traits were rated by independent judges. Statistical analysis confirmed several of the orthodox interpretations, particularly regarding intelligence and neurotic tendencies. But many of the more formal categories and inferences drawn from them were not verified. Sen concludes that an analysis of content, based on generally recognised principles and expressed in terms of generally recognised psychological factors, would be far more valuable for practical purposes.

Many other apperception or so-called projection tests have been designed, which give a perceptual stimulus that is not quite so near-formless as the inkblots. Pictures or sentences are used to portray a dramatic situation which could end in a variety of ways; and the testee apperceives the situation according to his previous experience. For instance, one picture shows a man crouched on the window-sill of an office many storeys up. He might be a thief or Batman or the window-cleaner; many other explanations, such as attempted suicide might be given, according to the mental inclinations of the testee. The Thematic Apperception Test, or TAT, is one such series of pictures and gets its name from the fact that the subject has to apperceive the picture and produce the theme which seems best to him. A certain percentage of a particular kind of reply to the whole series might well build up to valuable information of one kind of inclination or another in the subject's personality. The underlying assumption is that the testee will perceive in the pictures themes important in his own life.

There are a variety of ways in which a subject can be prompted to show his reactions to situations. For instance, a word can be given and the subject has to say the first word he thinks of on hearing it. This is the *word association* or free association test. When the list of stimulus words is compiled, at intervals down the list certain key words are inserted. Such lists can be seen in Appendix IV of *The Subnormal Mind* by Burt (1935), arranged in subjects of investigation. Another form of prompting is sentence completion, where the child is asked to finish such sentences as *I wish* ... or *I want*.... A well-planned list of this kind used with a class of children old enough to write the sentence completion can, amongst other things, pick out children whose reactions are in some way extreme. The same can be done with incomplete stories, for which the children can write or tell made-up endings. Or a child may be asked to put a set of ten pictures in order for interest, and if these, too, are well-planned they can be very revealing of what interests the child. When a whole battery of such apperception tests is used, insight into the subject's mental processes can be gained from a number of different aspects.

Fairly recently Bene (1957) has made an attempt to evolve more objective scoring of such apperception (or projection) tests. She proposes a new form of coding for replies by large numbers of subjects using two symbols: one representing the attitude expressed, and the other representing the object towards which the attitude has been expressed. When responses have been coded in this way, they can be treated statistically without much distortion of their original meaning. She used sentence completion (sometimes called open-ended questions), and gives examples of actual incomplete sentences used, grouped according to attitude and to object (the two symbols). For large numbers, always best for statistical work, she took 618 children, 317 in grammar schools and 301 in secondary modern schools. From her method of coding and subsequent statistical treatment she was able to draw some interesting conclusions about attitudes in the two kinds of secondary school, grammar and modern. She maintains that, although personality investigations have too many variables (aspects liable to change) for a single code to cover, this coding system can easily be adapted to a new area, once the worker has planned the required categories. This is an interesting article, as the idea seems to be original and the main theme is not the statistical processes used but the preparation of data for statistics. When statistical work is to be done, the test has to be designed to give answers that can be treated statistically, Bene gives many further references, largely American, for those wishing to study the important problem of how personality tests can be made more objective. It is the hitherto lack of objectivity which occasioned Burt (1965) to refer to such tests as 'would-be' objective tests.

In the first British scientific investigation of personality, by Burt and Moore in 1915, all the tests so far referred to were used: inkblots, thematic apperception, picture preferences, and teachers' ratings under controlled conditions. Because so much used on that occasion is still used today, that first research was called 'germinal'. Once Burt and Moore had the variety of scores on each of the 172 children of 9 to 11 years, they set out to find the mutual relationship in responses, the joint factors underlying the correlations, by factor analysis. They obtained all the correlation coefficients of each test with every other test. In terms of our split crystal (see p. 154), from information gained and related to other information, they were able to detect three kinds of pattern (or natural plane) within the matrix:

1. *general emotionality*, similar to McDougall's 'common fund of emotional energy', which had a high correlation with the teachers' rating of each child's temperament assessed along a stability/instability scale;
2. *a bipolar sthenic/asthenic* running from sthenic active approach to the environment (assertiveness, curiosity, anger, sociability, etc) to asthenic tending to withdraw from the environment (fear, disgust, grief, submission, etc.) (*Bipolar* means running from one extreme through zero to the other extreme.) This roughly corresponds to what Jung and later writers called extraversion and introversion;
3. a bipolar *euphoric/dysphoric*, running from pleasurable to unpleasurable emotions, not unlike optimistic-to-pessimistic reactions.

These are the main patterns which Burt and Moore were able to extract from the mass or matrix of information about test scores, by working out all correlations and then relating the correlations to each other.

Burt suggested that this statistically evolved classification of emotional propensities could also be used to classify persons into temperamental types or rather tendencies. There is a danger of misunderstanding over the word 'type', as so many people mistake a type for an exact copy of a prototype. We should think of Guilford's continuous line as a measuring scale, anywhere along which a person's measurement for a trait can be marked. In the same way, temperamental type means position on the measuring scale, *not* facsimile of an original. The four classes of sthenic, asthenic, euphoric and dysphoric seemed to provide a plausible basis for much of the traditional scheme of temperaments which has come down to us through Galen:

1. the *choleric* is an active dysphoric (pessimist),
2. the *melancholic* is an inactive dysphoric (pessimist),
3. the *sanguine* is an active euphoric (optimist),
4. the *phlegmatic* is an inactive euphoric (optimist).

Burt points out that the normal individual would therefore correspond to Galen's 'well-balanced' type, 'neither fantastically melancholy, too slowly phlegmatic, too highly sanguine, or too rashly choleric'.

Burt chose the words sthenic/asthenic from Wundt's studies of emotion, but they never became popular terms in this country. There was plenty of confirmation in the literature for what they meant: Pavlov used excitatory and inhibitive types of his dogs, Kretschmer used cyclothymic and schizothymic of his patients, James talked of explosive and obstructive types,

Guthrie of restrained and unrestrained children, and Jung of extraverted and introverted types. In order to bring his work in line with later research, Burt adopted Jung's (1923) terms, changing sthenic and asthenic to extravert and introvert, which have remained. However, as we saw from Adcock's (1965) glossary of terms used by Cattell and H. J. Eysenck (see p. 155), we always have to note carefully how each writer defines the terms he uses.

Before turning to personality research in the second half of the twentieth century there are three points directly related to the three aims of the original personality research which should be made. The first aim had been to find out whether differences of temperament and motivation were partly due to heredity; and in order to find out whether the three factors of general emotionality, extraversion/introversion and optimism/pessimism were peculiar to children, Burt and Moore carried out a parallel study with young adults (chiefly students and members of working men's clubs). They found virtually the same three factors in adults as in children.

The second aim was to see if an individual could be detected early as liable to neurosis or delinquency. Burt devotes the second half of *The Subnormal Mind* (1935) to describing the results of applying the same technique to neurotic (maladjusted) children. Factorial analysis of neurotic cases revealed a clear distinction between the two main types, extravert and introvert. For this later research Burt and his colleagues used a questionnaire consisting of 215 questions. This technique, which plays a very important part today, was devised by the American professor of psychology Woodworth, as a symptom-detector. In Chapter 5 of *Psychology: a study of mental life* (1922), Woodworth describes how such a questionnaire can be constructed. A form of it was used during the First World War as a 'mental hygiene group-test' for preliminary examination of recruits. The idea was not to find personality types, but to list neurotic symptoms, presumably to eliminate those with too many symptoms to make reliable soldiers. Burt's revised list can be seen in Appendix III of *The Subnormal Mind*. It is a searching list, well worth reading —and answering to oneself.

The third aim was to throw light on why so many children of average or above average ability failed to reach expected standards. In a series of later papers, Burt (1917, 1937, and refs) gave brief case histories illustrating the commoner types of temperament as they occur among school children of both sexes, and tried to show how the differences in motivation affected the child's educational progress in school. This aspect of Burt's work has been much overlooked, which has lead to a curious misunderstanding. His equally profound work on intelligence to which we shall refer later, so caught the imagination of educationalists that much research time was devoted to intelligence. Before long it transpired that IQ was not all; factors such as temperament, motivation and environment had immense influence. Had they read Burt's papers on these subjects they could have avoided attacking him for regarding inherited intelligence as so important. As Hearnshaw (1964) says: 'Burt has always recognised that cognition is only one side of mental functioning and that in real life the "orectic" or emotional side is equally important.' The emotional side is where we must look, to answer the third question as to why so many children fail to develop their intellectual potential.

Now let us turn to what personality research has been done in the last decade or so. Davidson *et al.* (1957) at Oxford made a combined psychological, psychiatric and somatotype (type of body) study of a hundred children within six months of their seventh birthday. Incidentally, their investigation is introduced by reference to Galen. The aim of this research was to correlate physique with behaviour in childhood. Though their findings were tentative they obtained evidence of one body-type being associated with introversion and another body-type with extraversion. The significant correlations between behaviour patterns and measurable bodily components lead them to hope that, even as early as age 7 years, children who are especially vulnerable might be picked out and given special care. In a future article they hope to give a report on a follow-up of these children at 11 years.

Since we are lamentably short of researches on young children in Britain, let us see something of how Cattell and Coan's (1958) work was done, with Illinois children of 6 and 7 years. Cattell and Grune (1954) had made an earlier questionnaire for children of 11 to 14 years, and taken the factors revealed by factor analysis for drawing up the questionnaire for younger children. Cattell and Coan modified some questions and added others which were suggested by observation of 6 to 7-year-old children. The final form was 200 questions which they gave to 151 children of this younger age. Details of explanatory pictures and administration can be seen in their 1958 article.

Each question has only two possible answers. The following are the first and last four questions, to give an idea of the kind of question asked:

1. Which do you like better: (*a*) cats, or (*b*) dogs?
2. Do you like (*a*) a friend who talks a lot, or (*b*) one who is quiet?
3. Would you rather play (*a*) school, or (*b*) cowboys and Indians?
4. If you wake up in the dark: (*a*) do you sometimes feel scared, or (*b*) do you like it because it's so dark and quiet?

197. When children play tricks on you: (*a*) do you cry, or (*b*) do you get mad?

198. Do grown-ups ever say you daydream too much? (*a*) Yes, or (*b*) no.

199. Are you as good-looking as other children in your class? (*a*) Yes, or (*b*) no.

200. Which would you rather be: (*a*) a bird, or (*b*) a horse?

The questions which have been omitted can all be seen in the original paper. Looking through 200 simple questions becomes more interesting as one sees something of the design. Several questions seem almost to repeat earlier questions, for instance questions on cats and dogs, or parents. These are check questions, to see whether the testee changes his mind or remains consistent throughout. Children greatly enjoy deciding about such questions, because they are about their own interests. The purpose underlying the questions was to throw light on different facets of both individual children and children of this age group; and replies are better if the children enjoy replying.

When the testing was completed, the 200 answers from each of the 151 children, a total of over 3,000 answers from children of 6 and 7 years, were analysed statistically. Amongst other findings the authors discovered that the responses of these children were comparable with adult replies to similarly planned personality questionnaires at the adult level. Cattell and Coan judged from their data that, with further research (being carried out), a questionnaire as reliable as existing questionnaires for older persons could be designed for children as young as 6 or 7 years. This was a very important discovery and confirms Burt's (p. 163) finding that temperamental traits are similar for children and adults.

Much research has been done with questionnaires, both in Britain and America. The terms 'questionnaire' and 'inventory' seem at times to be used interchangeably. For example, H. J. Eysenck (1959) reports that the Maudsley Personality Inventory or MPI is a '48-question inventory'. But strictly speaking, as already explained, a questionnaire is a set of questions to answer and an inventory is a list of items to check. Each series of questions or statements is drawn up with a particular investigation in mind. The aim is to make these tests more and more objective. Each statistical analysis reveals more accurate factors and components from which more accurate revision of tests or construction of new tests can be made. The set of questions which Cattell and Coan adapted for the children of 6 to 7 years was the American High School Personality Questionnaire (HSPQ). The British Maudsley

Personality Inventory (MPI), to which we shall refer in a moment, is based on H. J. Eysenck's (1953) theory of personality. The Q-technique designed by Stephenson (1953) is basically the same: the subject is given perhaps a hundred statements on different cards and has to sort them into piles according to how applicable they are to himself. Incidentally, the way in which the piles are arranged forms a distribution of traits, which carries out a first step of the statistical analysis for the experimenter. The best source of reference to the extensive American construction of such tests is the *Mental Measurements Yearbook*, edited by Buros (1959).

Since America is so much larger and the Americans construct so many more questionnaires, inventories, Q-tests, etc., it would be very convenient for us to use their forms of tests. But there are unfortunately three objections to simply adopting their proven tests, which can be illustrated from Cattell and Coan's work (1958) with HSPQ and children of 6 to 7 years:

1. There are differences in children's environment in the two countries. For example several questions refer to funny books, often called funnies, which are collections of strip cartoons far more common in the States than in Britain, and more usually called comic strips in Britain. Such questions would be easier for American than British children to answer.

2. Though both countries speak English, there are subtle differences in use of words which, in 200 questions, can make a difference to ease of comprehension for a British child. In question 197 above (p. 165), the term 'get mad' is one example. It comes in several questions and is definitely an Americanism. Other examples from this test are: 'Do you *like for* other children …', 'right now', 'act rude', 'go play', 'big bug' (meaning large insect), and so on. On the two counts of differing social environment and use of English, British children would be penalised in American tests, although America is another English-speaking country.

3. British statistical psychology, originating with Galton and carried to a very high level by Burt, is unquestionably the most precise in the world. We have seen that tests have to be planned with their particular statistical analysis in mind. Thus we have to construct our own tests to ensure that they can be subjected to what we consider the most suitable statistical analysis.

H. J. Eysenck (1959) produced the Maudsley Personality Inventory (MPI) in London; but he was most careful to state that it was still only a research instrument designed for experimental purposes, as it had only been tried out on 1,800 normal adults. Eysenck claimed that it differentiated between normal and various neurotic groups, 'neurotic' here apparently meaning mal-adjusted, not general emotionality. Furneaux and Gibson (1961) adopted the American Pintner inventory for use with our children; and this was tried out with varying degrees of success, on eighteen children aged 9 to 13 years at a school for difficult and maladjusted children. S. B. G. Eysenck* (1965) criticised the Pintner test on two counts: (a) the statistics were not satisfactory; and (b) it contained American-type wording from its American Pintner Scale origins.

Then H. J. Eysenck and S. B. G. Eysenck published the *Eysenck Personality Inventory* (EPI) (1964). This was adapted for children by S. B. G. Eysenck, as the *Junior EPI* (1965). She too emphasised that it is as yet only an instrument for experimentation, but it is of interest to us now for a number of reasons. First, she expects it to be of more use in schools than in clinics. Then, we are in urgent need of direct personality research, particularly of young children. Also, if we are better informed on how such research arises, we shall be better able to cooperate with further testing in schools. Because of our pressing need for such a test, we will look at this one in some detail, despite the fact that it is still in the experimental stage. Incidentally, something of a crisis seems to have occurred when the test had already been applied to nearly 7,000 children. The investigators saw how to add a section which should test scientifically whether the children were answering truthfully or not. At moments such as this research workers have to make radical decisions whether just to carry on or whether to start again with the fresh material. The extra section was added, and another 2,777 children were tested. How one can try to test children's truthfulness is interesting.

Both American and British psychologists have been much preoccupied with the possibility that children and adults might falsify their responses and put what they imagined the investigators would regard as 'desirable responses'. This is what happened in the Newsons' investigation on breast-feeding (see pp. 16–17), where responses to questions by health visitors were prejudiced in favour of what mothers considered medical opinion to be. In Britain Gibson (1964) of the Institute of Criminology at Cambridge, who has worked with children and adults of dubious ethical standards, has experi-mented with an eighteen-item lie scale in connection with the Maudsley Personality Inventory and the Junior MPI. Gibson describes the rationale of his test. The intention was to measure the tendency of children to distort their test responses by claiming an unlikely degree of moral perfection. The

* Dr S. B. G. Eysenck is the wife of Professor H. J. Eysenck and both work at the Institute of Psychiatry, University of London (formerly the Maudsley Hospital).

items were designed so that endorsement in the 'good' direction necessitated agreement with nine items and disagreement with the other nine. With ninety boys and seventy-one girls of 10 and 11 years in an urban district he found that the lie scale indicated much the same results with children as with adults. But the diagnosis was not quite so clear with children. Whereas adult replies made a fairly clear classification into 'honest' or' liar', many children's replies were not so extreme either way. As he points out, this could indicate a meaningful personality difference between adult and juvenile delinquents. One suspects, from Piaget's work (see pp. 72–3) that maturation of moral judgments plays a part here.

S. B. G. Eysenck *et al.* (1966) carried out an experiment on 'Desirability response set in children' with 575 children of 11 to 15 years, giving the same test twice within a month. The experimental group consisted of 286 children and the controls of 289 children. The controls were just given the test a second time without comment. But the second time the experimental group was tested, the children were told to 'fake good' (another Americanism, indicating the source of the lie scale idea). The actual words used were correct English: they were told that they 'should try to put themselves in the best light'. As predicted, there were highly significant changes in the experimental group when they changed from stating facts to trying to say what they thought would meet with adult approval.

The JEPI test to which the lie scale was added had been designed to measure three things: (*a*) neuroticism or emotionality; (*b*) extraversion and introversion; and (*c*) truthfulness of replies. We should note, with regard to the first aim, where neuroticism is equated with emotionality, that in 1915 Burt defined these two terms very differently: 'neuroticism' was maladjustment and 'emotionality' was inborn excitability.[*] Now the two terms are beginning to be correctly used once more. However, it is advisable to take particular care with definitions of these terms by any one writer, and particularly any research where the Maudsley or Eysenck Personality Inventories have been used. In the research now under review, the JEPI, the first objective was to measure emotionality.

When the preliminary trial of the Junior Eysenck Personality Inventory had been analysed statistically, sixty suitable items were selected for the final inventory. Emotionality was measured by twenty-four items; extraversion/introversion by twenty-four items; and lying by twelve items. The first

[*] H. J. Eysenck, appears to have borrowed the psychiatric term 'neuroticism' for 'emotionality'. He justifies this with many references in *Dimensions of Personality* (1947, p. 41); and on the previous page quotes Webb, also a student of Burt's, as prior to Burt. But the date is wrong.

results suggest that emotionality can be measured in this way with children of 7 to 16 years. But measurement of extraversion/introversion was not clear below the ages of 9 or 10 years. Further research should show whether this difficulty with the youngest children is due to a personality dimension which does not emerge clearly till 9 or 10 years; or whether it is simply due to the fact that questionnaires are too difficult for children of 7 to 8 or 9 to answer in writing. There was a steady decrease in lying, from the youngest to the oldest children. This is in accordance with other research quoted on children's lying, which shows that on an average, the older children become, the less they lie. The JEPI was based on the theory that emotionality and introversion/extraversion were independent of intelligence. However, two verbal intelligence test scores each, were obtained for 373 girls and 334 boys. There did seem to be some slight connection between personality and intelligence, which will require further investigation. The JEPI is not a personality test to be expected soon in the classroom, but there is value now in studying the care necessary for testing the personality of young children.

Astington's (1960) investigation (see p. 156) arose from the fact that 40 per cent of grammar school children passed the General Certificate of Education in fewer than three subjects. The children studied were in the Stockport area. Ratings of personality traits were made and personality tests were given to 300 boys in five primary schools and about 700 boys in maintained grammar schools. He found the ratings by teachers had a higher correlation with performance in GCE than the intelligence quotients. He therefore suggests that eleven-plus selection gives better prediction if teachers' personality ratings are added. Lynn and Gordon (1961) at Exeter, carried out an investigation on sixty male university students, based on H. J. Eysenck's theory of personality. Thus we expect to find emotionality along the stability/instability line called neuroticism here. Neither this factor nor extraversion showed any significant correlation with intelligence scores obtained from the progressive matrices intelligence test. But the authors concluded that extraverts are academically handicapped as they tend to give up more easily. This is a test with part of a design missing and some possible designs at the bottom. The testee has to choose the most suitable one to fill the gap.

Warburton et al. (1963) worked with a hundred students who were being trained to teach at Manchester Department of Education. Among the battery of tests employed, Cattell's 16PF personality questionnaire proved the best single predictor of the final teaching practice mark. They found the following three personality characters most closely related to a successful final teaching mark: *self-control, conscientiousness* and *sensitivity*. Evans (1964) at Southampton, compared personality characteristics with reasoning ability, in two representative samples of student-teachers: (*a*) 131 men and 158 women university graduates; and (*b*) 55 men and 90 women in four colleges of education. His findings on personality assessment for prediction of final teaching practice mark support Warburton and his colleagues (1963). He found that the students in colleges of education were significantly more extraverted than those in the university. The college of education students had a more active approach to their environment, with more curiosity, sociability, assertiveness and so on; while the university students, though just as stable, were inclined to be more introverted. But in agreement with many other researches, introversion, and not extraversion, was found to be the positive influence on academic attainment. Payne (1967) at Somerset used the MPI in an investigation of musical taste and found personality an important factor in motivation of taste: she found a correlation between classical/romantic music and stable/excitable personalities, the more stable preferring classical music and the more excitable preferring romantic music.

Since the two leading exponents of personality, Cattell in America and Eysenck in Britain, both regard personality questionnaires as important in personality assessment, it is encouraging to find so much research by others using questionnaires is going on. If emotionality and extraversion/introversion can be reliably estimated in this way, then their correlations with other aspects would be of great value. These figures could reveal to us the connections between personality and intelligence, scholastic attainment, scientific and artistic attainment, with different forms of education and post-school occupation, in fact with many areas of development where further illumination is urgently needed. Butcher *et al.* (1963) in introductory comments on a cross-cultural investigation of British and American children of 12 to 14 years, for which they had used Cattell's HSPQ (see p. 165), put the position clearly. They point out that

> neither questionnaires nor objective tests of personality have yet reached the stage of acceptance as practical instruments of selection and guidance, while ratings are very often so bedevilled with halo effect as to be even less satisfactory . . . From the theoretical point of view, however, there are enough suggestive and interesting findings in the literature to make it clear that research is getting warm, so to speak, and that real effects are there to be discovered when research instruments have been further standardised and refined.

Our brief look at twentieth-century scientific research on personality has shown us that much has been undertaken and that more has to be done before we can expect trustworthy objective assessments of personality. Even though some new insights into personality inevitably appear to conflict, thus calling for further research in a particular area, valuable information is already emerging: (a) in this most complex area of psychology, statistics have an important contribution to make, so that large numbers of subjects are required for these investigations; (b) where firsthand observation is linked to theory, the conclusions can have lasting value; (c) defining terms is always important, but clarity with personality can only be achieved by taking extra care over definitions; (d) results of different investigations can only be compared where definitions agree; and (e) much refinement of personality tests is in progress today.

A number of authorities are pressing for more research into young children's personality traits, e.g. Cattell and Coan (1958), Lynn (1959), Gibson (1964) and S. B. G. Eysenck (1965). Once there is common ground for assessing both children and adults, areas of difference begin to show, e.g. that lying decreases with age and the picture of dishonest children does not emerge so clearly as the picture of dishonest adults. The battery of tests used by Burt in 1915 are all used today and can all be used individually with younger children, on whom we urgently need personality data. There is also a possibility that the body type of children could help in prediction of behaviour (cf. Davidson et al., 1957).

Two interesting points about personality and intelligence, which psychologists and educationists have long suspected, now begin to receive statistical confirmation. First, personality takes precedence over high intelligence in teaching ability. Thus the best way to forecast a final teaching practice mark is to use a personality test as well as an intelligence test. This is true, even at the present level of personality test development, as is shown by Warburton et al. (1963) and E. G. S. Evans (1964). There are a number of reasons for this: (a) the living and learning contact with children essential for progressive education is best established by people more interested in other people than in themselves; those with highest intelligence often prefer academic studies and tend to withdraw into books. If those with highest intelligence are also endowed with highest creative ability, then the double gift might overpower the children, and such people would express themselves more effectively in one of the arts or in advanced science than in the classroom.

The second point about personality and intelligence is that level of intelligence is not the sole line of demarcation for college of education or university training. Outward-looking personalities, those more interested in others than themselves, are attracted to teaching and many of higher than average university intelligence frequently choose a college of education rather than a university. It has long been possible for graduates to take a teaching course, if they wished to work with children. Now it is possible for students at colleges of education to pursue their studies to degree level. The researches we have been looking at have included some MEd theses, resulting from such further studies by teachers. When children have to decide at school what further education they should take, they often have little notion of their personality potentialities. The stable extravert is more suited to teaching and the stable introvert is more suited to academic studies. It is now possible, on finding more of one's potentialities, to prolong studies on lines to which one is more suited. Nobody is going to deny that both the stable extravert and the stable introvert are more favourably placed if they have quite a good level of intelligence. But intelligence is rather like money: only stable personalities can put either to good purpose.

Meanwhile, teachers are constantly asked to assess children's personalities on permanent record cards. Yet many, for example Butcher *et al.* (1963), consider rating a somewhat unsatisfactory technique. For the present, it looks as if teachers should not only use rating, but also make every effort to improve their ratings. Rating is a technique which could be valuable with children too young to record their answers to personality tests, particularly as teachers of the youngest children are often most observant of behaviour. The best approach to the study of rating is threefold: examine first the construction of graphs, then the characteristics of judges, and lastly the traits to be rated.

1. *Graphs*

There should be only one trait on a page, to aid concentration; if there are more, cover them up. The whole group should be rated for one trait before going on to the graph of the next trait. The line representing the dimension of the trait should be continuous (to remind us that the trait in a particular group is not in discontinuous types but differentially graded) The line should be about 5 or 6 inches long and can have little guide lines pointing up to where to place the mark. The investigator can later put a stencil over the line to count how many marks fall within the required classes (for subsequent statistical analysis); he might later use fewer classes than he asked the rater to make, but must never use more classes than have been used in the rating. There are usually five or seven points or classes; the traits which are difficult to class should have a cruder scale with fewer points. The plus and minus ends to traits (e.g. on Leadership, 'Displays marked ability to lead his peers' and 'Probably unable to lead his peers') should alternate randomly at right and left of lines on successive sheets (to counteract any muscular tendency to bias marking in one direction). Each rating scale should begin with a question to be answered by a mark on the line. There should be an odd number of adjectives: two extremes, an average in the centre, and two or more on either side of the centre. First the likely number of extremes of a particular trait should be estimated (if there are none, less extreme descriptions must be used). The descriptive phrases should be universally understood (avoiding slang or colloquialism), and in small type with white spaces between them. There should be space to report the fact, if there has been no opportunity to observe this trait in an individual; and also space to state on what observed behaviour of each child the rating has been based.

Select one of the five rating scales in Figure 22 (p. 157), write it on a separate page, and check to how many of these criteria it conforms. Teachers who are asked to rate children for personality traits should examine the construction of the scale and report to the investigator any apparent defects they find. The investigator may be able to give a good explanation, such as very few classes for an obscure trait. The rater has to be very critical of the instrument he is given for rating.

2. Judges

There are various errors to which judges are universally prone. Some are too harsh; but many more are too lenient. Some have a central tendency, marking too many as average and not caring to mark any extremes. Some have an individual error to be seen in all traits rated, such as over- or under-estimating or having too wide a scatter to the extremes with not enough average markings; study of all one's own ratings can show if one has such a tendency.

Everyone's judgment is liable to suffer from halo effect (see p. 156), marking too much on general impression; this must constantly be checked by marking observed behaviour under standard conditions. Marking from general impression gives a spurious correlation of traits in one individual. Experience and determination to mark each trait from observed behaviour alone, greatly reduces the halo effect, even if it can never quite eliminate it. Halo effect is most common when a trait is not easily observable, not singled out or discussed, not clearly defined; also when traits involve reactions with others or when traits are of high moral importance. At times judges make a logical error, when two traits seem to be logically related and the judge assumes there must be a similar grading. Thus halo effect results from apparent linking of qualities in one individual; and the logical error results from an inferred linkage of traits irrespective of individuals. All these pitfalls can be reduced by judging a child from his observed behaviour. Of course, judges differ in ability to observe, to have insight into observed behaviour. Also, judges may, even after careful preparation, disagree. Therefore situations should be standardised. For instance, Vygotsky (see p. 97) would set a particular task, having arranged an obstruction, and then observe the young child's behaviour. Proper training, through discussion and study, improves rating ability. A judge who is sure of a trait ranks it more reliably than one who is not; so each trait must be precisely defined for all stages from one extreme to the other. More than one judge, with scores pooled, improves reliability; but there appears to be no improvement when scores of more than three or four judges are pooled. A judge can observe how he judges by comparing his score with the pooled scores of other judges. Raters should always be given enough time to base their markings on careful observation, and given opportunity to state the observed behaviour upon which their rating of a trait is based.

Ratings are influenced by the judge knowing the purpose of the investigation, so raters should be asked to make the ratings in advance of hearing the purpose to which the ratings are to be put. This means that teachers, while becoming informed about traits, about graphic scales and about how to judge reliably, should be prepared to assist research by rating first and finding out the nature of the research afterwards.

3. Traits

First and foremost, the traits must be carefully defined; so must each degree of the trait along the graphic line, from one extreme to the other. The definitions need to be objective and specific, with each trait related to a single type of behaviour. We still lack thorough scientific analysis of personality into independent variables, but we can try to avoid composites of several traits, by careful definition of both the trait and the linked observable behaviour. General terms, such as 'very', 'extreme', 'average' and 'excellent' (as used in many termly school reports) should be avoided. Rating should be on past or present observation but never on future potential, for the obvious reason that the future has not yet been observed. Rating should also not be used for any matter that can be more objectively assessed, e.g. health should be assessed from health records and intelligence from intelligence tests.

Guilford (1936), from whom many of these points have been taken, says that objections to rating on account of constant errors by judges can be met by a proof that (a) pooled ratings eliminate the force of these errors; and (b) certain statistical corrections can take account of such errors.

A great deal of preparation for rating can be done in colleges through students rating themselves. Incidentally there is a tendency for the able to underrate themselves and a stronger tendency for the less able to overrate themselves. These tendencies can be checked by careful study of the criteria for judges, by the definition of traits and by linking traits to observable behaviour. Students can rate small groups of the students they know best, pool their scores, compare individual scores with pooled scores, and also compare their self-rating with rating of themselves by others. Though students can be very good judges of some of their traits, they tend to have different opinions from other people on some traits. Rating scales can be constructed, with constant reference to psychological dictionaries and textbooks. The general discussion, rating, examination of results and subsequent improvement of performance, makes one familiar with the terminology of personality research, which can only be advantageous in other areas of personality testing, the so-called projection tests, the questionnaires, and so on. In the Staines experiment on the self (p. 116) we have already seen how preparing the one teacher to assess the children's self picture acted as a training for the teacher in the psychological processes involved. If students make a careful attempt to assess themselves and each other, this will prepare them for assessing the personalities of children.

There are many ways in which ingenious students can standardise conditions for rating their fellow students. For instance, invite several others to come singly on different days for a drink or discussion of some topic; then see there is no available chair and watch the visitor's reaction. Humour or sociability or anger or security might be rated in this way. The value of making up such standard conditions is that one becomes familiar with the concept of standardisation. The abstract concept of rating personality by direct observation under standardised conditions will be more firmly understood if students plan and carry out concrete situations in which to rate a succession of personality traits in their fellow students. Subsequent discussion of similar experiments with others will clarify a number of problems, such as faulty definition of degrees of a trait, lack of suitable observable behaviour for making a rating, and so on. But the children who are later rated, as part of school routine, will be better rated after such rehearsal; and until we have objective personality tests, rating is all that most teachers can do. If we make our ratings as reliable as possible, further research will show whether objective tests can surpass rating or not. Even if research should show that questionnaires and inventories are not as good as ratings by thoroughly trained judges of personality traits in known children, the objective tests have a most important role to play in obtaining large masses of data for statistical analysis.

There are a number of books from which further information on personality can be gained. Allport's *Personality, A Psychological Interpretation* (1937) is a classic. Allport is an erudite and reflective writer, and in this book he traces the development of the concept of personality over many centuries. Pear's *Personality, Appearance and Speech* (1957) is non-technical and entertaining, with a useful list of references. Ainsworth and Ainsworth have written a book, *Measuring Security in Personal Adjustment* (1958), which describes attempts to test the extent of a person's security and insecurity, now being carried out at the Toronto Institute of Child Study. Though the tests were devised for young adults, one hopes that suitable adaptation to young children will be successful. This is an interesting and valuable book.

In the past a clear distinction has been made between books for students and books for lecturers who have to teach students. But now that students are beginning to be orientated to research, some of this distinction goes. In carrying out an investigation, however modest, on a complex subject such as personality, the student has to be prepared to discuss the subject with the teachers. Therefore, the second Monograph from Keele University, edited by Halmos, *Papers on the Teaching of Personality Development* (1959), could have value to students. It is a report of a symposium and very practical in nature. It deals with students' attitudes, insight, human relations, identification, and so on.

Vernon's *Personality Assessment* (1964) is the most important modern survey of modes of assessing personality. It covers lay and specialist interpretations of personality and practical methods of assessment. As always with Vernon's books, it is clear and concise. Chapter 16 begins: 'It would be foolish to discard such a convenient and easily scored instrument as the self-report of personality, attitudes or interests, so long as we recognise its weaknesses and accept it simply as a method of approach to a person's conceptual system.' The reader wants to read on, to find out what Vernon considers are the advantages and disadvantages of this approach. What they are is set out in clear and completely logical sequence.

There is good reason for examining information on personality at the infant stage in the present account of developing children. Progressive educationists insist that teaching and learning establish a relation and human relations involve personality as well as intelligence. Therefore the personalities of children are of importance to teachers right from the beginning of schooling. So far, research on personality has been directed mainly to secondary school children and college students, to the neglect of the younger children. Scientific research on the personality of young children is just beginning and information from it will help to fill the gap in our knowledge of children aged 5 to 8 years.

15. Learning

The first thing people ask a child who has started to attend a primary school is, 'What have you learnt?' This is mystifying to the child who has been learning very rapidly all his life without having to report about it. The study of how anyone learns anything is very recent, a matter of little more than a hundred years. It really began with Bain's *The Senses and the Intellect* (1855), in which he linked the discoveries of physiologists about the nervous system with psychology. But Britain lost this initiative and experimental work was developed in America.

The first step in studying learning was to make an analysis down to simpler components, a task which proved far more complex than anyone had expected. We had better begin by ruling out what is not learning. *Reflex* action is not learning. If liquid gets into the throat of a newborn infant, its swallowing muscles respond; if there is too much liquid, it chokes. Though reflexes are not learning, they are involved in learning, so we should at least know that the simplest form of reflexes has four stages: a receptor (area sensitive to stimulus), a sensory neuron (a nerve cell to receive the sensory experience), a motor neuron (a nerve cell for muscle movement) and an effector (a muscle or gland of response). This sequence is known as the *reflex arc*.

In terms of evolution, it has taken a long time to develop the complex form of reflexes to be found in mammals. Figure 23 shows the stages which have been passed, on the way to the mammalian switchboardlike system with possible alternative responses. From the final stage of this sequence of diagrams, one can see that various alternatives of response are available in higher forms of life. Reflex action is far more complex than the simple statement of a reflex arc suggests. Many reflexes work at once or in close sequence. Sometimes they mutually strengthen or *facilitate* each other; and sometimes they cancel each other out, in mutual extinction or *inhibition*. The spinal cord inside the spine is like an underground (under flesh and bone) cable, carrying the incoming messages to the central switchboard (the brain) and carrying

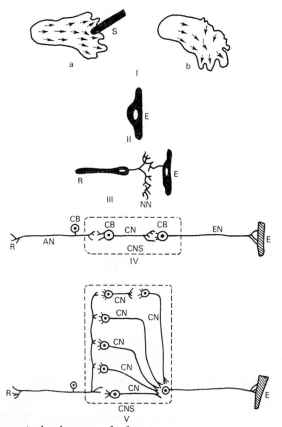

Figure 23. Stages in development of reflex arc.

   I. Amoeba. (*a*) Just stimulated by glass rod (S). (*b*) Change of flow of protoplasm and response of amoeba to such stimulation.
   II. Independent effector cell.
  III. Receptor-effector mechanism with some indication of nerve net (NN).
  IV. Simple receptor-adjustor-effector mechanism of reflex arc.
   V. More complex receptor-adjustor-effector mechanism. Abbreviations:
     S = stimulus, E = effector, R = receptor, NN = nerve net, AN = afferent neuron, CB = cell body of neuron, CN = connector neuron, CNS = central nervous system, EN = efferent neuron.

Source: Boring, Langfeld and Weld (1939).

back messages of behaviour. Figure 24 shows a flick of movement by a salamander. While this is going on, the salamander is also breathing, digesting, looking, hearing, circulating the blood and so on. The simple reflex action, as a working system, proves to be highly complex. But in itself it is automatic, and not learning.

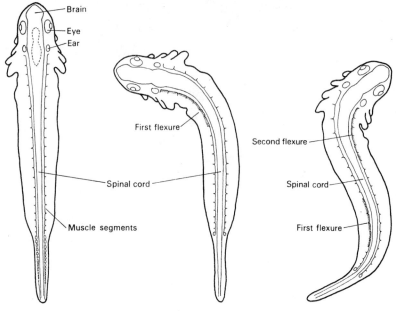

Figure 24. Swimming of the salamander.
Source: Boring, Langfeld and Weld (1939) (after Coghill).

The other important factor which we have to separate from learning is maturation, with which we are already somewhat familiar from the work of such people as Piaget. Maturation is the variance in developmental changes due to heredity. But all maturational aspects do, in fact, interact with the environment. So we might say maturation is an abstract concept, an aspect of developmental changes that take place more or less inevitably in all normal members of the species, so long as they are provided with an environment suitable to the species. It is very important to disentangle this abstract concept of maturation from learning, even though we see at once that it is deeply involved in learning. Separating the concept of maturation will help us to see whether the environment which we provide for normal young humans in primary schools is suitable to their stage of more or less inevitable developmental changes.

The Russian physiologist Pavlov (1849–1936), a Nobel Prize Winner, made a study of reflex action, at first of the circulation and digestion. His problem was that nobody had every devised a method of making accurate measurement of reflex behaviour. While studying the digestion of dogs, he noticed that a dog's mouth watered when powdered meat was put in front of it.

He hit on the brilliantly simple method of tapping the saliva and measuring the quantity of fluid each time the meat stimulus was set before the dog. He made a harness for the dog, which had to be trained to stand quietly in harness. Figure 25 is a diagram of the dog and harness. Then he tapped the fluid by means of a rubber tube leading from the salivary gland to a measuring container. In front of the dog was a bowl, and powdered meat could be put into the bowl by remote control. While he was studying the dog's digestion he wondered how the dog learned that the powder was really meat. He wondered whether a dog could learn that a light coming on meant that meat

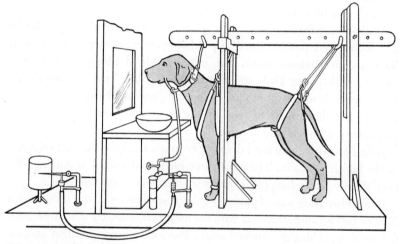

Figure 25. Pavlov's dog.
Source: Hilgard (1953) (after Yerkes and Margoulis).

was to follow. When he first put a light on, the dog's mouth did not water. But meat always followed the light; and after a few trials, the dog's mouth watered as soon as the light went on, before the meat appeared. So now Pavlov had two kinds of response: (*a*) the natural response of salivation at food, which he called an *unconditioned response*; and (*b*) the response to something that is a sign that food is coming, which he called a *conditioned response*. The dog had gone one step further than a reflex reaction to food and learned a changed or conditioned response. Dogs have no built-in mechanism to salivate at a light but the dog had learned a conditioned response. Pavlov spent the greater part of the rest of his life studying how many stages of conditioning the dogs could tolerate and how subtle the differences of stimulus could be; for instance, instead of a light he used a bell, and even a circle for meat and an oval for no meat. He experimented with reflexes that augmented or facilitated each other and with reflexes which cancelled each other out or inhibited responses. Amongst other important discoveries he found that inhibition, not performing a learned response, was a positive action; the learned action had to be stopped. Inhibition is a stopping of some action. After a few repeated inhibitions the conditioning is extinguished and the reflex can be conditioned again, in the same way or a different way. Because Aristotle had been the first to mention association in connection with learning, Pavlov's experiments with conditioned responses became known as *classical conditioning*. The work of Pavlov linked reflex action with learning, through conditioning.

We have seen from our study of work on the self, that British psychologists as a whole were not interested in psychological experiments. A few were interested in Pavlov's work. For instance, Lloyd Morgan (1852–1936) worked with young birds and first used terms like 'trial and error', 're-inforcement of successful modes of response', and 'inhibition of the unsuccessful'. But the Americans took up the suggestion from Bain of linking psychology with learning. People like Thorndike in the States carried on experiments with every level of living creature, from the simplest creatures to the higher primates. The most extensively used animal in America has been the rat. Hearnshaw (1964) refers to their 'cult of the white rat'.

But Pavlov's dog waited passively in harness while some such stimulus as a light or bell became associated with the meat that followed. The Americans followed up, with experimental work, Morgan's observation that animals frequently explored a situation actively, until by trial and error they happened to find a solution. They called this *operant learning* because the animals were active and operating. Once the animal's explorations result in success, then the correct solution is reinforced by success in classical conditioning. Therefore operant learning is basically classical conditioning, but the activity of the animal has chanced upon the stimulus associated with the reward through its own exploration.

Some psychologists felt that not all higher forms of learning could be fitted into classical conditioning and operant learning. For instance, learning to play games or to play a musical instrument involves taking in whole patterns. This kind of pattern learning is very noticeable in language, where whole sentences are treated as a single item, long before a child can isolate the separate words. Experiments have been done on maze learning by animals and men, mirror drawing, and so on, which require a whole situation to be grasped. The Americans have given the name *multiple response learning* to this. Neither operant learning nor multiple response learning have had anything like the amount of experimental work done on them that has been done on classical conditioning. Not everyone accepts multiple response learning. Hilgard of Stanford University has a lot to say about it in *Introduction to Psychology* (1953), but Deese of Johns Hopkins University does not mention it in *The Psychology of Learning* (1958). In fact Deese specifically says there are two types of learning, classical conditioning and operant learning. So we must leave the third kind as still an open question.

A theory originating from Germany is that the mind grasps a whole as something different in quality as well as quantity from the parts. The idea of pattern or (in German) *Gestalt* understanding is based on considerable experimentation. Subjects reported that a circle was something more than the sum of many arcs, that a melody remained a unit no matter in what key or with what instruments it was played, that a Bruegel picture of skating was more than a sum of many individual people skating, and so on. The Gestalt theory states that the properties of the whole as such are not derived by summation of its parts; and conversely, the parts derive their properties from their membership in the whole. This is a theory of considerable interest although, because of its subjective nature, it does not lend itself to the rigorous scientific procedures possible with classical learning.

Again from the subjective point of view, it seems that animals as well as people give evidence of *insight* at the moment of learning. A very famous example of this is to be seen in Köhler's *The Mentality of Apes* (1925). Köhler, a German, was in Tenerife when the First World War started and, unable to return home, studied the apes in the zoo, keeping careful records. He put bananas in difficult positions and left apparatus about, such as boxes and sticks, with which the apes could reach the bananas. At one time a banana could only be reached if all the boxes were put one on the other; at another time all the boxes were not enough, and the ape could not reach the banana until he had thought of hitting the banana with a stick. At such moments apes appeared to have insight about solutions. *Insight* is the process by which the meaning, pattern or use of an object or situation becomes clear and understanding is gained. It could be inferred to be occurring in apes because they surveyed the aim and the apparatus, paused, and then in a continuous set of movements put the apparatus correctly together. When the apes gave evidence of such insight, their learning was more effective. Here again, operant learning is involved in the active exploration, and success is reinforced by classical conditioning. But the insight shown refers to the animal's awareness of possible solution. This moment of insight is sometimes

7

very aptly called 'the AHA! experience'. Köhler's description of the behaviour of these apes is most interesting.

Experimenters with classical conditioning found there was a tendency for reflexes to shift to similar stimuli. For instance, if a bell was used instead of a light, then fairly similar sounds to the bell would act as a conditioning stimulus. The way in which similar stimuli can also cause a conditioned response is called *generalisation*. We have met this generalising, a mental activity which covers two or more similar items, in connection with Vygotsky's word meaning (see p. 93), where being able to use a word as a symbol involves generalising. The strength of generalising becomes less and less as the similar stimuli become less and less like the original stimulus.

The same thing happens with extinction. While one response to a stimulus is being actively inhibited, active inhibition also takes place with stimuli similar to the one being extinguished; and again, the strength of the extinction decreases as the stimuli become less and less similar to the original stimulus. So this generalising about similar stimuli happens both in conditioning a reflex response and in extinguishing a conditioned response. The generalising activity, for both response and extinction, is sufficiently constant for graphs of gradients of generalisation to be constructed. There is also an opposite activity, a tendency to notice when stimuli are dissimilar. This is called *discrimination*. Here again, we have met the idea of discrimination in connection with language. The more familiar people are with, for instance, camels or trees or snow, the more they discriminate among different kinds of camels or trees or snow, and the more words they have to describe different states of these things.

This type of learning proceeds by successive waves of conditioning, reinforcement, extinction, generalisation and discrimination. Some psychologists would claim that much of a child's learning proceeds in this way. Any green vegetable which looks like spinach may be disliked by a child because he dislikes spinach; all who wear trousers or have deep voices may be called *Dadda*. It is only by successive waves of reinforcement and extinction, subtler generalisations of what things are similar, together with subtler discriminations of what things are dissimilar, that the earliest crude learnings are refined to more accurate learning. The nasty flavour is associated with just spinach and the comfort-sounding word is reserved for just the one man at home; *doggie* is reserved for dogs and not used for cows or pigs. The more successful generalisations and successful discriminations can be reinforced, the more efficient the learning. This is what we have in mind when we reward a child for successful learning by appreciating his efforts.

Appreciation is a reward which reinforces the successful learning. A good teacher may give no more reward than a glance and an appreciative half smile, but the child receives the reward and the satisfactory behaviour is reinforced.

Much more of our learning proceeds along the lines of classical conditioning than we had realised before learning research was done. Solutions discovered by chance, through trial and error, are classically reinforced by success. The intellectual gratification of insight and emotional gratification of AHA! also aid the classical conditioning; and what proves unsuccessful is extinguished by active inhibition. Books of programmed learning are based on the discovery that success is a powerful reinforcement. When the steps in the learning are so small that the reader is successful nearly all the way, the outcome is securely reinforced learning. Unquestionably, the sphere of our greatest clumsiness in education has been that of extinguishing non-desirable behaviour. Instead of quietly conveying to a child that such writing, such spelling, or such calculation fails to win appreciation, we have created an emotional carnage; and what was slaughtered was the child's *self* respect.

The fact that we have underexploited pleasure in learning is amusingly revealed by an experiment now being conducted in a number of zoos with higher primates, especially chimpanzees. When the chimpanzees have learned something successfully, they are rewarded, not with food but with a metal disc which they can 'spend' at a chimp-o-mat, which is a coin-operated machine. A chimpanzee can learn to choose whether to put his disc in the slot for a grape or the slot for a chocolate. At the London zoo the monkeys immensely enjoy this new game. Indeed, they became so speedy in choosing rewards that elaborate devices were invented for them to unravel before gaining the reward. This kind of learning is called *token learning*. The important conclusion, which educationists should note, is that the monkeys enjoy the puzzle-solving as well as the reward.

There appear to be inborn differences in ability to form inhibitions. Many psychologists think that some people who are criminal or neurotic seek immediate gratification, not just because they have not been trained to carry out long-term projects, but because they have a marked inability to act on a basis of delayed reinforcement. The reason for this inability to tolerate delayed reinforcement may lie partly in the unstable disposition of the individual and partly in lack of ability to form inhibitions. The training necessary for forming inhibitions is much more difficult when the adults themselves are unreliable, sometimes giving and sometimes withholding deserved rewards. Then the child actually becomes conditioned to distrust success situations. Faced with a child who through temperament and/or home background lacks ability to form the inhibitions necessary for delayed greater gains, a good teacher goes out of his way to give this particular child excessively patient and stable encouragement. Such a teacher is, in the biblical sense, a 'good shepherd' because he can change his technique for the 'lost' child.

Another form of learning which should be mentioned is *imprinting*. Lorenz refers to it in *King Solomon's Ring* (1952); and so much information on learning is coming from ethnological studies such as those of Lorenz, that we should know of imprinting even if it is not yet clearly linked to learning theories. Lorenz's geese followed him because he was the first moving thing they saw after being hatched. The three characteristics of imprinting are: (*a*) it occurs with spontaneous rather than reflex behaviour (although the behaviour appears to be 'released' by external stimulus); (*b*) it seems to happen only in a very restricted period in the early life of young animals; and (*c*) it requires no specific reinforcement for activation. Jaynes (1956) has found considerable evidence of generalisation of imprinting, even to quite dissimilar objects. Those who wish to go more deeply into imprinting will find a full review of research in Slukin's *Imprinting and Early Learning* (1964); on p. 112 he tentatively links imprinting to early human learning. This subject is not yet sufficiently explored to be clearly related to human education. In 1968 the eminent zoologist Desmond Morris suggests that imprinting may be a factor when humans fall in love and form what he calls 'pair-bonding'. Further research will show whether imprinting can happen as late as this or, more likely, is revived when some characteristic of the loved one resembles that of the original imprinting stimulus. Statistically, the number of people who marry someone with a family resemblance is well above chance. This is one of the reasons why geneticists have to allow for 'preferential, not chance mating' (see p. 46, point 3).

During the first part of the twentieth century not many teachers thought that the findings of research into learning had any application to their classrooms. But gradually new information began to infiltrate schools and colleges; and much that teachers now take for granted originated in psychological research of the present century. For example, what we learn today depends both on our capacity to learn and on previous knowledge; learning arises from active interchange with the environment; recall of previous experience in a new situation can result in problem solving; and much of complex behaviour can be explained in terms of classical conditioning. Some information of this kind is so new that it still seems rather strange. For example, certain kinds of learning have to await maturation of the cortex of the brain, and this is particularly true of ability to think in symbols and to form concepts; situations for practice in manipulation of concepts have to continue much longer than we thought, not only throughout the junior school but well into the secondary school; if true abstract thinking is to develop, then all previous stages of thinking must first have been fully experienced.

People who work extensively by means of abstract concepts are traditionally described as 'lost in thought' and 'abstracted'. The highly abstract concepts that they manipulate can be symbolised in a variety of ways other than words; for instance, mathematics, music, painting and so on. The scientists and artists are seeking fresh arrangement of ideas. Such *conceptual learning* is the objective in much school work. Though this form of learning is not fully operative until the end of secondary school, many early factors of all-round development contribute to its attainment; for example, sensory-motor experience through which language has real meaning, intuitive thought, the manipulation of situations in problem solving, and wide exploration of the environment. The teacher's main concern is—or should be—to promote children's thinking as they advance towards conceptual learning.

We can learn much from the way in which outstanding men and women arrive at new insights. The mathematician Henri Poincaré, in *Science et Méthode* (1908), describes assembling all the relevant material for a problem, and waking after sleep to find the solution there. Rembrandt wished to give the impression of bright light in a picture, although white paint is much duller than light, and gave the illusion of light by darkening the knight's armour. Debussy gave an illusion of haunting strangeness to *L'Apres Midi d'une Faune* by opening it with a chromatic sequence which could not be fitted into any traditional scale. In the same way, Shakespeare broke from the traditional concept of a successful hero when he created the first hesitant hero in Hamlet. The great achievements of art and science come both through extensive well-organised knowledge and through insight which may be sudden or may come in a succession of small steps.

Perhaps our biggest reorientation of educational thinking today comes from realising that learning is neither a luxury nor a privilege; it is an essential for development and, like all essentials of life, it is a pleasure. Our most skilled work may well be in directing some of the children's inborn aggression towards the self-discipline necessary for tolerating the inevitable frustrations which accompany delayed reward. We can only do this if the objectives are ones which the children themselves understand and want to attain.

16. Mathematics

Mathematics is an aspect of education which has undergone one of the most revolutionary changes as a result of modern research on how children learn. To say we have underexploited pleasure in mathematics would be a classic understatement. In no area of education has the despairing teacher been so driven to resort to punishment, both physical and mental. Mathematics has its own system of symbols by which thinking can attain concept formation; and cortical maturation sets limits to the speed and nature of this learning. Abstract mathematical thinking can only be attained by means of full experience of all previous stages.

The child's environment has to suit his developmental level and he has to be free to explore it with enthusiasm. He has to make the discoveries for himself. We can no more impose insight on him than we can convert his nourishment into body-building. Rote learning has little to do with the main objective in introducing a child to mathematics, which is to foster problem-solving by recalling previous experience in a new situation. For this, much interesting experience of liquids, solids, lengths, weight and so on is essential.

A group of nursery school children playing with bottles, tubes, balls, etc. round a water trough are gaining foundations of mathematics. Some of what they learn will be wrong and will have to be altered after further experience and at later stages of maturation. Part of this training is in learning that information has to be checked. A teacher who, with the handling of money in mind, starts a shop in the classroom, has to introduce the children to the shop in ways that seem to have little to do with calculation. First the courtesies of shopping have to be enacted without any financial transaction; then a standard penny for all objects may be charged; then a more complex price and the exact money produced; and so on to change and keeping accounts. If this development is allowed to take a year or two, shopping in the classroom remains a pleasure. The environment is suited to the child's mental level and maturation can interact with environment.

In such learning, conditioned response plays an important part. If a child has two pennies to go shopping and receives two objects on his table, he can begin to see the two-ness of both pennies and objects. The success of getting the number of objects to fit the number of pennies he had, reinforces the process. The teacher strengthens the reinforcement by herself showing awareness of his success. When things go wrong the teacher's task is not to emphasise the obvious failure but to give the kind of help which enables the child to succeed on his own. The teacher's task is basically the same whatever the level of problem at which a child in the primary school is working. The progressive teacher does not so much give information as ask questions in small steps which enable the child to achieve his own insight. In order to ask these leading questions, the teacher is perpetually analysing the problems encountered by each child. This is such an interesting intellectual exercise for the teacher that many who had themselves taken an intense dislike to mathematics are now teaching the new mathematics with great enthusiasm.

The change of attitude to the teaching of mathematics has been due to the cooperation of many people. Interest came originally from two very different sources. First, the creative activity carried on in an increasing number of infant schools showed very clearly that children, left to themselves, take a lively spontaneous interest in learning the nature of liquids and solids, the weights of different substances, who has most or least, and so on. Teachers who were accustomed to working from children's own interests, saw that all the processes required on going up to good junior schools—and much more besides—could be carried out in practical situations, provided the teachers were alive to moments when mathematical discoveries were made, *and* what experiences should next be available.

The other source of the new attitude was the scientists. They said that the mathematics which children learned in school—and they did not just mean primary schools—was almost valueless. They maintained that arithmetic was for desk calculators, books of tables and slide-rules. They said children should begin with topology, binary logic, almost anything *but* arithmetic. Peel (1967) reports an interesting experiment by means of a game with children of 5 to 10, which demonstrates that children have an appreciation of binary logic. The author of this book on developing children took a physicist to a boys' junior school with a maths room equipped with desk calculators, slide-rules, paper for graph making, bicycle wheels and so on. After half an hour with a group of boys aged 8 and 9, going round and chatting about what they were doing, he said, 'Some of them are doing noncommutative algebra, others have arrived at the first stage of imaginary numbers. I had to do this stuff for my exhibition to Balliol.' These comments pinpoint a vital aspect of the new mathematics; the teacher has to recognise a child's mathematical discovery, and use the moment of discovery for handing on mathematical techniques.

The new approach was presented by the Mathematical Association in *The Teaching of Mathematics in Primary Schools* (1956). The ideas were so revolutionary that many interested teachers demanded courses and conferences. The Department of Education and Science gave full support, with a

Figure 26. Measuring Shadows.
Source: The Schools Council (1965).

series of study groups. Investigations were undertaken by such bodies as the National Foundation for Educational Research, and the British Association for the Advancement of Science. The Schools Council published *Mathematics in Primary Schools* (1965), which covers both the philosophy and the practical application of the new approach to mathematics. This is a most valuable reference book. It contains many illustrations and photographs, and suggestions for experiments. Indeed, the way the material is presented sets a standard for classroom presentation of children's discoveries. For instance, in a section on work with shadows (pp. 38–40), there are excellent examples of a six-year-old child's illustration, to be seen in Figure 26, together with her table and graph. In order to check whether the hourly changes in length of shadow were due to changes in her own height, she also measured her own height hourly.

A good popular book is *The Giant Colour Book of Mathematics, Exploring the World of Numbers and Space,* by Adler (1958). This is a book for parents to enjoy with their children, and many schools have it in the book corner. An excellent book in which a teacher can find fresh ideas is the Unesco *Source Book for Science Teaching* (1962). It is not presented as a new approach to maths but is full of material which can be adapted to this purpose, such as experiments in plant study, electricity, weights and pendulums, sounds and music. The illustrations are very clear and much of the apparatus is ingenious rather than expensive. Another useful book, which appeared a little too early to receive the appreciation it deserved, is *A Background to Primary School Mathematics* by Adams (1953). The author was an HMI and a prime mover in the mathematical revolution.

Educational Research has published many articles on the new approach to maths since the start of this journal in 1958. In the first issue Biggs (1958) gives a selected and annotated bibliography on the teaching of arithmetic; and in the same volume, but 1959, he introduces a symposium on 'The teaching of mathematics', with two articles on the development of number concepts in young children, and on the causes of anxiety over arithmetic. From the researches he mentions he concludes that there is a closer link of maladjustment with arithmetic than with any other school subject. This is supported by psychologists working in Child Guidance Centres, where arithmetic is given as the most disliked subject far more often than any other subject, by the children undergoing treatment. Biggs says much more research is required before we can say why this should be so. From his earlier article, on the development of number concepts, we already have a pointer to the causal connection of anxiety and expecting abstract number concepts from the children too early. In Chapter 6, we have seen that investigations by Lovell and others support the fact that practical situations in maths work should be the mode of learning for much longer than was previously thought. Biggs says attitudes of anxiety about mathematics seem to start in the infant school, and may affect a child's whole school career. He suggests that the teacher's attitude to maths is of prime importance, and asks how many teachers really like the subject. He looks forward to the day when classroom maths is such that 'fear of number' is a meaningless phrase. Wood (1968) has published a clear statement on the objectives in teaching mathematics.

The next articles in this symposium are concerned with practical experience for the children. Dienes (1959) writes on the growth of mathematical concepts through the use of apparatus which he has developed, and for which teachers have to undergo a course of training. This material has to be ordered through local education authorities direct from the National Foundation for Educational Research. Dienes maintains that children who have followed his whole course in their primary schooling will be equipped with a firm foundation for secondary school maths. J. D. Williams continues with a series of articles on: 1. Miming devices (1961); 2. Structural systems (1962); 3. Issues and arguments (1963a). The miming devices involve play at real life situations, using coins, measures, grouping, space, etc. The first part of this third article shows how much of the different systems overlaps or is complementary, and so the teacher needs to group all into a few general categories. The article on structural systems describes in detail eight sets of apparatus with which structures can be built. Williams ends this section by pointing out that many of these systems claim that they enable children to go beyond primary work. This will not surprise the reader, as we have already seen (p. 189) that children of 8 and 9 can spontaneously touch on such branches of mathematics as noncommutative algebra and imaginary numbers. Williams agrees that these claims may well be justified but, he says, there is little explanation of exactly how this is to be done. There has been insufficient research with new maths apparatus, on the vital point of exactly *how* the teacher develops the potential of a child revealed by his mathematical discoveries. In the article on issues and arguments, Williams reviews the various points raised and makes a plea that teachers should not swallow 'a scheme' whole but treat each one critically and make use of what each one has to offer.

In the final article of this symposium J. D. Williams (1963c) discusses arithmetic and the difficulties of calculative thinking. He gives four equally important areas of failure: (*a*) lack of understanding how to relate work to basic principles; (*b*) lack of understanding how to relate work to concrete situations; (*c*) lack of computing skills; and (*d*) lack of motivation. He then applies each of these categories to areas of difficulty for the children. On the first two points, basic principles and concrete or practical situations, we have already seen that *Mathematics in Primary Schools* (p. 190) covers both the philosophy and the practical application. On the third point, the computing skills, the teacher has both to hand on the traditional techniques and to see that there is sufficient practice, otherwise subsequent work is vitiated by needless inaccuracies. Tom Lehrer (1965) in 'The New Math'* makes a skit on this very point when he says that in the new approach one only has to

* In *That Was the Year That Was*, Pye Records R. 6179.

understand, not to get the right answer. With regard to motivation, the discoveries made by the children are so satisfying to their curiosity that these discoveries are in themselves sufficient reward—*provided* the teacher guides the children on to further discoveries.

During the publication of the series on Teaching of Mathematics, *Educational Research* also published an article by Biggs (1961) on the distribution of methods of teaching arithmetic in primary schools in England and Wales. A brief questionnaire was sent to over 7,000 primary school head teachers in sixty-one local education areas. The questionnaire asked for four types of information:

(1) *General details* of type and size of school; (2) *Arithmetical methods*, for instance whether structural apparatus such as Stern or Cuisenaire was used and if so how; (3) *Teaching practice*, for which there were two five-point self-rating scales: (a) for assessment of method, ranging from highly formal to almost entirely active; and (b) for assessment of how much or little concrete material and project work was used; and (4) *Willingness of head teachers to cooperate in further research work.* So much information was returned that analysis of it all proved impossible. This is a reminder to us that intended statistical analysis has to be part of the original design of an investigation and the information asked has to be tailored to what is to be treated statistically.

Two very interesting facts emerged from Biggs's enquiry. First, already in the early 1960s a quarter of the schools were using non-traditional ways of teaching arithmetic, such as miming devices and structural systems. These non-traditional techniques were used more in infant than in junior schools, but there were a number of indications that junior heads would like to make more use of the new approach. The second fact which emerged is that junior heads showed a keen desire to take part in further research.

Junior heads who have hesitated to introduce more progressive techniques naturally want to know at what point teaching takes place. As Williams, above, points out, we are in need of more research here. But it is not easy to design research from which many irrelevant variables are eliminated. Triggs (1966) investigated whether desk calculating machines had any value in primary school maths, and reduced his objective to no more than 'whether the machine had any intrinsic value *whatever*'. In order to concentrate on this one point, he arranged preliminary unaided experimental periods amounting to eighty minutes in all. Those who have used desk calculators will see at once that there is an educational fault here: children need help with these machines right from the start, if they are to learn much from them. Desk calculators are not dumb teachers. However, to have used them more educationally would have interfered with Triggs's investigation. The outcome was that the children who had experimental periods amounting to eighty minutes with the machines improved in maths facility, while the children who were not given time to experiment with such machines did not improve. Moreover, children of above average ability, who could more easily abstract the principles involved, improved even more than the rest. This highlights an important point about the new approach. Children can proceed according to their ability. The slow ones can achieve learning without being hurried so much that they miss vital steps; and those of above average, even those of exceptional ability, can also proceed at a pace which holds their attention, instead of their learning habits of boredom while waiting for the slower children.

In 1964 *Educational Research* began a series of three articles on 'Understanding and arithmetic' with some remarks on the nature of understanding by J. D. Williams. In 1966 this journal published another article by Williams, which gives guiding lines for research into the reform of primary school mathematics teaching. He says that pilot studies must precede educational change. Williams makes a number of suggestions about the planning of such pilot studies. The teachers involved should be enthusiastic about maths and should understand the new approach; where possible, more than one teacher in a school should be in the pilot study; there should be reasonable staff stability. Plans should be made for long-term follow-up from infant to secondary school of 'cohorts' or bands of pupils. The selected schools should be near an advisory centre, such as a college or institute of education; and if these schools are fairly near together, the teachers are able to confer. Schools will be less reluctant to abandon traditional methods in areas where the public examinations which the children have to take are not still completely traditionally orientated; and since the apparatus for the new approach is bulky, schools which still have space to accommodate it will be more willing to adopt it. Large schools with multistream organisation are also more willing to spare some teachers and classes for the experiment. And of course, such pilot studies are easier to arrange in areas where the local education authorities are already interested in the new approach to mathematics.

Williams then gives valuable suggestions on how to ensure that teachers who have begun the new techniques have a chance to sustain interest in them. These include in-service training on the basic teaching philosophy, individual responsibility within the scheme, an encouraging start with brighter children, time for preparation of lessons, and specialist consultations. Both those who plan such a pilot study and those who are to carry out the teaching will find this a most valuable article to read.

From these various articles it is evident that the National Foundation for Educational Research has given much thought to the new approach to mathematics. The research undertaken so far has produced evidence which persuades them to support the new approach; but they also indicate many areas where further research is necessary before this new approach can be fully exploited. There is one other piece of research in this journal which should be mentioned, although it concerns secondary school children. King (1965) reports differences in mathematical achievement related to types of secondary schools and their geographical location. This is part of a much larger study of fourteen-year-old children in south-east England and ninth grade children of the same age in two Minnesota cities of the United States. Many difficulties were met in this cross-cultural study. In the British schools there was considerable overlapping of scores in grammar, technical and secondary modern schools, but the mean scores of the different types of schools showed the expected differences. However, there was a very wide gap between the scores of the first two types and the secondary modern schools. This problem requires urgent attention because, King writes, the causes, motivation, and level of aspiration are not solely linked with differences of ability.

The *British Journal of Educational Psychology* has not in the last ten years been much concerned with the ways of introducing young children to mathematics. There were two articles on arithmetic in the 'fifties. The first article, by Meddleton (1956) of Queensland, Australia, who investigated systematic practice in arithmetic, arose from conversation with Schonell. In *Diagnosis of Individual Difficulties in Arithmetic* (1937) Schonell has much to say on the value of practice for children who are backward in arithmetic. He suggested to Meddleton that research was needed on the effect of practice on children of normal arithmetic ability. Meddleton made such an investigation with top juniors in London schools. He found that systematically planned mathematical practice was more effective than indiscriminate selection of practice examples; and what the children had learned more effectively this way they remembered after the vacation. He also found the practice slightly more beneficial to children of poorer socio-economic areas and more effect on multiplication and division than on addition and subtraction. Although this research is not concerned with the new approach, it could have an important indirect bearing on it. Further research on the new approach may well give us both information on well-designed practice periods for skills, and information on which particular skills, such as multiplication and division most need this systematic practice.

The other article is by Lynn (1957) of Exeter, on temperamental characteristics related to disparity of attainment in reading and in arithmetic. The subjects of Lynn's investigation were (a) eighty unselected normal children attending primary school, with age range 7·5 to 11 years; and (b) forty-five normal boys attending a secondary modern school, with age range 14·6 to 15·6 years. The children were given attainment tests in reading and arithmetic, and the juniors had two anxiety tests, while the moderns had one. In both groups there was a tendency for the more anxious children to be better at reading than at arithmetic. Lynn points out that cases of anxiety reported from clinical studies should be viewed as extreme cases of a general relationship found among normal children. He suggests that anxiety and poor reading coupled with poor arithmetic, may have a neurological foundation. In the next section we shall examine later work on this, which indicates that there may be neurological foundations for some reading problems. In conclusion, Lynn suggests that children who are anxious about arithmetic may retreat into reading as a way of dealing with their anxieties and finding satisfaction in fantasy.

Other articles in the *British Journal of Educational Psychology* concerning mathematics are about secondary and technical children. These include Wrigley (1958), Hebron (1962), Eifermann and Etzion (1964) and Taylor (1966b).

A Swedish experiment in maths is described by Vaigo in *New Scientist* 30th April 1970. During compulsory reorganisation along comprehensive lines work has for several years been directed towards inducting modern techniques into schools. The maths project is IMU (Individualised Mathematical Teaching) and even the youngest can proceed at their own pace, independent of classmates. One example will indicate the revolutionary of the experiment: all exercises with a solution rate below 80 per cent are either rewritten or withdrawn.

Part 5
Junior school age: 8 to 12 years

17. General development
8 to 12 years

One aspect of the years 8 to 12 has received considerable attention during the greater part of the twentieth century; this is mental development. Research into intelligence and scholastic attainment, which is the subject of the next section, together with the work by Piaget and others on the stages of this development, has begun to accumulate a considerable fund of information, and this information is now beginning to have a profound effect on work in junior schools. We now know, for instance, that when the majority of children reach the junior school they can carry out all forms of reasoning provided the problems are sufficiently simple; but we also know that throughout the junior school most children require actual situations which they can manipulate, before they can internalise and organise concepts for complex reasoning. This means that junior schools require far more activity than has been traditional. The number of junior schools beginning to arrange this is steadily increasing.

From the age of about 6 to puberty the rate of physical growth is nearly constant. At the beginning of junior school there is very little difference between boys and girls in height or weight or other bodily dimensions, except for the head, which in boys is always larger. Girls begin puberty on average a year earlier than boys, so that they tend to be taller and heavier than boys by the end of junior school, and may be stronger. But most boys are entirely prepubescent on leaving junior school. In terms of individual children these averages can be misleading. According to the Plowden Report (1967) the average age for menarche, the first menstrual period of girls, is 13 years in England at present; but the age range is from 10 to 15 years. Thus some girls in junior schools have fully developed breasts, are menstruating, and may even be fertile.

The average age for puberty in boys is nearly a year later, that is to say nearly 14 years; but the actual age extends over about the same range of age, being from about 11 to 16 years; thus some reach puberty while still in the junior school. Throughout this century records show that children reach puberty a little earlier in each decade. The reason for this is not yet quite clear; but if it is due to efficient diet fostering steadily better physical development, then we can expect an optimum age for puberty to be arrived at, beyond which diet has no effect.

Puberty is now a development which has to be taken into account with top juniors, if teachers are to show insight over the early developers. In physical terms, both excessively early and excessively late developers tend to be estranged from the general group of children; and the disadvantage works in opposite ways for boys and for girls. Boys are less mature than girls, and a boy who is also a later developer when compared with other boys suffers a double disadvantage. If a boy and girl have the same age and sit next to each other, when the boy is a late developer and the girl is an early developer the contrast is so great that it is difficult to believe they are the same age. Teachers who understand these matters can save the children very great personal suffering.

However, it is quite a small percentage of children who reach puberty during junior school years. The great majority are far more occupied with forming gangs than with the opposite sex. In their gangs they dare each other to feats of prowess. *The Lore and Language of School Children* by I. and P. Opie (1959) shows how important language is for the consolidation of such gangs who share both interests and rules of behaviour. Some of the chapters are just concerned with fun and wit and repartee; but others deal with oral legislation, adult authority and customs. Study of the wealth of examples shows how these little chants can weld a group together:

> Cross my heart and hope to die
> Drop down dead if I tell a lie.

This oath helps to ensure true communication at least within one's own gang.

Such a book which transfixes in language what one might call the 'half-jelled repressions' of the gang stage, is bound to have great significance for those who are natural interpreters of symbols. They are not surprised to see the content of the chants on matters about to be repressed. Chapter 6 has chants of parody and impropriety, the content of which should be familiar to all adults concerned with children of this age. We cannot guide the children emotionally or intellectually if we have ourselves totally repressed what children at the gang stage are struggling to discipline. One of the sadder sights of education is the teacher who does not know why the children get the giggles over the first verse of:

> This old man
> He played one,
> He played nick-nack
> On my drum

The children know a more appropriate rhyme than 'drum'. They now know that it must not be said, but they also know that it can still be thought in chants with your own gang. The most helpful teacher is the one who can see that 'drum' is a symbol for 'bum', and children in the gang stage are not yet quite able to concentrate on the symbol and forget the thing symbolised. This very situation is parodied in:

> Now Mary was a careful child,
> Avoiding every sham,
> She said—one little word that meant
> The mother of the lamb.

The forbidden word is 'damn' and the pun which replaces it is 'dam'; thus dam is a symbol for 'damn' and when adults fail to understand (remember) what the children really mean, this is extremely funny to the children.

Chapter 10 is another chapter which can help in guiding children of this age. It concerns cruelty, at all times an upsetting subject, both for those who inflict it and for those who suffer it. In this chapter one finds chants against unpopular children, with jeers and torments. We have already seen (p. 129) that social development lags behind individual development. It is the individual four-year-old who blames his teddy for a pool on the floor. But it is the eight- or nine-year-old gang which accuses an individual outside the group of giving offence. This gang stage of displacing blame onto others is a time when understanding adults can help children towards clarity of thinking. At this stage the children half-know what they are doing; but a couple of decades later, when displacement becomes racial or national hatred, expensive time-consuming specialist help may not be enough to overcome the damage caused by failure to outgrow the normal stage of gang thinking and displacement of unacceptable characteristics onto other groups.

As for the scapegoat on to whom the displacement is projected, an unpopular child is particularly in the teacher's care. As with less matters such as sneaking, swanking, and so on, all of which have relevant chants in this chapter, the teacher's responsibility is to analyse the situation, and take steps which will improve the behaviour of the individual, the gang, or both. A teacher who actively dislikes a child whose education is in his hands is probably making the very error under discussion: he has recognised something of himself in the child which he has repressed, and is projecting himself on the rejected child. The teacher can learn much by listening to the chants of a group of children, and extracting their emotional content. The Opies have arranged the chants under a score of themes, each theme revealing a particular kind of thinking, ranging from clever-dicks to intimidation, from nosey-parkers to tortures; and the chants reveal the way the children's thinking goes.

One example may show how this information might be used. There are many ways of dismissing a child. The teacher might some time ask each child in his class to make a list of all the ways he knows of sending an unwanted child away; after that, ask each child to draw two pictures, one of himself sending a child away and one of him being sent away himself. The general discussion resulting from this can be a step of intellectual integration: that of recognising that all of us feel at times superior and at times inferior; toleration of oneself is, as we have seen (p. 117), essential for toleration of others. Children who had been helped in this way would better remember when bullying or being bullied, that stability is gained by recalling the other extreme of the bully/bullying or dominant/subordinate relationship. They can then resolve their conflicts instead of crudely repressing them.

The twilight stage of repressing much that is too undisciplined or self-centred for normal social living, suggests that the junior school is a particularly bloodthirsty stage. But this is only because we have dared to look at what is being brought under control. In fact, the years from 8 to 12 are relatively calm years, between the storms of the nursery and the storms of adolescence. The children no longer accept uncritically what they are told. They are learning to find out for themselves; and in the process they sometimes find that they have been misinformed by adults. This gives a further spur to finding out facts for themselves. When children of this age are handled with understanding they are stable, and so this junior school stage is sometimes referred to as the 'latent period'.

While teachers are being trained they hear much about the aims of education and spend much time discussing the mainly moral issues involved. Since the years 8 to 12 cover a period when children are trying to discipline their emotional growth for social living and learning the discipline of seeking out facts, one would expect to find many reports of research on the link between junior school disposition and moral development. But there is so little recent research on moral development that one may suspect an irrational cause for this situation. Perhaps the reason is that a study of ethical behaviour would involve some study of unethical behaviour, of which most teachers are scared. This is most true of adults who have repressed unacceptable behaviour wholesale instead of resolving their conflicts.

We have nothing comparable with Piaget's *The Moral Judgment of the Child* (1932). Consequently lack of facts drives us to opinions which quickly become heated, emotion taking over when intelligence has nothing to add. We should look briefly at what research there is, although it has little to do with the junior school time of struggle towards integrated behaviour. A Symposium on 'The development of moral values in children' was held during the years 1957–9 in the *British Journal of Educational Psychology*, in which the word 'moral' is used, not in the sense of 'conforming to convention' but in that of internalising controls. The purpose of this series of articles was no more than to prepare the way for scientific study of the development of autonomous or self-contained behaviour.

J. Hemming (1957) opens the discussion with some aspects of moral development in a changing society; he discusses the problem of transmitting values from one generation to the next, when the older generation does not know for what kind of world the children are being prepared. Then J. F. Morris (1958) describes the way in which Piaget's 'morality of constraint' in early childhood develops towards a 'morality of cooperation'. He points out the lack of empirical information on this progression; he then draws conclusions from American research (of which there is more than is to be found in Britain), and finally recounts three researches in grammar schools. The grammar school investigations could quite well be adapted to junior school investigation. Next comes Staines's (1958) study of the self-picture in the classroom, already described in Chapter 11. Staines makes the important point that teachers who transmit their views of the children in their care to the children themselves have to recognise that such views so transmitted can affect each child's moral development.

Then comes an article by Crane (1958) of Australia. He asked his students to introspect on their childhood gang days and obtained information on 326 boys' gangs and 54 girls' gangs. If we are to profit by this information about 380 gangs, certain limiting factors have to be borne in mind: (*a*) events recalled about a decade later suffer from two defects; firstly, natural forgetting of outgrown phases and secondly, Freudian 'forgetting' or smoothing over by repression to make a more pleasing recollection; (*b*) the fact that gang rituals concern the stages of learning to forget the unacceptable, will give the information a bias towards this Freudian 'forgetting'; (*c*) this was a group of ex-gang members who had made good, so were probably rich in innate integrity, or in home background, or in both; far from being a random group it was a professionally selected group. Bearing these factors in mind, Crane's conclusions are interesting. He says that gang membership can be an important bridge between the kinship-based status conferred on the child by the family and the achievement-based status conferred by society at large. This conclusion highlights two matters which we have already discussed: that the teacher enables a child to incorporate in his self-picture a notion that he is acceptable through recognised achievements; and that gang membership is a sphere of prowess. If we see the out-of-school gang as a bridge between kinship-based status and achievement-based status, then we can reduce some of the unsavoury gang tensions by increasing the sense of achievement within the junior school group. The greater part of this achievement should be individual and non-competitive progression.

At this point we should interrupt the symposium to mention a book which counterbalances Crane's group, because it deals with adolescent gang members whose gang membership continued because they were unable to make good. This is *Group Processes and Gang Delinquency* by Short and Strodtbeck (1956). The authors made a study of a dozen Chicago gangs and evolved an imaginative way to contact the boys. Aided by many sociologists and psychologists, they gave responsibility to gang members, and those selected for responsibility proved a link between the adults and the individuals in the various gangs. This approach has great potentiality in bringing help to youngsters fixated at the gang stage.

Returning to the symposium, the fifth article, by Hilliard (1959), is on the influence of religious education upon the development of children's moral ideas in adolescence. Most of the researches quoted are connected with belief about God and heaven and whether religious people live better lives. The author points out that very little is known about the religious ideas of pre-adolescents. The fact that though it is compulsory in Britain for every school to hold a daily religious service, almost no investigation about its effect has been made, calls for consideration. The explanation may lie in the fact that the Churches have developed out of undue reverence for the arguments of Plato and Aristotle. They succumbed to the Greek notion of perfection with which they imbued all the works of Plato and Aristotle. The late Bertrand Russell, in *A History of Western Philosophy* (1946), says of Plato's theory of immortality, 'As a man, we may believe him admitted to the communion of saints; but as a philosopher he needs a long residence in a scientific purgatory'; and of Aristotle he says that, compared to his predecessors his merits were enormous, and for his demerits his successors are more responsible than he. If Russell is right the development of religious teaching has been mainly along the lines of Plato's particular treachery to truth, namely deciding what the object of the universe is, and then fitting an argument which proves it. The point at issue is not whether religious and ethical behaviour have value, but whether ultimate truth should be decided and argument tailored to fit it or whether scientific investigation with its steadily increasing approximation to truth is a better route. However, one or two investigators are beginning to use modern techniques, notably Goldman (p. 72), and the findings are valuable.

The next article, by Wheeler (1959), is on punishment, discipline and educational objectives in Australian secondary schools. He asked 765 children to introspect and found that most regarded punishment as retaliatory or a form of retribution or both. (Incidentally most letters to the press on prison call for punishment to be retributory and make it clear that the writers are moved by retaliation.) Wheeler took this to be a reflection of society's attitude and points out how far removed such attitudes are from educational aims; and how they can even retard the educational process. Punishment fails, he says, if teachers do not establish good rapport with children; and teachers who establish good rapport with children normally find punishment irrelevant to their educational objectives. Then follows an article by H. J. Eysenck (1960) which links learning with the development of internal controls and values. He says that moral values are learned during development and must therefore be linked to known facts and principles of modern learning theory. As a behaviourist he naturally thinks that 'conscience' is in fact a conditioned response built up during the child's formative years. By linking conditioned stimuli (arising from aggressive and other actions) with unconditioned stimuli (such as slaps, shaming and other punishments) immediately following the conditioned stimuli, we transmit, so he says, ideas on what may or what may not be done. (This would seem to underestimate how much children learn by simple imitation and identifying themselves with those they love, without any punitive conditioning.) Eysenck goes on to say that this conditioning should lead to an association of conditioned stimulus and the fear or anxiety response appropriate to the punishments. He quotes experimental evidence which indicates that this is apparently what happens. If so, he says, then individual differences in conditionability should be related to moral behaviour and the facility with which guilt-feelings are aroused. The treatment which children, adolescents and adults receive in response to immoral acts should be based on the recognition of individual differences between them, if this is to be beneficial. He points out that far too little research has been done on moral development for any conclusions to be reached; and, quoting Jeremy Bentham, Eysenck ends by saying we must wait to see whether punishment should fit the criminal rather than the crime.

R. S. Peters (1960) concludes the symposium with a valuable comparison of the theories of moral development presented by Freud and by Piaget. Piaget insists that there is a 'morality proper' apart from custom; he assumes that it is subject to maturation; and this he relates to cognitive maturation. His views provide a useful framework for research. We need much more information on conditions which favour or retard moral development; but, says Peters, Piaget makes no comment on the relics of earlier phases which persist in the adult mind. It would be out of place to offer a synopsis of what Peters says about Freud and his theory. He ends the whole symposium by saying, 'in this ill-explored field of moral development what is needed more than in almost any other field in psychology is a combination of concrete investigation with conceptual clarity'.

The most important articles on moral development following this symposium are by Goldman of Reading. In 1964 he reviewed some researches on religious thinking in a long and interesting article. Amongst his conclusions are the following: there is need to examine concepts central to understanding Bible material; experience and mental maturation set severe limits to religious thinking; concepts introduced too soon may retard or even prevent later thinking on religion; the time when childish concepts can be relinquished seems to be at about a mental age of 12 or 13 years; the Agreed Syllabus needs radical revision, so that it is related to ways of thinking at different stages of development; and there is clear indication that the prime influence on religious thinking is the home, and in particular comes from the parents.

The following year, in 1965, Goldman reported an investigation which he had made along modern scientific lines. As we saw in the section on Piaget (Chapter 6), he applied Piaget's scheme of operational thinking to religious stories and found that understanding of them is dependent on normal cognitive development. This confirms Piaget's view, expressed thirty-five years earlier in his book on the moral development of children. Goldman's data appears to suggest that religious thinking goes through stages in the same way that cognition develops in other fields; it is secondary to sensation, perception and conceptual thinking. Since religious thinking uses metaphor, simile, analogy and parable as its dominant form, Bible stories will become distorted if children have not yet had the original experiences from which the necessary inferences by metaphor, etc., can be drawn. Goldman himself has found in religious education that children go through conceptual stages, and his research indicates that these stages are what Piaget has called pre-operational, concrete operational, and formal operational.

Bradburn (1967) has also made an investigation of morality using modern methodology. She wished to find out whether modern children are really as ignorant of 'right' and 'wrong' as so many adults complain that they are. She used projection techniques, the limitations of which she fully appreciates. The pilot study was made of 380 children of different ages from 8 to 16 years and the final study was made of 600 children of 10 years. The children of 10 years showed in their replies that what they considered of value in the eyes of their parents was taking responsible action for the sake of others, even if it risked their lives. Seventy-eight per cent of replies described courageous actions, and more than a third of these referred to giving one's life to save another. This 'giving' is a striking result in a world where so much 'having' is advertised. Of the 22 per cent who completed stories with personal achievement, more than half stressed the importance of 'being' rather than 'having'. She concludes by saying that this and other researches indicate that many children have a fairly high degree of moral knowledge. They know what is generally accepted as right and wrong behaviour. But moral knowledge is no guarantee of moral behaviour. As a corollary Bradburn suggests that the motivational aspect of morality requires investigation, now that learning theory and the self-concept are linked to moral development.

Edwards (1965) has reviewed researches into moral development, including United States research, during the years 1920 to 1960. He rightly points out that the complexity of moral issues today, upon which young people have to exercise value judgments, means that more thorough study of moral development is urgent. In view of our ignorance of these matters it is startling to read in an article by Harris (1966) of the growing number of children who choose Religious Education for 'O' level examination. In 1951 over 22,000 took this examination, and by 1962 numbers had risen to nearly 53,000. But, he says, the level of failure is so high that no one concerned with this examination could feel complacent. Harris himself suggests that there is a slowly growing interest in religious examination, and this is not just because it is a 'soft option'; but he gives no evidence to support this contention. One should perhaps bear in mind that the reason for choosing this subject might be something a great deal shrewder than a 'soft option'; some may wish to be examined in a subject where the adults appear to have lost their way and so cannot afford to be too critical.

A book which can be valuable in starting discussion is *Introduction to Moral Education* by Wilson, Williams and Sugarman (1967). This is the first publication of a Trust with a Research Unit the main concern of which is research into moral education.

18. Speech and reading development 8 to 12 years

By the years 8 to 12, if children are fortunate enough to be in the care of progressive teachers, their language development is stimulated by a wide variety of imaginative approaches. The uses of language range from children's simple scientific statements, first spoken and then written, to their own poetry with nuances of experience beyond the reach of prose. There are two aspects of language development at this stage which all too often become submerged. First, the various media of verbal art have developed and formed part of the cultural heritage precisely because human minds develop in this way. A tiny child who has never heard a poem may make up a merry jingle which is nearer true poetry than some of the 'poems for children' which are foisted upon them. The major epics which are handed on over centuries arise from the phantasies of groups of adults in the same way that a child's individual phantasy life arises. Thus we should recognise that we can do no more than guide a spontaneously emerging verbal ability, much in the way that we guide the muscular coordination of spontaneously developing limbs in physical education.

Second, practice of an inborn ability is inherently pleasurable. We have lost our way here, because we knew that 'something' had to be done, if the spontaneously gay 'verbal scribbling' of little children was to develop to adult levels. We have bewildered them with adjectives, verbs and other parts of grammatical construction, with scanning and rhymes, with published dramatic forms, and so on. In our misguided efforts we have too often extinguished the inherent pleasure of manipulating words correctly. If one lays down guide lines for dramatic conversation most children cannot understand the abstraction. But if a boy of eight is producing an unscripted drama and tells the leading lady that she must sound more surprised when she says, 'How lovely to see you!' she may explode with, 'How *can* I sound surprised when I have only just left him!' After a general discussion, someone may suggest that she should say, 'Oh good! I am so glad you have come back!'

Between them they have all learned something about how words used in conversation should relate to thinking with feeling about the situation. Language development is far richer if we remember these two points: that the various media of literature are natural developments within a child; and that children have to find their own way to enjoyable repetitive practice in choice and arrangement of words.

But still the greatest stumbling block to delight in appreciation and creation of literature, for most children, is the junior stage of learning to read. The general expectation of junior school teachers is that the children should have learned to read before they leave the infant school. The fact that so many of them cannot read fluently appears to be a cause of frustration to the junior teachers rather than a reason for them to adjust their expectations. In a very sound popular article 'How soon should children read?' (*New Society*, 1966), Lytton points out that the real question is: at what age is reading taught most economically and most pleasurably to the majority? He says countries with phonic orthography all delay it; and we need to relax, because we are in danger of a middle-class neurosis on reading. We must not be obsessed by children doing under pressure what they could do easily a little later on. We need two things, he says: more research and more thought about our social values.

One area requiring more research is that of books suitable for the first two years in the junior school. We need information on the range and size of vocabulary and the length of words which can be expected of children who have progressed through all our better reading schemes. Now that we clearly appreciate the value of a controlled vocabulary the earliest stages of reading should be by means of one selected scheme. Otherwise control of vocabulary is vitiated. But when one scheme has been completed, the final stages of several schemes can give good practice. If we had some notion of what vocabulary learning is to be expected at 7 to 8 years, no matter what the scheme, then publishers could commission suitable reading for the first two years in the junior school, using this combined vocabulary as the main source of words. Such books would ensure the practice in reading which consolidates the newly learned skill after entering the junior school.

Because we have had so many reading casualties in the junior school, a great deal of attention has had to be given to reading backwardness. Indeed, there have been as many articles and books on backwardness in reading, in the last ten years, as on normal reading. This is an absurd situation. Had the time been devoted to research on normal reading, there would have been a reduction at source of reading problems. Children with reading difficulties suffer acutely. Research on their introspections would undoubtedly be startling. So much suffering is bound to affect adjustment and damage the self concept, thus undermining the courage to persevere. Sampson (1966) has written an article on 'Reading and adjustment: a review of the literature'.

In 1960–2 The *British Journal of Educational Psychology* published a symposium, 'Contributions to the diagnosis and remedial treatment of reading difficulties'. It is in the first article that M. D. Vernon (1960) of Reading states that despite many studies the problems are still very imperfectly understood. She is critical of some of the methods employed in investigating them; also of the methods employed in investigating ways of teaching reading, which are not scientifically controlled or carried on long enough. In conclusion she says that, at least in part, the problems arise from insufficient attention having been devoted to the nature of the reading processes itself. Then Curr and Gourlay (1960) of Birmingham write on 'The effect of practice on performance in scholastic tests'. Their main concern is mechanical reading, reading comprehension and arithmetic. They found practice had most effect on comprehension, less on mechanical reading and was almost negligible on arithmetic. More information along these lines would be valuable There is a notable difference between scholastic tests scientifically designed only to reveal the present stage of learning and the kind of test used by Piaget. Piaget's tests are, as Lovell and Ogilvie (1960) point out (see p. 75), in themselves learning situations. Curr and Gourlay's observation that comprehension is most improved by practice leads one to suspect that comprehension tests may be more of a learning situation in the Piaget sense than a mere assessment.

Hillman and Snowdon (1960) at Durham write on part-time classes for young backward readers. The aim of their investigation was to find out whether part-time teachers working with small groups could significantly improve reading achievement. They worked with 130 backward juniors who had been taught in small groups and a backward group as controls who did not receive help in small groups. Results showed a significant difference in favour of those who had been helped. The average reading age gained was 11 months in one term and nearly $2\frac{1}{2}$ years in three terms. The authors recommend these small groups with teachers, not specially trained for reading therapy, working part-time. They consider this as effective as more elaborate and expensive schemes. Dunham (1960), for a Manchester MEd thesis, studied the effects of remedial education on young children's reading ability and attitude to reading. There were twenty-seven retarded children of 9 years with about average intelligence, who attended classes of not more than six children once or twice a week for six months. These children were paired with a control group awaiting remedial treatment, for age, intelligence, reading ability and socio-economic environment. An attitude scale of twenty items was used. As with the previous experiment, the group receiving remedial help showed significant gains in reading ability. But their attitude to reading did not improve. Further research may show whether attitude scales are not yet sufficiently refined to be useful or whether much greater effort has to be made to counteract poor attitudes to reading established at an earlier age.

The next article in the symposium, on motivation in remedial reading by Roberts (1960) is a summary of an MA thesis at the University of Wales. This was a six months' experiment with children of 10 years, carried out once with three groups of six children and again with three groups of eleven children. Three ways of using motivation were tried: (a) curiosity and drive; (b) gregariousness; and (c) competition, with phonic drill. Curiosity and drive proved much the most effective and gregariousness the least effective. Roberts points out that a major problem with retarded readers is inability to learn new words; and the vivid meaningful associations formed with curiosity and drive gave greatest help in learning new words. The next article, on an experiment in selection for remedial education (1961), is by Lytton of Midlothian. The purpose was to find out whether selection was better if made by teachers' judgment or by objective tests. No significant difference between the two methods was found. An attempt to assess personality changes during remedial treatment proved inconclusive, and this may have been due to changeable standards in the teachers' ratings of seven personality traits in the children before and after the experiment. Lytton concludes that more reliable methods of assessing personality are needed. We have met this problem before in Chapter 14. Unless teachers train themselves to judge personality traits by direct observation of behaviour in controlled situations, their judgments prove unreliable.

Then Ravenette (1961) at West Ham reports an empirical approach to the assessment of reading retardation. He carried out a test with a sample of West Ham juniors aged 7 years 10 months to 10 years 10 months, using combined scores for prediction of reading attainment. In selecting a vocabulary scale and a word reading test, care was taken to relate both to established research. The Crichton Vocabulary Scale was chosen because of its British standardisation and because it correlates with the American Terman–Merrill Scale; and the Schonell Graded Word Reading Test was chosen because it is simple to administer and correlates well with the Neale (1958) prose reading test. In West Ham this became standard procedure in the following way:

(*a*) the head teachers select poor readers with good vocabulary; (*b*) the remedial teacher at each school gives both the Crichton Vocabulary Scale and the Schonell Graded Word Test; (*c*) children below the tenth percentile, equivalent to IQ approximately 80, are usually not selected for remedial work, which is reserved at this early stage of research for those who can profit more quickly; (*d*) children with a gap of more than two years between expected and observed reading score are top of the recommended list for remedial work; (*e*) the final selection is made in consultation with the head teacher on matters such as recent educational progress, school attendance, etc. If this system is effective in providing the right remedial reading classes for children who are of near average or average intelligence with good vocabulary but backward in reading, then perhaps the next step will be to provide a different remedial treatment for those of lower intelligence who are in reading difficulty.

The final article in this symposium is by P. Williams, on the growth of reading vocabulary and some of its implications (1961), is the summary of a PhD thesis at London University. The summary is too condensed to yield a clear picture, but it contains an interesting new approach to reading studies in general. The argument is that most measurement in child psychology and educational psychology is too much orientated to 'age-scale' and therefore puts too much emphasis on the group at the expense of the individual. Williams made two parallel word-scales of 100 words, based on random sampling of a dictionary, and gave them, together with Schonell's RI word recognition test, to 216 children aged 6 to 15 years. When results were combined, the following implications merited attention: (*a*) the very rapid development of word recognition skills between reading ages 7 and 8 years; (*b*) the apparent change in rate at a reading age of approximately $8\frac{1}{2}$ years; and (*c*) the relatively slow rate of growth in word recognition at higher reading ages. The part of this thesis which has direct bearing on the subject of the symposium is an appendix on educational retardation and season of birth. We will return to these findings in Chapter 21.

A whole series of articles has appeared on date of birth and educational achievement. The connection is not, as one might first think, to do with horoscopes. A child whose fifth birthday falls in the summer term can attend school for the last term of the year. Such a child has only one-third of the first year; but a child born in the autumn term has a full first year. Clark (1956) of Reading, in an area where competition for grammar school is extremely keen, investigated the effect of a candidate's age upon teachers' estimates of a child's chance of gaining a grammar school place. Her data come from 30,000 children. She found objective tests had similar distribution at all ages, but teachers' assessments were biased in favour of older children; also older children were more frequently selected for A streams than younger ones. This called into question certain current educational procedures.

Pidgeon and Dodds (1961) wrote on length of schooling and its effect on performance in the junior school. They made a fairly small investigation and decided that length of schooling should be allowed for in the same way that age is allowed for when testing. Jinks (1964) noted, when marking a batch of some 300 arithmetic tests for 11+ selection, a connection between length of schooling and results. He then examined the 11+ results of a whole borough, 657 girls and 658 boys, and found a marked influence of length of schooling. On further investigation he found that streaming widened the the gap between 'A' and 'C' streams, and surmised that some in 'C' streams had become discouraged, through shorter schooling, thus falling still further behind. The Appendix to P. Williams's PhD thesis, referred to in the previous paragraph, led him to conclude that the practice of annual promotion by age may be indirectly responsible for much mental ill-health in children. Williams (1964) then turned attention to schools for educationally subnormal children and made his own inquiry with 265 children attending such schools. There was an undue proportion of summer-born children in this group, and he concluded that increased flexibility of educational organisation is to be recommended.

Others who have written on the subject include Freyman (1965), who warns against confusing immaturity with retardation and hopes teachers will think again about streaming; and Pidgeon (1965), who makes a number of suggestions, including a change in teachers' attitudes and greater individualisation of learning. It is interesting to note here that the Plowden Report, while being temperate about streaming as a policy, makes a clear reference to attitudes in connection with it: 'Schools which treat children individually will accept unstreaming throughout the whole school' (p. 819). The whole new idea that younger children were being confused with backward children blew up to quite a furore in just a few years. But the matter is not yet clear. Armstrong (1966) of West Riding made a study of 24,000 children's scores in standardised tests at 11 and 16 years. He found with such large numbers no significant difference, whatever the organisation, between autumn- and summer-born children's achievement, by the end of schooling. He did, however, find a difference at 11 years, under test-free conditions; the summer-born children in large urban schools were at a disadvantage in comparison with summer-born children in small rural schools. We can expect quite a lot more research into possible connections between backwardness in reading and other subjects, and date of birth which affects length time in infant schools.

There have been a number of other attempts to pinpoint the value of remedial reading work. Ace (1956) at Plymouth made a comparative study of two methods of teaching in two different remedial reading centres, a mixed method in one and the Moxon method in the other, over a period of 117 sessions in the first half of 1955. The mixed method was combined 'look and say', sentence, and phonic approaches; the Moxon is phonic with visual approach, and the child does everything for himself—a method which needs to be seen in action. The Moxon group made significantly more advance and further research is now in progress. Friedmann (1958) at Oxford followed up an earlier article by Curr and Gourlay (1953) in the above symposium, on practice effect in reading. He makes a progress report on the significant amount by which children attending remedial classes catch up, and finds that backward readers not receiving remedial help remain retarded.

Schonfield (1956) at Bolton made a study of special difficulties at reading age 8+ years. In his remedial classes groups were small, some attempt was made to alleviate emotional problems, and the material was suited to the children. The problem of suitability of material with retardation is that the material has on the one hand to suit the reading age and on the other hand to suit the interests of the chronological age, thus the print may be at the six year level but the stories of interest to a child of perhaps 8 to 12 years. Consequently improvised material is usually best. Schonfield found a plateau at about 8 years, when no progress seems to be made. This is interesting, as P. Williams (1961), concluding the symposium above, suggests that there is normally a rapid increase in recognition between the ages of 7 and 8 years. More research on speed of progress in vocabulary at the age of 8+ is required. A plateau in speed of word recognition at the stage when others were leaping ahead could be a cause of backwardness, unless remedial action is taken.

Lovell, Johnson and Platts (1962) at Leeds also made a study of the reading ages of children who had been given remedial help, at a Child Guidance Centre. They followed up children assessed for reading age in January 1955 and they reassessed them in March 1960. There were two groups: A, which was rather older and more backward and made an average gain in reading age of 2:3; and B, which made a gain of 2:8. This is comparable with other reports on the effect of remedial teaching. Amongst the points which they note are the following: a small positive correlation between IQ and progress in reading age; the distribution of reading ages before remedial help was markedly asymmetrical, but became approximately normal by the end of remedial work; over half those who were in junior school at first assessment had progressed to reading age 9 by the second assessment and so were functionally literate. But not one went to a grammar school or an 'A' stream of a secondary modern. The study gave little help in picking out those most likely to improve under remedial care. There was so little difference between individual and small group teaching, that small groups are recommended as helping more retarded readers at one time and also as bringing the methods of specialist teachers to the notice of school staff.

As we have seen, reading casualties present such a problem that we can almost speak of a 'normal slow reading group'. For such, small groups enable the teacher to give sufficient individual help, and the work on reading together will be a needed social experience for the children. So far research has contributed more to diminishing the degree of retardation than to changing backward children's attitudes to reading. Since failure at reading has been a social disgrace, small groups are probably best for changing attitude to reading, once we have found how to do this, because the group in sharing the disability feels less isolated.

There has been much disagreement over specific dyslexia, a name for a group of deficiencies in speech, handedness (left-handed, cross-laterality, etc.), motor incoordination, and so on. Some, but not necessarily all, of these symptoms are liable to be found with some backward readers. M. D. Vernon (1962b) reviews the literature in an article entitled 'Specific dyslexia'. She reminds us that there are three kinds of reading disability: (a) moderate, due to environment, and the child can usually learn through phonics; (b) maladjusted, due to home problems, and the child needs therapy, after which reading problems disappear; and (c) organic, usually referred to clinics. This article is a valuable review of the situation today. At present a neurological basis for some reading retardation is highly speculative. There could be failure of normal development in some area of the brain, or an inherited deficiency; such an idea is supported by the effects of some accidents to the brain. The article concludes with indications of many areas where further scientific investigation is urgently needed. Of remedial treatment she says that no attempt has so far been made to differentiate dyslexics from emotional and environmental cases; and studies seldom make clear the exact nature of the disability.

We can, by the end of the 'sixties, say that the first two kinds of disability mentioned by M. D. Vernon are beginning to receive attention. Serious attention is at last being given to how best to teach reading to all children, and nobody would entirely leave out the phonic way today; and many authorities arrange for children with home disturbances to go to child guidance clinics, where both child and parents receive help, as we shall see in Chapter 22. But there has still been an almost complete divorce between the severe organic disruptions which are treated in hospitals and children still able to attend school who may have minor degrees of similar problems. All who have tried to teach extremely backward readers know a kind of shattered attention, which leaves the teacher sure that a child could read if only he would attend. In this connection, the work of Keating may be important.

Keating (1962) of Lingfield Hospital School, working with epileptic boys, reports such a situation. He tried intensive remedial reading work in groups but found this unsuccessful, since the children lacked the concentration to work on their own. He then gave individual attention for fifteen to twenty minutes a day, followed by silent practice. His techniques were eclectic, using all methods. Most of the children had emotional traits militating against reading progress: feelings of inferiority, lack of confidence, acquired boredom, lack of motivation, and so on. Keating found that this system worked provided there was enough intelligence, a will to cooperate, no organic lesion affecting visual and motor brain centres, work periods were short, frequent and regular, and the teacher had the will-power to give remedial care. He is now able to apply this individual care to small groups of five boys, who return to their own classes for three-quarters of the day. This report is a most valuable contribution, because an epileptic attack shatters concentration and is bound to affect normal integrative forces between attacks. Keating has developed a technique which gathers the children's attention.

Further research on reading backwardness has to cover a much wider field than previously. There has been a big Nuffield project on dyslexia at Leeds. At Edinburgh Ingram (1969) has written on the development of higher nervous activity in childhood and its disorders. Other universities concerned with language and speech development include Wales and Essex. A reading conference of the 'seventies has to concern itself with findings such as these can offer.

Kinsbourne and Warrington (1963) at the National Hospital, London, working with two groups of patients, selected for more than twenty points difference between verbal and performance intelligence quotient, applied their psychiatric knowledge of functional brain disorder to the problems. *Group I* (6 cases) had lower verbal ability and suffered language disorder;

but they had almost no difficulty in performance tests for mechanical arithmetic. *Group II* (7 cases) had lower performance ability and suffered specific difficulty with tests of finger differentiation and order, constructional tasks and mechanical arithmetic; but they had almost no language disorder. The authors diagnosed that these groups represented syndromes of failure in developmental cerebral deficit, Group I with deficiency in the language area of the brain and Group II with deficiency in the sequential ordering area of the brain. Each deficiency may give rise to a characteristic type of delay in leaning to read and write. The authors suggest that cerebral cortical deficiencies probably represent a minority within the population of retarded readers and writers. This may be true of such extreme cases as those with a difference of twenty points between verbal and performance intelligence quotients.

But there is reason to suspect that less extreme cases of cortical deficiency may account for a significant number of backward readers, as the next researches by Lovell *et al.* suggest. Lovell with the aid of his students, has carried out two investigations on cognitive and other disabilities, with backward readers of average non-verbal reasoning ability. Lovell, Shapton and Warren (1964) gave a sentence reading test and a non-verbal intelligence test to the whole third year group in twenty-two junior schools, in all 1,205 children. Of 139 children with reading quotient below 80, seventy had standardised non-verbal intelligence scores above 90. Fifty of these children were paired individually with average-to-good readers, matched for non-verbal test scores, social class, sex and school. These pairs were given a series of tests. There was a discrepancy in the number of errors made by backward readers with words of four letters or more, whereas normal readers did not make these errors with words of seven letters or more. The backward readers showed no deficit in performance on an oral language test but poorer performance on a variety of tests involving spatial relationships and left–right discrimination; also a greater 'rotation effect' on a test involving the copying of abstract designs, that is to say the design is correctly produced but wrongly orientated. They used a rotation test, produced by Shapiro *et al.* (1962), which yields significant differences between certain kinds of brain-injured patients and normal adults. Amongst the many interesting points discussed by Lovell *et al.* at the end of their paper, they suggest that there is a possible brain dysfunction with some backward readers, comparable with Shapiro's patients, which limits ability in the decoding and encoding processes involved in reading and, in some cases, disturbance of visual input. Many backward readers are capable of considerable powers of thought provided not too much reading and writing is demanded of them.

Lovell, Gray and Oliver (1964) used a reading test and a non-verbal intelligence test on the whole fourth year population in fourteen secondary modern schools, 981 boys and 872 girls. They found 426 children with reading quotient less than 80. Of these, 204 had standardised non-verbal reasoning scores more than 90. They paired thirty of the boys and twenty-five of the girls individually with average-to-good readers, matched for non-verbal scores, social class, sex and school. Again a number of individual tests were given. The boys who were backward had poorer performance on certain tests compared with non-backward boys, and greatly inferior performance to backward girls on the tests of copying and dictation. In conclusion they make the following four points: (*a*) marked reading failure remains about twice as frequent in the male as the female even at 14 to 15 years of age; (*b*) in spite of the fact that the mean reading score of the backward boys was $1\frac{1}{2}$ points lower than that of the backward girls, the mean vocabulary score of the backward boys was not below that of the backward girls; (*c*) in the case of the boys, but not the girls, two tests revealed a difference involving visual perception between backward and non-backward boys; (*d*) the mean error rate for certain important kinds of error was higher for boys than for girls on the copying test, and very much higher on the dictation test. They therefore suggest that the marked reading disability at 14 to 15 years is often part of a wider syndrome which affects the male more severely than the female; and the same seemed true at 9 to 10 years.

Four years later Lovell and Gorton (1968), from an experiment with fifty backward readers and fifty controls, were able to state more definitely that at least some of the backward readers showed signs of neurological impairment, though none of the controls did so; and that the five worst readers revealed the jerky movements symptomatic of the neurological disorder called Chorea. Needless to say, Lovell calls for more research. It would certainly be most valuable if many more lecturers in colleges of education would use the technique which Lovell has, over many decades, adapted from university practice. Just as the professors use students to gain the information which will solve their problems, so Lovell has used the students he educates. At the university it is the students who are awarded the PhD, but the staff in the colleges of education could receive the PhD. Then the higher degree would, in the true sense, be part of college work, instead of a midnight study which seems quite separate from college work.

We are still very ignorant about the development of the brain and what we know is, according to Tanner (1961), almost entirely dependent on the researches of Conel between 1939 and 1959, which were confined to the first two years of life. Tanner in Chapter 5 of *Education and Physical Growth* (1961), gives a brief account of what is known. There is considerable localisation of functions in the cerebral cortex, certain parts being necessary for vision, others for movement, and so on. Figure 27 gives some indication of areas. But as we look at these diagrams we should mentally impose dynamic electrical and chemical activity constantly operating over the whole area of the diagrams and also within the brain. Moreover, electrical currents generated in the brain flow in waves across the whole brain. These waves vary according to whether one is awake or asleep, preoccupied with a problem or idly dreaming. So, even though certain areas have specific functions, no isolated area becomes activated without the whole brain being involved. One of the regions in which M. D. Vernon suggests that we urgently need further research is the parietal lobe. A glance at the lateral view diagram will show that this is the area of auditory and visual association. Moreover, it is flanked by auditory and visual areas, and sensory regions for leg, arm, hand, lip, tongue and mouth. The research by Kinsbourne and Warrington (1963) referred to clinical indications of disturbance of two specific areas of the cortex. The investigation by Keating (1962) with epileptic boys was with children who suffered periodic chaotic disturbance of the electric currents which should flow in regular rhythmic waves over the whole brain. It is interesting that, with individual attention, Keating found a way to compel boys who wanted to cooperate, to concentrate on reading. Research into these 'brain waves' begins to suggest that at least some people can induce in themselves one of the wave rhythms, the alpha rhythm, at will.

We have dealt at some length with abnormal conditions, because of a suspicion, resulting from research, that neurological deficiencies may be differentially graded from normal to abnormal. Only further research will make clear what the relevance of this to backwardness in reading may be.

When books on backwardness in reading are considered, two classics, which precede the period from which most of the references here come, must be mentioned: Burt, *The Backward Child* (1937) and Schonell, *Backwardness in the Basic Subjects* (1942). It would not be too much to say that anyone who wishes to pursue any line of enquiry about children in trouble would be wise to see what Burt has said; but the book also makes fascinating reading. Schonell was one of Burt's students and his book is also based on very skilled direct observation of children. It is characteristic of books based on trained observation of children that they are interesting to read, because the details given are genuine and enable the reader to imagine the real people being described.

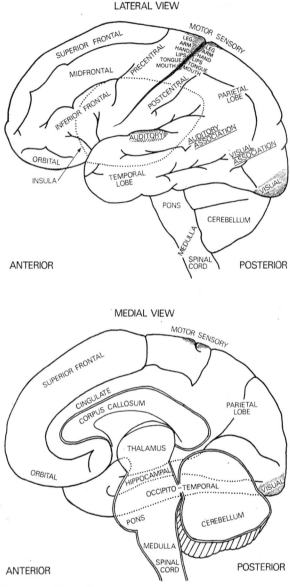

Figure 27. Map of brain.
Source: Tanner (1961).

Amongst more recent books, M. D. Vernon's *Backwardness in Reading* (1957) is a scholarly review of the position at that time. It is fully documented and the educational issues are clearly discussed. As we have seen, a good deal of research has been done since that time. But the account of remedial teaching in this book has a balance which we need to retain as research develops. R. Morris's *Success and Failure in Learning to Read* (1963), mentioned earlier, should be mentioned here as well. He has a final chapter dealing with backwardness and remedies. Future reading research would do well to keep the proportions of Morris's book: two-thirds on normal reading development and one-third on tests and casualties. Reviewing it, Collins (1964) writes: 'This book represents a genuine attempt to see the teaching of reading as the guiding of children's thinking processes rather than the inculcation of tricks with mechanical reading part-skills.' Thus we are not surprised to find that the chapter on backwardness is written from the point of view of helping the child to come to terms with his past reading failure. This is the approach most likely to assist in the difficult remedial problem we have met of changing a child's attitude to reading while helping him to read better.

According to the Plowden Report there is a marked rise in the standard of reading over the last twenty years or so. The standard of reading at 11 years today is that of children 17 months older in 1948. Of course, one has to remember that 1948 was very soon after the Second World War, with all its educational disruptions, children evacuated, teachers in the forces, and so on. It would be interesting to know how today compared with 1939, before the war had started. The report says that backwardness now has a different connotation. But it also says that nearly half the children in the representative sample of schools investigated continued to need, after transfer to junior school, the skilled teaching associated with the infant school—and did not get it. At least we have some figures from Lovell *et al.* (1964) about reading retardation in Leeds, and there is no reason to suspect anything exceptional in this respect about Leeds. Of 1,205 third year juniors 11·5 per cent had reading quotients below 80; and of 1,853 fourth-year secondary modern children 23 per cent had reading quotients below 80. Moreover, more than 50 per cent of the juniors and 48 per cent of the seniors had average intelligence when tested by performance tests instead of verbal tests. These children have fallen behind in reading because we have not understood the nature of their mental abilities.

Lovell *et al.* only found a small positive correlation between intelligence and reading achievement, yet none of the children in these groups went to grammar school or even reached 'A' streams of secondary modern schools. In this connection it is interesting to note a chapter by Crawford in *Education and the Urban Child* by Mays (1962). This is a study of an underprivileged district of Liverpool; and Crawford's contribution is a scientifically designed survey of reading attainment. The intelligence quotients of the children in her sample did not differ significantly from those of the city average, and yet, at 7 years 9 months these underprivileged children were 12 to 15 months behind in reading attainment.

In 1968 there were two articles on dyslexia. The first, by Reid (1968), on logical grounds aligns the two groups as believers and non-believers in dyslexia. The second, by Shearer (1968), reviews the literature and then produces evidence for there being some connection between reading disability and certain defects of physical skills, such as left–right discrimination and finger localisation. The following year Cashdan and Pumphrey (1969) make a powerful appeal for a more continuous programme of remedial reading as an integral part of normal junior activity, so that more children can enter secondary school as literate beings.

The sheer quantity of work that has gone into the articles and books on reading problems demonstrates that traditional methods of teaching reading have not suited a sizable proportion of children. Although we are all agreed in theory that there should be equal opportunity for education, data from research shows that reading is an important area where we have failed to organise it. The main reason appears to be our ignorance of the mental processes involved in reading, of individual differences in these processes, and of the influence on them of the different kinds of socio-economic environments from which our school children come. It seems that many children who cannot master the mechanics of reading at seven can do so with ease a year or two later. The real tragedy has been that problems in mastering the mechanics have masked the true level of intelligence of very many children. Many children of average or above average intelligence have, with considerable sense of failure, adopted into their self-picture the teacher's idea that they are stupid because they have difficulty in learning to read and so not much can be expected of them. This particular trouble falls most heavily on the boys.

Many kinds of research on reading are now required, and amongst them should be longitudinal studies of the connection between speech and reading, along the lines of Sampson (1956, 1959 and 1962, etc.). By the time her little group of fifty reached 8 years two had gone abroad. She was able to report of the remaining forty-eight an association between skill in language aspects of speech and reading; but the contribution of mechanical reading was not clear. Home influences contributed to skill and disability in reading; but personal maladjustment, though sometimes associated with reading disability was not incompatible with success. The methodology of this pilot study is extremely good. The Plowden Report (1967) states (p. 55) that language is central to education; but the Report's estimate that a child should know 3,000 words before starting to learn to read comes from America and (though the Report does not state this) dates back to 1933. We need recent information about language in our own country, if we are to enable the majority of children to enjoy enriching their language and experience through reading.

19. Tests of intelligence and attainment

Interest in testing intelligence was roused in Britain by the work first of Galton in London and then of Binet in Paris. The French government had followed Britain in making education compulsory for all children. They soon became aware of a problem familiar to all practising teachers, namely how to distinguish children who *won't* learn from children who *can't* learn. They asked Binet, Professor of Psychology at the Sorbonne in Paris, to help them, largely because he had just published a book about the reasoning capacity of his two daughters, both very clever but quite different in temperament. Binet acknowledged his indebtedness to both Galton and Spencer. He compiled a series of questions and problems and tried them out on a few children in Paris schools, spending hours with each child. These problems were arranged in hierarchical order, becoming harder and harder. But when he tried to establish at exactly what ages children could solve the problems, he was unable to do so, because some children could answer them much earlier than the majority, and some could not answer them until a much later age. Then Binet made one of those giant original abstractions for which mankind is permanently indebted. He invented the concept of mental age. Whatever a child's chronological age, his mental age was derived from the stage at which most children could solve these problems. Thus if a child of 6 solved problems which most children could not solve until 8, his mental age was two years above average; and conversely if a child of 6 could only solve problems which most children could solve at 4, his mental age was two years below average.

Binet enlisted the help of his colleague Simon and the Binet–Simon tests were designed to detect the children with mental age so far below average that they were too slow-witted to learn in a normal school, that is, children who *can't* learn in school, which is what the French government wanted to know. While Binet was seeking out children with mental age too low for them to profit from normal schooling, he also came across children with mental age too high for them to profit from normal schooling. In Chapters 20 and 21 we shall examine the educational implications of both these extreme divergences from average mental age.

Both anthropologists and doctors used a ratio to eliminate chronological age in dealing with children's height, weight, etc. In this way they could classify children as average, tall or short, light or heavy, and so on, irrespective of age. To do this also with intelligence must have been an obvious step. The first printed suggestion of such a ratio as an 'intelligence quotient' was that of L. W. Stern in 'Psychological methods of testing intelligence' (1914). The ratio of mental age to chronological age can be expressed mathematically as a fraction or as a percentage. A child of eight with a mental age of 4 would have a ratio of $MA/CA = \frac{4}{8} = \frac{1}{2} = 0.5$. The layman does not like measurements which are expressed as decimal; hence the fraction was multiplied by a hundred and such a child's IQ becomes 50. On the other hand, a child of four who can solve problems normally solved by children of 8 would have a ratio of $(MA/CA) \times 100 = \frac{8}{4} \times 100 = IQ\ 200$.

Many students have been frightened by mathematics, and it will be some time before the new approach to mathematics avoids this particular problem. Such students have to make a special effort to attend to terms such as *ratio* and *quotient*. Otherwise, like so many lay people, they will think of IQ as some kind of magic number. An ordinary fraction such as $\frac{3}{4}$ is a ratio; it is three of the quarters of a whole; and the answer that you get when you divide one number by another is called a quotient in mathematics. In an intelligence ratio the number which always stands firmly at the base of the fraction is the chronological age. When the mental age is put at the top, if it is less than that of most children, the answer is less than a whole number; and if it is more than that of most children the answer is more than a whole number. And with the special convention of the intelligence quotient, the first answer becomes less than 100, the second answer more than 100.

Just as we saw with personality, so with intelligence there are no sudden demarcations of 'types'. The grading is continuous. The best analogy is height. The heights of all the people in the world are smoothly graded from very tall to very short. If you stood them all in a row according to height, then a piece of string laid across the tops of their heads, from tallest to shortest, would fall in a curved line ('curved' because there would be very few tallest, and very few shortest). We can measure height very accurately, but we cannot yet measure mental age so accurately. The answers or quotients that we get depend entirely on how carefully tests have been constructed, standardised *and* administered. Standardisation of tests is discussed more fully later (pp. 232–3).

Burt gave the first set of intelligence tests ever given in Britain, in 1910. He saw that testing children individually was very time-consuming. Another way would have to be found, to test large numbers at each age for statistical purposes. Accordingly in constructing tests for higher mental abilities, using analogies, reasoning and so on, he compiled the questions in such a way that they could be given to groups of children by teachers who had themselves been trained in groups. These first group tests originally designed by Burt were later adopted and developed in the United States. His idea of group testing, together with many details of test construction, have remained features of modern intelligence assessment today.

Burt was the first psychologist to be appointed by an education authority (1913). His first major report to the London County Council was *The Distribution and Relations of Educational Ability* (1917). It is a survey of the educational abilities of the entire elementary school population of a representative London borough. His aims were: (a) to find the most suitable lines of demarcation between children in ordinary schools and the special schools for mentally defective children: (b) to estimate the number of backward children in ordinary schools; and (c) to verify the hypothesis of a 'general educational ability' underlying all school work.

From his statistical work, Burt came to the conclusion that at least 75 per cent of an individual's abstract component of intelligence as tested was due to that individual's genetic constitution. Thus rather less than 25 per cent is affected by environmental conditions. Although the innate capacity cannot be measured directly, the relative importance of heredity and environment can be calculated indirectly. This is a not unusual technique in science; for example, the temperature at the interior of the sun has never been measured, but can be calculated indirectly. For the relative importance of what Plato called 'nature and nurture', or heredity and environment, Burt and his colleagues have done extensive work on twins, particularly identical twins reared apart.

If the range of IQ is divided into a number of equal sub-ranges (say 41 to 45, 46 to 50 and so on), then the percentage of all individuals in each sub-range calculated and finally a graph is drawn to show these percentages vertically and IQ horizontally, this graph is called a *frequency distribution* of IQ. Such a graph, shown in Figure 28, consists of course of a number of steps climbing up as the IQ is possessed by more individuals, and then climbing down as the IQ becomes a rarer possession. A particular frequency distribution, expressed by a relatively simple mathematical formula and often appearing in physical phenomena, is called a *normal frequency distribution*; this is the dotted line in Figure 28.

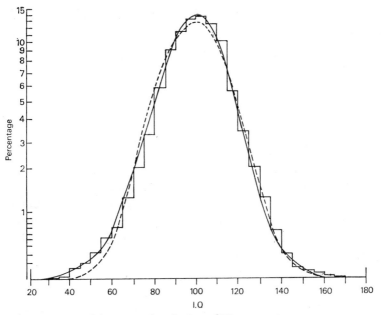

Figure 28. Normal frequency distribution of IQ
Source: Burt (1963).

In a statistical article entitled 'Is intelligence distributed normally?' Burt (1963) analyses the frequency distribution obtained by applying IQ tests to large samples of the school population and compares this with the commoner types of mathematically expressible frequency curves. The actually observed distribution is more asymmetrical and has longer tails than the normal curve, which in fact means that there are more children with very low and very high intelligence than the normal curve would suggest. In lists of the distribution of intelligence given in many text books, these extremes of very high and very low intelligence, individuals with IQ below 60 or above 150, have usually been omitted. Then the frequency does fit a normal distribution more closely. The full line in Figure 28 belongs to a class of somewhat less well-known distribution curves having mathematical formulae, proposed by Karl Pearson and classified by him as 'Type IV'. This curve fits the observed data much more closely, as it does most biological data.

Burt points out that surveys which have been taken from too small a sample of the population and with high and low IQs therefore omitted, have led to serious underestimates of the number of highly gifted and educationally subnormal children, a conclusion which is confirmed by data from other investigations. For example, the number of school children with IQ above

160 proves to be more than twelve times that which would be expected from a normal curve. And whereas the authorities assume from theory that there would be only three or four children with IQ over 175 in a million, the real figure appears to be more like 70 per million and possibly more. The data suggests that, if a very large survey were made, the number of gifted children to be expected might even be larger than that calculated from the Type IV formula. We have no arrangements for the education of such specially gifted children, partly because this discrepancy between theory and fact has been overlooked.

But the position is different with those who are well below normal in intelligence. Those who organise special schools for children who are educationally subnormal have known for a long time that insufficient accommodation was arranged because the authorities had underestimated numbers of children needing special schools. Their long waiting lists indicate this. It is interesting to note that parents with normal intelligence who had children of very low intelligence banded together before the Second World War and instigated research into the educational problems posed by their children's low IQs. Yet no such organisation existed for the other end of the curve of distribution, the gifted children who pose problems of education, until Mensa was formed for adults and later the National Association for Gifted Children was formed for children. One reason for the much earlier efforts made on behalf of the educationally subnormal was that the first intelligence tests were specifically constructed to screen out the ESN. Teachers were concerned for these children not able to attend school and a Royal Commission was formed to enquire what arrangements could be made for them. But the highly gifted mostly seemed to be doing quite well at school, sometimes even drifting to the top of the class, and this was taken to mean that they presented no educational problems. It is only now that we realise how little their minds are being stretched by work suited to their needs. We shall return to both these problems in Chapters 20 and 21.

Children in environments which foster intellectual curiosity through rich and varied stimulus would seem to have great advantage over those in poorer surroundings. In order to investigate such a matter it is necessary to try to group children according to the kind of home from which each one comes. The method normally followed is that of the Registrar-General, the central authority for registration of births, marriages and deaths, compiled from the periodic census. Tables are published showing the various ways in which occupations can be grouped. The one most frequently referred to is that for social class, which is very simple:

1. Professional occupations.
2. Intermediate occupations.
3. Skilled occupations.
4. Partly skilled occupations.
5. Unskilled occupations.

The middle three classes are subdivided into manual and non-manual. Foremen are generally in 3 and most managers in 2. The basis is the 'general standing within the community' and has no direct relation to earnings.*

In following research on the influence of home background upon children's development, it is important to realise that the initial source of most classifications of social class—the social class table of the Registrar-General—is very vague and quite arbitrary. As a general rule when social classification is important investigators make their own variation of this system. Carr-Saunders and Jones (1937) tried to classify by 'intellectual requirements'; Glass (1954) evolved a list specifically useful for research on social mobility; the Plowden Report (1967) endeavoured to keep very close to the original (vol. 2, p. 100); Nisbet and Gammie (see p. 267), in common with a number of other people, made the simple division of 'non-manual' and 'manual'.

Burt (1961) used the classification by fathers' occupation described by Carr-Saunders and Jones (1937) and he gives the following details:

Class I includes those engaged in the highest type of professional and administrative work (university teachers, those of similar standing in law, medicine, education or the church, and the top people in commerce, industry or the civil service);

Class II includes those engaged in lower professional or technical work (including most teachers, men of business, and executive clerks in the highest grades);

Class III includes those working in intermediate types of clerical, commercial, or technical work;

Class IV includes those ordinarily classified as skilled workers, but it also contains an appreciable number who are engaged in commercial or industrial work of an equivalent level;

Class V includes semi-skilled workers and those holding the poorest type of commercial position;

Class VI includes unskilled labourers, casual labourers, and those employed on coarse manual work.

* The author is indebted to Professor T. H. Marshall for much of this information on social class classification.

The basis of this classification is not prestige but the degree of ability required for the work.

For those concerned with the development of young children there is an even greater cause for dissatisfaction with the current method of classifying families and homes than the vague and arbitrary method of the Registrar-General; namely that homes are classified by occupational ability of fathers, whilst we have long known that the biggest single influence on a child's development is the mother (see, for instance, Chapter 5 of Burt's *The Backward Child*, 1937). However, at this moment of sociological flux it is difficult to see how best to assess the ability of mothers. Women are in increasing numbers taking up part-time jobs outside their homes; but these part-time jobs are not normally a main preoccupation and therefore fail to develop potentialities to the full. Thus a classification of women's jobs would tend to underestimate ability. Nevertheless, in spite of this danger the Newsons (1963) added the occupations of the 709 mothers they interviewed to the fathers' occupation for *Infant Care in an Urban Community*; they decided that this was a step towards better assessment of the homes. But the Plowden Report (1967) uses only the Registrar-General's assessment of social class of home (vol. 2, p. 100). The fact that the two columns of figures in that table agree must not be mistaken for confirmation that this technique is a good way to find social class of homes; the similarity of figures merely show that the Plowden Committee, using the same criterion for deciding social class (fathers' occupation) came to the same conclusion. The Plowden Committee must have considered other ways of classifying homes, and a summary of the points discussed could have influenced future thinking on socio-economic status and its classification.

Conway (1958) made a study of inheritance of intelligence and its social implications; and in his report he explains exactly how he arrived at a classification by fathers' occupation, based on the Registrar-General but with only three groups. He refers to the fact that Burt (1909) found unexpectedly wide differences in average performance between pupils at an ordinary elementary school and boys from the higher professional classes (sons of bishops, professors, etc.). It is often argued that children of professional people may do well because the tests are made by professional people and so biased in favour of such homes. Conway gives a number of reasons why this idea does not explain the differences found. In the early researches (1903–9) nearly all the tests were non-verbal; the elementary school selected for the first testing was not in a poverty area; many children said to be mentally deficient were shown by the intelligence tests to have normal capacity; many who failed at

230

11 years could have succeeded if intelligence tests had been added to the selection techniques; and the LCC school surveys a year or two later showed a wide average range when classed by father's occupational class, from unskilled workers whose children averaged IQ 89 to higher professional fathers whose children averaged IQ 120.

At that time the idea of inherited intelligence was generally accepted. What was not understood was that the sexual method of reproduction resulted in fresh recombinations of the genes transmitted by each succeeding generation. Intelligence tests showed that from time to time children from the poorest occupational class were found to have abilities equal to, and even far exceeding, the average level of those in the highest social classes. By arrangement with the London County Council, special scholarships were awarded to many of these children; and after-histories showed plainly that in nearly every case the awards were fully justified. Research between the wars showed that many children of ability were being missed from the poorer classes. Because individual variations were so wide and there were so many more children in lower occupational classes, the number of children of ability in the lower classes was even larger than the number of children of ability in the professional classes. *It was estimated that only half of the children in the poorer classes who had the ability to go to the university were actually reaching the university.*

Conway (1958) compares the work of Burt in 1922–7 with that of Floud et al. reported in *Social Class and Educational Opportunity* (1956), although the latter used slightly different social classification. There is a close measure of agreement between the two sets of figures, despite the gap of some thirty years. The vast improvement of social and educational conditions, since, for

TABLE 12: *Average IQ for different occupational groups*

Class	London 1922–7	S.W. Herts 1952	Middlesbrough 1953
I Highest administrative	120·3		
II Professional	114·6	113·0	115·2
III Clerical	109·7	109·2	108·2
IVa Commercial	104·8	103·7	104·4
IVb Skilled	101·5	100·1	99·0
V Unskilled	95·1	97·1	96·5
Average for working class	98·3	98·2	

Source: Conway (1958).

instance, the 1944 Education Act, has not yet made any impact on the intelligence level of the children of various occupational classes.

Once Binet had invented the concept of mental age and this had been related to chronological age, it was a relatively simple step to relate a child's scholastic attainment to the average attainment throughout the country. Thus he could be given a reading age, an arithmetic or spelling age and so on. These tests are now more often called attainment tests. Vernon, in *Intelligence and Attainment Tests* (1960), describes very clearly the elementary principles of testing, individual and group intelligence tests, and attainment tests. The scholastic attainment tests measure how well a child can use the knowledge *he has been taught*; but the intelligence tests measure how well a child can manipulate *data which he has not previously encountered*.

Now let us see how a test for intelligence or attainment is standardised. In the work on reading we have referred to vocabulary tests or scales, so we can look at how such a list of words is standardised. A committee of psychologists want a vocabulary list which will relate how many words a child knows to how many words most children know at various ages. They decide to have about forty-five words, beginning with an easy word like 'apple' and running to a difficult word like 'panopticon'. It is no good the committee suggesting words, because their own ideas might not be suitable for all children throughout the country. How do you get a random selection of words? First you decide how many words you want. They decide to have 150 words to begin with, in case a random selection produces too many suitable for one age group; and to ignore foreign words, proper names, etc. *The Concise Oxford English Dictionary* has 1,498 pages of definitions, so the top righthand word on every tenth page should give 149. So they decide to include also p. 205. This gives them: account, adverbial, aldehyde, ana, antipole, argute, astride, axis, banneret, beach, berm, black, boil, bracket, brotherhood. . . . Strictly, one should try every word with a thousand children of every age, stepping up by three-month steps; that is to say a thousand children of 5 years, a thousand of $5\frac{1}{4}$ years, a thousand of $5\frac{1}{2}$ years and so on. In practice some discretion might be exercised, as 150 words is too many for the younger ones to define.

Possible definitions have to be agreed, in order to standardise scoring. The vocabulary has to be meaningful to the child; he has to say what a word means. Eventually a list of the agreed forty-five words is arranged in order, according to the chronological age at which about 75 per cent of children can say what the word means. This is much the way in which Terman and Merrill (1937) standardised their list of forty-five words. *Measuring Intelligence* (pp. 304–23) gives all the words, together with the kinds of acceptable and unacceptable definitions agreed upon. They do not begin with 'apple' but another fruit. The examiner must not say to a child 'What is an apple?' because the 'an' would show that it is an object. He just ask, 'What do we mean by "apple"?' And he must be careful not to reveal whether the answer is right or wrong. But he must give enough encouragement and the reply 'Good' to the child's efforts is usually sufficient.

To allow for the chance element of a child never happening to have heard a particular word, this vocabulary test permits six successive failures, before the vocabulary questions stop. As you run down the list, it is clear that, in steps of six, the words become appreciably harder. Actual examples are not given here, because it is a matter of professional etiquette not to publicise standardised tests, in order to preserve the novelty element essential for testing intelligence. In order for the child's intelligence or governing power of the mind to be assessed, he has to manipulate data he has not previously encountered. Those who are studying intelligence and examine the book, will therefore see that, to the general public, it is almost incomprehensibly arranged. But a careful study, will show how it works. The *British Journal of Educational Psychology* discusses the Terman–Merrill and the Wechsler tests of intelligence in half a dozen articles during 1968–9. The Revised Stanford–Binet Scale is given individually, usually by a qualified tester. It has this name because Terman was a professor of psychology at Stanford University and he supervised both the revision of the original Binet test published in 1916 and the next two revisions, published in 1937 and 1960. Those who want to study the construction of tests can see the results of standardising many aspects of intelligence in the Manual for the third revision of the *Stanford–Binet Intelligence Scale* by Terman and Merrill (1960).

There is considerable dissatisfaction with the use of the 1960 revision in Britain. The uninformed mistake this criticism for complaint against intelligence testing as an objective measure. In fact, the criticism is of the statistics. For example, at age 11 the mean is about 107, but we maintain a mean of 100 throughout; and the standard deviation is about 20, but we have accepted a standard deviation of 15 throughout our investigations. Furthermore, we find too much importance is given to verbal reasoning in the higher levels, which is much to the disadvantage of the lower socio-economic classes, where homes do not have the constant exchange of concepts in lively discussion which is typical of so many middle-class homes. As Jensen (p. 245) says, the vicious circle of failure to exploit the verbal potential in the 'culturally disadvantaged' homes is exactly where the schools have to step in. Instead of attacking the tests as constructed by middle-class psychologists for middle-class children, we have to attack the educational system for failing to bring to the culturally deprived children the opportunity to develop their potential and thus grow to parents who provide culturally better homes for their children.

The solution for the British is to construct our own intelligence tests, properly weighted and statistically correct. When Burt retired he left at University College, London plans for such a British test. When the National Foundation for Educational Research was formed, this seemed the appropriate body to carry out the plans, but it has not done so. In the 'sixties the British Psychological Society undertook a preliminary investigation. During the 'seventies they will publish their findings and then we may hope for our own intelligence test, squarely based on the mental processes of reasoning to which the symbolism of words, mathematics, etc., can be put.

The National Foundation for Educational Research was created in 1946. It then became possible to undertake large national surveys. For instance Pidgeon (1960) reports a national survey of the ability and attainment of school children at three age levels: 7 to 8 years, $10\frac{1}{2}$ to $11\frac{1}{2}$ years, and 14 to 15 years. Tests of reading, arithmetic, and non-verbal ability were given to 10,000 children in schools all over the country; and their verbal intelligence was known from routine junior school testing. This is the start of a long-term investigation, results of which will be published periodically.

The initial investigation which demonstrated that intelligence consisted of both general and special abilities had established this through correlating the intelligence of children brought up in orphanages with the intelligences of their parents, and correlating the intelligence of twins. In more than forty years many identical twins reared apart have been discovered, both in the work initiated by Burt and in other research centres. Conway (1958) cites a now classic example from Burt's Bingham Lecture:

George and his brother were children of an Oxford don who died a few weeks before their birth. Unable with her slender purse to bring up two boys, the mother had secretly arranged for one to be boarded out. George remained with his mother; and, after a brilliant career at school, had obtained a first class degree in modern languages. His former teacher, encountering him (as he supposed) on the arrival platform at Paddington, was surprised to hear himself answered in a strong Welsh accent by a stranger who declared his name was Llewellyn Jones. It turned out that Llewellyn was the twin who had been adopted in infancy by an elderly Welsh couple, and brought up on an isolated farm in North Wales. He was now himself a young but successful farmer. Until this accidental meeting neither twin had the smallest inkling of the other's existence. We tested both. Llewellyn's reading and his verbal ability generally were those of a child of barely eleven; but his high IQ was practically the same as his brother's (137 as compared with 136 for George.) [The names are fictitious.]

Burt (1966) has reviewed his extensive work on the genetic determination of differences in intelligence through study of monozygotic twins reared together and apart. He begins with a brief account of the origins of the work and the correlation of intelligence first of children presumed to differ in inheritance (brought up in institutions) with that of their parents; and secondly the correlation of intelligence of identical twins reared apart. Identical twins reared apart are not as rare as was once supposed. By now there are 148 monozygotic twins in this research, fifty-three of the pairs reared apart. Burt compares his results with those of Shields (1962) and with those of a famous American research by Newman et al. (1936). Table 13 consists of correlations* in both his and Newman's researches. Each of them correlates monozygotes reared together, monozygotes reared apart, and dizygotes; but Burt also gives correlations for siblings reared together, siblings reared apart, and unrelated children reared together.

1. *Intelligence.* In both sets of figures there is a steady decline in correlations from monozygotes reared together, through those reared apart to dizygotic twins reared together. The figures given by Burt et al. are for larger numbers (see top row of figures) and these show a sharper decline from monozygotes to dizygotes. When the figures for twins and siblings or unrelated children are added, the difference is even more clearly marked. Identical twins reared together have cor. 0·925 and unrelated children reared together only cor. 0·438.

2. *Educational.* These correlations present a striking contrast with those for intelligence in both sets of figures. Monozygotes have close correlation

* Those who have not yet studied statistics, or have studied but lost their way, can make a rough interpretation of a correlation table by regarding the first two figures after the decimal point as a percentage e.g. cor. 0·944 as 94 per cent. Mathematicians do not approve of this because it is only a crude approximation; but it is far better than being afraid to look at a correlation table. The first four correlations in Table 13, results of correlating replies in a group test of intelligence, are roughly equivalent to the following percentages:

	Reared	*Estimated intelligence*
Monozygotes	together	94 practically identical
Monozygotes	apart	77 fairly similar
Dizygotes	together	55 ⎰ much less similar than
Siblings	together	54 ⎱ monozygotes reared apart

TABLE 13: *Correlations for mental, educational, and physical characteristics*

	Burt						Newman		
	Monozygotic twins reared together	Monozygotic twins reared apart	Dizygotic twins reared together	Siblings reared together	Siblings reared apart	Unrelated children reared together	Monozygotic twins reared together	Monozygotic twins reared apart	Dizygotic twins reared together
Number of pairs*	95	53	127	264	51	136	50	19	51
Intelligence									
Group test	0·944	0·771	0·552	0·545	0·412	0·281	0·922	0·727	0·621
Individual test	0·918	0·863	0·527	0·498	0·423	0·252	0·881	0·767	0·631
Final assessment	0·925	0·874	0·453	0·531	0·438	0·267	—	—	—
Educational									
Reading and spelling	0·951	0·597	0·919	0·842	0·490	0·545	—	—	—
Arithmetic	0·862	0·705	0·748	0·754	0·563	0·478	—	—	—
General attainments	0·983	0·623	0·831	0·803	0·526	0·537	0·892	0·583	0·696
Physical									
Height	0·962	0·943	0·472	0·501	0·536	-0·069	0·932	0·969	0·645
Weight	0·929	0·884	0·586	0·568	0·427	0·243	0·917	0·886	0·631
Head length	0·961	0·958	0·495	0·481	0·506	0·110	0·910	0·917	0·691
Head breadth	0·977	0·960	0·541	0·510	0·492	0·082	0·908	0·880	0·654
Eye colour	1·000	1·000	0·516	0·554	0·524	0·104	—	—	—

* Figures for boys and girls have been calculated separately and then averaged. In columns 3, 4, 5 and 6 the correlations for head length, head breadth, and eye colour were based on samples of 100 only.

Source: Burt (1966).

when reared in the same environment, but there is a considerable drop when they are reared in different environments. And the monozygotes have roughly the same educational attainment when reared apart as dizygotes reared together or unrelated children reared together or siblings reared apart. Note: the twins George and Llewellyn (above) were approximately the same for intelligence, but quite different for educational attainment.

3. *The physical characteristics* of monozygotes have a high correlation whether reared together or apart, in both sets of figures; and the correlations with other groups are considerably lower. Presumably the drop in correlation for weight of monozygotes reared apart is because weight can be affected by diet.

Burt concludes from this research that the correlation of intelligence for monozygotic twins is very high, whether reared together or apart. But the correlations for school attainment vary closely with similarity in environmental circumstances. From this it may be inferred that individual differences in 'intelligence', particularly when assessments have been carefully checked, are influenced far more by genetic constitution, or what is popularly called 'heredity', than by postnatal or environmental conditions. These figures and those of other writers agree satisfactorily with the view that the genetic tendencies which are responsible for individual differences in intelligence are in the main (though probably not exclusively) transmitted in accordance with a multifactorial hypothesis. It is quite feasible for intelligence to be mainly a matter of inheritance and at the same time for children to be much more or much less intelligent than their parents. The IQ of each child, though mainly determined by the genes of its parents, is not simply the average of their IQs.

There has in the past been much speculation as to whether different races or ethnic groups vary in general level of intelligence. Psychologists from different countries seem to agree that in spite of the difficulties some conclusions can safely be drawn: (a) although critics of the method declare that test results exaggerate differences, the main result of applying tests has been to show that the differences in intelligence are very much smaller than had previously been supposed, even though cultural differences are wide; (b) certain primitive races are much more homogeneous (owing to prolonged inbreeding) i.e. they have fewer individuals with extremely low or extremely high ability; and this has been erroneously taken to mean that the average is lower. In the United States intelligence tests for World War I the Negroes of the North had a higher average score than the white recruits of the South. As this instance shows, the real difficulty is not just to find suitable tests, but to be sure your samples are typical.

Wide cultural differences can have a marked effect upon tests of scholastic attainment, even when psychologists standardise the tests within a given community. Ortar (1960) working with new primary-school-aged immigrants to Israel from various cultures, abandoned the idea of testing the intelligence of such a varied group and devised a way of making a rough assessment of the children's 'learning potential'. She used the Wechsler Intelligence Scale for Children (WISC) and found the verbal section a much more valid predictor than the performance section.

There are very considerable problems when comparisons between ethnic groups are attempted. Lloyd and Pidgeon (1961) gave non-verbal tests to children in three ethnic groups, European, Indian and African, all in Natal. They concluded that standardised test scores of children from different cultural backgrounds cannot be considered comparable, even after a period of familiarisation with test material. The difficulty here may have been one of sampling.

McFie (1961) gave verbal and performance tests to thirty female African student nurses, all of whom had completed formal primary education, mostly in the vernacular; but only a few of them had had more than two years in secondary school. He gave them the Block Designs test, a series of patterned blocks which have to be put together to form various specified designs, with time limit and credits for finishing early. But when confronted with the unfamiliar blocks, they spent so long examining them and turning them over, that only five of the thirty gained any time-credits. Even those who managed to copy the designs correctly usually reproduced them in reverse or inverted.

McFie concluded that they were hampered by lack of experience of toys and practical education, so he devised an experiment to check the effect of practical education. He tested twenty-six African boys aged 16 to 19 years, at the beginning and end of a two-year course in a technical college, where they studied such practical occupations as building and carpentry. Although they had been educated in the vernacular, they had more trouble with non-verbal performance tests than with verbal tests. At the first test the boys had the same trouble as the student nurses; but after two years of practical education, they had no trouble in orientating designs, describing pictures or arranging in sequence a popular strip-cartoon. With the first test only four of the twenty-six boys got time credits with the Block Designs; but with the final test thirteen got time credits. Their two years of constructional training had so improved their ability to tackle performance test material that their whole attitude to the test had changed. McFie concluded that the ability to perceive visual material was as much dependent on the environment as the ability to talk or calculate.

Vernon and his wife (1965) carried out a series of performance and verbal tests with boys of 10 to 11 years from various cultures, using a hundred boys of the same age from south-west England as controls. Among the various groups was a group of fifty West Indian boys, who scored markedly below the British boys in practical tests and some non-verbal intelligence tests. But the difference between the West Indian and the British boys was not so great in formal educational attainments. The test the West Indian boys found hardest was Kohs Blocks, the block design of McFie's investigation. Forty per cent could not transfer the patterns from the cards to the blocks, whereas only 4 per cent of the British found this difficult. In the Matrix tests their score was only 75 as against the British median of 100. In the Vernon-Formboard, where seven different insets have to be fitted into seven different patterns, 50 per cent were as slow as, or slower than, the bottom two British boys. With a set of six black-and-white pictures showing perspective, such as an aeroplane in the foreground and a distant airport, 60 per cent made definite errors of perception or recognition on the relatively simple ones, as against half as many British boys in a more difficult series. With the Gottschaldt embedded figures the score was 87, as against the control 100 score. The West Indian boys were a year behind in the Draw-a-Man test, and also with the Porteus Maze tests.

On tracing the Porteus Maze Vernon points out that the West Indian boys would have had less opportunity to play with mazes in comics. But in point of fact all the tests he used show a marked resemblance to the toys to be found in any of our nursery schools and culturally stimulating homes. He found a substantial correlation, both with the West Indian and the British boys, between their test performance and an assessment of the cultural stimulus within their homes. Therefore Vernon concludes that cultural stimulus in the home strongly affects perceptual-practical abilities.

In the 1960s attention to the problems of cross-cultural testing shifted from the difficulty of constructing suitable tests, to the different effects upon the functioning of children's abilities of the various child-rearing patterns. Ferron (1966) compares the effects of early environmental stimulation upon nursery school Creoles in Freetown, Sierra Leone and a group of London nursery school children. There were thirty Freetown and thirty Deptford children and he found little difference between them on language. The

Creoles were descendants of slaves who had been established in the Freetown area after Britain abolished slavery. But the Creole children had great difficulty in discriminating geometric forms, even circles, squares and triangles; also in using a Formboard with insets building a tower, threading beads, and so on. In fact, the tests in which the London nursery school children were significantly better were those for which their many toys had given them much practice in perception and muscular coordination.

Others who have written in the 1960s on cross-cultural testing are Irvine (1966) on a rationale for testing attainments and abilities in Africa; Goldman and Taylor (1966) who have made two surveys of research and literature on the educational problems and potential of coloured immigrant children in Britain and America; Biesheuvel (1965) on the pitfalls of cross-cultural testing in connection with personnel selection; Bannister and Presly (1967) on testing student nurses; and Wober (1967) on differences of cognitive operations, the Americans predominantly visual and the Africans predominantly auditory or proprioceptive (sensitive to position and movement of the body), with national or cultural differences in response to test material. Ferron (1967) whose PhD thesis three years earlier had been on testing the intelligence of some West African children, concludes his discussion and research reports in *Educational Research* with an article on the linguistic factor involved. He says that educated Africans will have to launch a multidirectional attack on educational problems including the improvement of intelligence test performance in order to overcome the difficulties. By 1968–9 the *British Journal of Educational Psychology* had half a dozen more articles on cross-cultural testing. Interest is definitely roused. We should note that the differences between national cultures is no more than an extension of the difference between socio-economic environments within our own country.

All this might seem to have little to do with the testing of our own children's intelligence. But there are a number of reasons why it is directly our concern. First, largely because of western influences, many developing countries wish to develop western-type cultures and so select students to come to us for final education. This means we have to test them ourselves over here and we meet problems such as Bannister and Presley (1967) had over testing their student nurses. Principals of technical colleges in Britain find they cannot train such students in practical matters, to be architects, civil engineers, and other practical specialists, because of their lack of understanding of practical matters, map reading, drawing-board design and suchlike. They therefore have to recommend them for verbal professions, such as lawyers, and doctors (not surgeons). Those who teach have to understand the backgrounds from which their pupils come and these countries urgently need practical specialists. In our empire days we started educating these people. It is our responsibility now to help them to educate themselves.

Then we have our own immigrant problems. Mental testing, which is now a part of our educational practice, does not do justice to the intelligence of immigrant children, not so much because of language difficulties as because most of the children lack the practical perceptual-discriminative training which is part of our child-rearing practice long before our children reach school. According to the Plowden Report in 1967 there were in our primary and secondary schools 57,000 West Indian, 24,000 Indian, and just under 8,000 Pakistani children. Mental measurements such as suit our own children grossly underrate the mental abilities of these children from other cultures.

Lastly there is our initial purpose in studying cross-cultural testing; to see in the exaggerated form of widely differing cultures from jungle to Western capital, how varying environments can have varying effects upon the tests we use. The evidence shows that environmental stimulus at preschool and primary stage interacts with innate intelligence and so affects the development of inborn ability. Where the environment is stimulating, whether in home or school, intellectual development is better than where it is unstimulating. What applies to different countries throughout the world also applies to different socio-economic levels within our own country. As part of our educational attitude, we have to become far more sensitive to this.

Let us take from the Plowden Report information from one of their surveys about the number of books to be found in homes of different social classes. There were over 3,000 parents in the enquiry, well distributed through all the social classes. Table 14 shows the average of books in the homes. From this table we can see that 70 per cent of the children come from homes with more than five books and 19 per cent from homes where the parents either know they have no books or do not even know if there is a book in the

TABLE 14: *Number of books by social class*

Q.61 Number of books in home	I Professional	II Managerial	III Non-manual	III Skilled manual	IV Semi-skilled	V Un-skilled	Un-classified	Total
More than five books	95	88	85	67	61	43	55	70
One to five books	4	4	9	12	17	14	18	11
No books	1	7	6	21	22	42	27	18
Not known	0	1	0	0	0	1	0	1
Total number (100%)	(110)	(430)	(338)	(1,486)	(499)	(189)	(40)	(3,092)

house. On the same page there is a table showing that in 32 per cent of the families neither parent belongs to a lending library. Children from such a family will not see their parents absorbed in a book. Example of the joys of reading is one of the potent influences in encouraging children to master reading. Other tables in this survey report show that, through the social levels, the interest taken in the education of their children by fathers descends from 84 per cent with professional families to 40 per cent in families where the fathers have unskilled occupations. There is the same steady descent in the number of fathers who have been to school and talked to the head teacher, from 49 per cent of professional fathers to 17 per cent of unskilled fathers.

By means of factor analysis, the different aspects could be related. At one extreme there were parents who talked to head or class teacher on the first day, discussed education and teaching methods with them, and attended many school functions; and at the other extreme there were parents who never or rarely went to the school, were unlikely to talk to the class teacher or discuss education, and attended no school functions. Associations were found between social class and the responsibility and initiative taken by parents over their children's education. Pages 145–7 of vol. 2 give good examples of the clusters of related facts which can only be found by factor analysis.

The biggest factor in this social survey accounting for the children's variation in school achievement was not the variation in home circumstances or in schools. It was the variation in parental attitudes. It is possible that the bad attitudes to education of some parents stem from their own unhappy recollections of school failure. We need more research here. If this proved to be so, then for the sake of future generations as well as for the sake of individual children, it should become our educational policy to see that no child suffers from too much failure in school. As teaching machines and programmed learning show, the best learning of conditioned response is achieved by situations in which the child is almost certain to succeed. We have seen that attitudes, once established, are difficult to change; for example, in attitudes of backward readers to reading, and backward calculators to mathematics. There has been a little research on attitudes; for instance Baraheni (1962) with juniors, Hall (1963) and E. A. Allen (1960, 1961) with adolescents, and K. M. Evans (1966a) with teachers. But attitude scales do not yet appear to be sufficiently refined to produce any conclusive data. The Plowden Report has much to say on finding the right degree of persuasion, neither too much nor too little, augmenting a better attitude of parents to the education of their children. We shall see in the final chapter that research by Musgrove and Taylor (1965) and Banfield, Bowyer and Wilkie (1967) suggests that parents have the same objectives for education of their children as teachers, but teachers have not understood this nor given them sufficient information about school work. Regarding environmental influences upon intelligence and attainment, the two crucial appendices of the Plowden Report are in vol. 2, no. 4 (conclusions pp. 181–2) and no. 9 (summary pp. 368–71).

In *Genetic and Environmental Factors in Human Ability*, edited by Meade and Parkes (1966) Wiseman contributes a section on environmental and innate factors and educational attainment. He says that we can no longer separate our educational and social systems because they interact; and although we know so little about this interaction, we need to set out what we know rather than to proclaim what we believe. In an investigation with forty-four primary schools in the Manchester area he found that brightness and backwardness are not simple opposites; some special factors correlate with one and not the other, and vice versa. From the evidence he concludes: (*a*) that the influence of environmental factors on educational attainment is greatest at the youngest ages, and gets progressively less influential as the children get older; (*b*) that as far as social class is concerned—a very crude measure of environmental differences—its effect seems to disappear by the age of 17 or 18; (*c*) that factors in the home and neighbourhood, and particularly those associated with maternal care and material needs, are much more powerful determinants of educational achievement than are the factors within the walls of the school itself; (*d*) that the strong association between the intelligence test results and the 'home' variables suggest that their primacy of effect might be due largely to genetic factors; and (*e*) that adverse forces in the environment have their greatest effect on the more able children.

Wiseman says positive action must be taken but the situation is complex and it seems that the greatest harm is done before the child reaches school age. There is strong evidence that both animals and children suffering environmental deprivation not only slow down in development but may permanently suffer a lowered level of later performance. He suggests that the intellectual and logical schemata of Piaget may have their counterpart in the effective and creative life of children, and particularly of preschool children. The years before 5 are notoriously crucial for the development of mental health: they may be equally so for educational health. What is required is a reorientation of teachers. First they have to become aware of the nature of these adverse forces; and then they must expect to engage in positive action. A proportion of teachers should train themselves to act as general liaison between school and home.

S. Griffiths (1959) enquired into the causes of academic deterioration after successful juniors had gone to the grammar school. He came to the following conclusions: (a) where facilities for study in the home were good, there was no deterioration; where they were bad there was deterioration; (b) thirty-eight of thirty-nine parents lacked grammar schooling themselves; (c) the majority of parents were in the lowest category of socio-economic class; (d) those who deteriorated had less parental encouragement; (e) they were low in persistence; and (f) were frequently absent from school. If grammar schools knew which children were exposed to such hazards, they might be able to take at least some countermeasures, to ensure that these children had extra backing in schools.

In this complex area, environment has now been shown to affect the many types of test used for assessing intelligence. The best we can do at the moment is first to become aware of the situation and then to take special precautions to ensure that those children most likely to be environmentally handicapped have extra opportunity for success in school. On a long-term view, this should make a positive contribution through the next generation. We already know that positive attitudes to school can be fostered in children, no matter how low their intellectual endowments may be, from the remarkably fine work being done in schools for educationally subnormal children, to which we refer later. Also, in some progressive secondary modern schools, it is being done with children in the lowest streams. This is the true meaning of educating children according to their abilities and aptitudes, as laid down in the 1944 Education Act.

In 1961 Bernstein published an article on social structure, language and learning in *Educational Research* which was widely discussed by those interested in environmentally handicapped children. His theme is the relation of potential ability to developed ability. He points out that students now know the need for becoming aware of children's backgrounds; but we lack system in our approach to the problems in the educational programme for the 29 per cent from the lower working class. When no steps are taken in the primary school, the situation becomes progressively worse; and by the secondary school the environmental handicap which these children suffer becomes painfully clear. Bernstein is our advocate for the isolated, defenceless and inarticulate group of children for whom school learning never 'gets inside'. He says some teachers can reach them (and shows how), but some cannot. His article will make many more want to try.

A more recent article, again in *Educational Research*, is one by Jensen (1967) of California University on the culturally disadvantaged. He states the case paradoxically: we can hypothesise that there is a greater chance of finding a potential IQ of 130 to 150 among the culturally disadvantaged group whose measured IQ is 70 to 90 than among the middle-class group whose IQs are 100–130. His researches have shown that, amongst low IQ children, those from lower-class homes have greater learning potential than those from middle-class homes. This is because the abilities of children from middle-class homes are more likely to be developed than those from lower-class homes. Also the probability of finding a learning speed comparable with a middle-class 'gifted' child seems to be greater in the low IQ low socio-economic status than in the average IQ range of either social class group. On average the IQ test grossly underestimates learning ability among lower-class children.

Jensen points out that, except in the most extreme cases, economic factors have little effect on IQ, though a truly democratic society maximises genetic differences precisely because it minimises environmental conditions. He then seeks some non-genetic explanation of the present situation, in which democracy is failing to minimise environmental conditions. The trend today is away from crude socio-economic variables and towards more subtle intrafamily and interpersonal variables. He lists a dozen or so variables under the three headings: Press for Achievement Motivation, Press for Language Development, and Provision for General Learning. The culturally disadvantaged have three main handicaps: perceptual and attentional abilities, verbal and cognitive abilities, and orectic or motivational factors. The special training for all three handicaps differs from that for children who are innately slow learners. There is little research on perceptual abilities but the child who has not learned to discriminate sights and sounds is handicapped on reaching school. On attentional ability he cites Burt's *The Backward Child* (1937, pp. 479–85) as indicating its importance. On language he cites Bernstein (1961), as giving the best detailed analysis of social class differences in language characteristics important to the development of cognitive abilities. He then gives an analysis from his own research on verbal mediation of cognitive functions. In conclusion he gives examples from the United States of compulsory education for the disadvantaged. The brutal fact is that these children are in a cycle of poverty and cultural deprivation; and schools will have to take on responsibility for breaking the cycle.

Lynn (1959b), examining environmental conditions affecting intelligence, found that parental attitudes laid the foundations of development. He starts by accepting the assumption of such authorities as Burt and P. E. Vernon that intelligence is inherited. He then examines schools as an intellectual stimulus, the importance of the quality of the home, the importance to the child of communication with adults, the influence of the mother, and the attitude of the parents to intellectual attainment. He concludes by saying that the personality patterns are laid down in the home and teachers can inspire; but we have as yet little evidence on motivation. MacArthur and Elley (1963) explain the problem of finding the intelligence potential of children from deprived cultural and educational backgrounds and conclude that, so far, Progressive Matrices is the nearest we have to a culture-reduced test, because it has a high element of general intelligence and a low correlation with socio-economic status.

In our society today we have a vague impression that anyone worth his salt can rise to a higher social class. In *Intelligence and Social Mobility* (1961) Burt, basing his conclusion on observed facts, says that some 40 per cent do not take up the occupation for which they are mentally suited. Some 20 per cent could do more difficult work, and about as many are not intellectually up to the work they are doing. Also, the correlation of intelligence between parents and children is only 0·50; and the correlation between fathers' occupation and children's intelligence is lower still. If we were to attempt to keep men at jobs for which their intelligence fitted them, we should need an overall social mobility of 22 per cent. The greatest causes of rise and fall within society are, he says, intelligence and motivation. Elsewhere, in an article on Galton, Burt (1962a) gives a fascinating family history of one man, showing the social mobility within one family.

Since Burt regards motivation as such an important factor, we naturally turn to what he has to say on motivation. Burt and Williams (1962) have written on the influence of motivation on results of intelligence tests; although the article appears in the *British Journal of Statistical Psychology*, it is well within the ability of students not yet trained in statistics, provided terms such as SD, reliability and validity are known or can be looked up. The 'rewards' offered in the experiments are places in a grammar school or university, and, in the case of the younger children, money. Before the Second World War the 1·5 per cent of those at the university were not the top 1·5 per cent for intelligence. But in those days nearly half of the brightest (particularly women) did not go to university. Furneaux in *The Chosen Few* (1961) reminds us that Thomson said a quarter of university students in Scotland had IQs less than 115. However, the tests used were group tests and there was no strong motivation (as there would have been in an entrance examination). Moreover, an IQ for persons over 14 is a dubious measure. Such tests are not very reliable, particularly if only one is given. Originally tests were given individually, to determine borderline cases referred to the school psychologists. Then group tests, not quite so reliable, were introduced. In such cases the stronger the motivation, the higher the score. Results were more constant with a well-trained administrator. Although fewer tests were given to students, results showed the same trend. With children of 10 to 11 years and students of 17 to 22 years, where motivation was strong, the mean test performance was much higher and the tests proved much more reliable. Burt and Williams suggest two corollaries: (a) it is unwise to take test results at their face value, without knowing what were the motivational conditions; and (b) results from tests taken under different conditions cannot validly be compared.

J. Nisbet and Entwistle (1967) investigated the relation between size of family and scores on tests. They studied the results of verbal and non-verbal tests of intelligence and of attainment, from 2,868 children tested at 7, 9, 11 and 12 years. There was, as others have found, a correlation between larger families and poorer scores. The girls consistently suffered more than the boys. Within occupation groups I and II there was less difference. They interpret these results as evidence of environmental, rather than inherited, influence on test scores. Most people recognise both causes. Dull parents are more prolific. Another factor may be that the children spend more time together, and so lose the stimulus of adult interests and conversation. If this is so, it may also be a factor in the development of twins. On twins a number of authorities support Burt (1955), in giving as possible explanation for greater mortality, smaller physique and somewhat lower mental capacity compared with other children, their conditions of gestation and delivery, both environmental factors. We should also bear in mind the lack of language learning in twins through being too much thrown together. Greenberg (1966) writes of a 'parental exclusion' phenomenon in twins, whereby the twins have to deal with each other's aggression unmitigated by normal adult intervention. Here again is an environmental factor affecting mental as well as emotional development of twins. Sandon (1959), Chief Examiner for Somerset Education Committee, examined the 11+ results of well over 1,000 twins and found their average ability well below that of the general population.

Severe anxiety can impede the functioning of intelligence, though mild anxiety may act as a spur. There have been various researches on anxiety recently, for instance Bowyer (1961) with primary school children, Maguire

(1966) with secondary modern children, and Hallworth (1961) with secondary modern and grammar school children. But the findings are still somewhat confused. It may be that anxiety is a matter on which more depth psychology is required than is at present customary. Bene (1958) goes into unconscious motivation for behaviour in connection with suppression of heterosexual interests and aggression. She supports those who say suppression of such interests is due to occupational class, not intelligence; and she supports Gorer (1955), who says that for the English aggression is so confused with guilt that they will not even tolerate it in their children. We are aware that attitudes can impede the functioning of intelligence. However, it could well be that we find ourselves unable to make objective assessments of attitudes, and therefore are unable to change unsatisfactory attitudes, because we are unwilling to look into matters of aggression, guilt and anxiety dispassionately.

Another article that touches on anxiety, by Lynn and Gordon (1961), is on the relation of neuroticism and extraversion to intelligence and educational attainment. Here, it is as well to remember the comments (p. 168) on the psychiatric term 'neuroticism' in connection with normal children. The use of this now obsolete term corners these authors into writing of 'neurotics in normal groups' which is tantamount to saying 'abnormal normals'. Lynn and Gordon think that introverts are more socialised than extraverts, since they acquire conditioned anxiety reactions to social disapproval more readily than extraverts. They find extraverts handicapped in academic work, since they become fatigued more quickly and so give up more easily; and the so-called 'neurotics in normal groups' score more quickly. Not surprisingly, their article lead to 'correspondence'. Biggs attacks the work of Lynn and Gordon, Lynn replies, and Eysenck concludes the correspondence with an appreciation of the original article.

Amongst influences upon test results we should include some reference to practice effect, which results from children having much experience of the modern form of standardised tests. Heim and Watts (1957) at Cambridge attempted to reconcile opposing views on the effect of practice. They gave parallel tests to boys and girls of 13 and 14 years from six schools. But they found results not clear. Ortar (1960), with a group of students in Jerusalem who came from widely differing cultural backgrounds, found a marked practice effect. Indeed, she attempted to use the amount a student profited from practice as a measure of educability. Such an idea may have value, but should be divorced from use of standardised intelligence tests. Lloyd and Pidgeon (1961) made a study in Natal, where there was a mixed ethnic group, consisting of European, Indian and African children. None of the children were test sophisticated. The Europeans scored highest, which is to be expected with tests originating from western culture. But practice had much effect upon Europeans and Africans, and no effect on Indians. They conclude that standardised test scores of children from different cultural backgrounds are not comparable, even after a period of familiarisation with the tests. Elton (1965) of Kentucky experimented with a course on symbolic logic and syllogistic fallacies. But this caused no significant effect upon the results of reasoning tests, given at the beginning and the end of the course. Curr and Gourlay (1953), studying the effects of remedial education, set out what they considered more rigorous scientific standards. Then in 1960 they applied such standards to an investigation of the effect of practice on performance in scholastic or achievement tests with children in four primary schools. Practice was most effective for reading tests and least for arithmetic. There is no doubt that test sophistication through practice has an effect which must be borne in mind; but just how much or little the effect may be is not yet clear.

Since attitudes are closely bound up with personality Wisenthal's (1965) investigation of sex differences in attitudes and attainment in junior schools with over a thousand boys and over a thousand girls aged 7 to 11 years should be mentioned. Where there was a marked deterioration of attitude there was also a marked lack of attainment. Others who have linked investigation of personality with intelligence include: Astington (1960), Butcher et al. (1963), E. G. S. Evans (1964), and Child (1964). Then Eysenck and White (1964) make a re-analysis of some of the data purporting to show that stable children differ from labile (unstable) ones in the structure of their intellectual abilities and hint at a possible contrary explanation: that high stability subjects show greater organisation of abilities than unstable ones. 'It would almost appear', they write, 'as if greater stability and ability, respectively, went with greater degrees of organisation of ability and stability.' This is what one might call a 'virtuous circle'. Now, since we have seen that intelligence is the organising power of the mind, this new idea would mean that the hierarchical organisation of intelligence accepted by Burt (1949) and Vernon (1950) and many others as a useful model, would be affected. The more able and stable could arrange a better hierarchy. But as Eysenck and White (1964) say, more research is needed here. Thus we can see that personality has to be brought into the study of intelligence, but it brings with it not only the complexity of personality but also the many as yet unsolved problems of personality. Before the link between intelligence and personality can be satisfactory, much more research on personality will be needed in order to define personality more clearly.

Now let us look at research into children's intelligence according to age. If we begin with the nursery years, now generally recognised as of great importance, the first point we notice is that there is almost no British research from an educational standpoint in the last decade or so. Of the vitally important follow-up studies which conclude this section on intelligence, only one begins with nursery school children. The gap in scientific information on the intelligence of preschool children is so inexplicable on rational grounds that one is forced to speculate on possible irrational explanations. The gap is not just a British feature. Americans, such as L. J. Stone and Church (1957) complain bitterly, though much more research into the youngest children is now going on in America than in Britain. Could it be that pride in the high level of statistics in Britain has lead researchers here to go for only large numbers, forgetting that much information can only be gained by individual interviews? Originally, all intelligence testing was carried out entirely by individual interview. There is information only to be obtained from group tests (although they are somewhat less reliable than individual tests) because of the great numbers of answers which can be analysed statistically. But there is also information which can only be obtained individually. It would be a pity if the immense value of group testing with subsequent statistical work on hundreds, even thousands of scores, should blind us to other kinds of research on young children's intelligence. We need more Piaget-type research into the abilities of the youngest children.

Another possibility emerges. Not everyone knows how to handle young children. Are the research workers frightened to investigate children until they are of an age to be kept in order by a teacher? We have been shown how such research can be done. In Britain we have the work of such writers as R. Griffiths in *The Abilities of Babies* (1954), Sampson in 'Study of speech development in children 18–30 months' (1956), and Lewis in *Language Thought and Personality in Infancy and Childhood* (1963). From elsewhere we have such writers as Piaget in *Play, Dreams and Imitation in Childhood* (1951) and Murphy in *The Widening World of Childhood* (1962). It is very doubtful whether our primary schools can have either teachers working on modern lines or researches of real value, where teachers and psychologists undervalue data from children too young to be grouped for statistical investigations.

One of the reasons why Burt's surveys of young children have such value is that he has easy rapport with children of all ages. Hearnshaw (1964) says of him, 'As befits Great Britain's first professional psychologist Burt has never been an academic recluse. He has plunged into the stream of life (residing, for example, in social settlements in Liverpool and London).' Anyone who imagines that Susan Isaacs alone really wrote the passage in the *Infant and Nursery Schools* (Burt and Isaacs, 1933) referred to (p. 52), might be interested to read the following incident. When Burt's Department of Psychology was evacuated to Aberystwyth, he walked home one evening, coat flapping in the sea breeze, stick tapping and deerstalker-type hat pulled down. He saw two boys of about 3 and 6 years playing on the newly hearthstoned white steps of the students' hostel where the author lodged. Throughout the country, where steps are hearthstoned, children of all ages know that you do not play on them when they have just been done. The Professor evidently decided to get the children off the step and not to tell them what they already knew. So quite softly but suddenly he said, 'Boo!' The children scampered off at top speed as they were intended to do, down the road and round the corner. Then the older one stuck just his head back round the corner and hissed one four-letter word at him. The Professor accepted this under-standable 'retaliation of aggression' with the mixture of amusement and tenderness so often to be seen in nursery schools where similar anal references are considered part of normal development.

We shall not get the data we need about the youngest children's thinking from academic recluses who need teachers to stand by and keep order. May-be the nursery teachers themselves, who do indeed plunge into the stream of life, will have to learn the techniques of scientific investigation. The position concerning the infant school stage of intelligence research is almost as bad as at the nursery stage. However, Freyberg (1966) carried out an inves-tigation on the reliability of Raven's (1960) Coloured Progressive Matrices as a group test, with 159 children of 6 to 7 years. Because the subjects have at least to be able to read and write figures, the booklet form as a group test cannot be used with very young children. The original research with children on the Coloured Progressive Matrices had not appeared very reliable and Freyberg was testing it for reliability, rather than testing the children. Freyberg found it rather more reliable than Raven had claimed, which is an unusual situation, as research reports tend rather to exaggerate claims than to minimise them.

Some authorities (e.g. Garrett, 1941, and Burt, 1954) suggest that cognitive abilities appear to be relatively undifferentiated before 8 or 9 years. By 11 years intellectual versus practical types of intelligence are already beginning to appear. Hence our tripartite secondary scheme, which admittedly exagger-ates the differentiation. The apparent unreliability of the Coloured Progressive

Matrices might be due to this. But it is a useful test and certain errors of design pointed out by Banks and Sinha (1951) and Jordan and Bennett (1957) could be eliminated. It is such a convenient test to administer that it might well prove most profitable to standardise a third and even simpler form for nursery and younger infant school children. It would be given individually and the child could just point to the selected pattern. Although the higher mental abilities may be relatively undifferentiated before 10 to 12 years, it is likely that we might get some forewarning of later difficulties if, for instance, a test on the lines of Vernon's Formboard but without insets gave a child the chance to show whether he had ease or difficulty in orientating visual perception, upon which so much later cognitive work will depend, through reading, mathematics, and so on. We do not know what we shall find until more research is done with the youngest children.

Much more research is going on into the junior stage, when children can be expected to write their answers reasonably well. Here are two of special interest with regard to testing procedure. Jones (1962) used the Wechsler-Intelligence Scale for Children (WISC) on London primary children. This American test derives mental age and intelligence quotient by a procedure different from the usual practice. Jones found it gave a higher mean score than the Binet test. This reminds us again that one should not just accept an IQ for a child, but note which test has been used as well as under what conditions. Radford (1966) studied the effect of allowing the children to talk as they did a non-verbal test, a contribution on the lines of Vygotsky's study (p. 97) of the meaning of children's 'idle talk' as they solve problems. Radford used the Coloured Progressive Matrices test, and found that being allowed to talk while doing it improved the children's performance. If, as suggested above, a third and simpler form of this test were standardised for individual use, then note of the younger children's need to verbalise should be taken.

Naturally, the question of whether children for whom the mother-tongue is Welsh are handicapped by intelligence tests in English, has roused considerable interest. James (1960) gives a very good survey of work done on this subject, which indicates that Welsh bilingual children appear to be handicapped also by non-verbal tests of intelligence. But James re-analyses results of a 1951 Bangor survey in the light of socio-economic data made available to him by the School Welfare Officers in Caernarvonshire. James came to the conclusion that where monoglot and bilingual groups differ significantly in non-verbal intelligence scores, there is a corresponding difference in fathers' occupation. Thus bilingualism need not be the source of any intellectual disadvantage. Crude though judging class solely by father's occupation may be, it is the best gauge we have at present and socio-economic class should always be taken into consideration in regard to standardised testing.

Among the most interesting and valuable tests are the follow-up studies which begin in the junior school and go on to secondary, student and even adult life. Kellmer Pringle and Pickup (1963) report the junior stage of a study which will continue. Thirty-seven children were tested yearly with Goodenough's (1926) Draw-a-Man test (one of the tests Vernon used with the West Indian boys, see p. 239), giving 148 drawings which were analysed and intercorrelated with (a) each other; (b) Stanford-Binet IQ; and (c) WISC. Although they found the Draw-a-Man test unsatisfactory as a measure of intelligence in the junior school, it is an extremely good test for students to practise on, with both infants and juniors. Each child in the group requires lead pencil and standard size of paper, and nothing else at all on the desk. The atmosphere has to be relaxed and happy. As only the one instruction has to be given, any questions are pleasantly suppressed with a rather vague 'Just do the best you can'. Something has to be available for earlier finishers to get on with while slower ones complete their task of drawing a man. When all papers are taken in, the scoring requires practice. Since first times of group testing are in any case not very reliable, because easy atmosphere also requires practice, that this test is not a very reliable one is not so important. What is important is that students need training in testing. Therefore this article by Kellmer Pringle and Pickup is worth reading, together with Goodenough's *Measurement of Intelligence by Drawing* (1926). Above all, the student gains the experience of children enjoying a test as they enjoy the mazes and other puzzles in their comics.

There are not many books about testing the youngest children. R. Griffiths in *The Ability of Babies* (1954) is concerned with the first two years and consists of items of behaviour rather than standardised tests. A great deal of work went into this book and, although numbers were small for each month, it is a valuable book. Goodenough's *Measurement of Intelligence by Drawings* (1926) is also based on considerable research. As we have seen, measurement by drawings has limitations, particularly with older children; but it can be used from about 3 to 6 years with results that are interesting, if not reliable in producing a trustworthy mental age. The mental age produced is definitely not sufficiently reliable to warrant calculation of IQ. Piaget's *The Psychology of Intelligence* (1950) covers a wide age range.

Burt's *Mental and Scholastic Tests* (1921; 4th edn. 1964) is of much more than historic interest. It deals with the Binet–Simon Scale and the theoretical validity of tests. The tests themselves cover a very wide range of scholastic attainment (reading, spelling, arithmetic, writing, drawing, handwork and composition). P. E. Vernon's *The Measurement of Abilities* (1940) gives an introduction to statistical work in psychology; and his *Intelligence and Attainment Tests* (1960) is a lucid survey of recent trends. The National Foundation for Educational Research has brought out a small but extremely valuable catalogue of tests of all kinds. The booklet is to be reissued annually from 1970 onwards.

With regard to scholastic attainment, the two books by Schonell and his wife, *Diagnostic and Attainment Testing* (1950), and *Diagnostic and Remedial Teaching in Arithmetic* (1957) are valuable. The three books by Gardner which record scientific work are also relevant: *Testing Results in the Infant School* (1942), *Long Term Results in Infant School Methods* (1950), and *Experiment and Tradition in Primary Schools* (1966). We have seen that the best kind of testing for very young children may be the Piaget-type experiment, which is in itself a learning situation. Investigators have to train themselves to be fully conscious as to when they are being educators and when they are being scientific investigators. A first step here might be to study *The Rôle of the Teacher in the Infant and Nursery School* by Gardner and Cass (1965). This is a remarkable analysis of when teachers are educating, why and how. There are verbatim examples of teachers giving information, questioning to help a child towards the correct solution, demonstrating how something should be done, rejecting answers, correcting a child, all essential in sound teaching. But such assistance may not be given in objective testing. Before one can put aside the rôle of the teacher, that rôle has to be well understood.

20. Gifted children

Interest in scientific study of gifted people was first aroused by Galton's *Hereditary Genius* (1869). This is a study of the pedigree of nearly 1,000 eminent men, half of whom had one or more eminent relatives, which is 200 times as great as could be expected by chance for a parent chosen at random. Since that time there have been a number of studies in Britain and America. For example, Havelock Ellis's *A Study of British Genius* (1904); and in America, Cox, as part of a big Stanford investigation, produced *The Early Mental Traits of Three Hundred Geniuses* (1926). More recently, Goertzel and Goertzel have contributed *Cradles of Eminence* (1965) and Illingworth and Illingworth *Lessons from Childhood* (1966), both with reference to the early years of eminent people as reported in biographies.

Biographies are usually unduly biased in favour of the central figure and so are classed as unscientific. But they can be used with due care. In the 1920s Terman with his colleagues asked competent judges to assess the intelligence quotients of many famous people, from details in biographies and letters, and from their childhood accomplishments. The kind of information from which they have drawn their conclusion that Galton was a genius is that he knew his letters when he was twelve months old and when four wrote, 'I am four years old, and I can read any English book. I can say all the Latin substantives and adjectives and active verbs besides 52 lines of Latin poetry. I can cast up any sum in addition and can multiply by 2, 3, 4, 5, 6, 7, 8 and 10. I can also say the pence table, I read French a little and I know the clock.' From such evidence at four years, one is not surprised to hear that Terman's colleague Cox (1926) estimated that Galton would have had an intelligence quotient of about 200. In *Cradles of Eminence* biographies are used in another way. This is an account of over 400 eminent people of the twentieth century selected from more than 5,000 biographies, and with such a large number certain trends are discernible. Three in five of the 400 suffered at school in varying degrees, penalties ranging from utter boredom to serious persecution by teachers and/or children. Of the 240 children who suffered at school, four in five—192 children—were exceptionally gifted. Later, as eminent men and women, they criticised the curriculum, the merciless bullying and their school failures. Eleanor Roosevelt was considered delinquent, Albert Einstein mentally ill, and Thomas Edison retarded. Other 'dull' pupils included Trotsky, G. K. Chesterton, Proust, Cézanne, Rachmaninoff and Churchill. To give an example of the kind of attack to which these children were subjected, they quote Pierre van Paassen who felt his mind was scarred for life by the fury of his headmaster when he had dared to write such rubbish in an essay as: 'Snowflakes fluttering from a pitiless grey heavenly roof.' The authors found sufficient evidence, in these 400 cases, of common experience to devote sections to the subjects of opinionated parents, failure-prone fathers, 'smothering' mothers, and so on. In fact, a single chapter on homes which respected learning and achievement is followed by nine chapters on various kinds of maladjusted homes.

From a well-reasoned argument, the Goertzels conclude that, in the assessment of gifted people, creativity as well as intelligence has to be taken into account. They point out that teachers inducting children into the society of school, tend to lay too much stress on conformity, a point that we should bear in mind in the Terman study. In *The Gifted Child Grows Up* (1947), Terman and Oden describe (p. 5) the initial selection. Since teachers have to recommend the 'promising' pupils, they may well overlook children like Einstein, Chesterton or Churchill, whose teachers regarded them as mal-adjusted or retarded. As we follow the careers of the first 1,000 of Terman's gifted children, we must recognise that at least to begin with, nonconformists will have been screened off, however unintentionally. Indeed the Goertzels suggest that, between them, our schools and universities are selecting far too many conformist high-grade clerks for university education. During the 'sixties there have been a number of articles on creativity and 'divergent' or independent attitudes in the *British Journal of Educational Psychology* (five on creativity in the last two years). So far, no very clear picture has emerged, but at least the matter is now receiving due attention.

However, the study of creativity involves personality, an area of study which we have already seen is still far from clear. But the matter of creativity is discussed (among other things) in the 1962 edition of *The Year Book of Education: The Gifted Child*, one of the best issues of this series so far. Here the assessment of ability by intelligence tests, especially the popular type of group tests, when taken as they now stand, is critically discussed. Tests in current use are considered by Burt and others to furnish decidedly inadequate measures of gifted children, because (to use Burt's phraseology) 'they lay too much stress on *reproductive* and *analytical* thinking and too little stress on *synthetic* and productive or *creative* thinking'. The Robbins Report, *Higher Education* (1963), states that 'education ministers intimately to ultimate ends, in developing man's capacity to understand, to contemplate and to create'. Getzels and Jackson in *Creativity and Intelligence* (1962) survey studies of creativity and describe their own explorations with gifted students. In a critical note on this book Burt (1962d) says that, because of the limited range of the enquiry, this must be regarded as no more than the exploration which the authors claim it to be and he hopes that in the near future, the enquiry will be enlarged and extended, and also that other similar enquiries will be undertaken. Burt reminds us of the empirical approach to the subject of creativity by British psychologists, such as Hargreaves (1927), Spearman (1930), and even earlier, Burt and Moore (1911). Thus we can see that, difficult though it still is to assess, creativity as a factor in selection of the gifted is now becoming recognised.

Sultan (1962), for a London MA thesis, made a factorial study in the domain of creative thinking with ninety boys and eighty girls of 13 to 14 years attending grammar school. He was unable to support American work in some ways. But an Originality factor could be distinguished, showing itself more in creative leisure-time interests, Rorschach responses and artwork than in written tests or subjectively marked essays. No evidence is yet available as to how predictive this is of future creative achievement.

Lovell and Shields (1967) have made a study of fifty gifted children of 8 to 10 years who obtained a Verbal Score of 140+ on the Wechsler Intelligence Scale for Children. They examined four aspects of development in this group: personality, mathematical attainment, logical thought, and the relation between scores obtained when testing creativity and when testing logical thinking on the WISC scales. The findings suggest that their teachers rated their personalities very much as American teachers had rated Terman's comparable sample. This is an important point, because we are now adapting much American research to use in Britain. Although performance on tests of mathematical attainment was high, these gifted children had the greatest difficulty with certain kinds of series and numerical analogies. Only 10 per cent of the responses were at the level of formal thought in tasks of logical thinking; and tests of creativity do not measure intellectual functions entirely independent of those measured by the WISC scales and tests of logical thought. It is most valuable to be given this insight into regions where gifted children, while achieving a high level of mathematical attainment, may have problems in their thinking, and also to be shown that the selected tests of creativity did not prove entirely independent of the intelligence test used. Reports on similar investigations will be awaited with interest.

The importance now being given to creativity does not in any way minimise the importance of intelligence tests. We must therefore make clear exactly what levels of intelligence quotient should be the dividing line above which children should be classed as gifted, remembering always that even the most experienced testers allow a swing of about five points either way. That is to say a child competently assessed as having an IQ of 130 will be somewhere between 125 and 135. Wherever the dividing line is made, above it there are children who are moderately gifted, some rather more gifted, and some who are highly gifted. When the gradations of intelligence quotients above average were first studied there was a tendency to consider as 'gifted' only the exceptionally gifted. The performance of such children can be studied in *Children above 180 IQ* by Hollingworth (1942). This is a book which all students should read; it makes very clear what problems a teacher meets when he has such a remarkable child in the class. The parents of one child with almost as high a level of intelligence told the author that, at his first school, the headmaster said he could attend provided he did not speak; and he attended for three years without speaking in school because the parents did not know where else to send him.

In the 1920s, Terman decided that children with IQ 180+ were too rare, and he made the line of demarcation IQ 140+. But fresh data in America has caused American psychologists to lower it to 130+. They find that this is the level at which special provision of some kind should be made by schools for these children. When Burt began research into intelligence testing in 1911, he took a special interest for administrative purposes in the top 3 per cent of children so that his gifted group includes all over IQ 130. Thus British and American research have converged. As the 1962 *Year Book* referred to above is the best information to date, let us examine what is here considered to be the distribution of children with above average intelligence. From Table 15 we can see that about 2·25 per cent of children have IQs above

TABLE 15: *Distribution of gifted intelligence*

IQ above 130	2·25%	1 in 44
140	0·55%	1 in 180
150	0·14%	1 in 700
160	0·034%	1 in 2,900

Source: *Year Book of Education*, 1962.

130 and may be classed as of 'gifted' intelligence. When discussing intelligence (see pp. 227–8) we found a difference between the normal distribution and the actual number of children with very high or very low intelligence. Even from the normal distribution we would expect a small percentage of children to be found at either end of the intelligence scale. But for the educationist these rare cases are real children, such as the boy described in the previous paragraph; and what is more—the evidence of actual surveys shows that there are more of them than the simple statistical formula would lead us to expect. We can see this trend in Table 15; and according to Burt there are more than twelve times as many children with IQ 160+ than is to be expected from the assumption of a normal distribution. Thus children with the intellectual power approaching the phenomenal children described by Hollingworth in *Children above 180 IQ* (1942) are by no means as rare as we once thought.

Even when we have overcome the problem of identifying gifted children, the range of intelligence within the group is so great that it presents a problem within our problem. The 1962 *Year Book* states that the difference between a child with IQ 160+ and a grammar school child is greater than the difference between a grammar school child and an educationally subnormal child with IQ below 70. The 1944 Education Act states that education has to suit ability. We have to find ways to suit the wide range of ability within the 2·25 per cent of gifted children.

The first step is to identify the children with IQ over 130, and it would help if we had some idea as to where we are likely to find them.* Some psychologists have argued that Galton's 1,000 eminent men came from very cultured homes, and their high intelligence developed because of their stimulating environments. Burt (1961b), in the course of his observations on gifted children, found that many did not come from cultured homes. He therefore made a study comparable to Galton's, but of brilliant sons born in the humblest circumstances. Amongst them were: Carl Gauss, often acclaimed as the greatest of all mathematicians, the son of a German bricklayer; Laplace, almost as illustrious, the son of a Normandy farm labourer; Marlowe, Winckelmann and James Mill, the sons of cobblers; James Watt, Lincoln and Carlyle, the sons of carpenters; and equally distinguished sons of blacksmiths, tinkers and so on. The hypothesis that exceptionally favourable environments stimulated the intelligence quotients of Macaulay and Galton to 180 (according to Cox's 1926 estimate) falls down when we find equally high intelligence, despite unfavourable environments, in Kant, son of a strap-maker, Franklin, son of a soap-boiler, and Kepler, son of an innkeeper.

* See footnote p. 274.

This article by Burt gives very interesting case histories of some of these geniuses from poor environments.

Pursuing the same line of argument, Burt studied children brought up almost from birth in orphanages and residential institutions, and found a number of able boys and girls. In spite of the relatively uniform environments the variability of the children as a whole was actually greater than that of the general population. The average IQ was only 91, which is low in the average IQ 90–110 class; and there were a number of dull and defective children. But one in eighty had sufficient ability to merit a junior county scholarship although, because of their comparatively poor attainments in English and arithmetic, many who deserved a scholarship failed to pass the customary examination. Of eight children with IQ over 130, five were known to be illegitimate offspring of fathers of a comparatively high intellectual and social status; two others had fathers in professional classes who had died and left mothers in a state of extreme poverty. The high intelligence of these children obviously could not be explained by an exceptionally favourable environment.

Some psychologists argued that other variables might explain these results. So Burt took a group of 852 children of all levels of intelligence, but all from the same social and economic status, where the occupations of all the fathers of these children were classed as 'semiskilled'. Table 16 shows the wide range of intelligence of these children from similar cultural backgrounds. The majority of teachers hold the view that, since gifted children are commonly assumed to be the offspring of gifted parents, one looks to the professional classes or equivalent ranks in commerce and industry to find them. We can

TABLE 16: *Distribution of intelligence among children of similar home conditions*

IQ	Number	Percentage
Above 130	1	0·1
120–130	10	1·2
110–120	76	8·9
100–110	279	32·8
90–100	297	34·9
80–90	101	11·8
70–80	73	8·6
60–70	13	1·5
50–60	2	0·2
Total	852	100·0

Source: Burt (1961b).

see by the wide range of intelligence in the 'semiskilled' homes that some gifted children may be found here too. In a group of 1,000 children from homes where the father's occupation is semiskilled, we shall expect to find one gifted child.

But there is another reason why we should not assume that most of the gifted children are to be found in 'professional' homes. This is because relatively few homes are 'professional'. Burt (1961b) took a group of 2,172 children with above average intelligence, that is with IQ over 110, and found

TABLE 17: *Numbers of gifted children in different occupational classes*

Class	Occupation	Number tested No. (1)	% (2)	IQ over 110 No. (3)	% of group (4)	% of total (5)	IQ over 120 No. (6)	% of group (7)	% of total (8)	IQ over 130 No. (9)	% of group (10)	% of total (11)
I	Higher professional	74	3·4	52	70·3	9·6	25	33·8	11·5	15	20·3	27·8
II	Lower professional	330	15·2	136	41·2	25·1	69	20·9	31·8	23	7·3	42·6
III	Skilled	1127	51·9	260	23·1	47·9	96	8·5	44·2	13	1·1	24·1
IV	Partly skilled	356	16·4	69	19·4	12·6	22	6·2	10·2	2	0·6	3·7
V	Unskilled	285	13·1	26	9·1	4·8	5	1·8	2·3	1	0·4	1·9
	TOTAL	2172	100·0	543		100·0	217		100·0	54		100·0

Source: Burt (1961b).

what class of home they came from according to fathers' occupation (see p. 229).

From Table 17 we can see that kind of homes from which children in this group of 2,172 with above average intelligence came, at three levels of intelligence, above 110, above 120 and above 130 IQ. If we look down each row we find:

(1) is the number of children from each class of home. The figures show that most come from 'skilled' homes (1,127) and least from 'higher professional' homes (74).

(2) puts the same information as percentages of the whole group of 2,172 children. Thus we find the same order of classes, but can see at once that more than half (51·9 per cent) are from 'skilled' homes and only 3·4 per cent from 'higher professional' homes. Moreover, there are almost as many from 'unskilled' as from 'lower professional' homes.

(3) gives the number with IQ over 110.

(4) gives the same as (3) but by percentages.

(5) gives the percentage of the total 2,172. The rank order of classes is III, II, IV, I, V.

(6) gives the number with IQ over 120.

(7) gives the same as (6) but by percentages.

(8) gives the percentage of the total 2,172. The rank order of classes is now III, II, I, IV, V.

(9) gives the number with IQ over 130.

(10) gives the same as (9) but by percentages.

(11) gives the percentage of the total 2,172. The rank order of classes changes again, this time to II, I, III, IV, V.

Let us look at how the rank order of class of home from which these children come changes, according to the level of intelligence being considered. Table 18 gives this with the percentage of the whole group of 2,172 children in

TABLE 18: *Rank order of class of home**

IQ	Most children				Least children
over 110	III(47·9)	II(25·1)	IV(12·6)	I(9·6)	V(4·8)
over 120	III(44·2)	II(31·8)	I(11·5)	IV(10·2)	V(2·3)
over 130	II(42·6)	I(27·8)	III(24·1)	IV(3·7)	V(1·9)

* A loop has been put round the ranking of class I, children from homes where the fathers' occupations are highest professional and administrative. A sliding scale is necessary, to show that the rank order for class I changes, according to the level of intelligence being considered. If we are talking about all children with IQ over 110, then class I comes 4th; IQ over 120, then class I comes 3rd; IQ over 130, then class I rises to 2nd place. All the other classes are also liable to change their rank according to the level of IQ being considered.

brackets. If we are considering those with IQ over 110, or even over 120, then most come from class III. But if we are only considering those with IQ over 130, then the number from class I comes second only to class II; and class III has sunk to third place, but with still a substantial number of children. Class V, where the father has an unskilled job, remains bottom but may have a gifted child or two in every hundred such homes.

Some people apparently assumed that 'the lower classes' had very much larger families than 'the upper classes' and this was why there were so many more children in classes IV and V. But a look at column (1) of Table 17 shows that most children are not from classes IV and V; they are from class III. The crux of the matter is that in class III there are *more fathers* doing skilled work, so more homes, and therefore more children in this class. Where there are more children, the chance of finding gifted children increases. Conversely there are *very few fathers* doing higher professional work and therefore fewer homes from which to expect children who have inherited highest intelligence. Size of family does play a small part. Family planning has reduced the size of family in all levels of occupation, but so far it has had least effect (through least efficiency) in class V.

Thus, when we consider where we can expect to find gifted children there are three factors to be borne in mind: (1) the wide range of individual differences in intelligence within each class, causing considerable overlap; (2) the distribution through occupational classes of numbers, with peak figures in class III; and (3) the inheritance of intelligence, which causes highly intelligent professional parents to tend to have intelligent children. We have to seek gifted children in all occupational classes, but the figures in the research under review show that although the proportions are smaller, nevertheless the greatest number of gifted children come from the lower professional people, with rather more than half as many from higher professional people and almost, as many from skilled workers.

From the time Burt started surveys of intelligence for the London County Council in 1913, he followed up many of the children tested. He concluded from case histories of children above average intelligence, that at least a third of the children in the higher intellectual categories failed to obtain the type of education which their abilities deserved. Not all these failures can be ascribed to faulty selection. Motivation is as important as intelligence. Development after 11 years is as important as development before 11 years; and development is far harder to predict at a later age than at the earlier age. The history of intelligence testing shows that its aim has been to eliminate environmental influences and to judge reasoning powers, whatever the social class may be.

One of the earliest discoveries through intelligence testing was how grossly the ability of the more gifted children was underestimated. Burt found that 54 per cent of gifted children had attainment quotients below 120. The older children were deprived of more than half the educational equivalent of their natural advancement. The range of ability is so great within the gifted group that schools have failed to provide sufficiently varied environment for differing needs. Perhaps the most misleading fact has been that a child might come top of the class and still be educationally retarded, if the work of the class is far below his capabilities.

Within a decade of the commencement of Burt's work in Britain, Terman initiated and supervised an extensive programme of investigation of gifted children in America. Decade by decade the reports are published. The first was *The Mental and Physical Traits of a Thousand Gifted Children* by Terman *et al.* (1925). The 1,000 Californian children had IQs over 140 and were selected initially by the teachers of third and eighth grade, by filling in a form which asked for names of the three brightest and the youngest, and also the brightest child of the teacher's previous year. This was a fairly crude start and it may, as we saw, have missed some creative non-conformists. But all the children recommended by the teachers were subjected to intensive enquiries about interests, personality, homes, etc., as well as given individual intelligence tests. From this wealth of information, the thousand were selected. There is a good resumé of the research plan in the opening chapters of *The Gifted Child Grows Up*, by Terman and Oden (1947). The profiles of these children were very different from the popular notion of a genius as a weedy and sickly bluestocking or intemperate Bohemian. On the whole this gifted group was taller, healthier, better controlled and more stable than other groups of the population. Concurrently with the investigation, the Stanford–Binet test was restandardised for America, and published in 1937. Another revision was made in 1960. Eventually nearly 3,000 American children were given the two parallel forms of the 1937 test form L and form M.

The follow-ups of the original 1,000 Californian gifted children with IQ over 140, has shown that the great majority have fulfilled their promise. Table 19 gives their initial scores. A quarter of a century after these children were selected, by the time they were about 35 years old, they had published some ninety books or monographs and approximately 1,500 articles which appeared in scientific, scholarly or literary magazines. The publications cover a wide range. The books include eight college textbooks (four of them translated into foreign languages), fourteen volumes of fiction, three of poems, two medical treatises, two books of popular science, five on the social sciences, and several story books for children. Looking back over three decades, Terman and Oden (1947) had many regrets for omissions; for instance, that they had not made initial tests of mechanical, musical and artistic ability as well as intelligence; that they had not tested the intelligence of all parents and siblings; or noted the marital selection, fertility and mortality among parents and grandparents of their gifted thousand. Burt (1963) compared the results of Terman's investigation with his own and concludes that they are fairly consistent. The sampling was not directly comparable, since in the American study there were too few from the lowest occupational groups.

IQ	Boys	Girls	Boys and Girls
200	—	1	1
195–199	—	—	—
190–194	4	2	6
185–189	1	2	3
180–184	13	3	16
175–179	8	11	19
170–174	19	13	32
165–169	22	18	40
160–164	43	27	70
155–159	57	52	109
150–154	119	76	195
145–149	114	125	239
140–144	143	132	275
135–139	34	31	65
N	577	493	1,070
Mean	151·5	150·4	151·0
SD	10·8	10·4	10·6

Source: Terman and Oden (1947).

From his studies of gifted children in London schools, Burt concludes that we need to give more adequate recognition to the needs and numbers of the 'exceptionally gifted' with IQs over 160. Though their actual numbers are not large, they are twelve times more frequent than was thought. They form a group who constitute one of the nation's most valuable assets, and whose special educational requirements have hitherto been grossly neglected. Terman found between 300 and 600 per million in the general population. This is much higher than expected, and may be due to the fact that the intelligence average for California is higher than elsewhere in the States. In a later New York research, Hollingworth found at least a dozen with IQ above 180, that is, about 20 per million. Still later, the Counselling Center of New York University followed up over a hundred children tested when 5, who had IQs of 170 and more. In Britain, Burt finds that actual numbers vary widely from area to area. Near Oxford, in an enquiry with approximately 1,600 children in all, he found six children with test-scores equivalent to an IQ of 175 or above, nearly 0·4 per cent. But they were nearly all in one preparatory school, catering for children of dons. In Liverpool, with nearly eight times as many children of the same age, he did not find one child with such a high level of intelligence. However, outside the elementary school system he found a number of them, with proportional frequency just under 30 per million. In Figure 28 (p. 227) these are the children on the extreme right beyond the dotted theoretical line; from Table 15 (p. 258) they represent 0·034 per cent of the population, 1 in 2,900 children. They must be our most neglected children of all.

From a number of sources, information comes from adults who were gifted children, that the unhappiest time of all was the junior school years. This is understandable. Unless a junior school is run on lines of individual learning—and few junior schools are yet run this way—an intellectually gifted child is perpetually expected to think in ways he has outgrown. At the Piaget-stage of 7 to 11 years, when most children can reason given the concrete situation, the gifted child can reason formally or even in abstract concepts. But we have erred on the side of expecting too much abstract thought in the grammar school, so the gifted children would find this work somewhat more satisfactory. However, as we have seen from the research carried out by Lovell and Shields (1967) (see p. 257), the advancement may not be uniform for all types of mental process.

Nisbet and Gammie (1961), in 'Over 135 IQ', describe an interesting research technique now being evolved for follow-up study of gifted children at Aberdeen. They took 135 instead of 130 as the line of demarcation for gifted, as the average for Aberdeen, a university town, is four or five points above the national average. During 1950–3 these tests revealed 159 children out of the yearly group of 2,700 tested. The purpose was to find out what had happened to those who had not gone to the university; and the authors selected one of the four years for follow-up study. In 1953 there were thirty-six children who scored IQ 135 or above. Of these, twenty were at the university, so it was the remaining sixteen children whom they followed-up. Two were still at school, one having had a serious illness, and neither seemed likely to reach the university. Two others left school before sitting for the Scottish Leaving Certificate. Eight sat for this examination but failed to get university entrance; two of these were working in insurance, two in journalism, and the other four were continuing further education in colleges of technology, art, commerce and education. Four others gained university entrance but chose not to go there; one of these held a Commission in the Services; one was in the Executive Branch of the Civil Service; one was an apprentice chartered accountant; and one was a nurse.

The authors make the extremely pertinent comment that although nearly half did not go to the university, it would be wrong to classify this group as

266

'wastage'. They may yet distinguish themselves. A university education is not necessarily the best choice for all persons in this range of ability. It would have been interesting to know whether the educational attainment as compared with intelligence quotient fell lower in the non-university group than in the university group. However, another interesting line of enquiry was pursued. The occupations of the fathers in both groups was examined; and Table 20 shows this with the Registrar General's class III divided by a manual/nonmanual dichotomy. Here we can see that the proportion of high ability

TABLE 20: *1953 Group: Fathers' occupation*

	Fathers' occupation			
	Non-manual	*Manual*	*Not known*	*Total*
At university	15	3	2	20
Not at university	4	10	2	16

Source: Nisbet and Gammie (1961).

not going to the university is much greater for homes where the father's occupation is manual. This is all the more striking because of the fine Scottish tradition of value placed on education. Nisbet and Gammie explain that the purpose of this report is to show how easily a survey of gifted pupils can be made from readily available records. Although children gaining university entrance at Aberdeen schools would mostly choose Aberdeen University, most of the follow-up was done by post or telephone, so that the nearness of schools and universities was not of great importance.

A further research note by Macdonald, Gammie and Nisbet (1964) reports on the careers of a gifted group. Adding a further year, thus covering 1950–4, they now have 192 gifted children of whom 125 are boys and 67 girls. This proportion of boys to girls, they say, is supported by other research. The subsequent careers of 180, 94 per cent, were traced. Table 21 shows the university and non-university groups according to the fathers' occupation. Of the 180 whose careers were traced, 73 per cent of the men, but only 53 per cent of the women, went to the university; 80 per cent from homes where the father's occupation was non-manual, but only 52 per cent from the manual homes went to the university. When figures for sex and fathers' occupation are combined, 90 per cent (46 out of 51) of men from non-manual homes entered university, but only 41 per cent (14 out of 34) of women did so. The authors traced the careers of the 29 men and 34 women who did not go to the university. The careers chosen again suggest that it would be wrong to class this group as 'wastage'. Butcher and Pont (1968) report on a group of over

TABLE 21 : *Numbers at university: IQ 130+ group*

| | Fathers' occupation | | | | |
	Non-manual Classes I–III		Manual Classes III–V		Not known	Totals
At university: Men	46	90%	33	59%	1	80
Women	22	65%	14	41%	1	37
Total	68	80%	47	52%	2	117
Not at university: Men	5		23		1	29
Women	12		20		2	34
Total	17		43		3	63
Not traced					12	12
	85		90		17	192

Source: Macdonald *et al.* (1964).

1,000 Scottish school children of high ability. Both boys and girls rated as most interesting careers which they did not consider to be best paid, boys preferring engineering and girls teaching (arts).

Armstrong (1967) of West Riding reports an investigation of wastage of ability amongst the intellectually gifted. It is a follow-up study of 849 children with IQs 135+, out of 48,546 children admitted to grammar schools in 1956 and 1957. He found that more than twice as many who entered full-time higher education came from professional as came from working class homes. Yet performance at Ordinary and Advance levels of the General Certificate of Education showed significant differences between the two groups. This supports the findings on the influence of home background reported by many investigators, such as Burt (1961b) and Nisbet *et al.* (1961). But Nisbet and his colleagues would query the use of the term 'wastage', though many more years of follow-up will be necessary before definite information is available as to whether the non-university group distinguished themselves in later life. We may also hear later whether the non-university groups give signs of greater non-conformity, and whether they take up more creative work than the university group.

Following the work of the New York Counselling Center, Shouksmith of New Zealand and Taylor of Tonga (1964) wrote an article on 'The effect of counselling on the achievement of high ability pupils'. They are concerned about the underachievement of children of high ability (a problem of which we in this country are also becoming increasingly aware) and investigated the effects of counselling upon such children's educational attainment. Most of the literature about such gifted underachievers refers to various kinds of maladjustment, which might be eased by friendly discussion of worries, interests, aims and ideals. The counselling technique was made as simple as possible, so that if it proved successful it could readily be used by general teachers without special training. Three groups of twelve were chosen from 331 first-year children (12 and 13 years) in a New Zealand intermediate school. Groups were formed by trios matched for IQ, sex, age and attainment scores, one of the trio going to each group. All were of high ability with attainment below what should be expected. Those with IQ above 116 were identified, and from them the under-achievers selected. Group I was the Counselling Group and had extra tests. Each child was interviewed for twenty to forty minutes at approximately fortnightly intervals for six months, sometimes individually, sometimes in small groups. Group II, the 'Placebo' Group, were given the extra tests but no counselling; and Group III, the Control Group, was known only to the experimenters. Table 22 gives the procedure.

Counselling was non-directive, except occasionally when an impasse appeared to be reached. The results showed that non-directive counselling had a significant effect on the level of educational attainment. In four of the six attainment tests, final means for the Counselling Group differed significantly from the other groups. Improvement was not sufficient to bring all to their proper level of attainment according to their level of intelligence. But this first experiment was only for a short period, and many had long-standing low attainment. The seven parents who were most cooperative had children who improved most; and the three parents who cooperated least had children who profited least. The extra tests given to the 'Placebo' group caused a slight, but not statistically significant improvement. So the extra attention of extra tests was not sufficient, without the counselling, to make a significant difference. The authors conclude that a programme of simple counselling should be included in a school programme for pupils whose attainment is below what is to be expected of their intelligence level; and this is particularly true for those of high ability. Time spent this way should be rewarding to both child and teacher. Although this research includes children of only IQ 116+, and makes no specific reference to the gifted ones with IQ 130+, it suggests a line of research in non-directive counselling of gifted children which might prove most rewarding. Later (p. 278) we shall find that the 1944 Education Act lays a duty on Local Education Authorities to ascertain which children are educationally subnormal and provide for them.

	Group 1 Counselling Group	Group 2 'Placebo' Group	Group 3 Control Group	All other Form 1 pupils
Initial screening:				
Pre-experimental period	OTIS A,B	OTIS A,B	OTIS A,B	OTIS A,B
Pre-experimental period	ACER Achievement Battery	ACER Achievement Battery	ACER Achievement Battery	ACER Achievement Battery
Months 1 and 2	Sociogram Parents Interviewed	Sociogram	Sociogram	Sociogram
	WISC California Personality Test Sentence Completion Health Survey	WISC California Personality Test Sentence Completion Health Survey		
Months 2–6	Counselling			
Month 6	Sociogram Parents Interviewed	Sociogram		
Final appraisal beginning month 7	ACER Battery	ACER Battery	ACER Battery	ACER Battery

OTIS tests are devised in the United States by A. S. Otis.
ACER tests are Australian.

The same should be done for the supernormal, and counselling should be included in the provision for them.

The value of counselling for all children, urged long ago by Sully and others, is at last gaining attention and there is a valuable symposium in *Educational Research* 1967, no. 2, where Dawes, Raynor and Atcherly, Fuller and Juniper discuss the nature of school counselling. The Americans do more school counselling than the British at present, and Yates (1959) has written of their work. Preparation for counselling is excellent discipline for the teacher, and comes more naturally to the progressive educationist, whose work is far less noticeably directive than that of the formal teacher. The change from being an information-giver to being a sounding-board against which a child can, so to speak, hear his own thinking, is a dramatic one. It is a change not unlike the difference between being a teacher and giving an intelligence test. In both cases one has to step aside from being personally involved without losing sensitivity. Since good teachers are well aware of how deeply involved they become in the children's development, often to the extent of being overinvolved, training for counselling can give an extra quality to teaching, where objectivity as well as involvement is needed.

In a BBC broadcast given in 1945, Burt suggested that society should have a panel of highly intelligent people which could study problems. Before the end of that year an association was formed of people with intelligence above that of 98 per cent of the population. As it was a 'round table' discussion group it was called *Mensa*, from the Latin for a table. There is a Young Mensa for the 16 to 20 age group but nothing is arranged for children below 16 years. Consequently the National Association for Gifted Children was formed, to enable parents to seek advice, share problems and let their children meet intellectual equals. Mensa is essentially an association for adults and is international. The classes of problem with which they are concerned include: the part to be played by the highly intelligent person, the technological and sociological advances which create a demand for able people, and the nurturing of exceptionally able people. Members cooperate in research at a number of our universities. The National Association for Gifted Children is particularly concerned with the nurturing of exceptionally able children before they reach an age to qualify for Mensa activities. Groups have formed throughout the country. Parents express great relief at sharing problems and children who have been extremely unhappy at school benefit so much from days of creative activity together that they return to school better able to cooperate with their classmates. Colleges of Education are becoming interested to work with the children of exceptional intelligence brought together by the NAGC.

Before we consider books *about* gifted children, there is a type of book which teachers can recommend *to* gifted children. These books are based on *programmed learning* and are constructed from detailed research, with many small steps ('Frames') the great majority of which the reader understands immediately. Holland and Skinner constructed one, *The Analysis of Behaviour: a programme of self-instruction* (1961), which consists of 1,954 frames. Skinner said that, by the time students had worked through this they were just about ready to attend his psychology lectures. The frames can be put into a teaching machine or simply arranged as a book; but with the book the reader has to write the answers as instructed, because the time spent writing is required for learning a particular step. Teachers can hire such books when a gifted child shows special interests, for instance in advanced mathematics unsuited to most primary school work.

When students are training to teach they should study programmed learning. It does not replace the teacher. But it helps the teacher in two ways: (*a*) a child who has been away or needs extra practice can be given necessary individual help by allowing him to instruct himself with one of these sets of frames, in a machine or a book; (*b*) a child who needs extra opportunities for learning, for instance about the differential calculus, conditioned reflexes, or the basic principles of harmony, can also instruct himself, provided these specialised programmes are available. The students should also try to construct a programme and then test it on a number of people to whom the subject matter is new, to see which steps are too long and require breaking down into intermediate steps. An attempt to make a learning programme has a most salutory effect upon lesson notes, raising the standard of organisation.

Many articles have been written about programmed learning. In *Educational Research* (vol. 3, 1963) there is a series on 'Aspects of programmed instruction' by J. D. Williams, Curr, Peel and Leith; and there is a later article by Leedham (1965). In the *British Journal of Educational Psychology* there are two, by Poppleton and Austwick (1964), and Hartley (1965). An excellent advanced book is *Programmed Learning in Perspective. A Guide to Programmed Writing* by Thomas, Davies, Oppenshaw and Bird (1963).

Although the tests of intelligence constructed so far give indication of which children have IQ above 130 and various levels above this, many psychologists think that tests constructed for the population as a whole are not well suited to levels of intelligence at either extreme, the very subnormal or the exceptionally gifted. Tests for the very subnormal are examined in the next chapter. There has not yet been enough research on the mental processes of the highly gifted for satisfactory tests to be standardised for them. However, research has begun. Heim's (1947) AH4 and AH5 are tests for higher levels of intelligence. In 1953 Valentine produced *Reasoning Test for Higher Levels of Intelligence*. Others are in process of construction. The quality of intelligence tests for children with IQ above 130, and particularly for those in the highest levels, is bound to improve as we learn more of the ways in which young but able minds organise knowledge and adapt it to fresh information.

There are a number of valuable recent books about gifted children, in addition to those already referred to. But more specific reference should be made to one already referred to several times. This is the *The Year Book of Education: The Gifted Child* (1962); it is the sixty-fourth issue in this series. This is a joint publication by the Teachers College of Columbia University, New York, and the Institute of Education, University of London. Great trouble has been taken to base findings on research in many countries, and this effort to bring in line researches in many parts of the world is in itself of considerable value. There is a general introduction (66 pp.) by Burt which is one of the few contributions to rely chiefly on ascertained statistical data and detailed statistical analysis. Torrence, one of the others to cite statistical evidence, gives a useful survey of recent American work on creativity together with a four-page bibliography. A review by Moulton (1963) in the *British Journal of Statistical Psychology* can be very helpful to finding one's way in this substantial volume.

Cruikshank's *Psychology of Exceptional Youth* (1956) is about children with various handicaps, and has been criticised for including a very good chapter on gifted children. However, he makes a special point of including exceptional intelligence as a handicap, and in view of the research findings we have been examining, one must admit that, until we can develop gifted potential more efficiently, his contention is justified. Gottschalt of Germany contributes an interesting section on the subnormal and very gifted to the World Federation for Mental Health, ninth report, *Mental Health in Home and School* (1958). Hunter's article 'An exceptional talent for calculative thinking' (1962) reports the lightning calculations of Aitkin, born in New Zealand in 1895, who became a Professor of Mathematics at Edinburgh. This article shows how a special calculating ability, supported by high general ability, was fostered by long and intensive practice.

From the United States there are many important publications. A good introductory book is Hildreth's *Introduction to the Gifted* (1966). Torrance's *Talent and Education* (1961), No. 4 in The Modern School Practices Series, is sound and important. It is a symposium to which fifteen specialists contribute. Though it concerns the top 5 or 10 per cent of children, and we would term these 'above average' only some of them being 'gifted', it makes valuable suggestions on such matters as enriching the school environment and the formative rôle of experience which can be developed for gifted children. De Haan and Havighurst (1957), in *Educating Gifted Children*, revise and enlarge an earlier publication. This book is valuable for its description of discovering gifted children, and on the loss of talent with socio-economically underprivileged children. Although it is not specifically about gifted children, Torrance's *Education and the Creative Potential* (1963) is highly relevant.

Reviewing this book Nisbet (1964) makes the following thought-provoking comment: 'If we do not find this picture of creative youth entirely attractive, we must ask ourselves whether we in Europe are not too conformist.'

In 1960 the N.F.E.R. produced an article by Wall on highly intelligent children. Then in 1968 they produced a booklet, *The Gifted Child*, by Shields. His aim was to bring together the researches on gifted children and to draw out their significance for any person concerned with the education of children. The following year Bridges (1969) produced *Gifted Children and the Brentwood Experiment*, an account of work with gifted children one afternoon a week by a group of staff from Brentwood College of Education, carried on for a number of years. This is a valuable account of important pioneer educational work with gifted children. It would not have been possible to carry out the project without the sympathetic interest of George Robb, Educational Psychologist to Essex.

Footnote to p. 259
The Royal Commission on Reform of Local Government in England (H.M.S.O. 1970), known as the Redcliffe-Maud Report, if adopted, will greatly aid the detection of gifted children. Anyone informed on prediction of numbers of gifted children at the various levels of intelligence will be able to calculate approximate numbers. Now that parents are having their children independently assessed by psychologists, L.E.A.s will have to take steps to supply the gifted child's right for education suited to the ability and aptitude. Moreover, the public spirited will very likely be asking awkward questions about the expected number from classes IV and V.

21. *Educationally subnormal children*

When the London County Council appointed Burt as their psychologist in 1913, the Education Officer was influenced by Galton and Sully; he knew nothing of techniques in France. At that time teachers nominated children whom they thought mentally defective for certification by doctors on the grounds of educational backwardness. The point of introducing standardised intelligence tests is that if a child does fairly well at intelligence tests, you can be sure that he is *not* defective; if he fails you cannot be sure that he *is* defective without further clinical examination, case history, etc. Few teachers used intelligence tests in nominating children as possible mental defectives; but the use of tests also ensured that different school doctors adopted much the same borderline. Burt was appointed to check the certification of mental defectives. Just over two decades later he published the results of his researches in two deeply humane books, *The Subnormal Mind* (1935) and *The Backward Child* (1937). Burt also brought out a book specifically avoiding the use of technical terms, *The Causes and Treatment of Backwardness* (3rd edition 1954). The London County Council received a series of memoranda on his extensive surveys. Resulting from this work, schools for educationally subnormal children were begun long before people realised that the gifted also required special arrangements, at least for part of the time, if they were to develop their potential.

Segal (1961) makes an excellent summary of the history of work done for ESN children in an article on 'Dull and backward children: post-war theory and practice', which all students should read. He goes from Burt's first surveys, through changes in attitude to these children and the influence of various government reports, to picking up the threads again after the disruptions of the Second World War. One of the most difficult problems has been the unreliability of results, for these children, even from most careful individual testing. Consequently workers in this field take a keen interest in research into how much the IQs obtained with different tests may have been affected by environment, and inflexibility of organisation. Where the best possible is already being done for such a child, the results of testing are more stable. At present it is government policy, where possible, to place children who may be ESN in special classes for a probationary period to find out whether transfer to a special school is advisable; then to transfer back to normal schools children who prove to be within normal school range of intelligence and are able to return after a period of care in a special school. The present problems are to find more reliable methods of diagnosis and to find the most profitable kinds of environment. In Segal's view we need carefully planned education for these children as early as possible. This means earlier diagnosis than is customary, by an educational psychologist; and organisation of special nurseries. Teachers being trained for this work need to pay more attention to motivation in learning, and to maturation, possibly along the lines of Piaget's stages. Also language stimulation, to promote thinking, is of vital importance. There is a good bibliography at the end of this work, touching on important American research into educationally subnormal children.

One of the researches referred to in the above article is by Stott (1960) of Glasgow, reported in 'Observations on retest discrepancy in mentally subnormal children'. Stott examined retests with these children, both to check the reliability of previous tests, and to see whether discrepancies might reflect real changes in the rate of mental development as well as errors of test standardisation. The discrepancies were considerably greater than those obtained from standardisation of the Stanford–Binet Intelligence Scale. The gain through practice effect and losses through lapse of time between tests were much more than could be accounted for by test–retest error. Stott came to the conclusion that these discrepancies might in large part be due to real variations in the rate of mental development. He includes in these changes of rate of development those dependent on changes in motivation. He ends this article by speculating whether normal children of 4 to 5 years undergo a spurt of intellectual development; and whether this jump in development may represent changes in motivation, in mental organisation and conceptualisation resulting from new stages of mental development. Stott (1957) has also written on evidence for pre-natal impairment of temperament in mentally retarded children.

Cashdan (1962) at Cambridge has written an interesting survey on the intellectual powers of subnormal children. This survey begins with the fact that forty years' attention was focused on the limitations of these children; but during the subsequent fifteen years it has turned to their abilities and temperaments; and results have been surprising. She discusses the meaning and causes of subnormality, and the learning and educational measures required. As there are no theoretical grounds for assuming that any child is ineducable, there is no sharp separation of the educationally subnormal from the severely subnormal. Learning problems appear to be differentially graded from those of the mildly retarded to those of the severely subnormal. The most profitable approach at present appears to be the exploration of the learning abilities of normal and subnormal children of the same mental age. Insights are developing fast; and work with subnormal children is now a challenging and rewarding vocation. There is an excellent bibliography at the end of this article.

Some doubt has been expressed as to whether the Stanford–Binet Intelligence Scale standardised by Terman and Merrill is a suitable test for educationally subnormal children. In fact it is the most 'suitable' of those available at present, provided the English revision and standardisation is used, *and* the test is applied by a properly trained person. The problem is not whether such a test is 'suitable' but what are its limits and limitations. The notion that one relies on 'the IQ' (alone and unchecked) derives from popular journalism, though often wrongly attributed to Binet, Burt and Terman. It is only a third rate educational psychologist who wants a mechanical and foolproof test for assessing human beings.

Rushton and Stockwin (1963) used the Stanford–Binet Test with 111 boys in a residential special school and compared test scores on entry at 7 years with test scores before leaving between 14 and 16 years. They found a deterioration in mean score, despite certain statistical adjustments. The proportion of verbal subtests passed was consistently lower at all age levels than the proportion of non-verbal tests passed. On examination of the data they came to the conclusion that the deterioration of mean scores between $9\frac{1}{2}$ and $15\frac{1}{2}$ years was due to the fact that this test gives increasing weight to verbal intelligence. Because of this fact, the test was only of limited use for a group of children whose non-verbal intelligence scores surpassed their verbal intelligence scores. They quote the hypothesis of A. D. B. Clarke et al. (1958) that verbal assets are more seriously impaired in such children, and suggest replacing the Stanford–Binet Scale with a test especially constructed, with an equal balance of verbal/educational and performance/perceptual items. Such a test should give separate verbal and performance IQs, tap equally the established 'group factors' and measure them quantitatively, and distribute evenly throughout all age levels the different types of item. Rushton and Stockwin end by suggesting that these matters would be illuminated if a comparable research were undertaken with children at the other extreme of the normal curve, namely the educationally superior children.

Two years later, Stein and Stores (1965) at Manchester report an investigation on IQ changes in an educationally subnormal group at a special school. They refer to various researches which indicate that feeble-minded patients who have suffered extreme deprivation in early life may show a rise of IQ in a more fortunate environment. In their own research the aim was to find out whether the IQs in their group rose while in the special school, and what the predictive value of a test on entry might be, since evidence so far appears to be conflicting. They worked with 75 children attending a Lancashire special school for ESN children. The average age at the test on entry was 11·2 years, and on leaving was 16 years. They used the Terman–Merrill on entry and the Wechsler at the end of the time. They made allowance for the fact that the Wechsler test scores a little higher than the Terman–Merrill Stanford–Binet, and also for possible errors due to retest. Then they found three groups: (1) *improved*, with IQ gains of between 4 and 22 points (24 children); (2) *unchanged*, differences only ± 3 points (24 children); and (3) *deteriorated* IQ losses between 4 and 18 points (27 children). From these results the authors conclude that the predictive value of the Terman–Merrill test is limited, as it only gives consistent IQ with one-third of this group, despite marked changes with the rest—in a few cases sufficient to lift the children well into the range of intellectual normality. Thus their work with seventy-five children supports the findings of Rushton and Stockwin with their 111 boys. However, the Wechsler (until recently not properly standardised for English children) is far more liable to be affected by environmental changes, as is obvious from its contents. If one starts with Wechsler and ends with Terman, as one of Burt's students did, very different results are obtained.

The 1944 Education Act classes a certain group of children with low achievement in school work as educationally subnormal. It lays a duty on Local Educational Authorities to ascertain which these children are and to provide suitable forms of education for them. This might be remedial education, special classes, adjustment classes or special schools. P. Williams (1965) of Swansea discusses the ascertainment of such children, which we have seen from several researches presents particular difficulties. He goes into the history, from nineteenth-century voluntary organisations, to modern ways of ascertaining such children. Incidentally Burt did not suggest 'certification' but strenuously sought its abolition. 'Ascertainment', a word used today, goes back at least to 1890. Williams then discusses modern procedure, which bears marked resemblance to that initiated by Burt in County Hall. Before the removal of the word 'certification' the final decision was usually made by the school medical officer; but in London his decision might be reviewed by the psychologist (i.e. Burt), and this happened usually if a parent, teacher or inspector appealed against the doctor's decision. Today, according to Williams, it is not quite clear who makes the final decision. In Segal's (1961) survey of Local Educational Authorities, only 14 per cent had a full case conference of several experts to discuss each child and make a final inter-professional decision. There are a number of other problems still to be resolved, and Williams concludes by saying that work with mentally handi-capped children stands out as a field where cooperation between the profes-sions is essential. In the light of new research both the functions and the purpose of the special school may need rethinking so that this most valuable section of the educational service may make an even more effective contri-bution. We have already referred to earlier work by P. Williams (1964) on date of birth and its effect on educationally subnormal children (see p. 213). This particularly vulnerable group of children has suffered even more than most summer-born children through having less time in the infant school than autumn-born children.

Bookbinder (1967) made a study of the preponderance of summer-born children in ESN classes, hoping to find out whether age or length of infant schooling was responsible. He took the birth dates of all children in Bristol ESN classes in ordinary junior and secondary schools: 1,289 children, of whom 876 were boys and 413 girls, 745 in junior and 544 in secondary schools. He gives an interesting series of tables, but the situation is complex and he was unable to come to a clearcut conclusion. The evidence suggests that because of the time of year of their birth some borderline children of 7 years, who might otherwise be able to respond to the normal stimulation of an ordinary class, are placed in an ESN class and come to accept the low expectations of them as backward children. From this we can see that the borderline children are a special problem and are not to be confused with the severe cases for whom Segal (p. 354) advocates early diagnosis and special nursery schools. For reasons which have not yet been discovered, Bookbinder found—contrary to expectation—that by third and fourth year junior school, the season of birth of children in ESN classes becomes even more unevenly distributed. He puts forward two alternative possible explanations: that faulty ESN placement prevents the summer-born from catching up, or that the duller summer-born find it increasingly difficult to cope with the ordinary class and so more and more drift to the ESN class towards the end of junior school. Only further research will make the situation clear. But

Bookbinder puts forward a strong case for specialist teachers to coach retarded children, rather than having whole classes for the retarded. Such specialist teachers usually have the insight, sympathy and skill to diagnose the problem and to help each child. Armstrong (1965) has written a research note on special educational treatment in ordinary schools and considers that better arrangements for help at all ages will result in fewer casualties.

Half a century of work with educationally subnormal children has begun to accumulate valuable information about their problems. Ascertainment of these children has never from the start of testing been easy; and subsequent information about them suggests that techniques begun for testing high grade defectives, and now adapted for testing normal children, are not entirely suitable for use with intellectually subnormal children. This is the counter-part, the other extreme, of the 1962 *Year Book* contention that supernormal children are not suitably tested by means of tests constructed to differentiate intellectual levels of normal children. Thus we can see why Rushton and Stockwin (1963) suggest that comparable research with extremes of gifted children might throw light on ESN problems. One can see that it might be very illuminating to carry out parallel researches with subnormal and gifted children on the detailed analysis of their thought-processes, along the lines of Lovell and Shields (see p. 257). If such research revealed some continuum from subnormal, through normal (with whom, because of large numbers, we have more experience), to supernormal children, then we might get a clearer idea of the continuum of adaptation that should be built in to tests for both extremes as well as normals.

Lunzer and Hulme (1967) at Manchester carried out an investigation of normal and subnormal children of comparable mental age, to see whether differences existed between these two groups in learning by visual discrimin-ation, and in the formation of learning sets (generalised approaches to learning problems), or in both. They gave to twenty-eight older subnormal children and twenty-four normal preschool children of 2:7 to 4:4 years six visual discrimination problems. There was naturally some difficulty in matching them and the normal children proved to have a somewhat higher mean mental age. Nevertheless, little difference appeared either in the num-ber of trials to master the first problem, or in the subsequent improvement attributable to the learning set or attitude. But children who lacked self-confidence fared badly in the experiment. The subnormal children were as frequent as the normal children in spontaneously naming the colour forms on the six pairs of lids on $2\frac{1}{2}$-inch square boxes; and the subnormal ones were more vocal afterwards in explaining how they discriminated.

Amongst the references of Lunzer and Hulme to language research is Luria, *The Role of Speech* (1961) where Luria describes Vygotsky's experiments on what children actually say while working. But Lunzer and Hulme only describe what the children said *after* the tasks were completed. It would be most interesting to have reports of what educationally subnormal children say *while* they are performing a task. When the authors compared their results with others reported in the psychological literature, they came to the conclusion that specific deficiency of language is probably more noticeable at higher mental ages when the rôle of language may be more decisive. This suggestion that the younger intellectually subnormal are not so retarded in speech in comparison with younger normal children lends strong support to ascertaining these children early and arranging special nursery schools where their fairly normal level of speech can be developed under skilled guidance. Once this early opportunity is lost the gap becomes increasingly difficult to bridge.

Woodward and Stern (1963) made a study of eighty-three severely subnormal children at the Fountain Hospital, London. The children were all under 9 years of age and were studied in relation to Piaget's sensorimotor stages. They found that locomotor development was significantly in advance of speech development. Children classified according to sensorimotor stage varied considerably in both speech and locomotor development. Certain developments in language, drawing, performance ability and social responses were associated with the attainment of the last sensorimotor stage. This suggests that the achievement of the end of the sensorimotor period is an important step in the development of severely subnormal children. They give very clear descriptions of how they tested the children—always an achievement in reproducing Piaget's work—and conclude that children who have attained the last sensorimotor stage would benefit from attending a training centre, so that new skills of speech, drawing and performance can be fostered. Mannix (1960) for an MEd thesis at Manchester made a study of the number concepts of ESN children, along Piaget's lines, and amongst his conclusions were: that these children do pass through Piaget's three stages, that there are wide individual differences in how long they take to pass them, and that an individual may vary in rate of progress.

Bartlet and Shapiro (1956), of the London Institute of Psychiatry, give a detailed account of teaching a boy of 9 years with severe psychiatric disturbance to read. The precise account of tests to discover exactly what his problems were, would be of help to those working in special schools. In addition to associative problems this boy was liable to 'catastrophy responses' even when things were going well. It is refreshing to have a conclusion, after such patient work, which deals with the 'possible causes of success'.

Chazan (1964, 1965) has made two studies of maladjustment with ESN children in South Wales. In the first stage he compared 169 ESN children with a control group of normal children, matched for age, sex and socio-economic background. The ESN children were two complete age groups, 9–10 and 13–14 years. They came predominantly from the lower social strata and had more physical ailments and defects than the control group. Over a third of them were maladjusted, which was nearly three times as many as in the control group. They showed considerably more symptoms of depression, hostility towards adults, inhibition and emotional tension than the controls. There was also a high incidence of speech defects, unsatisfactory attendance at school and delinquency. In the second stage, Chazan made a special study of thirty of the most maladjusted of these ESN children. Significantly more of the maladjusted children showed some physical weakness or defect, were subjected to adverse psychological pressures and unsatisfactory discipline at home (related to parental instability), and had had interrupted or incomplete relationships with their parents. Significantly fewer of them had a positive relationship with their father; and in many cases maladjustment was associated with lack of progress in the basic subjects at the special school. He concludes by saying that we need comprehensive guidance services for the parents of educationally subnormal children.

In this connection, Cashdan and Jeffree (1966) have made a small study of the influence of the home background on the development of severely subnormal children. They made a pilot study with ten children of mental age $5\frac{1}{2}$ years and chronological age range 7 to 15 years at a training centre, matched with a group of ten normal children of $5\frac{1}{2}$ years at an infant school. They suggest in their conclusions that 'subnormality' may have roots in a variety of deprivation experience. But better counselling of parents and better educational procedures may alleviate or even prevent at least the secondary handicaps of many of these children, such as withdrawal, behavioural rigidity and poor language development. Comparison of the ten mothers of subnormal children with the ten mothers of the normal control children, by interview and rating, showed that the subnormal children had had less stimulating environments than the control children. A large-scale study is now being planned.

Two further researches should be mentioned. Morán (1960) of Puerto Rico University studied the levels of attainment of 300 ESN adolescents in the top class of a London special secondary school. He used specially designed or adapted tests and compared results with those of junior children of similar mental age. The ESN children showed a much wider range but fell below the junior school in every area tested except craft. Where there was enthusiasm for a subject there was relatively superior achievement. In conclusion Morán suggests that the curriculum of ESN adolescents should be directed towards vocational guidance and social maturity, instead of depending on verbal ability, which, as investigation shows, is specially weak in these children. Matthew (1964) for an MEd thesis at Manchester, studied the postschool social adaptation of sixty-two ESN boys in one borough. They were matched with controls in the same borough. Those boys who made adequate social adjustment merged inconspicuously into the workaday world. The partial failures and the failures were potential social problems and Matthew questions whether existing social services are adequate to deal with the postschool problems of the failures, and suggests the creation of a specialised service to cater for their needs during the transition period between school leaving and adulthood.

Although a great deal of work has been done for educationally subnormal children over many decades, and various government reports have secured better conditions for them, there is still a great deal more work to be done. In the first place, research has only just begun to get down to the nature of their learning problems. Until we know more of this we cannot make full use of the special schools now being run by increasingly well-qualified specialists. We do not know what we shall find. It is astonishing to hear, for instance, that ESN children have less language problems in the preschool years than later. Then, as with the gifted, there are many more subnormal children than the theoretical curve of normal distribution of intelligence leads us to expect. All who run special schools are fully aware of this, because of their long waiting lists.

If the study of subnormal intelligence can illuminate the nature of supernormal intelligence, we can be sure that the reverse is true. Whereas we find that the gifted ten-year-old may need access to the differential calculus and Dante's *La Divina Commedia* in the original, we shall see our way to stretch the minds of the subnormal by making similar adjustment, in the reverse direction, of the content of their syllabus. Our ascertainment of educationally subnormal children cannot become reliable until we possess better information as to how their minds work. Once we possess more information here, we shall be better able to educate them according to their ability.

22. Child guidance

The first edition of *The Young Delinquent* by Burt appeared in 1925, and in it Appendix II, 'The Psychological Clinic for Juvenile Delinquents'. The idea of a psychological clinic for helping maladjusted children was new to Britain. Burt gives a brief account of work in America along these lines, with the aim of making a scientific study of delinquent children referred by schools or courts. He then describes how small beginnings had been made in various parts of Britain. The staff suggested by Burt at this early stage include: (1) a senior psychologist; (2) a junior psychologist; he added that 'if no physician is on the staff one of them should possess medical and psychiatric experience and one at least should have had educational experience'; (3) one or more social workers trained in psychological investigation of social problems; (4) a shorthand typist for record keeping. The original drive towards child guidance was due to Galton, Sully, McDougall and Burt; and Burt's office in the Education Department at London's County Hall was in fact the first Child Guidance Clinic in Britain. The bias was psychological and not medical.

From this recommendation for dealing with delinquents a vast network of child guidance centres has developed throughout Britain for children with all kinds of behaviour disturbances. To the staff originally suggested there is now added a psychiatrist (a doctor with at least one year's study of the prevention, diagnosis, treatment, and care of mental illness). This addition became essential because a few of the children referred suffered from severe mental illness. Some centres are fortunate in having various other specialists, such as a speech therapist, a play therapist, or a teacher trained to help educationally retarded children to catch up in skills required for school work. The bias of the team of experts remains psychological, social and educational.

It is not easy to run an interprofessional team. Experts are accustomed to making final decisions themselves. This important development would probably have foundered on these grounds but for the fact that children in trouble awaken altruism in us. The chairman may be any one of the three specialists, psychologist, psychiatrist or social worker. In the discussions due weight is given to the views of each on his own area of expertise. The way in which each centre runs is unique, depending on the particular composition of personalities. Therefore it is impossible to describe 'the procedure'. Visits to clinics do not reveal much, because children in trouble cannot be treated as exhibits.

A brief account of what usually happened when the author was working at the Child Guidance Clinic of a London Teaching Hospital during the Second World War will give some indication of procedure. A child might be referred by various people, such as the head teacher or the family doctor or the minister. An appointment would be made as soon as possible to see the child with at least one parent. It would be almost useless to treat a child without any home cooperation. Usually the mother brought the child. The waiting room had toys, annuals, and such comics as were available in wartime. Occasional rowdy shouts could be heard from various rooms. The child went to the psychologist while the parent saw the psychiatric social worker. The psychologist chatted, gave various intelligence tests, usually including the newly published 1937 Stanford–Binet Intelligence Scale, with the Goodenough Draw-a-man thrown in if there was time; and gathered as much information on social development as possible, from attitudes expressed by the child towards school friends and enemies, and such matters as could be discussed. Meanwhile the PSW as the social worker is affectionately called, found out as much as possible on the history of the child, from conception onwards—even from the family situation before conception.

Before the PSW had finished, the child went from the psychologist to the psychiatrist. The psychiatrist's room was messy. There were paints and paper, a variety of toys from armed men to woolly animals. How the psychiatrist got the child talking was different in every case. Then the mother took the child home and the case conference was held. In theory this was to be held at a certain time in a certain room after a cup of tea, with several children on the list for discussion. In practice everyone was so deeply interested that the conference usually took place somewhere else over the cup of tea, and the formal procedure never happened unless visitors had been invited to witness it. The psychologist reported the IQ estimate, with data to indicate how reliable it might be, according to the degree of emotional adjustment of the child; also any other relevant information, e.g. the child said he had 'millions of school friends' but could not name a single one, which is somewhat contradictory. The PSW gave information on the home, whether there had been feeding troubles, nightmares, prolonged bedwetting; how the parents got on, what siblings there were, father's and mother's occupations and so on. Then the psychiatrist said what had emerged in his room; whether the child had seized a gun and shot down all woolly animals, been afraid to paint, whispered at a doll 'Damn!' It might be anything.

The purpose of the conference was to decide whether to treat the child or not. Reasons for not treating a child at the centre might range from the fact that the child was reasonably well adjusted and the parents showed great insight, to the fact that the child was so mentally ill that he should go to a special clinic for treatment. If it was decided that the child should be treated, who had time to take him on? Let us say the psychologist agrees to fit him in, beginning some time next month, when a present child's treatment should have terminated. Almost invariably the mother went to the PSW every time the child went to psychologist or psychiatrist. The psychiatric social worker is the backbone of the clinic, because she (or he) helps the parent to understand what happens to the child. Without some measurement of adjustment and increased insight in the home, improvement in the child's adjustment could not be sustained.

Often one good long chat with the PSW on the first visit is enough. The child no longer appears maladjusted at home and the parents no longer require help. Thus as many as a third of those on the waiting-list for treatment may say the problems have cleared up. When a child is treated, he may be too inhibited, and through play one helps him to become more conscious of what he really wants to do; or he may be too uninhibited and he has to be helped to form more inhibition of impulses. The treatment is largely through the symbolism of play, which we have already discussed in Chapter 7. The room is not beautiful. Children bump toys into walls, splash water around, throw plasticine at objects. The latitude allowed for expression of aggression is far greater than children normally require. There are just two absolute taboos: (1) treatment ends at a certain time, no matter how much the child wishes to continue, since there are other children awaiting help; and (2) no real damage may be done. Windows cannot be broken, nor can plasticine be thrown at the face of the therapist and so on. These two firm rules are part of the treatment, because they help the troubled patient to realise that the play activity is play. One cannot say 'just play' because this play under skilled guidance is a lifeline to the child.

High on the list of books about child guidance one should put Lowenfeld's *Play in Childhood* (1935), R. Griffiths' *Imagination in Early Childhood* (1935), Moodie's *The Doctor and the Difficult Child* (1940), Burbury, Balint and

Yapp's (1945) *An Introduction to Child Guidance*, and Jackson and Todd's (1946) *Child Treatment and the Therapy of Play*. Margaret Lowenfeld's book is based on observations at the Institute of Child Psychology, which she started as a child guidance clinic and training centre. She writes that play in childhood is the expression of the child's relation to the whole of life. Ruth Griffiths, working under Flugel at University College, London, collected a variety of phantasy material—drawings, stories, dreams, interpretation of inkblots—from children of 5. Her evidence shows that phantasy in children is not just a way of escaping from reality but is the child's way of coping with reality and resolving his problems. Dr William Moodie opened the London Child Guidance Clinic in 1929 and his books on the difficult child give much information on the kind of problems for which children are referred. There are other great names, such as Dr Emmanuel Miller who started a clinic in the East End of London under the auspices of the Jewish Health Organisation, and who writes in an introduction to the above Jackson and Todd book that they handle their material with reserve and a commendable absence of dogmatism.

A personal reminiscence is perhaps not out of place. While working on the Education Board of the Control Commission in Germany, the author had the privilege of taking the incomparable Sister Marie Hilda, who started the Catholic Notre Dame Clinic in Glasgow in 1931, to meet the Education Committee for North Rhine/Westphalia at the Ministry in Düsseldorf. She was minute, very deaf and spoke no German. The committee was almost entirely Catholic. They were charmed to hear of her dispensation from the Pope to go to America in the late 1920s to see how American clinics were run, but wanted her to describe actual cases. So she described two in detail, a girl of 14 who gave lurid accounts of her life as a prostitute, and a boy of the same age who rarely spoke. She said she had seen at once that the girl was describing a phantasy life and so arranged a nice, steady boy-friend for her. The boy was more difficult. He was pathologically shy, but also longed for a girl-friend. One day he arrived for treatment in a state of intense suppressed excitement. He had got a girl-friend. When she pressed him for details about her, he could tell nothing. Yet Sister Marie Hilda was sure the girl-friend was not just phantasy. He could not tell the colour of her eyes, her hair, anything. Eventually this little nun said, 'How do you know you were out with a girl at all?' Then the shy boy whispered, 'She has beautiful legs'. The insight shown by Sister Marie Hilda in both these cases had a profound effect on the Germans. They were particularly impressed at its being shown by a nun, and at hearing that this was typical of her work, as of most child guidance.

The behaviour of maladjusted children is partly due to the fact that, because of their problems, they have not learned to behave as other children of their age behave. It is also a cry for help. Therefore a study of what is done for them is also a study of society's attitude to them. There has been a fair amount of research on maladjustment since the Second World War. Chazan (1963) of Swansea has written a most valuable article on postwar trends in theory and practice with maladjusted children. He deals with the meaning of the term 'maladjustment', the classification of symptoms, the incidence of maladjustment, factors associated with it, the efficacy of treatment, and prevention and early detection. In conclusion he stresses the effectiveness of interprofessional cooperation and liason of all agencies concerned with the welfare of all children. There is a very good reference list.

Chazan (1962) has also written on a matter of increasing concern, now that the vast majority of children enjoy school, which is 'school phobia'. He analyses the cases of thirty-three children attending a child guidance centre between 1949 and 1959 who suffered school phobia. The findings support the work of others on intelligence, home background and personality features of such children; but they suggest that educational factors have been underestimated in consideration of both the aetiology (causes of origin) and the treatment. The account of these particular children is important reading: average plus intelligence, materially good homes, small united families with close mother–child bond but—about two-thirds showing marked dependency and emotional immaturity. There were few traumatic (mentally wounding) events; but in twelve homes at least one parent was chronically ill, physically or mentally; in six cases the school phobia started immediately after a period of illness or hospitalisation. Chazan concludes with a case history. Cooper (1966) has made a study of the part played by conditions in the school and home in 'school refusal' and finds much in common between school phobia and truancy. Tyerman (1958) made a study of truancy and found adverse home circumstances, together with lack of satisfaction in home or school a most important condition of truancy.

Mitchell and Shepherd (1966), of the London Institute of Psychiatry, made a comparative study of the behaviour of a random sample of over 6,000 Buckinghamshire children. Information from both parents and teachers showed that deviant behaviour at home was significantly associated both with lack of academic success and with behavioural deviance at school. This supports Chazan's contention that not enough attention has been paid to educational factors in children's problems of adjustment. Mitchell and Shepherd also found that many children showed deviant behaviour either at home or at school; and they stress the point that any attempt to estimate the distribution of maladjustment in the child population must utilise information from both teachers *and* parents. Howells and Lickorish (1963) at the Ipswich Department of Child and Family Psychiatry devised a family relations indicator, in the form of a projection test. They woeked on the assumption that a child draws on his own experience to explain ambiguous pictures. Six basic family scenes are repeated three times. The repetition is, of course, to test the consistency of the replies, that is, whether a child gave the same kind of response to a particular situation each time. The responses were compared with information from other sources, such as interviews with the families concerned. They concluded that such a technique could sometimes reveal information which is not otherwise available and that information obtained in this way can be used both for diagnosis and for therapy.

Lunzer (1960a) at Manchester made a study of forty-two aggressive and forty withdrawn children, selected by teachers from a total school population of 1,002 children, and matched them with a group of exceptionally well-adjusted children. Comparison was made by use of ratings and a battery of tests: Bristol Guides to Social Adjustment, a sociometric test, and a social adaptation test. Results indicated that there are probably rather more problems of aggression than withdrawal, but that the severity of the two behaviour problems is comparable. These indications are confirmed by a follow-up which is so far only of one year. Prompted by Lynn's (1957) suggestion that anxious children tended to show a higher performance in reading as compared with arithmetic (p. 196), Lunzer (1960a) gave tests of reading and arithmetic to the two groups of aggressive and withdrawn children. The aggressive children tended to do badly in arithmetic and Raven's Progressive Matrices. These results appear to Lunzer to contradict Lynn's results. But aggressiveness, though it may be laced with anxiety, is not anxiousness, so perhaps it is not fair to compare these results.

Most of the studies referred to have sections concerned with treatment, but some deal specifically with treatment. Kellmer Pringle (1957), while at the Birmingham remedial centre, made a comparative study of schools for the maladjusted and ordinary boarding schools and found all the symptoms of maladjustment were also to be seen to a lesser degree in ordinary boarding schools. Because the child–adult relationship is of great importance for maladjusted children, their schools need more liberal staffing. Kellmer Pringle (1961) also reported a long-term study of remedial treatment. Questionnaires were sent to 240 parents and 78 per cent were returned. The evidence suggested that the parents considered the remedial work had helped.

Petrie (1962) made a study of twenty-three maladjusted children in a special boarding school, in order to study progress in adjustment and relate this to other factors. The investigation included intelligence and attainment tests, the Bristol Social Adjustment Guides, and projection techniques; also the Warden classified the children into broad categories according to patterns of behaviour, severity of symptoms and degree of improved adjustment. Then results were compared. The Bristol Guides were moderately good in assessment of maladjustment, but assessment by projection tests was generally poor. All the techniques, except the WISC verbal scale, showed significant improvement but there was little agreement between them; and the only improvement on the Bristol Guides was significantly related to the Warden's own assessment of improvement. The children's rate of progress tended to be inconsistent, some doing better at the beginning, others at the end. An important factor was improvement in parental attitudes.

Two articles in the *British Journal of Medical Psychology* relate treatment to depth psychology. Gedo (1966) of Chicago writes on the psychotherapy of developmental arrest, where adolescent fixations are used as a means of resuming emotional maturation. Marks and Gelder (1966) of the London Institute of Psychiatry see common ground between behaviour therapy and psychodynamic techniques. In a good summary they show that each is complementary to the other. Two other articles concern grammar schools. Chazan (1959) studied sixty grammar school children referred for child guidance at Liverpool. He concludes with accounts of methods of treatment and also the outcome of treatment: nearly half the children showed considerable improvement and only five showed little or no progress.

Argyle (1963) has written an article on 'Introjection: a form of social learning'. Though this is not research specifically on maladjustment, it is an area where trouble can frequently be located in maladjusted children. The processes of introjection and projection which we discussed in Chapter 7 on children's play are seen in exaggerated form during treatment in child guidance. The symbolism of the children's play reveals a maladjusted child's attitude to the whole of life. Argyle's interesting article describes empirical research with children and their parents on the one aspect of introjection.

The young delinquent is also a matter of concern to the child guidance centre. Wilkins (1961) of the Home Office Research Unit, has written on 'Crime, cause and treatment: recent research and theory'. He says that as yet we have little positive evidence as to causes or treatment. (We have a good deal on causes, but less on the efficacy of treatments.) But now that the theories are better constructed and integrated, the future is more hopeful.

In a further article Wilkins (1963) evaluates some empirical studies and concludes by saying that the causes of delinquency will remain unknown until there is rigorous experimentation. Barbara Wootton (1966) in *New Society* writes that tradition in justice is slow to change, but now in connection with crime it is challenged by the scientific approach which argues that purely punitive treatment does not (always) discourage crime. Deacon (1965) gives a survey of delinquency in Somerset 1958–60. This follows several surveys in London and Liverpool, and gives much valuable information. Trasler (1963) at Southampton writes on theoretical problems in the explanation of delinquent behaviour. He describes the predicament of modern research, particularly regarding empirical definition, discusses the socialising process and effective social training, and concludes with theoretical problems in measuring potential criminality. If we cannot find the cues for specific reactions to environment that suggest possible delinquent tendencies, he says, then theory of delinquency will be overcome by sheer weight of facts. Others who have written on delinquency include Dell (1963) on social and school factors, McNally (1965) on school factors, Andry (1960) on parental pathology, Gibbens (1958), and Gibson (1964) on a test for use with delinquents.

Hearnshaw (1964) refers to a symposium in the *British Journal of Educational Psychology* (1951–3) as a 'somewhat acrimonious' discussion between psychologists and psychiatrists in the child guidance services. But it is still very interesting to read. It opens with Kennedy (1951) on the relations between psychologist and psychiatrist. Then Davidson (1952) writes on the relations of both to maladjusted children and adults, followed by Keir's (1952) history of child guidance (much fuller than given here), and McCallum (1952) on child guidance in Scotland; then Moody (1952) on the interprofessional conflict of disciplines and personalities, which those in the team would regard as 'airing their problems' rather than 'acrimonious'. The last two contributions are by Banks (1953) on research and Burt (1953) who insists, as he has done since he first proposed such centres, that only a small percentage of maladjusted children are pathological and the main bulk of the cases— some 90 per cent—require primarily psychological and educational guidance.

23. Decision about secondary education

At the end of the primary school years a decision has to be made for each child about which is the more suitable form of secondary educational system, the more academic or the more practical. In a comprehensive school there are usually many classes for each age and the bias from practical to academic work is graded from one extreme to the other. If the choice is between secondary modern and secondary grammar, the line of demarcation is sharp; but many secondary modern schools now arrange for more academic work in upper forms to suit children who might more suitably have been given grammar school education. Usually such children are unwilling to be transferred to grammar school as they have become attached to their present school. Transfer to more academic or more practical work within a comprehensive school does not involve change of school.

Whatever the organisation of secondary level, information has to be presented at the end of primary education upon which the decision must be made: which form of education best suits each child. A variety of ways of preparing children and presenting information have been tried out. Many schools have tried to prepare children by dividing predominantly practical from predominantly academic work during the primary school years, and by putting the children in classes where the work seemed best suited to their abilities. This has become known colloquially as 'streaming'. When this suggestion was first made Blair and Kimmins investigated it systematically. They concluded that, if the parents' cooperation was obtained and the lower classes were not given a bad name, normal, backward and supernormal children were all happier when working with those of about equal ability. Unfortunately this cooperation was not won, from either parents or teachers. Consequently the encouragement in learning to which every child is entitled became focused mainly on the academic or 'A' classes. Many teachers considered it a special honour to teach 'A' classes, and parents thought that to be in another class was some kind of disgrace for their children.

In order to break down this unfortunate situation there has been considerable research recently on so-called streaming. For example, in the *British Journal of Educational Psychology*, there are articles by Rudd (1958), Blandford (1958), Daniels (1961) and Veness (1960); in *Educational Research* by Yates and Pidgeon (1959), B. Jackson (1961), Svensson (1962), Willig (1963) and Pattinson (1963). The Plowden Report (1967), reviewing this and other research into streaming, comes to the conclusions (pp. 818–24) that the teachers' attitudes are more important than the organisation; and that teachers who treat children individually have no difficulty in accepting unstreaming throughout the school. Recent research indicates that—with present attitudes—streaming is harmful. But we have also to remember that it can be frustrating to bright and dull alike, causing confusion or boredom, to be taught in ways that suit a very different speed of thinking. We still have to find out which, given right attitudes of teachers and parents, is best for the children.

Whatever technique is used for selecting the suitable type of secondary education, follow-up studies are necessary to check success or failure of selection. S. C. Richardson (1956) followed up 813 children who entered four Plymouth grammar schools in 1949, using school marks as criterion. He came to the conclusion that some kind of test was necessary as teachers' estimates alone were not satisfactory. Intelligence tests had a significantly higher validity than any other single test, and validity was significantly reduced when attainment tests were omitted. He supported McClelland (1942) and Emmett (1954) in suggesting that highly speeded attainment tests are unsatisfactory as their appearance of objectivity is illusory. N. France (1964) made a six-year follow-up of a random one-in-fifteen group of all Kent children born in 1945, in all 1,300 children. This information included scores for tests of ability and attainment given annually in the junior school, and also assessments by teachings in the last year there. He concludes that a selection procedure using results of a series of tests throughout the junior school, together with teachers' assessments could be sufficient. Watts (1958) made a study of the effect of age and practice on intelligence testing with a group of grammar school girls in the north of England. She used the AH4 and AH5 tests for high-grade intelligence devised by Heim (1947). As a result of annual testing she concluded that improvement through practice rather than age goes on up to at least seven testings.

Nisbet and Buchan (1959) traced back the school history of 102 students who entered Aberdeen University from Aberdeen schools in 1953, and followed-up from end of primary school to fourth year university; they also studied a second group of forty-six entering the university in 1950. In both cases scores at 11 years were compared with subsequent university performance, but the correlations were not high, ranging only from +0·05 to +0·28. In the second group of seventy-seven who gained university entrance, nineteen had scored below IQ 110 in the test at 11 years. Examples of poor later performers and excellent performance by low scorers suggest that over an interval of years accurate prediction at 11 years of scholastic attainment is not possible. Tozer and Larwood (1958) studied IQ changes, with a group of 124 students, during their time at Liverpool University. They gave the National Institute of Industrial Psychology (NIIP) Group Test 33 (originally designed by Burt and still widely used), at the beginning of their degree courses and again, three years later, on entering the Department of Education for professional training. There was a highly significant gain in IQ irrespective of sex, honours or pass degree, arts or science. Here we have to remember that IQ obtained after 14 years is never so reliable. The writers leave what the cause may be an open question, but do not rule out the possibility that a college course could stimulate the functioning of intelligence.

There have been some recent researches on specific aspects of tests at 11 years. Sarnoff et al. (1959) of Yale University applied American tests of anxiety to British children, but they were not very successful here. Bowyer (1961) investigated individual differences in stress, with interesting results. Of 131 children, ten were definitely stressed, 106 variously stressed and only fifteen were little or not at all stressed. Middle-class children suffered most, apparently because of parental pressure. Children in homes where the test could be discussed freely suffered least; and some parents increased stress, when meaning to reduce it, by either banning talk about it or by reiterating that the results did not matter. The most stressed children were the sensitive ones of high ability or of borderline ability. Bowyer points out that stress is fatiguing.

Nisbet and Illesley (1963) at Aberdeen examined the effects of today's early puberty on tests at 11 years. They took a group of 1,385 girls, whose first menstruation date was known from medical cards, and analysed test results at 7, 9, 11 and 13 years. They came to the conclusion that early puberty gave no advantage at 11 years. Following this, Nisbet et al. (1964) examined results at 16 years and found that a slight superiority at $12\frac{1}{4}$ years diminishes as the late-developers reach puberty.

The value of essays as part of the selection procedure has been studied. There are many problems in trying to arrive at objective standards of marking. The *British Journal of Educational Psychology* published a symposium on the use of essays in selection at 11 plus, to which Penfold (1956), Peel and Armstrong (1956), Wiseman (1956), and Pidgeon and Yates (1957) contributed. No definite conclusion seems to have been reached. Wiseman points out that the number of children in an area, and therefore the number of essays to mark, can be decisive. The amount of labour involved if several independent markers have to be found to evaluate 10,000 essays would only be warranted if the outcome were very worthwhile. Ballard showed this long ago when essays were used in junior county scholarships at 11 years. So far, attempts to make essay marking part of the objective technique have not been successful. Others who have written in this journal on essays include Shouksmith (1958), Remondino (1959), Farrell and Gilbert (1960), and Young, D. (1962).

There have been some articles on English at secondary school level which should be mentioned here. They include Bate (1961), Paffard (1961), Powell (1963), Christie and Kline (1966) and Hewitt (1960). The last is on the performance in English Language at 'O' level, of a sample of 1,423 boys and 882 girls who went to the university.

Spoken English has also been studied. Hitchman (1964, 1966) gives a review of research and reports the situation in schools and colleges in the United Kingdom. King (1959) carried out an experimental investigation into the relative merits of listening and of reading for purposes of comprehension in primary schools. He reviews many relevant researches and describes how he got results by relating the final scores of 475 boys and girls in nine London primary schools to visual and auditory comprehension. Amongst his results are the following: the comprehension of boys was significantly higher when they listened to information than when they read it, but the comprehension of girls was not significantly higher with hearing it; and boys do better in tests which are orally presented than those in which they have to read the questions and write the answers. Thus a written test at 11 years would underestimate the comprehension of boys.

One problem raised by tests, at whatever age they are applied, has attracted a number of research workers. This is the influence of speed, which occasions a fast candidate to accumulate a high score through being able to tackle more questions in a given time than a slow but thorough candidate. Burt's solution was to arrange the items in the test in order of increasing difficulty; then the score is determined by difficulty of items as well as speed (and of course speed *is* a sign of efficiency). Amongst those who have studied speed are S. C. Richardson (1956), Yates (1966), and Moreton and Butcher (1963).

This problem of the slow but thorough child being handicapped by speed tests is an argument for keeping cumulative records throughout the primary school, from normal class work. France and Wiseman (1966) have devised an educational guidance programme for primary schools, suitable for use throughout the country. There is a 32-page workbook for each of first, second and third year junior stages, to be completed by every child individually, at his own pace, as part of normal school. The various separate items were tried out in the spring of 1964 throughout the whole country, from Aberdeen to Hampshire, then standardised and tried out on a random sample of Warwick and Solihull primary schools. These untimed tests produced satisfactory discrimination of ability, and results could be used both for guidance at the time and for information in deciding the best educational system at 11 years. As was to be expected, they found appreciable differences of achievement in different areas. Such information would be of value to local education authorities.

As the authors point out, the France–Wiseman Educational Guidance Programme was devised to meet a need. The ferment of change in education today necessitates a guidance programme firmly rooted in the primary school. Only the very largest local education authorities have an expert with the knowledge and experience necessary to devise, validate and standardise the objective tests necessary as basis for guidance. Teachers need a compact instrument which covers intellect and personality. Here, by means of short untimed tests and a specially designed record card, adequate data for guidance and also for prediction of development at 11 years, can be accumulated. Moreover, this gives the psychologist information about national norms which is rarely obtained within LEAs whose main concern is variations within their own area. They conclude with a point of greatest importance concerning research procedure of this kind, which we have already come across. 'It is far more valuable to the teacher and to the educationist to have available really comparable norms based on a population of known background of the order of size of 1,500 to 2,000 than to collate a mixed bag of populations numbering 20,000 and upwards.'

The *British Psychological Society* convened a committee of psychologists under the chairmanship of P. E. Vernon to study what had been done about selection since the 1944 Education Act. They published their findings in *Secondary School Selection*, edited by Vernon (1957), which reviews selection in historical perspective and makes recommendations intended to establish the 'parity of esteem' for all children envisaged by the Act. There are thirty-two recommendations, many of them suggesting in detail lines of further research. The overall trend of these recommendations is towards better understanding of children; and the final one is that cumulative records should be designed, not only as part of the selection technique but also for educational guidance throughout. This is a book which should be read by all who hope to move on to new ideas about decisions on selection of secondary education.

In the same year Yates and Pidgeon published *Admission to Grammar School* (1957), recounting the results of investigations by the National Foundation for Educational Research into the main problems of selection at 11 years. The problems fell into two categories: (*a*) problems associated with the fierce competition for grammar school places and (*b*) administrative problems associated with both provision of enough grammar schools and making valid allocations.

These last two books published in the same year marked the end of an epoch in selection. Indeed, one might well say that it was the information published in them which ended the epoch. From their different approaches both came to the conclusion that there must always be a borderline group of children for whom 'correct selection' was an impossibility. Some will be sent to the right type of school for them; others might do as well, or even better, at another type of school. In 1957 the unrealistic search for a fool-proof decision for all children at 11 years was given up. The objective is now to make the decision clear for the majority of children, and as clear as possible for borderline children.

24. The rôle of the teacher

There is a popular conception of the 'born' teacher who knows 'instinctively' how to handle children. This conception has some truth in it. Even as a student, such a person can get a group of children to do something with enthusiasm which another, perhaps more conscientiously prepared, cannot even persuade the children to try. But this gift for leading children is not enough in itself. Now, more than ever before, we have to find the most economic way of handing on the essentials of a swiftly evolving cultural heritage. Teaching in primary school is essentially a practical skill, and students have to learn many details of the most effective practice yet evolved. However, not only is every child unique; every group of children is unique. It would be impossible to equip students with practical details for all contingencies because in sheer quantity of advice this would be absurd, and because progressive teachers lead children on to levels of development hitherto unrecognised. The last few decades have shown this in many ways, for instance, in art, mathematics, poetry and music.

Cohen (1968), at Bradford, reviews research on how colleges endeavour to prepare students for the aims of teaching and concludes from results of research that such aims as 'promotion of independent judgment', 'development of critical thinking' and 'heightening of creativity and awareness' are assimilated by students through continuous exchange and interplay of individuals and groupings throughout the course. He calls the process whereby the student gradually acquires these attitudes 'teacher socialisation'. Others seeking the true nature of the teacher's rôle are Davey (1969), at York, on leadership in relation to group achievement, and King-Fun Li (1969) who sought objective measures of teachers' attitudes with ninety-seven Chinese students in Hong Kong.

Therefore students have to be given principles of education which can be guidelines for decisions in the classroom. The better the understanding of underlying theory, the better and the more flexible the practice. For instance,

298

a good grasp of how heredity operates leads to wiser adjustment of the environment, based on the limitations set by maturation. Knowledge of how and why intelligence testing has evolved in standardised form raises the probability of proper administration, with due regard for the effect of motivation upon a child's full use of his mental capacity. Modern discoveries about how children can best learn are now beginning to save children from having their time wasted in school; and they show how best to foster profitable attitudes to discovery. Awareness of the difference between wholesale repression and resolution of conflict equips a teacher to make sound decisions about all spontaneous activity from nursery school play to junior school art, both in many media.

When colleges of education have to select fifth and sixth form children to train as teachers, they would never willingly allow a born teacher to slip through their fingers. But what is probably a first interview can be a taxing occasion for the candidates, and it gives little scope for showing whether one can inspire a group of children. The colleges know that just to be a born teacher is not enough; there has to be the capacity and will to learn fast about both theory and practice. They also know that some candidates whose self-concept is too lacking in confidence for them to 'display' themselves at an interview, can in the classroom gain confidence as they see children grow under their care; and students who develop into teachers in this way remain particularly sensitive to children whose picture of themselves needs building up. Amongst the other things the colleges know is that a candidate who is clearly not a born leader, but is determined to teach, can, when equipped with the training, give children so much educational 'nourishment' that they and the teacher thrive; and such teachers, just because they cannot impose their personalities on the children, have of necessity to use modern methods. Born teachers have something to learn from teachers who are compelled to select material which children cannot resist.

Some research has been done into the best way of conducting interviews so that the required information is elicited from candidates. Burroughs (1958) and his colleagues at Birmingham made a list of fifteen items for interviewers to check as they affected their opinions of candidates, such as 'good first impression', 'pleasant voice' and 'enthusiastic about teaching'. When they compared these checklists with the final teaching mark of accepted candidates, they found three of the check items most useful as predictors of success: good impression, judgment of intellectual maturity, and ability to express himself or herself. Some colleges have wondered whether, as teaching is a group situation, it would not be better to conduct the interviews in groups. M. Allen (1962), for an MEd thesis at Manchester, compared interviews with eighty-nine candidates seen in small groups and 147 seen individually. Judgment of behaviour in small groups proved to forecast the final teaching mark better than did individual interviews; but the best predictor of all was the combined results of a verbal intelligence test, a vocabulary test, and a staff meeting of all who had interviewed the candidates. Since teaching is predominantly a verbal situation, one has to be able to reason verbally and also has to have a good command of vocabulary; and standardised tests give an estimate of these abilities.

Whereas the interview is much concerned with predicting the final teaching mark, the final teaching mark itself is a prediction of the kind of teacher which a student may become. Here we come up against two questions: (a) do we yet know enough about personality to analyse exactly which are the traits most necessary for the good teacher? and (b) are the educationists within the colleges and outside (for instance, head teachers and local education authorities) agreed as to what constitutes a good teacher? On the first question research is beginning to validate some traits which most teachers would be proud to acknowledge in themselves. Once more, this validation applies but little to primary school teachers, so we must again study investigations with older children, to see what we can glean and what we should demand of research with younger children.

K. M. Evans (1967) investigated whether the attitudes of students to values (by which they are often selected at interviews) underwent change during the Teacher's Diploma course at Cardiff. Only slight changes were detected, but this was no more than a seven-month course, and that any changes at all could be detected in so short a period suggests that further research here might be rewarding. Wiseman and Start (1965) found that teachers' satisfaction in teaching is an important concomitant of success. In order to have this satisfaction, teachers need confidence in their own ideas and have to be prepared to support these ideas in the face of opposition. They found in-service further training an important factor here. Successful and satisfied teachers proved to be warm, imaginative, sensitive, and able to make quick decisions. Their lively interest in children means that they are constantly learning more about the children and also about themselves; they are constantly critical of their own self-perception. Soloman (1967) found a certain level of tenseness necessary, giving a 'live-wire' quality in the classroom together with alertness to the children's needs. Fluency of pleasant ideas made learning enjoyable for the children. Such teachers were ranked by their tutors as extravert, more interested in others than themselves. They had warmth, sociability and cheerfulness; they had originality, took a liberal interest in progressive education and were critical of ideas and attitudes. Soloman concludes that these personality traits of stability, extraversion and radicalism are best detected by personality tests, which should be added to assessment of intelligence.

Others who support the use of personality tests for predicting the promising teacher are E. G. S. Evans (1964) who found students in colleges of education significantly more extravert than university students, and Warburton *et al.* (1963) who found self-control, conscientiousness and sensitivity the traits most closely related to successful teaching. Sometimes a student gives evidence of so many of these traits now known to be associated with successful teaching that the college confidently gives a high final teaching mark; and yet, once entered in the teaching profession the quality of teaching deteriorates rapidly. J. D. Williams (1966) made a study of this 'backsliding' in connection with modern mathematics in primary school, specifically in the use of constructional apparatus designed by Cuisenaire and by Dienes. He found some who had started apparently with the best intentions had made so many adaptations that the apparatus could no longer be regarded as based on scientific research. He found the causes included lack of space, material or time, and also unconscious persistence of previous ideas. His recommendations include further research on what causes stress when new techniques are introduced, what can be done at early stages to improve time-budgeting, etc., and what tactics a teacher can employ as a means of sustaining changed attitudes.

Murdoch (1966) suggests that teachers should think of themselves as people who have insight in classroom situations. Amongst the most important insights touched on in previous chapters are the connection between self-acceptance and good adjustment, both for teacher and for child (Taylor and Combs, 1952), the teacher's influence on each child's self-awareness (Staines 1958, Chadwick 1967); and the way in which self-acceptance relates to the whole personality structure (Zahran 1967). There does not yet appear to be any research on the self picture of tutors in colleges; whether they see themselves as having insight over students, building the students' self concept, etc. All the qualities of the good teacher listed so far, as resulting from modern research, are in close accord with the hopes and expectations of specialists in child development, who are well aware that the hitherto unrecognised potentialities of developing children call for hitherto largely unrecognised qualities in teachers.

On the second question which faces those who have to select and train students for teaching, whether educationists inside and outside the colleges agree as to exactly what constitutes a good teacher, the picture is not so clear. Wiseman and Start (1965) made an enquiry covering all kinds of school from 'infants' to university, and found little correlation between the college assessment and the various criteria of success in the teaching profession. Rudd and Wiseman (1962), investigating sources of satisfaction and dissatisfaction within the teaching profession, found only a low correlation between college assessments and the views of head teachers. They also found that, though the majority experienced a high degree of satisfaction, this too had little correlation with the college assessment.

Finlayson and Cohen (1967) compared the views of students and head teachers on the role of the teacher and found wide differences of opinion. They also found the students in their investigation becoming steadily less progressive and more authoritarian from first to final teaching practice, and put this down to the greater influence of head teachers in the last and longest practice. They also suggested that the discrepancy of views of tutors and head teachers, between which the student oscillates, is due to the fact that the tutor is now detached from the every day running of the school while the head teacher has responsibility for the children no matter how adverse conditions may be. J. H. Clarke (1968) got from over 1,000 sixth form boys and girls (in connection with choice of careers) their image of the teacher. Of 1,511 eighteen-year-olds only about 3·5 per cent of boys and 7 per cent of girls considered teaching as a career. The main objections were the low pay, the unruly classes and the monotonous work. Clarke expresses the hope that better learning situations will result in more children wanting to become teachers.

Since there is as yet no contrary evidence, we must assume that the rôle of the teacher is seen quite differently by educationists inside and outside the colleges. As there is abundant evidence that both parties in the disagreement are on the whole extremely conscientious and self-sacrificing in the profession they have chosen, this is not a matter on which professional people can be content merely to take sides. Only further research can show how both can reach greater understanding, thus sparing the student and young teacher unnecessary confusion and conflict about his or her role.

But there is an even greater influence on the child than the teacher's; that of the parents. Some people have investigated how parents see the role of the teacher and whether this agrees with the teachers' own views. Musgrove and Taylor (1965) constructed a questionnaire to find the views both of parents and teachers on moral training, instruction in subjects, social training, education for family life, social advancement (getting on in life), and education for citizenship. In all types of schools teachers saw their work as primarily intellectual and moral; moreover, all teachers saw parents as comparatively indifferent to moral objectives in the education of their children and primarily concerned with instruction on subjects and getting on in life. This picture of parents projected by teachers differs from the views of the parents themselves. The 237 parents rated educational priorities in substantially the same order as the teachers. It is interesting to note that teachers unjustly ascribe to parents an indifference to moral development, since we have already seen that moral development is the very area in which teachers are least well informed. One must suspect that the withdrawal of educationists from analysis of the concomitants of moral development may be due to projection of their own irrational withdrawal upon the parents, at an extremely elementary level of thinking.

Since parents appear to have the same educational priorities as teachers, some people have wondered what opportunities parents are given to take detailed interest in their children's education. Banfield, Bowyer and Wilkie (1966) investigated parents' knowledge of trends and organisation in education and came to the conclusion that parents are not given enough information particularly about the 'infant' stage of education. Here is another area where insufficient has been done to clarify the teacher's rôle, and it is a particularly serious indictment since the parents who have an even greater influence on their children than teachers, appear to have more or less the same educational objectives as teachers. In an article on the rôle of the teacher, Westwood (1967) reviews the many social and cultural influences which may also be at work here. He rightly says that much more research is needed before we can draw conclusions about the chain of relationships at work. Those who wish to pursue the matter further will find that Westwood's article has a valuable reference list.

It is right that the first step in scientific investigation of the teacher's work should be an analysis of the most suitable personality traits; and what we know is no more than a beginning. We should next analyse the ways in which life in college fosters in a student those traits which we begin to see are essential to good teaching. For example, decision making is an important element in the classroom. Lovell and White (1958) studied what is often almost the first important decision which students have to make after entering college: which subjects to select for study. They drew up a questionnaire and gave it to 102 male students to find out what influenced their decision. The students chose the subjects which they had enjoyed most or done best in at grammar school; and there was a significant correlation between these subjects which they enjoyed and the interests of their parents. The authors also found a close correlation between choice of science subjects and attitudes to arithmetic at junior school. What appears to be a free choice at a given moment is profoundly influenced by previous experience, and wise decisions are made by those who can sort out and weigh up the influences affecting their choice. Lovell and White suggest a number of lines for further research, such as junior school attitudes to arithmetic, particularly those of girls; and the relation between good motivation towards mathematics and science on the one hand and personal needs and temperamental qualities on the other.

Another important factor for the successful teacher is a liberal attitude. One of the major obstacles to accepting fresh ideas is that various mistaken beliefs have become entrenched. Warburton (1956) made a questionnaire consisting of popular beliefs, such as:

Most children are born bad.
All men are born with equal powers.
Red-headed people are likely to be temperamental.

He gave this to 143 graduates at the beginning and end of a one-year training at Manchester, and found that, despite a training which included psychology, a considerable number of superstitious beliefs were still held at the end of the course. The biggest improvement was shown in those areas which the students found most difficult at the beginning. Presumably in these areas they had not arrived at the course with preconceived mistaken ideas.

The actual processes of learning and teaching need far more study than we have yet given them. According to Jahoda and Thomas (1966) teaching, particularly at the university level, has for centuries been an unskilled occupation, in the sense that university staff are not taught, and sometimes do not learn, how to encourage learning in their pupils. These authors conducted action research with students in the learning situation. One of their objectives was a study of how to increase staff flexibility. Tutoring is highly skilled and students have to be encouraged to examine their own learning processes in order that they can increase the range and penetration of their individual learning skills.

We must not slip into the error of seeking a scapegoat for our ignorance about teaching and preparation for teaching, particularly not at the moment when we are beginning to face our ignorance. This fault in educational development runs through the whole educational system from the highest university administration to the most modest nursery school. In 1962 the British Psychological Society and the Association of Training Colleges and

Departments of Education produced a joint report on the teaching of educational psychology in training colleges. Only a third of the psychology lecturers had a degree in psychology. Reviewing the report Hollins (1963) said the picture it painted was an unfavourable one and he doubted if it was improving much.*

A year after the BPS and ATCDE report on educational psychology in colleges, the 1963 *Year Book of Education* took as its theme 'The education and training of teachers'. Here the distinguished contributors state that teachers, old and young, exhibit a paralysing conservatism, and they demand a research-minded profession. Wiseman (1964) immediately pointed out that, in the whole 600 pages of this joint publication by the Teachers' College, Columbia University, New York and the Institute of Education, London University, there was no reference whatsoever to research on teacher training. Four years later *Educational Research* (1967) published a symposium on the rôle and function of educational research by distinguished authorities who claim that the situation has much improved during the mid-'sixties and the opportunity of this quickened thinking must not be lost. There seems to be some justification for their optimism, judging by the number of recent articles on teacher training. Amongst those not already mentioned are: K. M. Evans (1959a, b, 1961a, b, 1966), Flook (1959), J. D. Williams (1960, 1965), Collier (1960), E. A. Allen (1963), Shipman (1967), Johnson (1966), Baird (1968), Clarke (1968), and Penfold and Medlon (1969). Johnson, who planned an extensive investigation of attitudes to educational research, was restricted to using only a London area because of opposition by local education authorities elsewhere; and even in the London area individual sessions with each head teacher were necessary and promises had to be made before head teachers would agree, that answering would not take long, that the answers would be anonymous, and that nothing would be published that the teachers would not like. This uninformed attitude to research by those who have to grant permission for it to be conducted, draws attention to the need for high-level overall planning which is too well sponsored to be obstructed. Burroughs (1962) has written an article on the particular responsibility of institutes of education to carry out research internally, with other institutes, and with the cooperation of lecturers and teachers outside their institutes.

So the quickened thinking about educational research still seems to be mainly in the colleges of education. We must take steps to see that the first-hand knowledge of developing children possessed by progressive teachers is not withheld from research-workers through lack of understanding by

* This may well be why Fleming (p. 3), found the schools at least 30 years behind research.

officials. Nursery school teachers, who are the first educational experts to induct children into society, daily handle raw aggression and lead it gently towards social living. They have to widen their own horizons, so that, for instance, they are familiar with such modern trends in thinking on mankind's biological aggression as are expressed by Lorenz (1966), Ardrey (1967) and Desmond Morris (1967). Teachers who are, for instance, interested in very gifted children can show how sufficient intellectual stimulus, even when possible within a normal classroom, is not enough. These children need creative expression and have to be coaxed back from their isolation to social living, if they are to be wise leading men and women of the future. Those teachers who are particularly interested in behavioural problems of children find that knowledge of child guidance work acts as a microscope enlarging the nature of behavioural problems which we all undergo. Since these teachers are frequently the ones to help children through temporary difficulties, they spare our over-burdened child guidance clinics many borderline children. The experience of the practising teacher as a source of a wide variety of research material will more easily link up with educational research as colleges raise their standards of both educational psychology and the smattering of educational research which students must experience if they are to cooperate later with high grade research.

There are some community issues which urgently need the support of teachers, no matter what the age or social background of the children they teach. The training of a teacher enables him to grasp, in a way the layman cannot, the principles of development involved. High amongst these issues are two which are particularly germane to this book: (a) the cultural value to the community as a whole of nursery schools for all who think their children would benefit from them; and (b) a breakthrough which schools can make, of the downward spiral of poverty and cultural deprivation which affects a significant section of the population. Only when teachers see their rôle in relation to the whole community for which they are preparing children, does their profession become truly distinguished.

Bibliography

ACE, P. W. (1956) 'A remedial teaching scheme. Introducing a new reading method', *Brit. J. Ed. Psychol.* 26-3.

ADAMS, L. D. (1953) *A Background to Primary School Mathematics*, London: Oxford Univ. Press.

ADAMS, R. S. (1962) 'A further approach to attitude scaling', *Brit. J. Ed. Psychol.* 32-3.

ADCOCK, C. J. (1965) 'A comparison of the concepts of Cattell and Eysenck', *Brit. J. Ed. Psychol.* 35-1.

ADLER, I. (1960) *The Giant Colour Book of Mathematics. Exploring the World of Number* (1st edn 1958), London: Paul Hamlyn.

AINSWORTH, M. D. AND AINSWORTH, L. H. (1958) *Measuring Security in Personal Adjustment*, London: Oxford Univ. Press.

ALLEN, E. A. (1960) 'Attitudes of children and adolescents in school', *Ed. Res.* 3-1.

ALLEN, E. A. (1961) 'Attitudes to school and teachers in a secondary modern school', *Brit. J. Ed. Psychol.* 31-1.

ALLEN, E. A. (1963) 'Professional training of teachers: a review of research', *Ed. Res.* 5-3.

ALLEN, M. (1962) 'A comparison between group and individual selection procedures in a training college', *Brit. J. Ed. Psychol.* 32-3.

ALLPORT, G. W. (1937) *Personality. A Psychological Interpretation*, New York: Holt.

AMES, L. B. AND LEARNED, J. (1946) 'Imaginary companions and related phenomena', *J. Gen. Psychol.* 69.

ANDRY, R. G. (1960) *Delinquency and Parental Pathology*, London: Methuen.

ARDREY, R. (1967) *The Territorial Imperative*, London: Collins.

ARMSTRONG, H. G. (1965) 'Special educational treatment in ordinary schools', *Brit. J. Ed. Psychol.* 35-2.

ARMSTRONG, H. G. (1966) 'A comparison of the performance of summer and autumn-born children at eleven and sixteen', *Brit. J. Ed. Psychol.* 36-1.

ARMSTRONG, H. G. (1967) 'Wastage of ability amongst the intellectually gifted', *Brit. J. Ed. Psychol.* 36-2.

ARGYLE, M. (1963) 'Introjection: a form of social learning', *Brit. J. Psychol.* 55-4.

ASTINGTON, E. (1960) 'Personality assessment and academic performance in a boys' grammar school', *Brit. J. Ed. Psychol.* 30-3.

BAIN, A. (1855) *The Senses and the Intellect*, London: Parker.

BAIRD, C. L. (1968) 'The role of the teacher of six- and seven-year-old children', *Brit. J. Ed. Psychol.* 38-3.

BANFIELD, J., BOWYER, C. AND WILKIE, E. (1966) 'Parents and education', *Ed. Res.* 9-1.

BANKS, C. (1953) 'Research in child guidance', *Brit. J. Ed. Psychol.* 23-1.

BANKS, C. AND SINHA, U. (1951) 'An item-analysis of the progressive matrices test', *Brit. J. Stat. Psychol.* 4-2.

BANNISTER, D. AND PRESLY, A. S. (1967) 'Test selection of overseas nursing candidates', *Bull. Brit. Psychol. Soc.* 20-68.

BARAHENI, M. N. (1962) 'An inquiry into attitudinal concomitants of success and failure at school', *Ed. Res.* 5-1.

BARRINGTON, H. (1966) 'The teaching of elementary science by television and other methods', *Brit. J. Ed. Psychol.* 36-1.

BARTLET, D. AND SHAPIRO, M. B. (1956) 'Investigation and treatment of a reading disability in a dull child with severe psychiatric disturbance', *Brit. J. Ed. Psychol.* 26-3.

BARTLETT, F. C. (1916) 'An experimental study of some problems of perceiving and imaging', *Brit. J. Psychol.* 8.

BATE, S. M. (1961) 'The teaching of English in secondary schools', *Ed. Res.* 3-2.

Beacon Readers (1933) London: Ginn.

BEETON, I. (1861) *The Book of Household Management*, London: S. O. Beeton.

BENE, E. (1957) 'The objective use of a projective technique, illustrated by a study of the differences in attitude between pupils of grammar schools and of secondary modern schools', *Brit. J. Ed. Psychol.* 27-2.

BENE, E. (1958) 'Suppression of hetero-sexual interests and of aggression by middle class and working class grammar school boys: a comparative study', *Brit. J. Ed. Psychol.* 28-3.

BERLYNE, D. E. (1957) 'Recent developments in Piaget's work', *Brit. J. Ed. Psychol.* 27-1.

BERLYNE, D. E. (1958) Review of Eysenck (1957) *Brit. J. Psychol.* 49-2.

BERNSTEIN, B. (1958) 'Some sociological determinants of perception', *Brit. J. Sociol.* 9.

BERNSTEIN, B. (1961) 'Social structure, language and learning', *Ed. Res.* 3-3.

BIESHEUVEL, S. (1965) 'Personnel selection', *An. Rev. Psychol.* 16.

BIGGS, J. B. (1958) 'The teaching of arithmetic: a selected and annotated bibliography', *Ed. Res.* 1-1.

BIGGS, J. B. (1959) 'The teaching of mathematics: I. Development of number concepts in young children; II. Attitudes to arithmetic—number anxiety', *Ed. Res.* 1-3.

BIGGS, J. B. (1961) 'Distribution of methods of teaching arithmetic in primary schools in England and Wales', *Ed. Res.* 3-2.

BINET, A. (1903) L'Étude Expérimental de l'Intellect, Paris: Schleicher.

BLANDFORD, J. S. (1958) 'Standardised tests in junior schools with special reference to the effects of streaming on the consistency of results', *Brit. J. Ed. Psychol.* 28-2.

BOOKBINDER, G. E. (1967) 'The preponderance of summer-born children in E.S.N. classes. Which is responsible: age or length of infant schooling?' *Ed. Res.* 9-3.

BORING, E. G., LANGFELD, H. S. AND WELD, H. P. (1939) *Introduction to Psychology*, New York: Wiley.

BOWLBY, J. (1953) *Child Care and the Growth of Love*, Harmondsworth: Penguin.

BOWYER, R. (1961) 'Individual differences in stress at the eleven-plus examination', *Brit. J. Ed. Psychol.* 31-3.

BRADBURN, E. (1967) 'Children's moral knowledge', *Ed. Res.* 9-3.

BREARLEY, M. AND HITCHFIELD, E. (1966) *A Teacher's Guide to Reading Piaget*, London: Routledge and Kegan Paul.

BRIDGES, S. A. (1969) *Gifted Children and the Brentwood Experiment*, London: Pitman.

BRITISH PSYCHOLOGICAL SOCIETY *and* ASSOCIATION OF TRAINING COLLEGES AND DEPARTMENTS OF EDUCATION (1963) *Teaching Educational Psychology in Training Colleges*, London: BPS or ATCDE.

BROOKS, F. D. (1937) *Child Psychology*, New York: Houghton Mifflin.

BROWN, J. A. C. (1963) *Techniques of Persuasion from Propaganda to Brainwashing*, Harmondsworth: Penguin Books.

BROWN, N. O. (1959) *Life Against Death: the psychoanalytical meaning of history*, London: Routledge & Kegan Paul.

BROWN, R. W. AND LENNEBERG, E. H. (1954) 'A study in language and cognition', *J. Abnormal Soc. Psychol.* 49.

BROWN, W. (1881–1952) Psychologist.

BRUCE, D. J. (1964) 'The analysis of word sounds by young children', *Brit. J. Ed. Psychol.* 34-2.

BURBURY, W. M., BALINT, E. M., AND YAPP, B. J. (1945) *An Introduction to Child Guidance*, London: Macmillan.

BUROS, O. K., ed. (1959) *Fifth Mental Measurements Yearbook.* New Jersey: Gryphon Press.

BURROUGHS, G. E. R. (1957) *A Study of the Vocabulary of Young Children*, Edinburgh: Oliver & Boyd.

BURROUGHS, G. E. R. (1958) 'A study of the interview in the selection of students for teacher training', *Brit. J. Ed. Psychol.* 28-1.

BURROUGHS, G. E. R. (1962) 'Cooperative research in institutes of education', *Brit. J. Ed. Psychol.* 32-2.

BURT, C. L. (1909) 'The experimental study of general intelligence', *Brit. J. Psych.* 3.

BURT, C. L. (1917) *The Distribution and Relations of Educational Ability*, London County Council Report.

BURT, C. L. (1921) *Mental and Scholastic Tests*, London: Staples.

BURT, C. L. (1925) *The Young Delinquent*, Univ. London Press.

BURT, C. L. (1935) *The Subnormal Mind*, London: Oxford Univ. Press.

BURT, C. L. (1937) *The Backward Child*, London: Univ. London Press.

BURT, C. L. (1949) 'The structure of the mind. A review of the results of factor analysis', *Brit. J. Ed. Psychol.* 19-2.

BURT, C. L. (1953) 'Symposium on psychologists and psychiatrists in the child guidance service: conclusion', *Brit. J. Ed. Psychol.* 23-1.

BURT, C. L. (1954) *The Causes and Treatment of Backwardness*, London: Univ. London Press.

BURT, C. L. (1955) 'The evidence for the concept of intelligence', *Brit. J. Ed. Psychol.* 25-3.

BURT, C. L. (1958) 'Definition and scientific method in psychology', *Brit. J. Stat. Psychol.* 11-1.

BURT, C. L. (1958) 'A note on the theory of intelligence', *Brit. J. Ed. Psychol.* 28-3.

BURT, C. L. (1959) 'Class differences in general intelligence III', *Brit. J. Stat. Psychol.* 12-1.

BURT, C. L. (1961a) 'Intelligence and social mobility', *Brit. J. Stat. Psychol.* 14-1.

BURT, C. L. (1961b) 'The gifted child', *Brit. J. Stat. Psychol.* 14-2.

BURT, C. L. (1961c) 'The structure of the mind', *Brit. J. Stat. Psychol.* 14-2.

BURT, C. L. (1962a) 'Francis Galton and his contribution to psychology', *Brit. J. Stat. Psychol.* 15-1.

BURT, C. L. (1962b). Review of Lovell (1961) *Brit. J. Stat. Psychol.* 15-1.

BURT, C. L. (1962c) 'The sense datum theory', *Brit. J. Stat. Psychol.* 15-2.

BURT, C. L. (1962d) Review of Getzels and Jackson (1962) *Brit. J. Ed. Psychol.* 32-3.

BURT, C. L. (1963) 'Is intelligence distributed normally ?' *Brit. J. Stat. Psychol.* 16-2.

BURT, C. L. (1965) 'Factorial studies of personality and their bearing on the work of the teacher', *Brit. J. Ed. Psychol.* 35-3.

BURT, C. L. (1966) 'The genetic determination of differences in intelligence: a study of monozygotic twins reared together and apart', *Brit. J. Psychol.* 57-1 and 2.

BURT, C. L. AND HOWARD, M. (1956) 'The multifactorial theory of inheritance and its application to intelligence, *Brit. J. Stat. Psychol.* 11-2.

BURT, C. L. AND ISAACS, S. *Infant and Nursery Schools*, London: H.M.S.O.

BURT, C. L. AND MOORE, R. C. (1911) 'Experimental tests of higher mental processes', *J. Exp. Psychol.* 1.

BURT, C. L. AND MOORE, R. C. (1915) 'The general and specific factors underlying the primary emotions', *Brit. Ass. Ann. Rep.* No. 84.

BURT, C. L. AND WILLIAMS, E. L. (1962) 'The influence of motivation on the results of intelligence tests', *Brit. J. Stat. Psychol.* 15-2.

BUTCHER, H. J., AINSWORTH, M. AND NESBITT, J. E. (1963) 'Personality factors and school achievement: a comparison of British and American children', *Brit. J. Ed. Psychol.* 33-3.

BUTCHER, H. J. AND PONT, H. B. (1968) 'Opinions about careers among Scottish secondary school children of high ability', *Brit. J. Ed. Psychol.* 38-3.

CANNON, W. B. (1934) 'Hunger & thirst' *Hbt. gen. exp. psychol.*, Worcester, Mass: Clark Univ.

CARR-SAUNDERS, A. M. AND JONES, D. C. (1937) *Social Structure in England and Wales*, London: Oxford Univ. Press.

CARTHY, J. D. AND EBLING, F. J. (1965) *The Natural History of Aggression*, London: Academic Press.

CASE, D. AND COLLINSON, J. M. (1962) 'The development of formal thinking in verbal comprehension', *Brit. J. Ed. Psychol.* 32-2.

CASHDAN, A. (1962) 'The intellectual powers of subnormal children', *Ed. Res.* 4-2.

CASHDAN, A. AND JEFFREE, D. M. (1966) 'The influence of the home background on the development of severely subnormal children', *Brit. J. Med. Psychol.* 39-4.

CASHDAN, A. AND PUMPHREY, P. D. (1969) 'Some effects of the remedial teaching of reading', *Ed. Res.* 11-2.

CASS, J. E. (1966) *The Under Fives in the Welfare State*, London: Nursery Sch. Assn.

CATTELL, R. B. (1946) *Description and Measurement of Personality*, London: Harrap.

CATTELL, R. B. (1964) 'Cattell on Eysenck', *Occup. Psychol.*

CATTELL, R. B. AND COAN, R. W. (1958) 'Personality dimensions in the questionnaire response of six- and seven-year-olds', *Brit. J. Ed. Psychol.* 28-3.

CATTELL, R. B. AND GRUNE, W. (1954) 'Primary personality factors in the questionnaire medium for children 11 to 14 years old', *Ed. Psychol. Meas.* 14.

CHADWICK, J. A. (1967) 'Some effects of increasing the teachers' knowledge of their pupils' self picture', *Brit. J. Ed. Psychol.* 37-1.

CHAZAN, M. (1959) 'Maladjusted children in grammar schools', *Brit. J. Ed. Psychol.* 29-3.

CHAZAN M. (1962) 'School phobia', *Brit. J. Ed. Psychol.* 32-3.

CHAZAN, M. (1963) 'Maladjusted pupils: trends in post-war theory and practice', *Ed. Res.* 6-1.

CHAZAN, M. (1964) 'The incidence and nature of maladjustment among children in schools for the educationally subnormal', *Brit. J. Ed. Psychol.* 34-3.

CHAZAN, M. (1965) 'Factors associated with maladjustment in educationally subnormal children', *Brit. J. Ed. Psychol.* 35-3.

CHILD, D. (1964) 'The relationship between introversion–extraversion, neuroticism and performance in school examinations', *Brit. J. Ed. Psychol.* 34-2.

CHOWN, S. M. (1959) 'Personality factors in the formation of occupational choice', *Brit. J. Ed. Psychol.* 29-1.

CHRISTIE, T. AND KLINE, P. (1966) 'The effect of studying classics to "A" level on the writing of English', *Ed. Res.* 9-1.

CHUKOVSKY, K. (1963) *From Two to Five.* Trans. Morton, Berkeley: Univ. of California Press.

CLARK, H. (1956) 'The effect of a candidate's age upon teachers' estimates and upon his chances of gaining a grammar school place', *Brit. J. Ed. Psychol.* 56-3.

CLARKE, A. D. B., CLARKE, A. M. AND REIMAN, S. (1958) 'Cognitive and social changes in the feeble-minded—3 further studies', *Brit. J. Psychol.* 49-2.

CLARKE, J. H. (1968) 'The image of the teacher', *Brit. J. Ed. Psychol.* 38-3.

CLAY, M. M. (1969) 'Reading errors and self-correction behaviour', *Brit. J. Ed. Psych.* 39-1.

COHEN, L. (1968) 'College and the training of teachers', *Ed. Res.* 11-1.

COLLIER, K. G. (1960) 'The teaching of psychology in training colleges', *Brit. J. Ed. Psychol.* 30-2.

COLLINS, J. E. (1964) Review of J. Morris (1963), *Brit. J. Ed. Psychol.* 34-1.

COLLINS, M. (1959) 'A follow-up study of some former graduate student teachers', *Brit. J. Ed. Psychol.* 29-3.

COLLINS, M. (1964) 'Untrained and trained graduate teachers: a comparison of their experiences during the probationary year', *Brit. J. Ed. Psychol.* 34-1.

CONEL, J. L. (1939–59) *The Postnatal Development of the Human Cerebral Cortex*, Cambridge, Mass: Harvard Univ. Press.

CONWAY, J. (1958) 'The inheritance of intelligence and its social implications, *Brit. J. Stats. Psychol.* 11-2.

CONWAY, J. (1959) 'Class differences in intelligence II', *Brit. J. Stat. Psychol.* 12-1.

COOPER, M. G. (1966) 'School refusal: an inquiry into the part played by school and home', *Ed. Res.* 8-3.

COX, C. (1926) *The Early Mental Traits of Three Hundred Geniuses*, Stanford Univ. Press.

CRANE, A. R. (1958) 'Pre-adolescent gangs and the moral development of children', *Brit. J. Ed. Psychol.* 28-3.

CRESSWELL, D'A. (1953) *Margaret McMillan*, London: Hutchinson.

CRUIKSHANK, W. M. ed. (1956) *Psychology of Exceptional Youth*, London: Staples.

CURR, W. (1963) 'The significance and implications of programmed learning', *Ed. Res.* 5-3.

CURR, W. AND GOURLAY, N. (1953) 'An experimental evaluation of remedial education', *Brit. J. Ed. Psychol.* 23-1.

CURR, W. AND GOURLAY, N. (1960) 'The effect of practice on performance in scholastic tests. *Brit. J. Ed. Psychol.* 30-2.

DANIELS, J. C. (1961) 'A comparison of streamed and unstreamed schools', *Brit. J. Ed. Psychol.* 31-2.

DARWIN, C. (1871) *The Descent of Man, and Selection in Relation to Sex*, London: Murray.

DAVEY, A. G. (1969) 'Leadership in relation to group achievement', *Ed. Res.* 11-3.

DAVIDSON, M. (1952) 'The relation between psychologists and psychiatrists in the service of maladjusted adults and children', *Brit. J. Ed. Psychol.* 22-1.

DAVIDSON, M. A., MCINNES, R. G. AND PARNELL, R. W. (1957) 'The distribution of personality traits in seven-year-old children: a combined psychological, psychiatric and somatotype study', *Brit. J. Ed. Psychol.* 27-1.

DAVIS, E. A. (1937) *The Development of Linguistic Skills in Twins, Singletons with Siblings, and Only Children from Age Five to Ten Years.* Inst. of Child Welfare Monograph No. 14, Univ. Minnesota Press.

DAWES, P. P. (1967) 'What will the school counsellor do ?', *Ed. Res.* 9-2.

DEACON, W. J. (1965) 'A survey of delinquency in Somerset 1958-60', *Ed. Res.* 7-3.

DEESE, J. (1958) *The Psychology of Learning*, New York: McGraw-Hill.

DE HAAN, R. F. AND HAVIGHURST, R. J. (1957) *Educating Gifted Children*, Univ. Chicago Press.

DELL, G. A. (1963) 'Social factors and school influence in juvenile delinquency. An analysis of police cases in the Belfast Juvenile Court, July '61–June '62', *Brit. J. Ed. Psychol.* 33-3.

DESCŒUDRES, A. (1924) 'La mesure du langage de l'enfant', *J. de Psychol.* 21.

DIACK, H. (1960) *Reading and the Psychology of Perception*, Nottingham: Skinner.

DIENES, Z. P. (1959) 'The growth of mathematical concepts in children through experience', *Ed. Res.* 2-1.

DIRINGER, D. (1962) *Writing*, London: Thames and Hudson.

DIXON, B. (1968) 'The way some scientists talk', *New Society*, 11 April 1968.

DOUGLAS, J. W. B. AND ROSS, J. M. (1964) 'The later educational progress and emotional adjustment of children who went to nursery schools or classes', *Ed. Res.* 7-1.

DOWNING, J. A. (1962) 'The relationship between reading attainment and the inconsistency of English spelling at the infant school age', *Brit. J. Ed. Psychol.* 32-2.

DOWNING, J. A. (1963) 'Is a "mental age" of six essential for "reading" readiness?,' *Ed. Res.* 4-1.

DOWNING, J. A. (1969) 'The perception of linguistic structure in learning to read', *Brit. J. Ed. Psych.* 39-3.

DOWNING, J. A. AND GARDNER, K. (1962) 'New experimental evidence on the role of the unsystematic spelling of English in reading failure', *Ed. Res.* 5-1.

DOWNING, J. A. AND JONES, B. (1966) 'Some problems of evaluating i.t.a. A second experiment', *Ed. Res.* 8-2.

DOWNING, J. A. AND LATHAM, W. (1969) 'Research Note: A follow-up study of children in the first i.t.a. experiment', *Brit. J. Ed. Psych.* 39-3.

DREVER, J. (1952) *A Dictionary of Psychology*, Harmondsworth: Penguin Books.

DUNHAM, J. (1960) 'The effects of remedial education on young children's reading ability', *Brit. J. Ed. Psychol.* 30-2.

EDWARDS, J. B. (1965) 'Some studies of the moral development of children', *Ed. Res.* 7-3.

EIFERMANN, R. R. AND ETZION, D. (1964) 'Awareness of reversibility; its effect on performance of converse arithmetical operations', *Brit. J. Ed. Psychol.* 34-2.

ELLIS, H. (1904) *A Study of British Genius*, London: Hurst & Blackett.

ELTON, C. F. (1965) 'The effect of logic instruction on the Valentine Reasoning Test', *Brit. J. Ed. Psychol.* 35-3.

EMMETT, W. G. (1954) 'Secondary modern and grammar school performance predicted by tests given in primary schools', *Brit. J. Ed. Psychol.* 24-2.

ENGLISH, H. B. AND ENGLISH, A. C. (1958) *A Comprehensive Dictionary of Psychological and Psychoanalytic Terms*, London: Longmans.

EVANS, E. G. S. (1964) 'Reasoning ability and personality differences among student-teachers', *Brit. J. Ed. Psychol.* 34-3.

EVANS, K. M. (1959a) 'Research on teaching ability', *Ed. Res.* 1-3.

EVANS, K. M. (1959b) 'The teacher–pupil relationship', *Ed. Res.* 2-1.

EVANS, K. M. (1961) 'An annotated bibliography of British research on teaching and teaching ability', *Ed. Res.* 4-1.

EVANS, K. M. (1966a) 'The Minnesota teacher attitude inventory', *Ed. Res.* 8-2.

EVANS, K. M. (1966b) 'Group methods', *Ed. Res.* 9-1.

EVANS, K. M. (1967) 'Teacher training courses and students' personal qualities', *Ed. Res.* 10-1.

EYSENCK, H. J. (1947) *Dimensions of Personality*, London: Kegan Paul.

EYSENCK, H. J. (1953) *The Structure of Human Personality*, London: Methuen.

EYSENCK, H. J. (1957) *The Dynamics of Anxiety and Hysteria: an experimental application of modern learning theory to psychiatry*, London: Routledge and Kegan Paul.

EYSENCK, H. J. (1959) *The Maudsley Personality Inventory*, Univ. London Press.

EYSENCK, H. J. (1960) 'The contribution of learning theory', *Brit. J. Ed. Psychol.* 30-1.

EYSENCK, H. J. (1961) 'Eysenck on Cattell', *Occup. Psychol.*

EYSENCK, H. J. AND EYSENCK, S. B. J. (1964) *The Eysenck Personality Inventory*, Univ. London Press.

EYSENCK, H. J. AND WHITE, P. O. (1964) 'Personality and the measurement of intelligence', *Brit. J. Ed. Psychol.* 34-2.

EYSENCK, S. B. G. (1965) *The Junior Eysenck Personality Inventory*, Univ. London Press.

EYSENCK, S. B. G. (1965) 'A new scale for personality measurements in children', *Brit. J. Ed. Psychol.* 35-3.

EYSENCK, S. B. G., SYED, I. A. AND EYSENCK, H. J. (1966) 'Desirability response set in children', *Brit. J. Ed. Psychol.* 36-1.

FARRELL, M. J. AND GILBERT, N. (1960) 'A type of bias in marking examination scripts', *Brit. J. Ed. Psychol.* 30-1.

FERRON, O. M. (1966) 'The effects of early environmental stimulation among Freetown creoles—a comparative study', *Ed. Res.* 8-3.

FERRON, O. M. (1967) 'The linguistic factor in the test intelligence of West African children', *Ed. Res.* 9-2.

FINLAYSON, D. S. AND COHEN, L. (1967) 'The teacher's rôle: a comparative study of the conceptions of colleges of education students and head teachers', *Brit. J. Ed. Psychol.* 37-1.

FISHER, G. H. (1965) 'Visual and tactile–kinaesthetic shape perception', *Brit. J. Ed. Psychol.* 35-1.

FLEMING, C. M. (1946) *Research and the Basic Curriculum*, London: Univ. London Press.

FLOOK, A. J. M. (1959) 'Note on the use of new-type tests for improving the quality of discussion in discussion groups', *Brit. J. Ed. Psychol.* 29-3.

FLOUD, J. E., HALSEY, A. H. AND MARTIN, F. M. (1956) *Social Class and Educational Opportunity*, London: Heinemann.

FLUGEL, J. C. (1933) *A Hundred Years of Psychology*, London: Duckworth.

FOSS, B. M. (1969) *British Psychological Society Supplement*, London: B.P.S.

FOSS, B. M. ed. (1963) *Determinants of Infant Behaviour, II*, London: Methuen.

FRANCE, N. (1964) 'The use of group tests of ability and attainment: a follow-up study from primary to secondary school', *Brit. J. Ed. Psychol.* 34-1.

FRANCE, N. AND WISEMAN, S. (1966) 'An educational guidance programme for the primary school', *Brit. J. Ed. Psychol.* 36-2.

FREUD, S. (1904) *The Psycho-pathology of Everyday Life*, Eng. Trans., London: Unwin 1920.

FREUD, S. (1919) *Totem and Taboo*, London: Kegan Paul.

FREUD, S. (1920) *General Introduction to Psychoanalysis*, New York: Liveright.

FREYBERG, P. S. (1966) 'The efficacy of the coloured progressive matrices as a group test with young children', *Brit. J. Ed. Psychol.* 36-2.

FREYMAN, R. (1965) 'Further evidence on the effect of date of birth on subsequent school performance', *Ed. Res.* 8-1.

FRIEDMANN, S. (1958) 'A report on progress in an L.E.A. remedial reading class', *Brit. J. Ed. Psychol.* 28-3.

FULLER, J. A. (1967) 'School counselling: a first inquiry', *Ed. Res.* 9-2.

FULLER, J. A. AND JUNIPER, D. F. (1967) 'Guidance, counselling and school social work', *Ed. Res.* 9-2.

FURNEAUX, W. D. (1961) *The Chosen Few. An examination of some aspects of university selection in Britain*, London: Oxford Univ. Press.

FURNEAUX, W. D. AND GIBSON, H. B. (1961) 'A children's personality inventory designed to measure neuroticism and extraversion', *Brit. J. Ed. Psychol.* 31-2.

GABRIEL, J. (1964) *Children Growing Up. The Development of Children's Personalities*, Univ. London Press.

GALTON, F. (1869) *Hereditary Genius*, London: Macmillan.

GALTON, F. (1875) 'The history of twins as a criterion for the relative powers of nature and nurture', *J. Roy. Anthrop. Inst.* 5.

GARDNER, D. E. M. (1950) *Long-term Results of Infant School Methods*, London: Methuen.

GARDNER, D. E. M. (1942) *Testing Results in the Infant School*, London: Methuen.

GARDNER, D. E. M. (1956) *The Education of Young Children*, London: Methuen.

GARDNER, D. E. M. (1966) *Experiment and Tradition in Primary Schools*, London: Methuen.

GARDNER, D. E. M. AND CASS, J. E. (1965) *The Rôle of the Teacher in the Infant and Nursery School*, London: Pergamon Press.

GARRETT, H. E. (1941) *Statistics in Psychology and Education*, 2nd edn, London: Longmans.

GATES, A. I., JERSILD, A. T., MCCONNELL, T. R. AND CHALLMAN, R. C. (1942) *Educational Psychology*, New York, Macmillan.

GEDIKE (1791) 'Children's book for first practice in reading without the ABC or spelling', From: Tuer (1896).

GEDO, J. E. (1966) 'The psychotherapy of developmental arrest', *B. J. Med. Psychol.* 39-1.

GESELL, A. AND ILG, F. L. (1943) *Infant and Child in the Culture of Today*, London: Harper.

GESELL, A. AND THOMPSON, H. (1929) 'Learning and growth in identical infant twins: an experimental study by the method of co-twin control', *Genet. Psychol. Monog.* 6-1.

GETZELS, J. W. AND JACKSON, P. W. (1962) *Creativity and Intelligence*, London: Wiley.

GIBBENS, T. C. N. (1958) 'The Porteus Maze Test and delinquency', *Brit. J. Ed. Psychol.* 58-3.

GIBSON, H. B. (1964) 'The spiral maze. A psychomotor test with implications for the study of delinquency', *Brit. J. Ed. Psychol.* 34-2.

GLASS, D. V. ed. (1954) *Social Mobility in Britain*, London: Routledge & Kegan Paul.

GODDARD, N. L. (1958) *Reading in the Modern Infants' School*, Univ. London Press.

GOERTZEL, V. AND GOERTZEL, M. G. (1965) *Cradles of Eminence*, London: Constable.

GOLDMAN, R. J. (1964a) 'The Minnesota tests of creative thinking', *Ed. Res.* 7-2.

GOLDMAN, R. J. (1964b) *Religious Thinking from Childhood to Adolescence*, London: Routledge & Kegan Paul.

GOLDMAN, R. J. (1964) 'Researches in religious thinking', *Ed. Res.* 6-2.

GOLDMAN, R. J. (1965) 'The application of Piaget's scheme of operational thinking to religious story data by means of the Guttman scalogram', *Brit. J. Ed. Psychol.* 35-2.

GOLDMAN, R. J. AND TAYLOR, M. F. (1966) 'Coloured immigrant children: a survey of research, studies and literature on their educational problems and potential in Britain', *Ed. Res.* 8-3.

GOODACRE, E. J. (1967) *Reading in Infant Classes*, Slough: National Foundation for Educational Research.

GOODACRE, E. J. (1969) 'Published Reading Schemes', *Ed. Res.* 12-1.

GOODENOUGH, F. L. (1926) *Measurement of Intelligence by Drawings*, London: Harrap.

GOODENOUGH, F. L. (1949) *Mental Testing*, New York: Rinehart.

GORER, J. (1955) *Exploring English Character*, New York: Cresse Press.

GOTTSCHALDT, K. (1958) *Mental Health in Home and School*, London: World Fed. Men. Health.

GREENBERG, H. R. (1966) 'Notes on the parental exclusion phenomenon in twins,' *Brit. J. Med. Psychol.* 39-1.

GREGORY, R. L. (1966) *Eye and Brain*, London: Weidenfeld & Nicolson.

GRIFFITHS, R. (1935) *A Study of Imagination in Early Childhood and its Function in Mental Development*, London: Kegan Paul.

GRIFFITHS, R. (1954) *The Ability of Babies*, Univ. London Press.

GRIFFITHS, S. (1959) 'An examination of the causes of deterioration in academic performance among pupils in a grammar school', *Brit. J. Ed. Psychol.* 29-2.

GUILFORD, J. P. (1936) *Psychometric Methods*, New York: McGraw-Hill.

HALL, M. (1963) 'A study of the attitudes of adolescent girls to their own physical, intellectual, emotional and social development', *Ed. Res.* 6-1.

HALLWORTH, H. J. (1961) 'Anxiety in secondary modern and grammar school children', *Brit. J. Ed. Psychol.* 31-3.

HALLWORTH, H. J. (1964) 'Personality ratings of adolescents: a study in a comprehensive school', *Brit. J. Ed. Psychol.* 34-2.

HALMOS, P., ed. (1959) *Paper on the Teaching of Personality Development*, The Sociological Review. Monog. No. 2. Keele: Univ. Col. of N. Staffs.

HALSEY, A. H. (1959) 'Class differences in intelligence, I', *Brit. J. Stat. Psychol.* 12-1.

HARGREAVES, H. L. (1927) 'The faculty of imagination', *Brit. J. Psychol. Monog.* 10.

HARRIS, J. G. (1966) 'Examinations in religious education—statistics and inferences', *Ed. Res.* 8-2.

HARTLEY, J. (1965) 'Linear and skip-branching programmes: a comparative study', *Ed. Res.* 35-3.

HAVIGHURST, R. J., ROBINSON, M. Z. AND DORR, M. (1946) 'The development of the ideal self in childhood and adolescence', *J. Ed. Res.* 40-4.

HAYAKAWA, S. I. (1966) 'On communication with children', ETC: *A Review of General Semantics.* 23-2.

HEARNSHAW, L. S. (1964) *A Short History of British Psychology.* 1840–1940. London: Methuen.

HEBB, D. O. (1958) *A Textbook of Psychology*, Philadelphia, Pa.: Saunders.

HEBRON, M. E. (1962) 'A factorial study of learning a new number system and its relation to attainment, intelligence and temperament', *Brit. J. Ed. Psychol.* 32-1.

HEIM, A. W. (1947) 'An attempt to test high grade intelligence', *Brit. J. Psychol.* 37-2.

HEIM, A. W. AND WATTS, K. P. (1957) 'An experiment on practice, coaching and discussion of errors in mental testing', *Brit. J. Ed. Psychol.* 27-3.

HEMMING, J. (1957) 'Some aspects of moral development in a changing society', *Brit. J. Ed. Psychol.* 27-2.

HENLE, M. AND HUBBLE, M. B. (1938) 'Egocentricity in adult conversation', *J. Soc. Psychol.* 9.

HEWITT, E. A. (1960) 'The performance in English Language at 'O' level of a sample of university students', *Brit. J. Ed. Psychol.* 30-1.

HILDRETH, G. H. (1966) *Introduction to the Gifted*, New York: McGraw-Hill.

HILGARD, E. R. (1953) *Introduction to Psychology*, London: Methuen.

HILLIARD, F. H. (1959) 'The influence of religious education upon the development of children's moral ideas', *Brit. J. Ed. Psychol.* 29-1.

HILLMAN, H. H. AND SNOWDON, R. L. (1960) 'Part-time classes for young backward readers', *Brit. J. Ed. Psychol.* 30-2.

HITCHMAN, P. J. (1964) 'The testing of spoken English: a review of research', *Ed. Res.* 7-1.

HITCHMAN, P. J. (1966) 'The testing of spoken English in schools and colleges in the United Kingdom', *Ed. Res.* 8-3.

HOLLAND, J. G. AND SKINNER, B. F. (1961) *The Analysis of Behaviour: a programme for self-instruction*, New York: McGraw-Hill.

HOLLINGWORTH, L. H. (1942) *Children above 180 IQ*, New York: World Books.

HOLLINS, T. H. B. (1963) 'Critical comment: teaching educational psychology in training colleges', *Brit. J. Ed. Psychol.* 33-2.

HOPKINS, W. S. (1960) 'Review of Diack' (1960), *Brit. J. Stat. Psychol.* 13-2.

HOWELLS, J. G. AND LICKORISH, J. R. (1963) 'The family relations indicator. A projective technique for investigating intra-family relationships designed for use with emotionally disturbed children', *Brit. J. Ed. Psychol.* 33-3.

HUEY, E. B. (1908) *The Psychology and Pedagogy of Reading*, New York, Macmillan.

HUNTER, I. M. L. (1962) 'An exceptional talent for calculative thinking', *Brit. J. Psychol.* 53-3.

ILLINGWORTH, R. S. AND ILLINGWORTH, C. M. (1966) *Lessons from Childhood*, Edinburgh: Livingstone.

INGRAM, T. T. S. (1969) 'The development of higher nervous activity in childhood and its disorders', in *Handbook of Clinical Neurology*, Vol. 4, Amsterdam: North-Holland Co.

IRVINE, F. E. (1966) 'School-based social work', *New Society* 10 March 1966.

ISAACS, N. (1961) *The Growth of Understanding in the Young Child: a brief introduction to Piaget's work*, London: Educational Supply Assn.

ISAACS, N. (1967) *What is Required of the Nursery-Infant Teacher in this Country Today?* London: Nat. Froebel Foundation.

ISAACS, S. (1929) *The Nursery Years*, London: Routledge & Kegan Paul.

ISAACS, S. (1930) *Intellectual Growth in Young Children*, London: Routledge & Kegan Paul.

ISAACS, S. (1932) *The Children We Teach*. Univ. London Press.

ISAACS, S. (1933) *The Behaviour of Young Children*, London: Routledge & Kegan Paul.

JACKSON, B. (1961) 'Teachers' views on primary school streaming', *Ed. Res.* 4-1.

JACKSON, L. AND TODD K. M. (1946) *Child Treatment and the Therapy of Play*, London: Methuen.

JACKSON, S. (1965) 'The growth of logical thinking in normal and subnormal children', *Brit. J. Ed. Psychol.* 35-2.

JAHODA, M. AND THOMAS, L. (1966) 'The mechanics of learning', *New Scientist* 14 April 1966.

JAMES, C. B. E. (1960) 'Bilingualism in Wales: an aspect of semantic organisation', *Ed. Res.* 2-2.

JAYNES, J. (1956) 'Imprinting: the interaction of learned and innate behaviour. I. Development and generalisation', *J. Comp. Physiol. Psychol.* 49.

JENSEN, A. R. (1967) 'The culturally disadvantaged: psychological and educational aspects', *Ed. Res.* 10-1.

JERSILD, A. T. (1952) *In Search of Self*, New York: Columbia Univ. Press.

JERSILD, A. T. (1957) *The Psychology of Adolescence*, New York, Macmillan.

JINKS, P. C. (1964) 'An investigation into the effect of date of birth on subsequent school performance', *Ed. Res.* 6-3.

JOHNSON, M. E. B. (1966) 'Teachers' attitudes to educational research', *Ed. Res.* 9-1.

JONES, J. K. (1967) *Research Report on Colour Story Reading*, Nelson.

JONES, J. K. (1968) 'Comparing i.t.a. with colour story reading', *Ed. Res.* 10-3.

JONES, S. (1962) 'The Wechsler Intelligence Scale for children applied to a sample of London primary school children', *Brit. J. Ed. Psychol.* 32-2.

JORDAN, T. E. AND BENNETT, C. M. (1957) 'An item analysis of the coloured progressive matrices', *J. Consult. Psychol.* 21.

JOYNT, D. AND CAMBOURNE, B. (1968) 'Psycholinguistic development and the control of behaviour', *Brit. J. Ed. Psychol.* 38-3.

JUNG, C. G. (1923) *Psychological Types*, New York: Harcourt, Brace.

KEATING, L. E. (1962) 'A pilot experiment in remedial reading at the Hospital School, Lingfield', *Brit. J. Ed. Psychol.* 32-1.

KEIR, G. (1952) 'A history of child guidance', *Brit. J. Ed. Psychol.* 22-1.

KELLEY, P. J. (1961) 'An investigation of the factors which influence grammar school pupils to prefer scientific subjects', *Brit. J. Ed. Psychol.* 31-1.

KELLOGG, R. (1955) *What Children Scribble and Why*, Palo Alto: Nat. Press.

KELLOGG, R., KNOLL, M. AND KUGLER, J. (1965) 'Form-similarity between phosphenes of adults and pre-school children's scribbling', *Nature* 11 December 1965.

KENNEDY, A. (1951) 'Psychologists and psychiatrists and their relationship', *Brit. J. Ed. Psychol.* 21-3.

KIDD, D. (1906) *Savage Childhood. A Study of Kafir Children*, London: A. & C. Black.

KING, W. H. (1959) 'An experimental investigation into the relative merits of listening and reading comprehension for boys and girls of primary school age', *Brit. J. Ed. Psychol.* 29-1.

KING, W. H. (1965) 'Differences in mathematical achievement related to types of secondary schools and their geographical location', *Ed. Res.* 8-2.

KINSBOURNE, M. AND WARRINGTON, E. K. (1963) 'Developmental factors in reading and writing backwardness', *Brit. J. Psychol.* 54-2.

KIRKMAN, A. J. (1967) 'Command of vocabulary among university entrants', *Ed. Res.* 9-2.

KNOLL, M. AND KUGLER, J. (1959) 'Subjective light pattern spectroscopy in the encephalographic frequency range', *Nature* 5 December 1959.

KÖHLER, W. (1925) *The Mentality of Apes*, 2nd edn, trans. Ella Winter, London: Kegan Paul.

LEE, C. (1969) *The Growth and Development of Children*, London: Longmans.

LEE, T. (1957) 'On the relation between school journey and social and emotional adjustment in rural infant children', *Brit. J. Ed. Psychol.* 27-2.

LEEDHAM, J. (1965) 'Programmed learning: revision in small groups', *Ed. Res.* 7-2.

LEITH, G. O. M. (1963) 'Teaching by machinery: a review of research', *Ed. Res.* 5-3.

LEWIS, M. M. (1936) *Infant Speech*, London: Kegan Paul.

LEWIS, M. M. (1963) *Language, Thought and Personality in Infancy and Childhood*, London: Harrap.

LI, A. K-F. (1969) 'Student Attitudes and teacher training performance', *Ed. Res.* 12-1.

LILLEY, I. M. (1967) *Friedrich Froebel. A Selection from his Writings*, Cambridge Univ. Press.

LLOYD, F. AND PIDGEON, D. A. (1961) 'An investigation into the effects of coaching on non-verbal test material with European, Indian and African children', *Brit. J. Ed. Psychol.* 31-2.

LORENZ, K. (1952) *King Solomon's Ring: New Light on Animal Ways*, trans. Wilson. London: Methuen.

LORENZ, K. (1967) *On Aggression*, trans Latzke, London: Methuen.

LOVELL, K. (1958) *Educational Psychology and Children*, London: Oxford Univ. Press.

LOVELL, K. (1959) 'A follow-up study of some aspects of the work of Piaget and Inhelder on the child's concept of space', *Brit. J. Ed. Psychol.* 29-2.

LOVELL, K. (1961) *The Growth of Basic Mathematical and Scientific Concepts in Children*, London: Oxford Univ. Press.

LOVELL, K. (1963) 'Informal v. formal education and reading attainments in the junior school', *Ed. Res.* 6-1.

LOVELL, K., BYRNE, C. AND RICHARDSON, B. (1963) 'A further study of the educational progress of children who had received remedial education', *Brit. J. Ed. Psychol.* 33-1.

LOVELL, K., GRAY, E. A. AND OLIVER, D. E. (1964) 'A further study of some cognitive and other disabilities in backward readers of average non-verbal reasoning scores', *Brit. J. Ed. Psychol.* 34-3.

LOVELL, K., JOHNSON, E. AND PLATTS, D. (1962) 'A summary of a study of the reading ages of children who had been given remedial teaching', *Brit. J. Ed. Psychol.* 32-1.

LOVELL, K., MITCHELL, B. AND EVERETT, I. R. (1962) 'An experimental study of the growth of some logical structures', *Brit. J. Psychol.* 53-2.

LOVELL, K. AND OGILVIE, E. (1960) 'A study of the conservation of substance in the junior school child', *Brit. J. Ed. Psychol.* 30-2.

LOVELL, K. AND OGILVIE, E. (1961) 'A study of the conservation of weight in the junior school child', *Brit. J. Ed. Psychol.* 31-2.

LOVELL, K., SHAPTON, D. AND WARREN, N. S. (1964) 'A study of some cognitive and other disabilities in backward readers of average intelligence as assessed by a non-verbal test', *Brit. J. Ed. Psychol.* 34-1.

LOVELL, K. AND SHIELDS, J. B. (1967) 'Some aspects of the study of the gifted child', *Brit. J. Ed. Psychol.* 37-2.

LOVELL, K. AND WHITE, G. E. (1958) 'Some influences affecting choice of subject in school and training college', *Brit. J. Ed. Psychol.* 28-1.

LOVELL, K. AND WOOLSEY, M. E. (1964) 'Reading disability, non-verbal reasoning, and social class', *Ed. Res.* 6-3.

LOWENFELD, M. (1935) *Play in Childhood*, London: Gollancz.

LUNZER, E. A. (1960a) 'Aggressive and withdrawing children in the normal school', *Brit. J. Ed. Psychol.* 30-1.

LUNZER, E. A. (1960b) 'Disparity in attainment', *Brit. J. Ed. Psychol.* 30-2.

LUNZER, E. A. AND HULME, I. (1967) 'Discrimination learning and discrimination learning sets in subnormal children', *Brit. J. Ed. Psychol.* 37-2.

LURIA, A. R. (1961) *The Role of Speech in the Regulation of Normal and Abnormal Behaviour*, London: Pergamon.

LYNN, R. (1957) 'Temperamental characteristics related to disparity of attainment in reading and arithmetic, *Brit. J. Ed. Psychol.* 27-1.

LYNN, R. (1959a) 'Environmental conditions affecting intelligence', *Ed. Res.* 1-3.

LYNN, R. (1959b) 'Two personality characteristics related to academic achievement', *Brit. J. Ed. Psychol.* 29-2.

LYNN, R. (1963) 'Reading readiness and the perceptual abilities of young children', *Ed. Res.* 6-1.

LYNN, R. AND GORDON, I. E. (1961) 'The relation of neuroticism and extraversion to intelligence and educational attainment', *Brit. J. Ed. Psychol.* 31-2.

LYTTON, H. (1961) 'An experiment in selection for remedial education', *Brit. J. Ed. Psychol.* 31-1.

LYTTON, H. (1966) 'How soon should children read?', *New Society* 14 July 1966.

MACARTHUR, R. S. AND ELLEY, W. B. (1963) 'The reduction of socioeconomic bias in intelligence testing', *Brit. J. Ed. Psychol.* 33-2.

MCCALLUM, C. M. (1952) 'Child guidance in Scotland', *Brit. J. Ed. Psychol.* 22-2.

MCCARTHY, D. (1930) *The Language Development of the Pre-school Child*, Univ. of Minnesota Press.

MCCARTHY, D. (1933) *Language Development: Handbook of Child Psychology*, Clark Univ. Press.

MCCLELLAND, W. (1942) *Selection for Secondary Education*, Univ. London Press.

MACDONALD, B., GAMMIE, A. AND NISBET, J. (1964) 'The careers of a gifted group', *Ed. Res.* 6-3.

MCDOUGALL, W. (1908) *An Introduction to Social Psychology*, London: Methuen.

MCFIE, J. (1961) 'The effect of education on African performance on a group of intelligence tests', *Brit. J. Ed. Psychol.* 31-3.

MCGRAW, M. B. (1935) *Growth, A Study of Johnny and Jimmy*, New York: Appleton-Century.

MCNALLY, J. (1965) 'Delinquency and the schools', *Ed. Res.* 7-3.

MAGUIRE, U. (1966) 'The effects of anxiety on learning, task performance and level of aspiration in secondary modern school children', *Brit. J. Ed. Psychol.* 36-1.

MANNIX, J. B. (1960) 'The number concepts of a group of ESN children', *Brit. J. Ed. Psychol.* 30-2.

MARKS, I. M. AND GELDER, M. G. (1966) 'Common ground between behaviour therapy and psychodynamic methods', *Brit. J. Med. Psychol.* 39-1.

MATEER, F. (1918) *Child Behaviour. A Critical and Experimental Study of Young Children by Methods of Conditioned Reflexes*, Boston: Badger.

MATHEMATICAL ASSOCIATION (1956) *The Teaching of Mathematics in Primary Schools*, London: G. Bell.

MATTHEW, G. C. (1964) 'The post-school adaptation of educationally subnormal boys', *Brit. J. Ed. Psychol.* 34-3.

MAYS, J. B. (1962) *Education and the Urban Child*, Liverpool Univ. Press.

MEAD, M. (1956) *New Lives for Old*, New York: Morrow.

MEADE, J. E. AND PARKES, A. S. (1966) *Genetic and Environmental Factors in Human Ability—a Symposium*, Edinburgh: Oliver & Boyd.

MEDDLETON, I. G. (1956) 'An experimental investigation into the systematic teaching of number combinations in arithmetic', *Brit. J. Ed. Psychol.* 26-2.

MERRIMAN, C. (1924) 'Intellectual resemblance of twins', *Psychol. Monog.* 33-152.

MILLER, D. (1966) 'Leisure and the adolescent', *New Society* 9 June 1966.

MITCHELL, M. E. (1966) *The Child's Attitude to Death*, London: Barrie & Rockliff.

MITCHELL, S. AND SHEPHERD, M. (1966) 'The child who dislikes going to school', *Brit. J. Ed. Psychol.* 37-1.

MOODIE, W. (1940) *The Doctor and the Difficult Child*, New York: Commonwealth Fund.

MOODY, R. L. (1952) 'A conflict of disciplines and personalities', 22-3.

MORÁN, R. E. (1960) 'Levels of attainment of educable subnormal adolescents', *Brit. J. Ed. Psychol.* 30-3.

MORETON, C. A. AND BUTCHER, H. J. (1963) 'Are rural children handicapped by the use of speed tests in selection procedures?', *Brit. J. Ed. Psychol.* 33-1.

MORRIS, D. (1967) *The Naked Ape. A zoologist's study of the human animal*, London: Jonathan Cape.

MORRIS, J. F. (1958) 'The development of adolescent value-judgments', *Brit. J. Ed. Psychol.* 28-1.

MORRIS, J. M. (1958) 'The relative effectiveness of different methods of teaching reading, A—the place and value of phonic', *Ed. Res.* 1-1.

MORRIS, J. M. (1959) 'B—the place and value of whole-word methods', *Ed. Res.* 1-2.

MORRIS, J. M. (1966) *Standards and Progress in Reading*, Slough: N.F.E.R.

MORRIS, R. (1963) *Success and Failure in Learning to Read*, London: Oldbourne.

MORRISON, A. AND HALLWORTH, H. J. (1966) 'The perception of peer personality by adolescent girls', *Brit. J. Ed. Psychol.* 36-3.

MOULTON, E. (1963) Review of 1962 *Year Book of Education:* 'The Gifted Child', *Brit. J. Stat. Psychol.* 16-2.

MULLER, H. J. (1925) 'Mental traits and heredity', *J. Hered.* 16.

MURDOCH, W. F. (1966) 'The effect of transfer on the level of children's adjustment to school', *Brit. J. Ed. Psychol.* 36-3.

MURPHY, G. (1947) *Personality*, New York: Harper.

MURPHY, L. B. (1962) *The Widening World of Childhood*, New York: Basic Books.

MUSGROVE, F. (1967) 'University freshmen and their parents' attitudes', *Ed. Res.* 10-1.

MUSGROVE, F. AND TAYLOR, P. H. (1965) 'Teachers' and parents' conception of the teacher's role', *Brit. J. Ed. Psychol.* 35-2.

NATIONAL FOUNDATION FOR EDUCATIONAL RESEARCH IN ENGLAND AND WALES (1969) *Test Agency Catalogue. Tests of aptitude, ability, intelligence, personality, interest, attitudes and achievement*, Slough: Nat. Found. Ed. Res.

NEALE, M. D. (1958) *Analysis of Reading Ability: Manual of directions and norms*, London: Macmillan.

NEWMAN, H. H. (1942) *Twins and Super-twins*, London: Hutchinson.

NEWMAN, H. H., FREEMAN, F. N. AND HOLZINGER, K. J. (1937) *A Study of Heredity and Environment*, London: Hutchinson.

NEWSON, J. AND NEWSON, E. (1963) *Infant Care in an Urban Community*, London: Allen & Unwin.

NEWSON, J. AND NEWSON, E. (1965) *Patterns of Infant Care in an Urban Community*, Harmondsworth: Penguin Books.

NISBET, J. (1964) Review of Torrance (1963) *Brit. J. Ed. Psychol.* 34-1.

NISBET, J. AND BUCHAN, J. (1959) 'The long-term follow-up of assessments at age eleven' *Brit. J. Ed. Psychol.* 29-1.

NISBET, J. AND ENTWISTLE, N. J. (1967) 'Intelligence and size of family', *Brit. J. Ed. Psychol.* 37-2.

NISBET, J. AND GAMMIE, A. (1961) 'Over 135 IQ', *Ed. Res.* 4-1.

NISBET, J. D. AND ILLESLEY, R. (1963) 'The influence of early puberty on test performance at age eleven', *Brit. J. Ed. Psychol.* 33-2.

NISBET, J. D., ILLESLEY, R., SUTHERLAND, A. E. AND DOUSE, M. J. (1964) 'Puberty and test performance: a further report', *Brit. J. Ed. Psychol.* 34-2.

OBRIST, C. AND PICKARD, P. M. (1967) *Time for Reading*, Teacher's Manual, London: Ginn.

OPIE, I. AND OPIE, P. (1959) *The Lore and Language of School-children*, London: Oxford Univ. Press.

ORTAR, G. R. (1960) 'Improving test validity by coaching', *Ed. Res.* 2-2.

OSTER, G. (1970) 'Phosphenes', *Scientific American*, Feb. 1970.

PAFFARD, M. K. (1961) 'The teaching of English literature in secondary schools', *Ed. Res.* 3-3.

PARROT, A. (1960) *Sumer*, London: Thames & Hudson.

PATTINSON, W. (1963) 'Streaming in schools', *Ed. Res.* 5-3.

PAYNE, E. (1967) 'Musical taste and personality', *Brit. J. Psychol.* 58-1 and 2.

PEAR, T. H. (1957) *Personality, Appearance and Speech*, London: Allen & Unwin.

PEEL, E. A. (1959) 'Experimental examination of some of Piaget's schemata, concerning children's perception and thinking, and a discussion of their educational significance' *Brit. J. Ed. Psychol.* 29-2.

PEEL, E. A. (1959) 'The measurement of interests by verbal methods', *Brit. J. Stat. Psychol.* 12-2.

PEEL, E. A. (1962) 'Priorities in educational research', *Brit. J. Ed. Psychol.* 32-2.

PEEL, E. A. (1963) 'Some psychologial principles underlying programmed learning', *Ed. Res.* 5-3.

PEEL, E. A. (1967) 'A method for investigating children's understanding of certain logical connectives used in binary propositional thinking', *Brit. J. Math. and Stat. Psychol.* 20-1.

PEEL, E. A. AND ARMSTRONG, H. G. (1956) 'The predictive power of the English composition in the 11+ examination', *Brit. J. Ed. Psychol.* 26-3.

PENFOLD, D. M. E. (1956) 'Essay marking experiments: shorter and longer essays', *Brit. J. Ed. Psychol.* 26-2.

PENFOLD, D. M. E. AND MEDLON, R. P. (1969) 'Social Sensitivity in Relation to Teaching Competence', *Ed. Res.* 12-1.

PENROSE, L. S. (1963) *Outline of Human Genetics*, London: Heinemann.

PETERS, M. L. (1967) *Spelling: Caught or Taught*, London: Routledge and Kegan Paul.

PETERS, R. S. (1960) 'Freud's theory of moral development in relation to that of Piaget', *Brit. J. Ed. Psychol.* 30-3.

PETRIE, I. R. J. (1962) 'Residential treatment of maladjusted children. A study of some factors related to progress in adjustment', *Brit. J. Ed. Psychol.* 32-1.

PHILLIPS, A. S. (1963) 'The self concepts of trainee-teachers in two sub-cultures', *Brit. J. Ed. Psychol.* 33-2.

PHILLIPS, A. S. (1964) 'Self concepts in children', *Ed. Res.* 6-2.

PIAGET, J. (1926) *The Language and Thought of the Child*, trans. M. Warden, London: Kegan Paul.

PIAGET, J. (1928) *Judgment and Reasoning in the Child*, trans M. Warden, London: Kegan Paul.

PIAGET, J. (1932) *The Moral Judgment of the Child*, London: Routledge & Kegan Paul.

PIAGET, J. (1950) *The Psychology of Intelligence*, London: Routledge & Kegan Paul.

PIAGET, J. (1951) *Play, Dreams and Imitation*, London: Routledge & Kegan Paul.

PIAGET, J. (1960) *The Child's Concept of Geometry*, London: Routledge & Kegan Paul.

PIAGET, J. AND INHELDER, B. (1956) *The Child's Conception of Space*, London: Routledge & Kegan Paul.

PIAGET, J. AND INHELDER, B. (1958) *The Growth of Logical Thinking from Childhood to Adolescence*, London: Routledge & Kegan Paul.

PICKARD, P. M. (1961) *I Could a Tale Unfold*, London: Tavistock.

PICKARD, P. M. (1965) *The Activity of Children*, London: Longmans

PIDGEON, D. A. (1960) 'A national survey of the ability and attainment of children at three age levels', *Brit. J. Ed. Psychol.* 30-2.

PIDGEON, D. A. (1965) 'Date of birth and scholastic performance', *Ed. Res.* 8-1.

PIDGEON, D. A. AND DODDS, E. M. (1961) 'Length of schooling and its effect on performance in the junior school', *Ed. Res.* 3-3.

PIDGEON, D. A. AND YATES, A. (1957) 'Experimental inquiries into the use of essay-type English papers', *Brit. J. Ed. Psychol.* 27-1.

PITCHER, E. G. AND PRELINGER, E. (1963) *Children Tell Stories*, New York, Internat. Univ. Press.

PLATO. *Phaedrus*. The Loeb Classical Library, London: Heinemann.

PLOWDEN REPORT (1967) *Children and their Primary Schools*. Vol. 1, *Report* Vol. 2, *Research and Surveys*, London: H.M.S.O.

POINCARÉ, H. (1908) *Science et Méthode*, Paris, Bibliotheque de Philosophie Scientifique.

POPPLETON, P. K. AND AUSTWICH, K. (1964) 'A comparison of programmed learning and note-making at two age levels', *Brit. J. Ed. Psychol.* 34-1.

POTTS, E. (1960) 'A factorial study of the relationship between the child's vocabulary and his reading progress at the infants' stage', *Brit. J. Ed. Psychol.* 30-1.

POWELL, J. P. (1963) 'The teaching of English literature in secondary schools: some remarks on "unteachable" and "unexaminable"', *Ed. Res.* 5-2.

PRINGLE, M. L. K. (1957) 'Differences between schools for the maladjusted and ordinary boarding schools', *Brit. J. Ed. Psychol.* 27-1.

PRINGLE, M. L. K. (1961) 'The long-term effects of remedial treatment: a follow-up enquiry based on a case-study approach', *Ed. Res.* 4-1.

PRINGLE, M. L. K. AND MCKENZIE, I. R. (1965) 'Teaching method and rigidity in problem solving', *Brit. J. Ed. Psychol.* 35-1.

PRINGLE, M. L. K. AND PICKUP, K. T. (1963) 'The reliability and validity of the Good-enough Draw-a-Man test', *Brit. J. Ed. Psychol.* 33-3.

PRINGLE, M. L. K. AND SUTCLIFFE, B. (1960) *Remedial Education—An Experiment*, Birmingham Printers.

RADFORD, J. (1966) 'Verbalisation effect in a "non-verbal" intelligence test', *Brit. J. Ed. Psychol.* 36-1.

RAVEN, J. C. (1947) *Guide to Progressive Matrices*, London: Lewis and Harrap.

RAVEN, J. C. (1958) *Guide to Using the Mill Hill Scabs*, London: Grieve & Lewis.

RAVEN, J. C. (1960) *Guide to Using the Coloured Progressive Matrices*, London: Lewis.

RAVENETTE, A. T. (1961) 'Vocabulary level and reading attainment: an empirical approach to the assessment of reading retardation', *Brit. J. Ed. Psychol.* 31-1.

RAYNOR, J. M. AND ATCHERLEY, R. A. (1967) 'Counselling in schools—some considerations', *Ed. Res.* 9-2.

RAZRAN, G. H. S. (1936) 'Salivating and thinking in different languages', *J. Psychol.* 1.

REEDER, R. R. (1900) 'Historical development of school readers and of methods in teaching reading', (Columbia Univ. Contribs. to *Philos., Psychol., and Ed.* 8-2) Macmillan.

REID, J. F. (1968) *Dyslexia: A Problem of Communication*, London: Allen & Unwin and *Ed. Res.* 10-2.

REMONDINO, C. (1959) 'A factorial analysis of the evaluation of scholastic compositions in the mother tongue', *Brit. J. Ed. Psychol.* 29-3.

RICHARDSON, M. (1935) *Writing Patterns*, Univ. London Press.

RICHARDSON, S. C. (1956) 'Some evidence relating to the validity of selection for grammar schools', *Brit. J. Ed. Psychol.* 26-1.

ROBERTS, G. R. (1960) 'A study of motivation in remedial reading', *Brit. J. Ed. Psychol.* 30-2.

ROBBINS REPORT (1963) *Higher Education*, London: H.M.S.O.

ROBBINS, W. J. (1928) *Growth*, New Haven: Yale Univ. Press.

RORSCHACH, H. (1911) *Psychodiagnostics: a diagnostic test based on perception*, trans. Lemkan and Kronenberg, Berne: Hans Huber 1942.

ROWLANDS, R. G. (1961) 'Some differences between prospective scientists, non-scientists and early leavers in a representative sample of English grammar school boys', *Brit. J. Ed. Psychol.* 31-1.

RUDD, W. G. A. (1958) 'The psychological effects of streaming by attainment', *Brit. J. Ed. Psychol.* 28-1.

RUDD, W. G. A. AND WISEMAN, S. (1962) 'Sources of dissatisfaction among a group of teachers', *Brit. J. Ed. Psychol.* 32-3.

RUSHTON, J. (1966) 'The relationship between personality characteristics and scholastic success in eleven-year-old children', *Brit. J. Ed. Psychol.* 36-2.

RUSHTON, C. S. AND STOCKWIN, A. E. (1963) 'Changes in Terman–Merrill IQs of educationally subnormal boys', *Brit. J. Ed. Psychol.* 33-2.

RUSSELL, B. (1946) *History of Western Philosophy*, London: Allen & Unwin.

SALK, L. (1962) 'Mothers' heartbeat as an imprinting stimulus', *Transac. New York Ac. Sc.* Series II, 24-7.

SAMPSON, O. (1956) 'A study of speech development in children of 18-30 months', *Brit. J. Ed. Psychol.* 26-3.

SAMPSON, O. (1959) 'The speech and language development of 5-year-old children', *Brit. J. Ed. Psychol.* 29-3.

SAMPSON, O. (1962) 'Reading skill at eight years in relation to speech and other factors', *Brit. J. Ed. Psychol.* 32-1.

SAMPSON, O. (1966) 'Reading and adjustment: a review of the literature', *Ed. Res.* 8-3.

SANDERSON, A. E. (1963) 'The idea of reading readiness', *Ed. Res.* 4-1.

SANDON, F. (1959) 'Twins in the school population', *Brit. J. Stat. Psychol.* 12-2.

SARNOFF, I., SARNOFF, S. B., LIGHTHALL, F. F. AND DAVIDSON, K. S. (1959) 'Test anxiety and the "eleven-plus" examination', *Brit. J. Ed. Psychol.* 29-1.

SHEARER, E. (1968) 'Physical skills and reading backwardness', *Ed. Res.* 10-3.

SHIELDS, J. B. (1968) *The Gifted Child*, Slough: N.F.E.R.

SCHONELL, F. J. (1937) *Diagnosis of Individual Difficulties in Arithmetic*, Edinburgh: Oliver & Boyd.

SCHONELL, F. J. (1942) *Backwardness in the Basic Subjects*, Edinburgh: Oliver & Boyd.

SCHONELL, F. J. AND SCHONELL, E. (1950) *Diagnostic and Attainment Testing*, Edinburgh: Oliver & Boyd.

SCHONELL, F. J. AND SCHONELL, E. (1957) *Diagnostic and Remedial Teaching in Arithmetic*, Edinburgh: Oliver & Boyd.

SCHONFIELD, D. (1956) 'Special difficulties at a reading age 8+', *Brit. J. Ed. Psychol.* 26-1.

SCHOOLS COUNCIL (1965) *Mathematics in Primary Schools*, Curric. Bull. No. 1, London: H.M.S.O.

SCHWEINITZ, K. DE (1931) *How a Baby is Born*, London: Routledge & Kegan Paul.

SEGAL, S. S. (1961) 'Dull and backward children: post-war theory and practice', *Ed. Res.* 3-3.

SEN, A. (1950) 'A statistical study of the Rorschach Test', *Brit. J. Stat. Psychol.* 3-1.

SETH, G. AND GUTHRIE, D. (1935) *Speech in Childhood*, London: Oxford Univ. Press.

SHAND, A. F. (1896) 'Character and emotions', *Mind* 5.

SHAPIRO, M. B., BRIERLEY, J., SLATER, P. AND BEECH, H. R. (1962) 'Experimental studies of perceptual anomaly VII, *J. Ment. Sc.* 108.

SHERIF, M. AND CANTRIL, C. W. (1947) *The Psychology of Ego Involvements*, London: Wiley.

SHERRINGTON, C. (1955) *Man on his Nature*, Penguin.

SHIELDS, J. (1958) 'Twins brought up apart', *Eugen. Rev.* 50.

SHIELDS, J. (1962) *Monozygotic Twins*, London: Oxford Univ. Press.

SHIPMAN, M. D. (1967) 'Theory and practice in the education of teachers', *Ed. Res.* 9-3.

SHORT, J. F. AND STRODTBECK, F. L. (1965) *Group Process and Gang Delinquency*, Univ. Chicago Press.

SHOUKSMITH, G. (1958) 'Fluency and essay writing', *Brit. J. Ed. Psychol.* 28-3.

SHOUKSMITH, G. AND TAYLOR, J. W. (1964) 'The effect of counselling on the achievement of high-ability pupils', *Brit. J. Ed. Psychol.* 34-1.

SLUKIN, W. (1964) *Imprinting and Early Learning*, London: Methuen.

SMITH, M. E. (1926) 'An investigation of the development of the sentence and the extent of vocabulary in young children', *Univ. Iowa Stud. Child Welf.* 3-5.

SOLOMAN, E. (1967) 'Personality factors and attitudes of mature training college students', *Brit. J. Ed. Res.* 37-1.

SOUTHGATE, V. (1965) 'Approaching i.t.a. results with caution', *Ed. Res.* 7-2.

SOUTHGATE, V. (1968) 'Formulae for beginning reading tuition', *Ed. Res.* 11-1.

SPEARMAN, C. E. (1930) *Creative Mind*, London: Nisbet.

SPENCER, H. (1855) *Principles of Psychology*, London: Williams & Norgate.

STAINES, J. W. (1958) 'The self-picture as a factor in the classroom', *Brit. J. Ed. Psychol.* 28-2.

STANDISH, E. J. (1959) 'Reading readiness', *Ed. Res.* 2-1.

STANDISH, E. J. (1960) 'Group tests of reading readiness', *Ed. Res.* 2-2.

START, K. B. (1966) 'The relation of teaching ability to measures of personality', *Brit. J. Ed. Psychol.* 36-2.

STEIN, Z. A. AND STORES, G. (1965) 'I.Q. changes in educationally subnormal children at special school', *Brit. J. Ed. Psychol.* 35-3.

STEPHENSON, W. (1953) *The Study of Behaviour: Q-technique and its methodology*, Univ. Chicago Press.

STERN, C. AND W. (1928) *Die Kindersprache*. Leipzig, Barth.

STERN, L. W. (1914) 'Die intelligenzprüfung an kindern und jugendlichen', *Fortschritte auf dem Gebiet der Intelligenzeprüfung*, 1912-15.

STONE, C. AND FAIRBANK, A. (1957) *Beacon Writing*, London: Ginn.

STONE, L. J. AND CHURCH, J. (1957) *Childhood and Adolescence*, New York: Random House.

STOTT, D. H. (1957) 'Evidence for pre-natal impairment of temperament in mentally retarded children', *Vita Humana* 2.

STOTT, D. H. (1958) *The Bristol Social Adjustment Guides*, Univ. London Press.

STOTT, D. H. (1960) 'Observations on retest discrepancy in mentally sub-normal children', *Brit. J. Ed. Psychol.* 30-3.

STRANG, R. (1957) *The Adolescent Views Himself*, New York: McGraw-Hill.

SULLY, J. (1893) founded *British Assn for Child Study*.

SULTAN, E. E. (1962) 'A factorial study in the domain of creative thinking', *Brit. J. Ed. Psychol.* 32-1.

SVENSSON, N. E. (1962) 'Ability grouping and scholastic achievement', *Ed. Res.* 5-1.

SWALES, T. D. (1967) 'The attainments in reading and spelling of children who learned to read through the initial teaching alphabet', *Brit. J. Ed. Psychol.* 37-1.

SYMONDS, P. M. (1951) *The Ego and the Self*, New York: Appleton.

TALLMAN, G. G. (1928) *The Intelligence Resemblances of Twins*, 27th Yrbk of Nat. Soc. for Study of Ed.

TANNER, J. M. (1961) *Education and Physical Growth. Implications of the study of children's growth for educational theory and practice*, Univ. London Press.

TAYLOR, C. AND COMBS, A. W. (1952) 'Self acceptance and adjustment', *J. Consult. Psych.* 16.

TAYLOR, P. H. (1962) 'Children's evaluation of the characteristics of the good teacher', *Brit. J. Ed. Psychol.* 32-3.

TAYLOR, P. H. (1966) 'Does initial training prepare teachers to understand and take part in educational research?', *Ed. Res.* 9-1.

TAYLOR, P. H. (1966b) 'A study of the effects of instructions in a multiple-choice mathematical test', *Brit. J. Ed. Psychol.* 36-1.

TEMPLIN, M. C. (1957) *Certain Language skills in Children*, Univ. of Minnesota Press.

TENSUAN, E. S. AND DAVIS, F. B. (1965) 'The psychology of beginning reading: an experiment with two methods', *Brit. J. Ed. Psychol.* 35-2.

TERMAN, L. M. AND MERRILL, M. A. (1937) *Measuring Intelligence. A guide to the administration of the new revised Stanford–Binet tests of intelligence*, London: Harrap.

TERMAN, L. M. AND MERRILL, M. A. (1960) *Stanford–Binet Intelligence Scale Manual for the Third Revision*, Boston: Houghton Mifflin. Harrap 1961.

TERMAN, L. M. et al. (1925) *Mental and Physical Traits of a Thousand Gifted Children*, Stanford Univ. Press.

TERMAN, L. M. AND ODEN, M. H. (1947) *The Gifted Child Grows Up*, Stanford Univ. Press.

THACKRAY, D. V. (1965) 'The relationship between reading readiness and reading progress', *Brit. J. Ed. Psychol.* 35-2.

THOMAS, C. A., DAVIES, I. K., OPPENSHAW, D. AND BIRD, J. B. (1963) *Programmed Learning in Perspective*, United Kingdom: Lawson Technical Products.

THORPE, J. G. (1959) 'The value of teachers' ratings of the adjustment of their pupils', *Brit. J. Ed. Psychol.* 29-3.

TORRANCE, E. P. (1961) *Talent and Education. The Modern School Practices Series* No. 4, Minnesota Univ. Press.

TORRANCE, E. P. (1963) *Education and the Creative Potential*, London: Oxford Univ. Press.

TOZER, A. H. D. AND LARWOOD, H. J. C. (1958) 'The changes in intelligence test score of students between the beginning and end of their university courses', *Brit. J. Ed. Psychol.* 28-2.

TRASLER, G. (1963) 'Theoretical problems in the explanation of delinquent behaviour', *Ed. Res.* 6-1.

TRIGGS, E. (1966) 'The value of a desk calculating machine in primary school maths', *Ed. Res.* 9-1.

TUER, A. W. ed. (1896) *History of the Hornbooks*, London: Leadenhall Press.

TYERMAN, M. J. (1958) 'A research into truancy', *Brit. J. Ed. Psychol.* 28-3.

UNESCO (1962) *Source Book for Science Teaching* (1st edn. 1956), Paris, Unesco.

VAIGO, A. C. (1970) 'Tailoring maths to the individual', *New Scientist* 30 April 1970.
VALENTINE, C. W. (1942) *The Psychology of Early Childhood*, London: Methuen.
VALENTINE, C. W. (1950) *Psychology and its Bearing on Education*, London: Methuen.

VALENTINE, C. W. (1953) *Reasoning Tests for Higher Levels of Intelligence*, Edinburgh: Oliver & Boyd.

VENESS, T. (1960) 'Goal-setting behaviour, anxiety and school streaming', *Brit. J. Ed. Psychl.* 30-1.

VERNON, M. D. (1957) *Backwardness in Reading*, Cambridge Univ. Press.

VERNON, M. D. (1960) 'The development of perception in children', *Ed. Res.* 3-1.

VERNON, M. D. (1962a) *The Psychology of Perception*, Harmondsworth: Penguin Books.

VERNON, M. D. (1962b) 'Specific dyslexia', *Brit. J. Ed. Psychol.* 32-2.

VERNON, P. E. (1933) 'The German and the American approach to personality', *Brit. J. Psychol.* 13.

VERNON, P. E. (1940) *The Measurement of Abilities*, Univ. London Press.

VERNON, P. E. (1950) *The Structure of Human Abilities*, London: Methuen.

VERNON, P. E. (1957) 'Educational psychology', *Chambers's Encyclopaedia*.

VERNON, P. E. (1957) *Secondary School Selection*, London: Methuen.

VERNON, P. E. (1960) *Intelligence and Attainment Tests*, Univ. London Press.

VERNON, P. E. (1964) *Personality Assessment*, London: Methuen.

VERNON, P. E. (1965) 'Environmental handicaps and intellectual development', *Brit. J. Ed. Psychol.* 35-1 and 2.

VERNON, P. E. (1968) 'What is potential ability?', *Bull. Brit. Psychol. Soc.* 21-73.

VYGOTSKY, L. S., trans. Hanfmann and Vakar (1962) *Thought and Language*, Cambridge Mass: M.I.T. Press.

WADDINGTON, M. (1965) 'Colour blindness in young children', *Ed. Res.* 7-3.

WALL, W. D. (1960) 'Highly intelligent children', *Ed. Res.* 2-2 and 3.

WARBURTON, F. W. (1956) 'Beliefs concerning human nature among students in a university department of education', *Brit. J. Ed. Psychol.* 26-3.

WARBURTON, F. W., BUTCHER, H. J. AND FORREST, G. M. (1963) 'Predicting student performance in a university department of education', *Brit. J. Ed. Psychol.* 33-1.

WARD, J. (1885) 'Psychology', in *Encyclopedia Britannica*, 9th, 10th and 11th editions.

WARREN, H. C. (1934) *Dictionary of Psychology*, New York: Houghton Mifflin.

WATTS, K. P. (1958) 'Intelligence test performance from 11 to 18: a study of grammar school girls', *Brit. J. Ed. Psychol.* 28-2.

WEBB, L. (1967) *Children with Special Needs in the Infants' School*, London: Colin Smythe.

WECHSLER, D. (1949) *Wechsler Intelligence Scale for Children Manual*, New York: The Psychological Corporation.

WEST, M. (1964) *A General Service List of English Words*, London: Longmans.

WESTWOOD, L. J. (1967) 'The role of the teacher', *Ed. Res.* 9-2.

WHEELER, D. K. (1959) 'Punishment, discipline and educational objectives', *Brit. J. Ed. Psychol.* 29-2.

WHITE, D. (1954) *Books Before Five*, London: Oxford Univ. Press.

WHORF, B. L. (1950) *Four Articles on Metalinguistics*, Washington: Foreign Service Inst.

WHORF, B. L. (1954) *Language, Thought and Reality*, London: Wiley.

WILKINS, L. T. (1961) 'Crime, cause and treatment: recent research and theory', *Ed. Res.* 4-1.

WILKINS, L. T. (1963) 'Juvenile delinquency: a critical review of research and theory', *Ed. Res.* 5-2.

WILLIAMS, J. D. (1960) 'Teaching problem-solving', *Ed. Res.* 3-1.

WILLIAMS, J. D. (1961) 'Teaching arithmetic by concrete analogy: I. Miming devices', *Ed. Res.* 2-3.

WILLIAMS, J. D. (1962) 'II. Structural systems', *Ed. Res.* 4-3.

WILLIAMS, J. D. (1963a) 'III. Issues and arguments', *Ed. Res.* 5-2.

WILLIAMS, J. D. (1963b) 'Aspects of programmed learning I. Some Notions and Arguments', *Ed. Res.* 5-3.

WILLIAMS, J. D. (1963c) 'Arithmetic and the difficulties of calculative thinking', *Ed. Res.* 5-3.

WILLIAMS, J. D. (1964) 'Understanding and arithmetic. I. The importance of understanding', *Ed. Res.* 6-3.

WILLIAMS, J. D. (1965) 'Some Problems involved in the experimental comparison of teaching methods', *Ed. Res.* 8-1.

WILLIAMS, J. D. (1966) 'Method-revision: the problem of sustaining changes in teaching-behaviour', *Ed. Res.* 8-2.

WILLIAMS, P. (1961) 'The growth of reading vocabulary and some of its implications', *Brit. J. Ed. Psychol.* 31-1.

WILLIAMS, P. (1964) 'Date of birth, backwardness and educational organisation', *Brit. J. Ed. Psychol.* 34-3.

WILLIAMS, P. (1965) 'The ascertainment of educationally subnormal children', *Ed. Res.* 7-2.

WILLIG, C. J. (1963) 'Social implications of streaming in the junior school', *Ed. Res.* 5-2.

WILSON, J., WILLIAMS, N. AND SUGARMAN, B. (1967) *Introduction to Moral Education*, Harmondsworth: Penguin Books.

WINGFIELD, A. H. AND SANDIFORD, P. (1928) 'Twins and orphans', *J. Ed. Psychol.* 19.

WINNICOTT, D. W. (1957) *The Child and the Outside World*, London: Tavistock.

WINNICOTT, D. W. (1958) *Collected Papers: Through Paediatrics to Psycho-Analysis*, London: Tavistock.

WISEMAN, S. (1956) 'Essays in selection at 11+. Reliability and validity', *Brit. J. Ed. Psychol.* 26-3.

WISEMAN, S. (1959) 'Trends in educational research', *Brit. J. Ed. Psychol.* 29-2.

WISEMAN, S. (1962) 'The tools of research—men and machines', *Brit. J. Ed. Psychol.* 32-3.

WISEMAN, S. (1964) 'Critical note on the *Year Book of Education* 1963', *Brit. J. Ed. Psychol.* 34-2.

WISEMAN, S. AND START, K. B. (1965) 'A follow-up of teachers five years after completing their training', *Brit. J. Ed. Psychol.* 35-3.

WISENTHAL, M. (1965) 'Sex differences in attitudes and attainments in junior schools', *Brit. J. Ed. Psychol.* 35-1.

WOBER, M. (1967) 'Adapting Witkin's field independence theory to accommodate new information from Africa', *Brit. J. Psychol.* 58-1 and 2.

WOBER, M. (1968) 'Towards an ecological and informational theory of aesthetics', *Bull. Brit. Psychol. Soc.* 34-2.

WOLFF, P. (1963) 'Observations on the early development of smiling', see Foss, B. (1963).

WOOD, R. (1968) 'Objectives in the Teaching of Mathematics', *Ed. Res.* 10-2.

WOODWARD, M. AND STERN, D. J. (1963) 'Developmental patterns of severely, subnormal children', *Brit. J. Ed. Psychol.* 33-1.

WOODWORTH, R. S. (1922) *Psychology. A Study of Mental Life*, London: Methuen.

WOOTTON, B. (1966) 'Crime and its rewards', *New Society* 23 September 1966.

WRIGLEY, J. (1958) 'The factorial nature of ability in elementary mathematics', *Brit. J. Ed. Psychol.* 27-1.

WUNDT, W. (1910) *Grundzüge der Physiologischen Psychologie*, II, Leipzig, Engelmann.

YATES, A. J. (1959) 'Guidance services in the United States', *Ed. Res.* 1-3.

YATES, A. J. (1960) 'Level, speed and personality factors in the intellectual performance of young children', *Brit. J. Ed. Psychol.* 36-3.

YATES, A. J. (1963) 'A further study of progressive matrices (1947)', *Brit. J. Ed. Psychol.* 33-3.

YATES, A. J. (1966) 'The relationship between level and speed on two intelligence tests', *Brit. J. Ed. Psychol.* 36-2.

YATES, A. J. AND PIDGEON, D. A. (1957) *Admission to Grammar Schools*, Newnes.

YATES, A. J. AND PIDGEON, D. A. (1959) 'The effects of streaming', *Ed. Res.* 2-1.

Year Book of Education: 'The Gifted Child' 1962, London and New York in association with the Teachers' College, Columbia Univ., N. York and the Inst. of Ed., London, Evans.

Year Book of Education: 'The Education and Training of Teachers', 1963, Evans.

YOUNG, D. (1962) 'Examining essays for eleven plus classification', *Brit. J. Ed. Psychol.* 32-3.

YOUNG, J. Z. (1964) *A Model of the Brain*, Oxford Univ. Press.

ZAHRAN, H. A. S. (1967) 'The self-concept in the psychological guidance of adolescents', *Brit. J. Ed. Psychol.* 37-2.

Index